W9-BVP-341

Your Money and Your Life

Your Money and Your Life

A Lifetime Approach to Money Management

Robert Z. Aliber

STANFORD ECONOMICS AND FINANCE

An Imprint of Stanford University Press

Stanford, California

Stanford University Press
Stanford, California

Special discounts for bulk quantities of Stanford Economics and Finance titles are available to corporations, professional associations, and other organizations. For details and discount information, contact the special sales department of Stanford University Press. Tel: (650) 736-1782, Fax: (650) 736-1784

Printed in the United States of America on acid-free, archival-quality paper

Library of Congress Cataloging-in-Publication Data

Aliber, Robert Z.
    Your money and your life : a lifetime approach to money management /
Robert Z. Aliber.
       p.   cm.
    Includes index.
    ISBN 978-0-8047-4853-7 (cloth : alk. paper)
    1. Finance, Personal—United States.   I. Title.
HG179.A433   2010
332.024—dc22   2010024886

Typeset by Westchester Book Group in Sabon, 10/14

Contents

Figures and Tables

Your Money and Your Life

1   Introduction and Overview

During your lifetime you've made—and will make—thousands of financial decisions. Should you rent a home or should you buy one? If you buy a home, when is a fixed-rate mortgage preferable to an adjustable-rate mortgage? Should you buy a new or a pre-owned car? Is a term life insurance policy a smarter choice than a permanent life insurance policy? How much life insurance do you need—and when do you need it? Are stocks a better investment in the long run than bonds? Should you buy shares in a mutual fund or, instead, should you buy the shares of the firms that the mutual funds own? Should you drink Grey Goose or Absolut vodka rather than Smirnoff or Popov, or some other generic or near-generic? How can you best protect yourself from a health care problem that could cost tens of thousands of dollars? How can you determine how much you need to save for a comfortable retirement? How can you best protect yourself from financial disasters, like the sharp decline in stock prices from 2001 to 2003 or the collapse of home prices in many states that began in 2007?

Some of your choices involve current consumption—the amounts you spend for food, housing, and transportation. Some are related to investments as you seek to increase your accumulated savings so you'll have the money for the down payment on a home, your children's education, and your retirement.

You have to deal with two types of uncertainty as you make these decisions. One type involves changes in your personal circumstances—the size of your family, health issues, and changes in your employment or income. The second type of uncertainty centers on changes in the financial environment, including changes in the consumer price level and inflation rate and changes in the prices of real estate, bonds, and stocks. American household wealth declined by 10 percent between 2007 and 2009; millions of families that had recently purchased homes for the first time or had traded up to more expensive homes and had mortgage indebtedness that was 70 or 80 percent of the purchase price of their homes lost nearly all of their wealth as real estate prices declined.

America is one of the richest countries in the world as measured by the standard of living, the education its universities and colleges offer, the diversity of family vacations, the quality of housing, and the level of health care. Yet tens of millions of Americans are worried about their financial futures. Despite the country's great wealth, the incomes of more than 20 million Americans are below the poverty level. Many of those are below this level temporarily while they grapple with their bootstraps and search for new employment opportunities. Sadly, some millions will remain bogged below this level, perhaps because of the lack of skills. Many of those with poverty-level incomes are seniors who are partially or fully retired. You may have read that fewer than 15 percent of Americans save enough for a comfortable retirement, and you're concerned that you may be among the other 85 percent.

These apprehensions in part reflect U.S. economic uncertainties. The large U.S. imports of automobiles, electronics, and apparel and the country's massive trade deficit have led to concerns about a diminution of U.S. dominance in global competition. General Motors (GM) and Ford, once the icons of American production prowess, have stumbled, losing market share to firms headquartered in Japan, Germany, and South Korea; GM and Chrysler have become bankrupt and have received loans from the U.S. Treasury because their futures seemed so challenged that no private bank or institution would lend them any more money. The U.S. industrial hegemony strikingly evident in the first seventy-five years of the twentieth century has been challenged by the rapid expansion of Toyota, Sony, Canon, Daimler-Benz, and Hyundai. Increased dependency on imported energy has led to a sense of vulnerability, especially when prices at the gasoline pumps have climbed above $4 a gallon. Many Americans once assumed that they would be part of a corporate family—IBM or the

Pennsylvania Railroad or Sears Roebuck or Eastman Kodak or Chase Manhattan Bank—for thirty or thirty-five years, but that kind of employment security has become a relic.

Once-great firms such as United Airlines, Delta Airlines, and Bethlehem Steel have gone bankrupt, and their pension obligations to their retired workers and their current workers have been shunted to the Pension Benefit Guaranty Corporation (PBGC), a U.S. government agency that had a deficit of more than $11 billion at the end of 2008—a deficit that will surge when PBGC takes over responsibility for the pensions of the workers in the failed U.S. automobile firms and their suppliers. Tens of thousands of retired workers have taken "haircuts" on their anticipated pensions, which in some cases have been reduced by more than 70 percent. The health insurance coverage for hundreds of thousands of retirees has shrunk.

U.S. firms in an array of industries are shifting from defined-benefit pension plans to defined-contribution pension plans; formerly these firms guaranteed monthly payments of a specified amount and carried the investment risk so that they had to come up with more cash for the payments if the rates of return on their investments were below average. Now the employees carry the investment risk, and their pension benefit checks when they retire will depend on their choices among bonds, stocks, and mutual funds. The two major U.S. government programs for those over age 65, Social Security and Medicare, are financially challenged as the number of retired Americans increases relative to the number of active workers.

Individual Americans increasingly will be on their own as they move along the life cycle toward retirement, with less assistance from both their employer (unless their employer is the U.S. government) and from various government programs. If you're concerned about your financial future, this book is for you. It will help you make three basic types of financial management decisions—consumption and saving; investment choices among bonds, stocks, and mutual funds; and the financial planning that brings together the amount you will need to save in anticipation of retirement with the amount you think you will need to maintain your standard of living after you retire. These decisions are closely related. In these pages you'll learn how to develop a financial planning framework that will help you determine how much you need to save each year so you'll have enough money in retirement to maintain your standard of living.

Your investment decisions—your choices between bonds and stocks, and your reliance on mutual funds—have a big impact on how rapidly your savings accumulate; you'll be guided through these decisions. You'll learn a lot about the big dent that costs and fees charged by the mutual funds can make between the rates of return on bonds and on stocks, and the rates of return that you will earn as an owner of mutual funds that own bonds and stocks.

One of your major problems is that those who want to sell you something control much of the information. These sellers may be friendly and charming, but their primary commitments are to their families, not yours. The sellers control the information flow, and they are much more knowledgeable—they are specialists as sellers, and you are a generalist because you buy from sellers in so many different areas. You need to un-bundle the source of information from the purchase decisions—a practice that has become much easier because of the tremendous amount of information available on the Internet. If you're interested in a mortgage, look up "The Mortgage Professor's Web Site" (www.mtgprofessor.com); if you want to know more about Social Security, look up "Social Security benefits."

This book will help you with the key spending and investment decisions as you move from your twenties to your forties, fifties, sixties, and seventies. You'll be able to determine the amount that you need to save each year when you're employed so that when you retire, the money available from your Social Security benefits, any employment-related pension, and your accumulated savings will be sufficient to maintain your standard of living. When you're in your twenties and thirties, saving is difficult because there are so many seemingly urgent consumption needs. Most individuals spend first, and the amount they save is like a "leftover." If you are to achieve your accumulated savings targets, you'll have to reverse the arrangement; follow the adage "pay yourself first," and initially save 10 percent of your income; as your income increases, save 20 percent of the increase. Paying yourself first means that you are likely to make more efficient consumption choices.

Saving and consumption are the flip sides of the same coin. More efficient consumption decisions help you to achieve the same level of satisfaction by spending fewer dollars, and a small increase in the efficiency of your consumption spending will allow you to double the amount you save each year with minimal effort. If you are going to accumulate the funds for retirement, you'll need to become promiscuous (i.e., indiscriminate, less discerning) when choosing among national brands and store brands and generics. "Brand loyalty"—a habit encouraged by the marketing geniuses on Madison Avenue—can be very expensive to your efforts to increase the amount you save each year. Benjamin Franklin's portrait is on the $100 bill because of the wisdom of his observation "A penny saved is a penny earned." He might have added, "A dollar saved is like having $20 in the bank." If you follow the straightforward suggestions in Chapter 2, the annual savings on your consumption spending could easily match the interest income you might earn if you had $250,000 in the bank.

The money you save from savvy consumption decisions becomes money you can invest. You've heard about the power of compound interest and the virtues of an early start—some wit said that Einstein said that "compound interest was the most powerful law in the universe." Probably not, but the idea is powerful. You've heard that the rates of return on stocks are higher than the rates of return on bonds, and that in turn the rates of return on bonds are higher than the rates of return on Treasury bills, certificates of deposit (CDs), and money market funds. You've seen the ads of the firms that own and manage mutual funds bragging about the rates of return on their funds in the last year, the last three years, and the last five years—although the number of these ads declined sharply after stock prices plummeted in 2008. One of your major investment choices is how much of your accumulated savings should be used to buy bonds and how much should be used to buy stocks; a related decision is when to increase and when to reduce the proportion of bonds in your portfolio. This book helps you sort through your investment options and avoid paying a financial advisor to make decisions that you can better and more thriftily make yourself.

Financial planning combines savings and investment choices. The framework in Part III of this book will help you estimate a target value for your accumulated savings on the date you plan to retire and some intermediate target values fifteen, ten, and five years prior to the retirement date. You can estimate the amount you need to save each year to achieve your target values for these various dates. Your need to tackle financial planning methodically would be less pressing if you had been born rich, but in reality being rich is a state of mind, a matter of matching your consumption expenditures to your income. Tragically, millions of Americans will never have enough income to pay for the minimum necessities.

But millions more—many millions more—have enough income so that they will develop a new sense of freedom once they gain control of their financial lives.

If you're like most Americans, your saving and investment decisions have been ad hoc and responsive to immediate opportunities. Some of these decisions have been impulsive and reflect whether you feel cash rich or cash poor at the moment. This book provides a more systematic approach than this ad hoc opportunism. The first step in gaining financial freedom is to develop a framework that should assist you with time-consistent decisions so that the amount you save each year should be enough (together with the anticipated benefits from Social Security and employment-related pensions) to maintain your standard of living in retirement. That won't just happen. You need to position yourself so that a major surprise when you leave the active labor force will not have a detrimental impact on your ability to maintain your standard of living. Unless you win one of the major lotteries or marry someone who has, you will need a savings program. Having a savings program won't guarantee that you'll have a hassle-free retirement, but not having one will almost guarantee that you'll feel financially challenged.

Traditionally, 65 was the retirement age for Americans, and for seventy years it was the age at which Americans could begin to receive the full retirement Social Security benefits; when that age was set, life expectancy was in the low seventies. The increase in longevity in the last seventy years has been dramatic. The retirement age now is creeping up after having declined in the 1980s—and Social Security is ratcheting up the age at which it pays out full benefits. The life expectancy of the average American couple at age 65 is nearly twenty-five years—and increasing. Many will be retired for about as long as they were in the active labor force. An increase in your life span requires planning so you won't outlive your assets.

The income for Americans over age 65 comes from four principal sources. About 40 percent comes from Social Security, about 20 percent from employment-related pensions, and about 20 percent from personal savings. The remaining 20 percent comes from wages and salaries; more than 11 million Americans over age 65 continue to work, some because of the challenges and some to alleviate boredom, but most because they need more money. Too late they realized that they hadn't saved enough for retirement while they were in their forties and their fifties.

If you want to maintain your standard of living after you retire, you will need between 65 and 75 percent of your preretirement income. Your annual financial needs will be less than when you were actively employed because you will no longer have employment-related expenses. Moreover, you'll be on the receiving rather than the paying end of the Social Security program—although you may be one of the 10 million individuals who pay Social Security taxes at the same time that they receive Social Security benefits. Your home mortgage loan may be paid off—or it may be much smaller so that you can reduce your monthly payments by refinancing. You won't need to save for retirement because you'll already be retired. But you'll have more time to spend and to travel, and that might be expensive.

The bedrock program for paying the living costs of most Americans in retirement is Social Security. Ninety-five percent of Americans over age 65 receive Social Security retirement benefits; most of the remaining 5 percent receive some other type of government pension. There is a great deal of chatter in Washington and in the news predicting that the Social Security program will become bankrupt. Not to worry. The program is the biggest "profit center" in Washington because the taxes that employed Americans pay each year exceed pension and other benefits that the Social Security Administration pays to the retired. Social Security will remain a profit center for at least the next ten years. As Americans age and benefits increase relative to taxes, the rate of increase in benefits will be slowed and taxes will be increased. But even a perfectly healthy Social Security program is not sufficient for most Americans to maintain their standard of living once they retire.

Yogi Berra once said, "If you don't know where you're going, you'll end up someplace else." For most individuals, the ten or fifteen years prior to retirement are the high savings years. You need to develop target values for your accumulated savings on the date of retirement and intermediate targets for earlier dates, say, five and ten years before you plan to retire. Then you need to develop a "savings program" that is time-consistent between these target values, the feasible rates of return on your savings as they accumulated, and x dollars each month that must be added to these savings.

Planning your financial future isn't quite this formulaic, of course. It's complicated by financial uncertainty. The prices of bonds, stocks, and real estate are unpredictable; 2007 and 2008 were miserable years because American household wealth declined by more than 10 trillion. U.S. stock prices had declined by 40 percent between 2000 and 2003, and half of the households that owned stocks experienced even larger losses. Then there's the U.S. inflation rate: the U.S. consumer price level in 2008 was five times higher than it was in 1965. Severe U.S. inflations have been episodic, almost one a generation. Finally, your personal circumstances are a wild card in your financial future. Your annual income, family size, and health may change abruptly. Forecasting your income and your family needs five years into the future is difficult, and yet the financial planning gurus want you to project your family circumstances ten, twenty, sometimes thirty years down the road. But if you don't map out the trip and head for a destination, you can be sure you won't arrive there.

The Range of Financial Decisions: Ten Big Questions

The menus in many Chinese restaurants provide a useful analogy for the range of decisions you'll make when you undertake financial planning. The number of individual dishes is the product of several primary ingredients, including chicken, beef, shrimp, and pork, and a number of sauces and complements. Some of your basic financial decisions are more or less comparable to such a mix-and-match menu. One set of decisions involves your consumption pattern and the amount you save each year; another set involves the allocation of your accumulated saving between bonds and stocks or whether instead you'll buy CDs from a bank. It's important to distinguish between the handful of decisions that are central to your financial well-being and the mass of decisions that are secondary.

Consider some of the more important decisions:

—How much should I save each year to ensure that I will have a comfortable retirement?

—How can I modify my everyday spending on food, shelter, and clothing to increase the amount that I can save comfortably each year?

—When and how should I buy a home, and when is it more cost-effective to rent?

—When is an adjustable-rate mortgage preferable to a fixed-rate mortgage?

—When should I increase my life insurance, and when should I reduce it? When is term life insurance a better buy than permanent life insurance? Which types of insurance are rip-offs?

—What proportions of my accumulated savings should be invested in bonds and in stocks, and when should I change these allocations?

—When should I buy shares in a mutual fund, and when should I buy the bonds and the stocks that mutual funds buy?

—How can I best protect my income and wealth against another surge in the U.S. inflation rate?

—Should I buy an annuity to ensure that I will not outlive my assets?

—When should I take more than the minimum annual distribution from tax-advantaged accounts, such as individual retirement accounts?

—Are health care policies cost-effective, or are there less costly ways to ensure that I am well taken care of if I should become physically or mentally handicapped?

There are two ways to get comfortable answering these questions. You can develop and enhance your personal knowledge through reading and discussion, or you can rely on a financial professional—a broker for a large or small investment firm, a mutual fund salesperson, or a personal financial advisor. Most want to be paid for their services, either through a fixed annual fee or through a commission calculated according to the value of the assets they help you manage. Four thousand people considered Bernie Madoff their "best friend" and trusted advisor—before the Feds hustled him to prison. Bernie had a lot of company in his scamming activity—at least four other large Ponzi schemes surfaced in 2008. And there has been a massive amount of misrepresentation by those connected with the major financial institutions. You might rely on a personal financial advisor to help you choose mutual funds, and you might have to pay 1 percent to the advisor and another 1.5 percent to the manager of the mutual fund—a total of 2.5 percent. An awful lot of money compared to the price of this book.

This book has three major sections. The chapters in Part I (chapters 2–8) will help you save money as you avoid wasteful expenditures. They address the major consumption decisions, including the purchase of items for the home, housing, insurance, and college education. The chapters in Part II (chapters 9–11) focus on your investment decisions. Should you buy bonds or stocks, and should you buy these securities directly or rely on one or several mutual funds? The chapters in Part III (chapters 12–17) deal with planning for your retirement, offering suggestions that will assist you in relating the amount you should save each year to your employment-related pension and to your Social Security benefits, deciding whether to purchase an annuity, and assessing the merits of a reverse mortgage.

This book will help you develop a framework for making basic decisions about your financial well-being using everyday language. A back-matter glossary explains the meaning and the relevance of technical terms, and there are shorter glossaries in boxes in the text. Most financial decisions involve trade-offs, and periodic "calculators," suggestions, and references are provided throughout the book to help you make the choice that's right for you.

You can read this book straight through or refer to chapters as they become pertinent to your financial decision making. If you're moving, read Chapter 4 as a guide to the rent-or-buy decision. If you're established in your home, you may want to read the section in that chapter on when to refinance the mortgage. Before you buy any more insurance and whenever you receive a policy renewal notice, you might want to read Chapter 5, on insurance. Read Chapter 10, on mutual funds, before you buy mutual funds and even if you own them; half of those who read that chapter will likely question whether they own the most appropriate funds. Should you buy a health care policy that would cover some of the cost of daily care if you require it in your senior years? Read Chapter 15.

This book won't tell you what decisions to make, but rather it will take you, step by step, through the decision-making process so that you'll arrive at the choice that's right for you. A one-size-fits-all approach to financial management—for example, "Buying is better than renting"—isn't the way to achieve the peace of mind that comes with knowing that your financial planning has been made with your individual interests in mind. Every now and then, however, you'll be nudged in a particular direction because the advantages of one choice over another seem overwhelming.

The message of the book is straightforward: you're an amateur continually competing against a range of professionals who have specialized in seeking to enhance their income at your expense. Be prepared, and know the data.

A Note on Terminology

The words "savings" and "investment" often are used to mean the same thing, namely, the securities or assets that you have accumulated.

In this book the word "savings" follows standard economics usage and means that portion or share of your annual income that is not spent on consumption of goods. "Investment" at the personal or household level involves purchasing bonds, stocks, real estate, and other assets with the cash you have acquired because your consumption spending has been less than your income. "Accumulated savings" is the sum of the assets that you have purchased and inherited.

Is your monthly payment on your home mortgage loan consumption or savings? The most likely answer is that the interest component of this payment is consumption and the loan-reduction component of this payment is savings. It gets a bit complicated because an inflation premium may be embedded in the interest rate on the mortgage; the counterpart of this statement is that the value of the house might increase.

Part I EXPENDITURE DECISIONS

2   "Day-Old Bread" Is Worth $20,000 a Year

Tweedle Dee and Tweedle Dum are identical twins. Their annual incomes are in the same ballpark and their consumption patterns are similar. The only significant difference in their lifestyles is that Tweedle Dum prefers top brands like Mercedes and Rolex, and Tweedle Dee has no loyalty when choosing among national brands, store brands, and generic versions of the same goods and services. Tweedle Dum used to drink Absolut vodka but switched to Grey Goose when this more expensive brand became available. Tweedle Dee chooses Cossack or Popov or Zhenka, depending on which brand is on sale. Tweedle Dum always buys Coke. Tweedle Dee alternates between Pepsi and Coke, always going with the lower-priced soft drink. Tweedle Dum buys a lot of Procter and Gamble bathroom and kitchen items, and Tweedle Dee buys versions of the same products with the Walgreen's and CVS store labels—unless the national brands are priced lower. Sometimes the brothers buy the same products. Often they purchase their shirts and suits at the same stores, but Tweedle Dee shops later in the season to take advantage of sales. Tweedle Dee doesn't have the faith Tweedle Dum does that price is an indicator of quality, and follows four rules of thumb: buy generics, be indiscriminate when choosing among national brands, buy on sale, and buy on the basis of unit pricing.

Tweedle Dee knows that newly born children begin life without clothes, and he knows that every product begins as a generic; some are just born again as recognizable national brands.

Consider that kitchen staple, coffee. When coffee first appeared in cans on store shelves in the early years of the twentieth century, the "one pound" can contained sixteen ounces. But in the 1970s, the one-pound can shrank to thirteen ounces. The sellers then offered the marketing message that there were as many cups of coffee in the smaller can as in the sixteen-ounce can. (They might have continued selling the same-sized can and indicated there were more cups of coffee in it—but they didn't.) The coffee companies wanted to raise their prices, but they feared that if the cost of the then-standard sixteen-ounce can increased, buyers would shift to a less expensive brand. Their bet was that they could get most consumers to pay the same price for a smaller can—and they would need to buy three or four more of these smaller cans each year. The "one-pound coffee" again lost a few ounces for a second time in the 1980s. Now the traditional "one-pound" coffee can has eleven and a half ounces and the "two-pound" can of coffee has twenty-three ounces.

The sellers of standard products for the kitchen and bathroom want you to believe that prices have increased because the costs of the basic materials have increased, but the extra dollars you pay are spent on more advertising so that you become more strongly attached to their brands so they can raise the prices even further. They make their money from the branding, not from selling coffee and soaps.

When Abraham Lincoln was president, there were no national brands or even regional brands of basic household items. Products in general stores were sold in barrels and in bins. Abe had a reasonably successful life even though he relied completely on generic products. Manufacturers began to "brand" their products to distinguish them from those of their competitors at the end of the nineteenth century. Branding involved endowing the generic products with "exceptional" attributes. Uncle Ben enhances rice with a few spices and raises the price of the product several hundred percent. (A pound of generic rice costs about $0.50, and a pound of branded rice sells for $2.50.) The basic raw material for Coke and Pepsi is tap water; the distributors add caramel-colored syrup and either sugar or a sugar substitute and sell a gallon at a price that is often twice that charged for gasoline. Imagine Abe Lincoln's remark if he visited Schnucks supermarket in Springfield, Illinois, and noticed that there were eight or ten different bottled waters—including some that had been imported.

Consumption spending is a battle of wits with the tens of thousands of marketing geniuses who want you to buy many goods and services that you don't especially need and to pay more than the minimum for many of the items you need—or think you need. Their success depends on their ability to convince you that their brands are more valuable than those of their competitors and more valuable than the store brands and the generics. These practical and clever men and women work full time trying to discover your irrationalities and insecurities so they can exploit them. They've hired thousands of consulting psychologists to identify your foibles.

The Price of Branding

Every branded product has an embedded generic. When you buy a branded product, you're buying a generic and a lot of marketing messages. These messages add 30 or 40 percent or more to the cost of the product. The profits of the sellers come primarily from the marketing messages—but clever as they are, they haven't figured out how to sell these messages without attaching them to a generic.

Twenty or thirty different brands of vodka are available in the typical neighborhood liquor store. A few sell for as little as $5 or $6 for a standard 750-milliliter bottle, and a few sell for $25 to $30. Large stores sell a few vodkas that range from $50 to $60. Many vodkas, especially the more expensive ones, are imported; you can buy two kinds of Russian vodka, several Polish vodkas, a French vodka, a Finnish vodka, an Icelandic vodka, and a Dutch vodka. You can also buy vodkas made from Vermont maple syrup, Maine potatoes, New Hampshire apples, and organic corn distilled on Nantucket Island.

U.S. government regulations require that the output from the distilling process must be at least 95 percent pure alcohol. Virtually all the flavor that might have been imbued by the basic ingredient is removed in the distilling process. Local tap water is then added to reduce the alcohol content to 40 percent, which is called 80 proof. (One and one-half gallons of water are added to each gallon of alcohol.) Vodka is distinctive because it is colorless, odorless, and tasteless. Most individuals mix vodka with tomato juice, tonic, orange juice, lemonade, vermouth, or wine so that any slight taste of the original ingredient is overwhelmed. Ninety-five percent of vodka drinkers could not identify the brand in a blind taste test; 99 percent could not identify the vodka in a Bloody Mary. Yet the manufacturers of expensive vodkas advertise their performances in taste tests to attract buyers who fancy they can detect such subtle differences.

You can buy a 750 milliliter bottle of vodka for $6, $7, or $8, and at nearly every $1 increment up to $25. Vodka producers have concluded that some individuals want to spend $9, others want to spend $12, and still others $15 on the standard 750-milliliter bottle. The bottles of the more expensive vodkas are more attractive; that's part of the marketing gambit. Imported vodkas have cachet because they are foreign. Taking that cue, domestic producers have slapped Slavic names on some of their vodkas. (Until the 1980s most of the vodkas bought by the Russians in Moscow were generic; the communists weren't long on marketing.) American vodka producers would like to price their vodkas in the $15 to $20 range, but they have likely concluded that their share of the premium market would be modest because those who are spending this amount want an imported brand. (The story with gins is similar, except that the brand names are British—or sound British.)

Grey Goose has become the brand that other vodka marketers would like to emulate. When it debuted on store shelves, it was priced $3 higher than any of the other leading brands. Made in France and sold in an attractive frosted glass bottle, Grey Goose was an instant success. A large group of buyers wanted the most upscale brand available, as long as the hit to their pocketbooks was not too great, and they knew Grey Goose was the best because it was the most expensive. Only a few of these buyers could afford a BMW or Cadillac, but they could afford a "top-of-the-line" vodka. The brilliant entrepreneur who developed the brand sold it to Bacardi for more than $2.5 billion.

The "Nothing Is Too Good for My Daughter" Syndrome

Many consumers strongly believe that higher prices mean better quality. Gasoline refiners traditionally sell three octanes, 87, 89, and 91. The higher octanes have a few more additives that are supposed to prolong engine life. Virtually all U.S. automobiles—and almost all the cars in the Hertz, Avis, and National rental fleets—are designed to run on 87 octane; a higher octane is needed only in a few imported sports cars or in cars with turbo-chargers. The additives are not necessary, but the refineries have provided a modest rationale for why you might want to pay ten cents or twenty cents more than you would for the basic 87 octane. The profits that the refineries earn from the higher octanes are a multiple of those that they earn from selling the basic gasoline. It's the same old story: they can't sell the additives without attaching them to the generic product.

The production costs of the most expensive vodkas exceed those of the cheaper vodkas by a few pennies—probably less than ten or twenty cents a bottle. (Okay, I'm guessing.) The differences in the costs of the bottles are probably more significant than the differences in the costs of the vodka. Still, the difference in the cost of manufacturing an elaborate glass bottle and a polyethylene one is trivial relative to the difference in the prices charged for the vodkas they contain. Most of the price difference among vodkas reflects the marketing dollars spent. It's a safe bet that the larger the marketing expenditures per bottle, the higher the profits. These firms spend a lot on marketing because the "sale" of these messages is highly profitable—but none of the marketing geniuses have yet figured out how to sell the marketing messages without attaching them to a vodka bottle.

The same is true for many consumer products—gasoline, toothpaste, breakfast cereals, toilet paper, detergents, paper towels, crackers, canned soup, coffee, rice, spaghetti and other pasta products, disposable diapers, cigarettes, soaps, apples, bananas, and coffee. Many of the branded products are packaged foods. Most fresh fruits, vegetables, meats, and fish are sold without a brand attached. (Frozen meats and frozen fish are exceptions.) Hot dogs and sausage are branded, although hamburger usually is not. Branding is expanding to fresh foods—Mr. Perdue hustles his chickens, Chiquita promotes its bananas, and the State of Washington advertises its apples. Specialty firms in Kansas City and Omaha market steaks in national publications at three or four times the price of top grades of beef in quality supermarkets.

Brand Loyalty and Buying Clubs

Every producer and firm wants loyal customers. Loyal customers are repeat buyers and are not particularly price sensitive. Decades ago, "green stamps" were awarded to customers in some grocery stores and gas stations based on the number of dollars they spent—spend $10 and get 100 stamps. The "Green Stamp Company" sold the stamps to the grocery stores and the gas stations. Americans pasted the stamps into books; ten books of stamps could be exchanged for a toaster, twenty-five books for a vacuum cleaner, and seventy-five for a TV set. The stamps were as good as cash—eventually. "Stamp collectors" could calculate a full book of stamps had a retail value of about $3 based on the observation that four books of stamps were needed to obtain a toaster that might be purchased for $12, and thirty-six books were needed to obtain a modestly priced vacuum cleaner. The managers of the stamp companies designed attractive products that would take 100 or 200 books of stamps; customers were eager to accumulate enough books of stamps to obtain one of these awards, and in the meantime the stamp company had free use of the money they had obtained from selling the stamps to the stores and gas stations that would distribute the stamps as a patronage incentive. The company that promoted the stamps limited the number of stores in each local market that could offer the stamps to induce loyalty to those stores. The success of green stamps prompted imitative behavior by entrepreneurs that developed blue stamps and red stamps.

Several large superstore chains have "buying clubs"; an annual membership might cost $25. By itself the membership fee would deter customers, but the implicit benefit of the membership is access to a store with lower prices achieved through bulk purchasing. Once a family has paid the membership fee, it is more likely to return to the store a second and a third time to amortize the fee across a large number of visits. Loyalty to the club reduces their sensitivity to lower prices that might be charged by competitors.

Producers of appliances and other goods offer "cash-back" coupons— and the grocery stores offer cents-off coupons. Often the buyer would have to mail in proof of purchase. Assume that the price was $100 and the cash-back coupon was worth $20. Every buyer could immediately do the calculation that the effective price was $80. Forty percent of the buyers failed to mail in the coupons and another 15 percent forgot to include the proof of purchase from the carton. Neat. The buyers thought they were paying $80 and the sellers ended up receiving an average price of $95.

Individual stores often place an item or items on sale for a few days; the price reduction may be 20 or 30 percent. Often the reduction is larger than the store's traditional markup over the price it paid the wholesaler or distributor. The store may use the sale item as a loss-leader to induce you to visit; the hope is that you will stick around long enough to buy lots of other goodies. Another explanation is that the distributor has a bulging inventory and needs to unload merchandise quickly.

Lots of firms are enticed to enter the markets for these branded products because the difference between the prices at which the products are sold and the costs of production is so large. Established firms use the tens of millions they spend on marketing to complicate entry for potential competitors.

Now the marketing wizards are involved in "product extension." Stoli offers four or five flavored vodkas. Smirnoff is available in an abundance of fruit flavors—orange, citrus, watermelon, strawberry, and others. Toothpastes come in various flavors, gels, and stripes—as well as three or four different sizes. These firms extend the product line to get more shelf space in the supermarkets and to increase their market share—but the inflated prices they charge are extremely large relative to their production cost increases.

Day-Old Bread and Planned Obsolescence

If you're like most Americans, you buy a loaf of bread, use two or three slices a day, and store the rest of the loaf in the refrigerator or in a breadbox. A loaf may last a week or more. Four or five days pass before you eat the entire loaf of bread. You can also buy "day-old bread," which often sells for 40 to 50 percent of the price of a fresh loaf. If you continually bought day-old bread you might save $40 to $50 a year.

Now consider last year's model of those products where technological obsolescence is rapid—electronic equipment, TVs, high-fidelity components, CD players, CAM recorders, automobiles, appliances, clothes, skis, and tennis rackets. You can buy this year's model or last year's; in both cases you're likely to keep the model for five years or longer. The price of last year's model at the end-of-the-year sale often is lower by 20 or 30 percent.

The manufacturers of these products have a major dilemma. Competition (and the high costs of product recalls and lawsuits) has forced them to improve the quality of their products. Now many products are "perfect" or "nearly perfect" and built to last a "lifetime." Future sales of these products would be modest if they were based primarily on replacement demand. The only way these firms can maintain sales growth is to introduce new features to last year's model so you are dissatisfied with the one you have.

The surge in U.S. auto imports from Japan that began in the late 1970s compelled General Motors (GM), Ford, and Chrysler to improve quality and reliability. Now many of the cars built by Detroit will provide 150,000 miles of service without major problems. That's ten to fifteen years of relatively trouble-free driving. Obviously as the car ages and the mileage builds up, the cost of repairs increases. Your automobile expenses may consume from 5 to 20 percent of your annual living costs, depending on the initial price of the model, how long you own the car (let's call this the turnover cycle), whether you buy a new car or a preowned car, and how many miles you drive each year.

Many automobile purchases are made because someone in the family decides that the current car is too prone to breakdowns or too dowdy. The range of choice is large—you can spend between $40,000 and $60,000 or more to buy a luxury imported or domestic model, or you can spend between $10,000 and $15,000 to buy a basic economy car—a smaller cabin, less horsepower, fewer amenities. Consider developing a lifetime strategy toward the ownership of an automobile that includes four variables: the type or model or brand, the price bracket, the new or preowned choice, and your "turnover cycle."

When you buy a new car, you may have the choice between buying this year's model or last year's model; the odds are nine out of ten that this year's model is last year's model with a few more bells and whistles. At the end of the model year, last year's model sells for 80 to 90 percent of the price of this year's model. Most models are in the production pipeline for six or eight years before being replaced by a completely new model—there are annual face lifts, more or less like a new lipstick. When you buy a new automobile model soon after it arrives in the showroom, you have greater choice about the color and style and the packages of options. As the dealers' inventories become smaller, the dealers reduce the prices of the still-unsold units to appeal to more economically sensitive buyers. You can save several thousand dollars by buying a car at the end of the model year when the dealers are eager to clear their showrooms and their lots to make room for next year's models.

One group of expenses—depreciation, sales taxes, registration fees, and liability insurance—associated with owning an automobile is more or less fixed, regardless of whether you drive 1,200 or 12,000 miles a year. The annual depreciation expense is much larger than all of the other ownership costs combined during the first four or five years after the car has been purchased. The dollar amount of these fixed costs depends on the initial purchase price of the car and its age; the older the car, the smaller the annual depreciation. The second group of "variable" expenses depends on the number of miles driven each year; if you drive 10,000 miles a year, the costs of gasoline, oil changes, tolls, and tires are twice those if you drive 5,000 miles a year. Parking expenses are also in this group. These mileage costs are sensitive to the model; however, the difference between owning a gas guzzler that gets fifteen miles to the gallon and an economical model that gets thirty miles to the gallon is likely to be in the range of $400 to $500 for those who drive 10,000 miles a year. If you drive many more thousands of miles in a year, the depreciation costs will be modestly higher and become more like a variable expense. Mileage expenses increase modestly if you own a car for five or ten years because tires, mufflers, headlights, and other parts will need to be replaced.

Consider the financial decisions of Adam Smith, now 25 years old, who contemplates owning a car for the next fifty years; he is trying to decide how frequently he should buy a new car. If Smith follows a two-year ownership cycle, he will purchase twenty-five cars in the fifty-year period; if he follows a three-year cycle, he will buy seventeen cars. Each time Smith buys a car, the depreciation clock starts running; similarly, each time he buys a car, he has to pay the state sales tax.

Assume that Smith spends $30,000 on a new car. One rule of thumb for depreciation is that the market value declines by one-third when he drives the car off the lot and for the first year, and thereafter the market value declines by 20 percent a year; this "rule" is sensitive to the make and model. If Smith owns the car for two years, the first year's depreciation is $10,000, the second year's is $4,000, and the average annual depreciation for the first two years is $7,000. The total projected depreciation over the fifty years is $350,000. Smith will write twenty-five checks for the state sales tax, each for $1,500 if this tax is 5 percent of the market price. The total for depreciation and sales tax over the fifty-year period is $387,500.

If, instead, Smith owns the car for three years, the year-three depreciation of $3,200 should be added to the total depreciation of $14,000 for the first two years; the average annual depreciation for the first three years is a bit more than $5,700. The total depreciation over fifty years is $285,000, and the state sales tax totals $25,500 for aggregate costs of $310,500. Smith has saved nearly $80,000 in depreciation expenses and state sales taxes by lengthening the turnover cycle from two years to three. Lengthening this cycle to four years means that Smith would buy twelve cars in the fifty-year span, and his aggregate ownership costs would decline to $278,000.

Now assume that Smith decides to run each car into the ground. It is a bit uncertain how long it will take before he concludes that the time and money paid on maintenance for an auto that is ten, twelve, or fifteen years old are too high. Using a conservative assumption that the ownership cycle is twelve years, he will buy four cars in the fifty-year span. The total purchase price will be $120,000. The sales tax will sum to $6,000, and the total ownership costs sum to $126,000. The less conservative assumption is that the car lasts sixteen years; the total purchase price is $90,000 and the sales tax will add $4,500 to the costs. Annual average depreciation is $2,500 in the former case, a bit less than $2,000 in the latter. Smith will, of course, have some repair bills. As the market value of the car declines, Smith may decide that collision insurance and comprehensive insurance are too expensive and may self-insure, saving a few hundred dollars more each year. This strategy will save Smith $300,000 over the fifty-year period compared with a two-year turnover cycle.

Now assume that Alfred Marshall decides to buy the three-year-old car that Smith is selling and run the car until annual repair expenses are too high. Marshall is likely to buy five cars in the fifty-year span. (This conservative assumption assumes that each car is worn out when it is fifteen years old.) Each time Marshall buys a car he pays $12,800, which is the difference between the $30,000 that Smith paid for the new car and the depreciation of $17,200. Marshall's total depreciation expense of the five cars is $64,000; he pays $3,000 for state sales tax.

You can save a lot of money by minimizing your purchases of depreciating assets.

Smith faces two more choices. Rather than buy the new car for cash, he might buy the car on an installment plan with monthly payments for three, four, five, or six years. Or he might lease the new car for a period of two, three, or four years.

First, consider the choice between a cash purchase and a purchase on the installment plan. To move cars out of their dealers' showrooms, GM and Ford periodically offer promotions, which often take the form of a reduction in the sales price for cash transactions or "free credit" for an installment sale over five or six years. Almost always these offers are limited to selected models that have been selling sluggishly. Consider the promotion in the form of a reduction of the sales price by $1,500 for a cash payment or "free credit" for forty-eight months—at the end of the period you would then pay $25,000 for the car.

Is the "free credit" for forty-eight months worth more than $1,500? The answer depends on the rate of return you could earn on the money you would have to invest if you take the free credit. If you invested the $23,500 for one year at a 5 percent rate, you'd earn $117.50 in investment income; in four years you'd earn less than $700. And you'd pay income tax on the investment income. Take the lower sales price. It's probably worth twice as much as the "free credit." (There are lots of calculators on various Web sites that will help you identify the lower cost choice. Go to an Internet search engine and type in "auto calculators.")

Now consider the choice between a cash purchase and leasing the car. The standard features of the auto lease include a front-end fee that might approximate four to six monthly lease payments, and a fixed monthly payment for twenty-four or thirty-six or forty-eight months. You will also have to pay the sales tax, the registration fee, and the title fee, much as if you had purchased the car. No additional payment is necessary to the leasing company unless the fenders or the paint have been excessively dinged or there are over-the-limit miles on the odometer. At the end of the lease period, you have the option to buy the car for a fixed amount stipulated in the lease agreement; if the market in used cars is soft, you might be able to buy the car for an even lower price than the one stipulated in the leasing contract.

Leasing has several advantages. It's easy and uncomplicated. The leasing company may be able to buy the car for a lower price than you can because it buys in volume and has more experience in negotiating auto purchases. And if you lease, you won't have your own financial wealth tied up in the ownership of a depreciating asset; instead, you can use the money that you otherwise would have used to buy the car to buy bonds and stocks. (One of the standard arguments for leasing is that the monthly payment is smaller than if you bought the car on the installment plan—but this argument is misleading. What you must determine is whether the all-in cost of owning is less than the all-in cost of leasing. If you buy the car even on the installment plan, you will own the automobile at the end of three, four, or five years and then not have any payments to make until you buy your next automobile.)

The leasing company is in business to make a profit. When you lease the car, in effect you're "renting" the use of the wealth of the leasing company—which almost certainly is renting the use of wealth from a bank or some other financial institution. The leasing company has concluded that the rate of return that it can earn from leasing is higher than the rate of return that it could earn when investing in bonds and in stocks. Your monthly lease rate and the associated fees are set by the leasing company to cover its costs, including the depreciation of the car and its own profit. If you buy, you bear the depreciation risk—the monthly decline in the market value of the car. If instead you lease, the lessor bears the depreciation risk—but the lessor has estimated the depreciation and your monthly lease payments are set so that they will reimburse its costs of depreciation. (Some of the lessors have lost millions because they underestimated the depreciation. Perhaps some will make the same mistake again, but that seems unlikely.)

Leasing is less hassle, at least until the end of the lease period when you may be dinged for $675 because of nicks to the paint. The lease is a contract, and it is likely to be costly to change the terms.

There are two principal uncertainties in the buy-or-lease choice. One is the rate of return you can expect to earn on the funds that you would use to buy bonds and stocks if you lease; the other is the rate of depreciation of the market value of the auto if you buy.

Since you know the lessor's estimate of depreciation already is embedded in the monthly lease payment, the major uncertainty is the rate of return on bonds or stocks.

The seller may tell you credit is free; if you believe this statement, his brother-in-law may call to sell you a bridge over the East River. Someone has to pay for the cost of the car, and the automobile dealer is probably paying an interest rate of 7 or 8 percent for his "floor plan"—to finance the new cars that are on his showroom. If the automobile dealer is offering you "free credit" at a time when he is paying 7 or 8 percent interest, then the price you are charged for the car must be sufficiently high to reimburse the cost of the "free credit." Otherwise he is burnt toast.

Should you buy or lease?

The answer depends in part on the rate of return you anticipate you can earn on your capital and the interest rate built into the lease. If you can earn 12 or 15 percent a year on your own investments, leasing is likely to be the low-cost alternative. But if you can earn only 4 or 5 percent on your investments, leasing is likely to be more costly.

Teasers and Price Discrimination

Sellers always are trying to figure out how to charge each customer the largest amount that the traffic will bear. Firms continually practice price discrimination to induce you to change your behavior and buy from them. They know you're slow to break habits, and so they have to offer something super-duper up front to get you to change your expenditure pattern.

Teaser prices and interest rates are polite forms of "bait and switch." The sellers offer you a "signing bonus" with the bait of a low interest rate or three months' free service or a no-annual-fee credit card for a year if you switch to their brand. The sellers hope that you will become lethargic once you have switched. You need to become an indiscriminate switcher among the teaser prices and interest rates offered by competing sellers. The firms have raised the prices in the "out months" to get the money to pay for the signing bonus that they've given you. Teasers were once frequent with adjustable interest rate mortgages; the interest rate in the first year was exceptionally low, and then after twelve months the interest rate would bump up. The credit card companies offer you teaser interest rates often below those that they would pay on a certificate of deposit for a year on balances transferred to them. Of course they hope you will continue to dance with them for the second song after they have raised the interest rate. But you're under no compulsion to stay with them if one of their competitors then offers a similar deal. Consider the pay-off to your consumption—your ability to pay for a vacation—with the amount that you will have saved from switching when you're offered the bait.

Traditionally banks made their money by paying 3 percent on deposits and charging 6 percent on loans; the three percentage point difference was more than enough to cover their costs and provide them with profits. Increasingly banks are charging their customers fees; the most profitable activity in many banks is the fee charged depositors when they write "bad checks"—the banks almost always collect the funds, and the fee for the bad check is $30, $40, or more.

Banks that issue credit cards charge merchants and restaurants between 1 and 5 percent for providing immediate cash and relieving the merchants of credit risk. The merchants, restaurants, and other firms that accept credit cards have raised their prices to cover this cost. In effect, you are paying for the advantages of a credit card regardless of whether you use one. If you use the card and pay the balance due each month, you're getting a "free loan" for several weeks—but you've already paid for "this loan" in the higher prices that you were charged when you paid for the restaurant meal and the gasoline and the thousand other items with your credit card. (You may be able to negotiate a cash price with some sellers that is modestly below the credit card price. Good luck.) Similarly, you've already paid for the frequent flyer miles or the other rebates. If you pay with cash, you're not obtaining the fringe benefits that you paid for in the higher price.

In part the profits of the credit card companies come from the interest rates on the credit card balances—which often are in the range of 15 to 20 percent. At one stage, cardholders had nearly a thirty-day grace period before being charged interest; now the banks have shortened this grace period. The strategy of the card companies is to position the cardholders so they can be charged fees, which can add much more to companies' bottom lines than a 1 or 2 percent increase in their interest rates. Now the banks want you to carry a significant debit balance so they can apply fees or penalties for overshooting payment due dates or going over your credit limit or some other infraction of the small print in their contracts.

The three major credit card companies now charge 3 percent when you use a credit card issued in the United States for purchases in Canada, Mexico, Japan, or Great Britain. This charge is one more effort by the banks to fleece you with fees. You would be better off using traveler's checks as a source of cash when you travel abroad or obtaining cash from the local ATM.

How Many Credit Cards Do You Need?

The credit card business is very competitive—and very profitable. The issuers of cards include major banks, some freestanding card companies, travel specialists such as American Express, and the stores such as

L.L.Bean and Brooks Brothers. When one of the credit card companies comes up with a new feature designed to enhance the attractiveness of the card, there is nothing to prevent its competitors from copying it. Each card issuer has to figure out how to remain distinctive.

From your point of view, the key features are the annual membership fee, the fee for using the card in other countries, and the "freebies"—the frequent miles, the cash dividends, the "free" plane tickets, the two-for-one airfares, and the number of days you have to pay the bill before you begin to accrue interest. If you don't pay the balance monthly, then you will want to know about the interest rate, the various penalties if you fail to pay on time or if you overstep your credit line, and other charges. But pay the balance monthly.

The airlines practice price discrimination 24/7. They are continually trying to discriminate between those who travel on business and other travelers and to stick the business travelers with higher fares, often much higher fares. Hence the excursion fares are lower if you stay at your destination over a Saturday night; the airlines know that the employers of the business travelers will pay the higher fares to get their employees home for the weekend. At times the excursion fare may be lower than the one-way fare, and you might consider buying the excursion fare and throwing away the return coupon. If the airline has sold only a few seats on a particular flight, you'll be quoted a low fare. As the number of seats reserved on a flight increases, the airline will raise the fare. If the plane has 100 seats, the airline may sell 120 reservations, counting on "no-shows" and the probability that some passengers won't make the flight because of a missed connection. Moreover, the fares charged the last few passengers who make reservations are much higher than the fares that were charged those who made their reservations four and six weeks earlier. If the number of individuals who arrive for the flight exceeds the number of available seats, the airline will ask for volunteers willing to travel on a later flight and receive a free ticket—maybe two free tickets. Nevertheless, the airlines already have figured out that the fares charged the last few passengers on the flight will more than cover the cost of the free tickets to the volunteers who will take the later flight.

Price Discrimination and Seniors

Sellers often discriminate among buyers on the basis of age; "seniors" are a favored group. A large number of sellers have lower prices and "special deals" for those over age 62 or 65 or 69, either continuously or on certain days of the week. The age thresholds for graduating into the class of seniors differ; if you're 50, you're old enough to join AARP (which used to be known as the American Association of Retired Persons) and take advantage of special rates that hotels and the auto rental firms offer AARP members. Movie theaters and public transportation generally use age 65 as the senior threshold. Several ski resorts reduce the daily lift ticket prices for those 65 and over. From time to time, airlines have special prices for seniors.

If sellers are to be successful with their two sets of prices, it must be difficult or impossible for those who are charged the lower price to resell or transfer the good or the service to someone else. Beauty salons often have lower prices for seniors on Tuesday. It is very hard to resell the shampoo and cut. Hence lower prices for seniors are much more readily available for services than for goods, although some stores offer discounts for seniors in the middle of the week when traffic is relatively light and sales are modest.

Hotel chains and car rental firms have lower prices for seniors. Banks often have lower service costs for the maintenance of accounts for seniors. American Express has a gold card for seniors that costs a few dollars less than the company's regular gold card. Similarly, the green card for seniors costs less. This card leads to savings of 20 percent on flights on American Airlines, one free day with two paid days with Budget Rent A Car, a 20 percent discount on Amtrak train tickets, one night free with two paid nights at selected Sheraton Hotels, and low rates at Westin Hotels.

The Consumption Mind-Set Strategy and Family Savings

The almost universal lament is that saving is difficult. The easiest way to save is to develop a mind-set toward daily consumption decisions—you can save a great deal by becoming a fan of store brands and generics and by buying day-old bread and lengthening the ownership cycle of your car and your TV. Remember that the primary reason that sellers want you to become loyal to their brand is so that they can charge you higher prices— and prices that are much more profitable.

The game with sellers and producers is that they are trying to determine the highest price you will pay, and you in turn are trying to determine the lowest price at which they will sell. Their advantage is that they are professionals, and thousands of hours are devoted to strategizing how to get you to trade up to buy the goods and services that are their highest profit items. But you can be selective. Take full advantage of their "bait and switch" teasers by switching whenever they change the bait.

ACTIONABLES

1. Develop a lifetime consumption strategy. Estimate your annual savings from buying generic and store labels rather than national brands. Buy any brand as long as it offers the lower price. Develop an annual target for these savings. For example, resolve, "This year my objective is to save $1,500 by using store labels and generics."

2. Estimate your savings over the next ten years if you buy a two-, three-, or four-year-old pre-owned automobile. Estimate how much you will save annually if you adopt a buy-and-hold automobile strategy.

3. Develop the habit of asking for the lowest price. When you're quoted a price, show some indifference and ask whether there is a lower price.

4. Never buy anything that is at the end of the aisle in the supermarket unless it was on your shopping list before you entered the store.

5. Become comfortable being a serial user of sellers' "bait and switch" strategies. Never ignore the advantages of teaser interest rates. If you're a senior or a near-senior, identify the sellers that have special prices for seniors.

6. Always pay your credit card balance monthly. If you don't have the cash to pay the card monthly, go on a consumption diet or famine and tear up your cards. Remember that the credit card companies will earn much more from the fees they charge you than from the interest.

3   Managing Your Credit and Your Cash

Let's begin with a quiz. Assume the average middle-class American family, annual income of $60,000, the head of the household is age 55. The quiz question is: What is the value to this family from the time of marriage until 70 of a high "credit score," say, an "A" rather than the gentlemanly "C"? $100? Or $500? Or $1,000 or $5,000? Or $10,000 or $50,000? Or $100,000? Read on, and you should be able to figure out the answer after the next few pages.

Your credit score—the estimate of how likely you are to repay money that you might borrow to finance the purchase of a car, a home, or a refrigerator—is a valuable asset. This score determines whether you will be able to borrow money from anyone besides a pawnshop, your brother-in-law, or a loan shark and the interest rate you will pay when you obtain a mortgage to buy a house or use an installment sales contract to finance the purchase of a car.

Credit is very helpful in managing your financial life, and in two different ways. In the long run, the money going out more or less must match the money coming in—but in the short run, there will be shocks that will lead to a surge in the money going out relative to the money coming in, and access to credit can smooth the adjustments—and minimize the sharpness of the decline in your expenditures when there is a sudden drop in income or a one-time surge in emergency expenditures.

Moreover, credit often is needed to finance the purchase of "big-ticket items"—homes, cars, refrigerators, and other durables that provide a flow of services over time. You can rent these assets, or you can "buy to rent," or you can buy them with credit and repay the loan over three, seven, or thirty years. In each case, you make a series of monthly payments, and hence you need to know which form of acquiring the use of the assets is less costly. Credit usually is the lower cost choice—if you qualify for the credit. (The "rent-to-buy" stores that rent or sell appliances and furniture are high-cost operations; the buyers are charged too much for the goods and too much for the credit.)

One of the two basic types of credit is secured or asset backed; home mortgages and auto loans are asset backed because the terms of the credit contract provide that the lender has the right to acquire ownership of the asset if the borrower fails to adhere to the repayment terms. A loan from a pawnshop is a secured credit; the borrower leaves an electric guitar or the motorcycle or the diamond ring at the shop and receives a loan for ninety days. If the borrower fails to repay within ninety days, the pawnshop is likely to offer the goods for sale.

Unsecured credit means that the borrower's credit reputation is on the line. The borrowers usually sign a note—an IOU that specifies the terms of the loan, primarily the interest rate and the repayment schedule. Most unsecured credits are for less than $5,000. The lenders rely on the assumption that most borrowers will repay on time to protect their credit reputations and their ability to borrow in the future. The lenders can always pursue the borrowers into the courts and force them into bankruptcy—which will make it difficult for them to secure credit for the next seven years.

Interest rates on secured credit are lower than on unsecured credit, because the risk of loss to lenders is smaller. Ideally the lenders would set the interest rate charged each borrower based on the likelihood that the borrower would not repay. The greater the likelihood that the borrower would not repay, the higher the interest rate. You might think that the lenders would like to set the structure of interest rates so that they are indifferent between low-risk borrowers and high-risk borrowers after adjusting for losses and the costs associated with managing these losses—for example, the costs associated with homes that they have acquired through foreclosure or the costs associated with repossessing an auto if the

Table 3.1

Interest Rates by Type of Loan

Secured Credits	Interest Rate
Home Mortgage	
15-year fixed	4.72
15-year fixed jumbo	5.77
30-year fixed	5.27
30-year fixed jumbo	6.13
5/1 adjustable rate	4.57
5/1 adjustable rate jumbo	4.92
Home Equity Loans	
$75,000 line, good credit	4.99
$75,000 line, excellent credit	4.80
$75,000 loan, good credit	8.45
$75,000 loan, excellent credit	8.30
Auto Loans	
36-month used car	8.13
60-month new car	7.45

Source: Data from "The Data Bank," New York Times, September 1, 2009.

borrower has not repaid in a timely manner. In fact, the lenders set the interest rates so that high-risk loans are more profitable than low-risk ones, even after adjusting for the greater likelihood and higher costs of the losses. One reason that high-risk loans are more profitable is that these borrowers have fewer alternatives; they can't easily take their business to other lenders. The firms that make "payday loans" are immensely profitable.

The interest rates on different types of loans or credit are illustrated in Table 3.1.

Payday Loans and Pawnshops

If you've ever seen a pawnshop, you'll remember the three suspended balls, a sign from a medieval guild. A loan from a pawnshop is secured; you've left your saxophone or your engagement ring or coin collection at the shop. The amount of the loan is likely to be about a third of the retail market value of the property you left. The interest rate on the loan is likely to be in the range of 20 to 30 percent a year. You have up to ninety days to repay the loan, but you can renew the loan.

Payday loans are a sophisticated, high-cost version of the pawnshop. Not quite the terms from the Budd Shulberg movie *On the Waterfront*— borrow $5 this week, repay $6 next week. The interest rate seems a nickel shy of 17 percent—but remember, that's the weekly rate; the annual rate is nearly 900 percent.

Payday loans are a marvelous convenience for those who are broke and need to get through the next three or four days. The lenders require that you pledge your auto—you leave the title to the car with them. You might borrow $100 and agree to pay $120 when you receive your next paycheck. $20 for the convenience of a short-term loan. The interest rate can be several hundred percent when calculated on an annual basis.

The difference between having a high credit score and a low one can amount to several thousand dollars a year—more than $100,000 over a lifetime. Savvy management of your credit will enable you to increase the amount you can spend on food and clothing and travel by 5 to 10 percent.

Three closely related topics are discussed in this chapter. The first is your credit score, what it means, why it is valuable, and how you can increase your score. The second is your choice of the means of payment— whether to pay for goods and services with currency or by check or by a debit card or by a credit card and when to pay by using green stamps or "points" or frequent flyer miles. Some of these means of payment are more costly than others, some are riskier than others, and some generate information that will be used to enhance—or reduce—your credit score.

One of the most important means of payment is by credit card, which "bundles" a payment and a bank loan. The loan may be short term, but often short-term loans morph into long-term loans. The third topic is your management of a "rainy day fund" to help see you through those periods when your payments are larger than your receipts; you need to decide on how much reliance to put on your own savings and how much reliance to put on borrowed money. The higher your credit score, the stronger the case for using borrowed money to cope with those periods when you've come up short, and the larger the share of your own money that you can invest in bonds and stocks and other long-term securities and assets.

The gambits in this chapter could increase your real income by 5 to 10 percent. It's like finding money because you've become more systematic and more disciplined in your payment habits.

Managing Your Credit Score

Four different parties are involved in credit scoring. First, millions of borrowers provide the basic data on their payment habits, which is collected by the lenders. Second, the lenders report on the millions of transactions that occur each month—are the borrowers paying their mortgage loans and their credit account balances on time? Third, three credit rating agencies—Experian, TransUnion, and Equifax—use these data to produce a credit score for each borrower on a month-to-month basis. These firms have the data on the payment habits of tens of millions of families. The fourth participant is the Fair Isaac Corporation, a firm based in San Francisco that developed the scoring technique—and presumably the most effective way to use the data that the lenders have collected on the borrowers. These scores are made available to the lenders whenever they request new information.

The higher the credit score, the greater the likelihood the lenders will get their money back, and the lower the interest rates they will charge.

Your credit score is like your DNA—one number that summarizes your willingness and ability to pay your mortgage loan, your car loan, your credit card debt, and your installment sales contract on time. Credit scores—sometimes known as FICO scores (after the Fair Isaac Corporation)—summarize hundreds and even thousands of items of data on particular individuals into a single number. Experian, TransUnion, and Equifax use virtually the same data on virtually each of your dozens of credit transactions to produce one number that summarizes their views on how likely you are to repay on time. The FICO score summarizes data on your payment history, the relationship between the outstanding balances on your credit cards relative to the limits on your credit cards, the number of credit cards you have, and how long you have had these cards. Experian, TransUnion, and Equifax collect the data from tens of thousands of lenders—credit bureaus in the major cities and states, mortgage lenders, installment sales companies, and other sources.

Table 3.2
Distribution of Credit Scores

Outstanding	A+	Over 800	13%
Excellent	A	750–799	27%
Very good	B+	700–749	18%
Acceptable	B	650–699	15%
Marginal	C	600–649	12%
Low pass, Maybe	D	550–599	8%
Unacceptable	D–	500–549	5%
Deadbeat	F	Below 500	2%

Sources: Data from The Credit Scoring Site, http://www.creditscoring.com; The Credit Score Blog, http://blog.creditscoring.com/; Federal Trade Commission, "Facts for Consumers," http://www.ftc.gov/bcp/edu/pubs/ consumer/credit/cre24.shtm; Equifax, http://www.equifax.com/: Experian, http://www.experian.com/; Transunion, http://www.transunion.com.

Credit scores vary from 850 to 300; the distribution of scores is summarized in Table 3.2. The median credit score is about 720—half the borrowers have higher scores. There is a modest variation in the scores provided by the each of the three credit rating agencies at each moment. And your score changes as more information becomes available.

Remember how the grades you received in elementary school could be paired with different scores. There has been the equivalent of grade inflation in scoring credit—40 percent of the borrowers are in the excellent or outstanding groups.

Assume that you want to buy a $125,000 home and that the amount of money you will have for the down payment might be as low as 5 percent or as high as 40 percent, depending on how much of the money needed for the down payment you have accumulated in liquid savings and how much you might borrow from relatives and friends. Five percent down means a loan-to-value ratio of 95 percent down, 10 percent down means a ratio of 90 percent, 20 percent down means a ratio of 80 percent, and 40 percent down means a ratio of 60 percent. The higher this ratio, the larger the risk that the lender incurs. Each of these loan-to-value ratios is a row in Table 3.3. Each column shows a different value for the credit scores. The figures in the cells show the interest rates the lenders are likely to charge. These rates are those set by the two government-sponsored mortgage lenders, Fannie Mae and Freddie Mac.

Table 3.3

Interest Rates and Credit Scores (annual percentage rate)

Loan-to-Value Ratio	Credit Score					
	620	660	680	700	720	740
95%	NA	NA	5.50*	5.38	5.38	5.38
90%	NA	5.75*	5.50*	5.38	5.38	5.25
80%	6.25	6.00	5.63	5.38	5.25	5.25
60%	5.38	5.25	5.25	5.13	5.13	5.13

Notes: *Requires private mortgage insurance; NA = not available.

Sources: Data from The Credit Scoring Site, http://www.creditscoring.com; The Credit Score Blog, http://blog.creditscoring.com/; Federal Trade Commission, "Facts for Consumers," http://www.ftc.gov/bcp/edu/pubs/consumer/credit/cre24.shtm; Equifax, http://www.equifax.com/: Experian, http://www.experian.com/; Transunion, http://www.transunion.com.

Assume that you have enough money to make a 20 percent down payment (the 80% row) and manage to increase your credit score from 620 to 720 and that the mortgage loan is $100,000. You would save $1,000 in interest in the first year, and over the life of the thirty-year loan you would save $15,000. That's a lot of money. If you want a $200,000 mortgage, you could save $2,000 in the first year. That's an awful lot of money.

Obviously it pays—a lot—to increase your credit score. There are four major ways to do this. The first is to repay on time. The second is to keep large unused credit lines—that is, to use only a modest part of the amount that you might borrow—say, no more than 30 percent. The third is to keep your credit cards with particular lenders and stores for a long period. The fourth is to limit the amount of your indebtedness relative to your income, especially the total of your outstanding credit card debt, to 20 to 30 percent. And it helps to repay the credit card indebtedness monthly.

If you're at the early stages of the life cycle and do not yet own a home, your credit history will be based primarily on your success in paying your bills on time, especially your credit card bills. If you already own a home, it's important that you pay the mortgage on time. Credit card payments—you will find more on this in the next section—can be viewed as small-ticket items. Mortgage indebtedness is a big-ticket item, and when you first buy a home, that might be two or even three times your annual income.

Assume your annual income is $60,000—a monthly income of $5,000. Limit your monthly charges to $1,500, and have three credit cards, each with a $5,000 limit. Charge $500 on each card each month. Because the amount that you will have borrowed on each card is about 10 percent of your limit, you will be far from being "maxed out."

Once you have a credit card, keep it; don't change cards even if some other vendor has a card with a low teaser rate—the lenders take the stability in your relationships seriously.

Zero Interest Rates on Seventy-two Monthly Payments

The automobile industry is sophisticated in its use of credit to move the cars out of the showrooms and off the lots. The auto firms are geared to produce cars; not producing is expensive because their fixed costs are so high. But the firms are extremely reluctant to cut price—or to cut price directly by more than a nominal amount. If they cut price directly, those who bought the cars in the previous several months would become very angry because the amounts owed on their installment loans would be larger than the market price of a new car.

Consider the following. An auto company offers to sell you a $30,000 car with a zero interest rate and a loan amortization of seventy-two months. How much is the cheap credit worth? That is an easy question to answer once you know the interest rate. You could use the interest rate of 10 percent, and the "free credit" amounts to a price cut of $4,500, or 15 percent of the price of the car (see Table 3.4).

Table 3.4
Cash Value of a Zero Interest Rate Loan on a $30,000 Auto

Interest Rate	Amortization Period (months)					
	12	24	36	48	60	72
2%	$150	$300	$450	$600	$750	$900
4%	300	500	900	1,200	1,500	1,800
6%	450	800	1,350	1,800	2,250	2,700
8%	600	1,000	1,800	2,400	3,000	3,600
10%	750	1,500	2,250	3,000	3,750	4,500

Source: Author.

Improving your credit rating by reducing your average monthly balances relative to the limits means that you may need to reduce your spending relative to your income. But that's a one-time adjustment that may take three or six months—once you've dieted, you will have the benefit of lower interest rates for an extended period. For example, assume that you are stretched and that you are carrying $8,000 of credit card debt from one month to the next. The interest rate probably is in the range of 20 to 25 percent—so you are paying $1,600 to $2,000 a year in interest. As you work off the debt, the interest payments decline. Commit to a few rules that will enable you to reduce your indebtedness by delaying some purchases until you are able to pay the monthly bill in full when it arrives.

Why Paying by Credit Card Is Less Expensive than Paying by Cash or Check

The most profitable department in any U.S. bank is the group that deals with bounced checks. A lot of banks make more money from the fees they charge when checks bounce than they do from lending money. But it's like that popcorn in the movie theaters. The theaters can't sell you the popcorn until you've bought the ticket, and the bank can't collect the fees until you've become a depositor. The bank never—well, hardly ever— incurs a loss when a check made out to Macy's or to Home Depot bounces; the bank sends the check back to Macy's or Home Depot and subtracts the amount of the bad check from the values of the stores' deposit accounts. A bounced check is like an unintentional loan from the seller of the goods to the writer of the check. (Amusingly, the banks charge more when they bounce a check than the sellers do, even though the sellers have the credit risk.)

Few of those who bounce checks complain that the fee is too high. The bankers get away with collecting these fees because they have convinced those who have written the checks that they have committed a mortal sin, even though the cause may have been an error in arithmetic.

Similarly, Americans paid tens of billions more in fees on their credit card accounts because they "violated" one of the rules of the contract set by the credit card companies.

In the early stages of the life cycle, there never seems to be enough money. Individuals are acquiring durables—automobiles, furniture, children—and may be paying off student loans. In the later stages of the life cycle, the cash drain is much less severe, receipts may exceed payments, and you'll have a lot of excess cash—and you're likely to have a lot of equity in your home.

Consider the several different ways you can pay for a vacuum cleaner. You can pay by

—currency

—check

—debit card, alternatively known as an ATM card

—cashier's check or bank check, postal money order, and travelers checks

—food stamps

—vouchers

—green stamps, frequent flyer miles, "points"

—credit card, no rewards (CCNR)

—credit card, rewards in the form of cash, points, or frequent flyer miles (CCR)

Some of these methods are less costly than others. These payments incur different risks, from theft or loss of the currency to fraudulent use of your credit card or your debit card. Hence it's important to know the risks of each form of payment.

Moreover, the form of your payment may have an impact on the prices set by the sellers of the vacuum cleaner. The prices charged by the sellers when payment does not involve cash are likely to be higher than when payment is by cash or a credit card or a debit card.

Using currency to make a payment seems straightforward. A payment of $100 using five $20 bills seems like it would cost $100, no more and no less. But where did you obtain the currency? If you obtained the currency from an ATM, you may have been charged a fee of $1.00, $1.50, or even $3.00. (The nonbank ATMs charge higher fees. Some of the fees charged by the ATMs in convenience stores are two dollars, and some in strip clubs are three dollars.)

Payment by check seems straightforward. No obvious cost is attached to using a check. But you can pay by check only if you have money in your deposit account, and the interest rate on that money is trivially low. One of the costs of keeping a deposit account is the interest income you might earn if you used the money to buy some other security.

A debit card is like an immediate check. The use of the card sends an electronic signal to the bank to transfer money from your account to that of the seller. Saves the bother of writing a check. One advantage of a debit card is that you can obtain currency when you're at the supermarket; you don't have to go to the bank or to an ATM. There is no "apparent" concern with forged signatures as long as you keep the card in your possession. But it's not risk-free, since the clerk at the store might have used a cell phone to photograph your card and then will use your information to withdraw money from your account. And you are at risk, much more so than if the clerk forged your name to a check.

Cashier's checks, money orders, and travelers' checks are "high-powered" checks—you usually pay a fee to "rent" the signature of someone who has a higher credit rating than you have. These fees can be 1 percent or more of the amount of the payment. Expensive, low risk.

Food stamps initially were a form of U.S. government social welfare assistance made available to individuals and families that had low incomes to enable them to buy agricultural products that were in excess supply. The recipients would receive the stamps in the mail and use them as a form of currency—but only to buy a particular range of products. Now the program is more directly a direct form of financial assistance or supplemental income—the recipients in effect have a debit card, and their accounts are credited each month.

Vouchers are tied to the purchase of a particular type of good or service. There are many different types of vouchers, but almost all are tied to the purchase of a particular good or the purchase from a particular supplier. Cents-off coupons that are in Thursday's newspapers are vouchers. You might have received the voucher to buy x because you had paid cash or check to buy y; the voucher then is like a rebate. And if you forget to mail in the voucher, too bad. "Cash for Clunkers" was a voucher program; so is a "buy one, get one free."

Credit cards differ from checks and debit cards because they bundle the payment with an "automatic loan," since you pay with "other people's money"; you prequalified for what in effect is an unsecured loan when you received the card with its credit limit. (Often the credit limit when you receive the first card is $3,000.) Once you've received the card, you're free to draw on the line of credit.

The rewards credit cards differ from the no-rewards credit cards in that you receive something back, often cash or frequent flyer miles. One rewards card provides 1 percent back on purchases of x, 2 percent back on purchases of y, and 3 percent back on purchases of z. Another type provides "points"—for example, accumulate 10,000 points (often you earn a point for each $1.00 of expenditure) to buy a vacuum cleaner—or you can accumulate frequent flyer miles (FFMs) that will be added to the FFMs that you accumulate when you fly on the airlines. (In effect, the airlines sell FFMs to the banks and the others which they "give" to you when you buy their goods and services.) Figure that these rewards amount to 1 to 2 percent of the value of your purchases.

The supplier of the line of credit is likely to be a bank, but it could be a specialized lender or travel firm like American Express. If you pay the bill from the lender within the grace period—say, fifteen or twenty days after you receive your monthly bill—you are not charged interest. In effect, the lender makes you an interest-free loan for two or three weeks, twelve months a year. The firms that issue the credit cards are not charities; they incur costs of $150 to attract one more user of credit cards. These firms view you as a profit center. They have three sources of income to offset the costs incurred in attracting more users of the cards and in making the interest-free loans.

These lenders buy the IOUs from the gas stations and the supermarkets and the department stores that you have produced when you used your credit card for $0.97 or even $0.95. (These sellers hate these fees; they feel they are being gouged. But they have little choice, because if they didn't take the cards, many customers would take their business to their competitors that take cards.) Most of these sellers have raised their prices to offset most or all of the haircut they take when they sell $1.00 of IOUs to the lenders for $0.97. (Some of these sellers have established their own cards to reduce the amount they have to pay the credit card companies.) Assume that you charge $1,000 a month, or $12,000 a year—that's $360 of income to the lenders from being able to buy your IOUs at a discount.

Moreover, these lenders have a lot of data that indicate no more than 50 percent of those who use credit cards will repay the amounts due within the grace period, so they now have a set of borrowers who are on the hook and paying interest initially that is in the range of 12 to 18 percent.

Finally, you may have paid an annual fee of $60 or $85 for the card. Some upscale cards have annual fees of $395.

FFMs and points are rebates tied to purchases of specialized goods and services. These forms of payment differ from vouchers in that they have been earned because you bought an airline ticket or stayed at a hotel or charged something on a credit card. Initially FFMs could be used to obtain tickets for airplane flights or upgrades. Now they can be exchanged for vacuum cleaners and hotel stays and other goods and services. Usually the airlines offered one FFM for each mile traveled, regardless of the purchase price of the ticket; a few airlines offered one point for each trip. Some airlines combined both; if the trip was a short distance, say, less than 500 miles, you received one point; if the trip was longer, the number of FFMs received was based on mileage. And if business was slow and there were a lot of empty seats, the airlines often increased the number of FFMs offered for a particular flight.

Which form of payment is lower cost? Assume that you are at Wal-Mart or Home Depot or the local supermarket. Using a CCNR is less costly than using cash or currency because you get an interest-free loan. If your monthly credit card balance is $2,000 and the interest-free loan is for fifteen days and the interest rate is 10 percent, you've reduced the cost of those payments that are made by the use of credit card by 1 percent, so you've saved $100 a year. (Remember, $100 here, $100 there, and it adds up.) The amount of cash you need to carry with you is smaller.

If instead you use a CCR, the savings are even greater. If the reward is a cash reward, then you might save $200 or $250 a year with the same expenditure pattern. If you collect and use FFMs, the savings can be even greater. See the box on the alternative ways to use FFMs.

Now consider that you want to buy an airline ticket. Should you use currency, your debit card, or FFMs? How much is an FFM worth? That depends primarily on how it is used, since you can use an FFM to buy a coach-class ticket or a business-class ticket, or an upgrade of a coach-class ticket to a business-class ticket. Note that the FFMs that accrue to your account are a form of untaxed income.

How Much Is a Frequent Flyer Mile Worth?

It depends, both on the method of earning the FFMs and how you choose to spend them. Often a free domestic ticket "costs" 30,000 FFMs.

You could earn 30,000 FFMs if you made five round trips between Washington, D.C., and San Francisco, or eight round trips between Chicago and Los Angeles. Assume that each round trip between Washington and San Francisco costs $600, and each round trip between Chicago and Los Angeles costs $500. The free ticket costs $3,000 for the first set of round trips and $4,000 for the second set. If you used the 30,000 FFMs to "buy" another ticket between the two coasts, you will have saved $600. Similarly, if you used the 30,000 miles to obtain a ticket between Chicago and Los Angeles, then the ticket is worth $500.

The airlines have two sets of prices for the same trip. Generally, a domestic ticket will cost 30,000 FFMs, regardless of the pair of cities involved. The cash price of a ticket between domestic pairs of cities might vary from $150 to $1,200. Hence the value of each 30,000 FFMs depends on the cash price of the ticket, and that in turn depends on how competitive the airline business is between each pair of cities. For example, Delta has a "lock" on flights to and from Cincinnati and accounts for 80 or 90 percent of total flights. So ticket prices to and from Cincinnati are especially high for the miles involved. You can use FFMs to upgrade from coach or economy to business class, or from business class to first class. Now analyzing the value is more complex, because the coach-class fares if you want to upgrade are higher than the minimum coach-class fares. And the difference between the price of a business-class seat and of a coach seat is both larger and more variable.

A business-class ticket across the Atlantic Ocean may cost $4,000 or $5,000, and the coach ticket might cost $1,000; you can upgrade for 30,000 FFMs. If you had intended to upgrade, the use of FFMs is a bargain. The bargains are even greater if you are upgrading to first class.

What, then, is the low-cost way to make a payment?

First, use currency or a check or a debit card if you can get the seller to reduce the price by 2 percent.

Second, use a rewards credit card, either for cash or for FFMs.

Third, rarely if ever use a nonrewards credit card; there are no advantages relative to the rewards card.

Fourth, if you don't trust yourself to limit the amount that you charge each month to the amount that you can repay, throw away the cards. The interest costs of carrying that balance monthly are too high relative to the advantages.

Fifth, don't use a debit card until you can get your bank to agree to accept a $50 limit on your liability in case of fraudulent use of the card.

The Credit Card Debt Treadmill and Trap

Several million families a year file for bankruptcy because of the burden of their credit card debt. The usual pattern is that when the monthly bill arrived, they took the easy way out—they paid the minimum required by the lender, which might have been as little as 5 percent of the amount due.

The interest rate was probably in the range of 12 to 15 percent, so the amount due would be increasing even if they paid the minimum. In effect the borrowers are on a treadmill; the indebtedness on their credit cards has morphed into a "permanent loan," and they have little hope of paying down the indebtedness unless they either win the lottery or adopt exceptional measures to squeeze their consumption spending relative to their incomes. Assume that their indebtedness is $8,000 and their income is $40,000. The interest rate on the indebtedness is 24 percent, and so their interest bill is $1,920 a year. A lot of money. It didn't start out that way. But compound interests compounds, and if you are slightly late with one payment, then you are charged a fee—yes, the fee was noted in the fine print, but you ignored the print.

There are five ways to get off the treadmill. Declare bankruptcy. Negotiate a reduction with the lender (good luck). Semi-starve. Refinance by increasing your home mortgage, or sell the car and other big-ticket items.

Getting off the treadmill is so difficult that you are well advised to avoid getting on the treadmill. Pay your credit card balance in full every month.

A Rainy Day Fund

Because payments and receipts are not perfectly synchronized, you need a rainy day fund to carry you through the periods when payments are larger. You probably need an "ordinary" rainy day fund to cope with shocks like the explosion of the hot water heater, and then you need an "extraordinary" fund to cope with a sudden decline in income because of a period of unemployment.

Consider the possible sources of money for a rainy day:

Your own money
—Cash under the mattress
—A bank savings account

Other people's money
—Credit card line
—Bank overdraft line
—Home equity line
—Your brother-in-law

In the early stages of the life cycle, you probably will have to use your own money for the rainy day fund. As you move along the life cycle and your assets increase relative to your income, you will be able to use other people's money for the fund. You can then invest your own money for long-period returns.

ACTIONABLES

1. Obtain the values for your credit score from each of the three firms that provide these scores.

2. If your credit score is less than 750, develop a strategy for raising your credit score. One major element in the strategy is to reduce the amount you owe relative to your credit limit, which means that you may need to reduce sharply your use of the credit card for the next three or six months. The rate of return on this investment—on reducing your consumption relative to your income—will be enormously high.

3. Develop a strategy for paying for your purchases of goods and services. Recognize that the prices of most goods and many services have been increased by the seller to reflect that the seller is going to have to discount the credit card receipts with a bank. When you're purchasing big-ticket items, ask the seller whether the price is lower when you pay by check or cash. If you can't get a lower price, then pay with a credit card.

4. Arrange an overdraft credit line with your banker as a backstop for your checking account so you will never have to pay a fee for a bounced check. But before you do so, figure out in advance how you will repay the overdraft. Still, the interest rate on the overdraft is likely to be several percentage points lower than the interest rate when you do not pay the balance due on the credit card on a timely basis. *Never* fail to pay the monthly balance on your credit card within the month.

5. If you travel in other countries and use a credit card when you are in those countries, then obtain a credit card that does not charge a special fee.

6. If you have the willpower to limit the amount of your purchases to the amount that you can pay off each month—or at least ten or eleven months of the year—use an RCC.

7. A difficult decision: should you accumulate your FFMs, or use them up as soon as they accumulate? Save them for travel between the city pairs that require high cash prices.

8. If you travel to foreign countries on business and are reimbursed by your employer or the sponsor of a trip for business-class airfare, consider obtaining a credit card that will enable you to buy a two-for-one ticket.

9. If you accumulate FFMs because you're one of the road warriors who are on the airlines once or twice a month, develop a strategy toward the use of these miles. Usually the most profitable way to use these miles is to purchase upgrades.

10. If your monthly charges on a credit card are more than $1,000, ask the bank to waive the annual fee.

4   To Rent or to Buy: That's the Question

The year 2008 was a bummer of a year for American homeowners. The price of the average home declined by 20 percent; the price declines in the previous year had been 6 percent. Moreover, prices continued to decline in 2009. The geographic pattern of price declines was very uneven; the declines were sharpest in those regions that had experienced the most rapid price increases. Most of the price declines had occurred in the sixteen states that had experienced the most rapid increases in prices, which also were the states that had been experiencing the most rapid rates of economic growth. Increases in real estate prices had been modest in Texas, even though the state had grown rapidly. Price declines and home foreclosures were severe in several of the Midwest states, especially those associated with the production of automobiles.

The sharpness of the price decline challenged the adage "Real estate is a great investment—the price of real estate always rises." Another canard is that home ownership is financially more attractive than renting in part because of tax advantages—3 to 5 million foreclosures challenged that bit of folklore. The sharp decline in property prices meant that renting was the much more attractive choice for millions of families.

Each time you move—and on average Americans change their residence six or seven times in the four decades or so that each is in the active labor force—you will face the rent-or-buy decision. These moves often are prompted by a change in employment or finances, a desire for better

schools, or a decline in the quality of your neighborhood. Once you retire, you may move two or three more times—to a warmer climate, perhaps, or to be nearer children and grandchildren. Every year, 40 million
Americans pack up their households and move. Each time you move
you'll have to decide whether renting is likely to be more financially rewarding than owning. If you rent, you pay others for the use of their
money to provide you with housing. If you buy and finance much of the
purchase with a mortgage, you also pay others for the use of their money.

Ask twenty-five of your friends whether renting or owning is financially more attractive. Most will answer that owning is the better deal. If
you ask why, you'll receive three or four different answers. Some will say
that the U.S. income tax system favors home ownership, others that
house prices almost always increase. Most of your friends won't consider
that if you rented, you could have used the money you aren't spending on
mortgage payments, which generally are higher than rental payments, to
buy bonds or stocks. The key question is whether your wealth would
have increased more rapidly if you had bought real estate or if instead
you had bought one of these securities.

The data on average rates of return on U.S. stocks and on residential
real estate can indicate long-term trends, but your rent-or-buy decisions
are made at a particular point in time and in a general area, when stock
prices or real estate prices may be very high or low relative to their long-
run values. Moreover, real estate prices vary extensively among the many
U.S. regions and metropolitan areas and even within these areas. In 2003,
2004, and 2005, real estate prices increased sharply in about half the regional housing markets; renting in these areas thus became relatively
more attractive.

Between 2003 and 2007, the price of U.S. residential real estate increased sharply relative to U.S. gross domestic product (GDP). Much of
this increase, but not all, was the bubble that was fed by the ready avail-
ability of credit. The surge in real estate prices led to an increase in the
ratio of the median home price to the median family income. The increase
in home prices led to the decline in the rental rate of return.

Three Basic Housing Rules of Thumb

Real estate experts often quote the "three threes" housing rules. The first
rule is that buyers should spend no more than one-third of their income on
housing, including operating expenses such as utilities and maintenance

and the capital costs including the interest on the money borrowed to buy the house or the interest income forgone if you bought the house with cash. Because of the surge in real estate prices after 2000, many recent buyers are spending more than a third of their income on housing—in some cases nearer one-half. Remember Yogi Berra's quip: "The neighborhood is so expensive nobody can afford to live there." He might have wondered how anyone could afford to live in Manhattan or San Francisco. Prices there are very high, say, relative to Cleveland and Phoenix and Nashville, because lots of people want to live there and have figured out how to get the cash to pay the rent and to make the mortgage payments, or at least they had this figured out when mortgage interest rates were very low. Individuals adjust to steep housing costs by living in smaller units. Singles in Manhattan share apartments. Families—especially immigrant families—"double up"; several families share the same apartment or home.

The second of these rules of thumb is that the annual costs of a home are likely to be 3 percent of its market value. These are the costs of maintenance, utilities, and local property taxes. If the home has a market value of $200,000, figure $6,000 a year. In addition, the cost of capital of the property is likely to be about 5 percent regardless of whether the home is owned or rented; this is like the interest rate after adjustment for inflation. So the sum of these two costs is 8 percent; figure $16,000 a year on a $200,000 home.

One of the basic inputs to the rent-or-buy decision is the monthly rent set by the landlord. Unless the landlord is the U.S. government or Habitat for Humanity, the landlord sets the rent at the highest level that "clears the market"—if the rents are too high, the landlord may have vacant apartments that incur costs without any counterpart revenues. The landlord wants a rate of return after paying all expenses that will be higher than the rates of return on U.S. Treasury bonds and corporate bonds. In addition, the landlord wants compensation for the aggravation of dealing with difficult tenants—and for the deadbeats who don't pay the rent for months before they scoot from the property. If you rent, the landlord hopes that your monthly payment will cover these costs. If you own, then you will pay these costs directly. But most of these costs are more or less the same and should not affect or bias the rent-or-buy decision.

The third "three threes" rule is to rent if you intend to live in a property for less than three years because the transaction costs of buying a home—payments to the broker, payments for a mortgage, real estate transfer taxes—are likely to be 8 percent or more of the value of the home. Add another 2 percentage points for the costs of moving, and the ballpark total is 10 percent of the market value of the home. These one-time transaction costs associated with the purchase of a home should be amortized over the number of years you own the property. If you own a home for only a year before you sell and move, the annual cost of home ownership is the sum of the 8 percent in the previous paragraph and the 10 percent in this paragraph. Buy only if you plan to live in a home long enough to amortize these costs over at least three or four years so they have a modest impact on raising your annual housing costs.

Why Rent?

Assume the year is 1965 and you've won a $1 million lottery prize, but there's a catch: you must use all of the prize money to buy stock either in GE or in GM. You will want to know both the dividend that GE pays on each share and the dividend that GM pays. And you will need to estimate how rapidly the earnings and dividends of both companies will increase. The outcome of this scenario now is known; the rate of return on GE stock trounced that on GM stock. In 1965, of course, few would have made such a prediction: GM was then the dominant automaker in the world, and GE was identified with light bulbs and washing machines.

The GE-or-GM choice is a metaphor for the rent-or-buy decision. Again assume you've won the lottery, and the cash on hand from the lottery prize is sufficient to pay for a home that is especially attractive to you—or you can use the money to buy stocks. The current owner of this home has set both the monthly rent and the sales price and will agree either to rent the house or to sell it to you. In effect, the owner has projected that the increase in his or her personal wealth if you rent will not be significantly different from the increase if you buy. (Note that the landlord is projecting that the rate of return on bonds and stocks is not significantly different from the anticipated rate of return on real estate.)

If you rent, then the money that you would otherwise have used to buy the home can be used to buy bonds and stocks, and your financial wealth will accumulate at the rates of return on bonds and stocks. If you buy, then your wealth will increase as the market value of your home increases. One of the limitations in using the GE-or-GM metaphor for the rent-or-buy choice is that it may be difficult to rent a home for an extended period in many neighborhoods, especially if you are not in one of the major cities with lots of apartment buildings; if you want to live in one of these neighborhoods, you must buy. Another flaw in the comparison is that the market in stocks is more liquid than the market in real estate and hence transaction costs in stocks are much lower. The apparent rate of return on real estate must be slightly higher than the rate of return on stocks to compensate for these higher transaction costs.

The rate of return on real estate depends on whether the neighborhood is growing rapidly or slowly, but then the rate of return on stocks will depend on whether you bought GE or GM.

Patterns in the U.S. Housing Market

The great raconteur Will Rogers once said, "Buy land. They ain't making any more of the stuff." Clever, but incorrect. Bays are filled in, mountains are leveled, and forests are cut down. Land is a "great investment" only if its rate of return in the long run from the sum of the increase in price and the rental income is higher than the rates of return on bonds and on stocks. It's often said that the price of land always rises. This, too, isn't historically true. The price of land often has declined during economic downturns, especially in regions that have experienced significant declines in employment. Even that old cliché "Location, location, location" is misleading, for the properties in favored locations are likely to be "overpriced" relative to other properties. Still, the supply of land in very attractive locations— on the shores of lakes, rivers, and oceans and close to urban cultural amenities—is more or less fixed, and the prices of land in these areas has been rising more rapidly than the prices of other parcels.

The U.S. housing market consists of more than 120 million freestanding homes, condos, co-ops, and rental apartments. Two-thirds of American families own their own homes, a modestly higher proportion than the number of homeowners twenty-five years ago and a sharply higher figure than that of half a century ago. The proportion is somewhat lower in larger cities. The U.S. government has stimulated home ownership through low interest rates on mortgages and reductions in the required minimum down payments. A powerful real estate lobby in Washington touts home ownership as the bedrock of democracy to induce the U.S. Congress to adopt laws that favor home ownership.

U.S. home prices increased by 70 percent between 2001 and 2007, more rapidly than at any previous time in American history. (U.S. stock prices increased more rapidly between 1995 and 1999 than at any previous time.) There are nearly 200 metropolitan areas and many different neighborhoods within these areas; the price increases in older industrial cities, such as St. Louis, Cleveland, and Detroit, have been much below average. Even though Texas is one of the most rapidly growing states, home price increases there have been modest. The areas with the most rapid price increases include both the Atlantic and Pacific coasts, especially southern California and southern Florida.

Some analysts described the rapid increases in real estate prices between 2001 and 2007 as a "bubble"; they suggested that real estate prices would tumble once they stopped climbing. Toward the end of this period, there was a surge in the share of homes purchased with subprime mortgages; these homes generally were less expensive than the median home. Purchases of these homes led to significant increases in the prices of more expensive homes as individuals traded up. Some of the buyers were motivated by the anticipation of capital gains from further increases in property prices; those who bought early had large profits from increases in market prices. Property prices in many areas were increasing at rates two to three times the interest rate, and hence the rate of return from real estate investment—or speculation— was high, especially when much of the money needed for the purchases was borrowed. The proponents of the housing bubble theory suggested that once property prices stopped increasing, many who purchased for capital gains would find that their interest payments on the borrowed money were larger than their rental incomes, and these buyers would become distress sellers.

Property prices began to decline toward the end of 2006, and fell in both 2007 and 2008. Generally, the price declines were largest in those areas where the increases had been the most rapid. Foreclosures surged, especially in those homes purchased with subprime mortgages; the buyers of many of these properties had "upside-down" mortgages, and the amounts owed were larger than the market value of the property. Because of the surge in foreclosures in some areas, the declines in prices may undershoot the long-run trend of prices.

In the long run the ratio of home prices to family income, as measured by the ratio of the median price of the newly built home to the median family income, has been relatively constant and varied around a value of three—that ratio approached four toward the end of 2006. (Remember that the median is the midpoint value in a distribution of values—half the values in the distribution are larger than the median value and half are smaller.) The median value for the ratio of home prices to family income declines when unemployment increases because families then are less eager buyers. The median value also declines when interest rates increase because higher monthly mortgage interest payments squeeze affordability.

The surge in home prices after 2001 was triggered by the combination of a sharp decline in interest rates, which greatly reduced the cost of home mortgages and the monthly cash payment associated with each $1,000 of mortgage indebtedness, and much greater availability of money for mortgages, especially for those with low credit scores. (Homes are like bonds; they provide a steady stream of rental services that are comparable to the interest income on bonds. When interest rates decline, the prices of bonds increase because investors will pay more for the interest income on the bonds; similarly, when interest rates decline, home prices increase because homeowners will pay more for the rental services provided by homes.) Sales of new homes generally have accounted for 15 to 20 percent of total annual sales.

The prices of new homes are much higher than those of fifty years ago partly because the new homes are larger and have more amenities— more bathrooms and more appliances in the kitchen. A much larger share of the newly produced homes have central air conditioning and central vacuum systems and central alarm systems.

The prices of new homes have increased more rapidly than the consumer price level. The American population today is more than twice as large as it was fifty years ago, and many of the new homes have been built on what had been farmland or forests at greater distances from the central business districts. Commuting time and costs have increased. As Americans have become richer, the price of a unit of time—an hour, a minute—has increased. Individuals and especially the DINKs (double incomes, no kids) pay higher prices for living units that are nearer their workplaces to reduce the implicit and explicit costs of commuting. Many families prefer to live near the "action"—the movie theaters and museums and restaurants.

Innovations in the mortgage market have made it easier for families to buy more expensive homes relative to their incomes and have contributed to the surge in real estate prices. Mortgage debt has increased relative to family incomes and to home values. The new mortgage products have included adjustable interest rate mortgages, interest-only mortgages, and negative amortization loans. (The key feature of a negative amortization loan is that the indebtedness increases for the first five years of the loan because the interest payment on the mortgage is less than the interest rate on the loan. For example, the interest rate might be 7 percent, but the interest payments for the first three or five years would be 4 percent of the amount of the loan.) These innovations reduced the monthly cash payment associated with each $1,000 of mortgage indebtedness. Moreover, there were more first-time home buyers with small down payments, and the increase in their indebtedness contributed to the increase in the ratio of mortgage debt to home equity.

Are Timeshares a Rip-Off?

The timeshare concept is straightforward: rather than buy an apartment that you would own all year, you buy an apartment that you "own" for just a week or two. The developer of a timeshare apartment sets the price of each of the 52 weeks; the prices for the weeks in prime-time busy winter seasons and around school vacations are higher than the prices for the off-season summer weeks. Buyers of timeshares use the apartment without any significant additional payment beyond an annual maintenance fee of several hundred dollars.

Now consider two scenarios. In the first, you buy the fifty-one timeshare weeks of a particular apartment (the developer generally reserves one week of each year for maintenance and redecorating). Now add the purchase prices for these weeks. Assume that the sum of purchase prices for the fifty-one weeks is x. Now compare x with the price of the identical condominium apartment that you would own for the entire year. X is much higher than the price of the identical apartment, perhaps twice as high. (Much of your payment when you purchase a timeshare is for the charm of the sales agent, the timeshare counterpart of the frosted glass bottle of Grey Goose vodka.) Moreover, despite the low prices for the summer weeks the developer may not be able to sell all of the fifty-one weeks, so the prices of the weeks that are readily sold are higher to cover the losses on the weeks that are difficult to sell.

Now the second scenario. Rather than buy the timeshare, you use the money to buy a bond or a stock. Each year you use the investment income on the bond or the stock to rent a timeshare for a week. The likelihood is high that renting the timeshare for a week will be less expensive than owning it; the first-time buyers were snookered into overpaying for the marketing associated with the sale of the timeshare. Owners of time-shares become bored with returning to the same apartment year after year, so there is a vibrant market in previously sold timeshares. Generally, renting a timeshare is less expensive than owning one.

The pervasive belief—and a standard argument of real estate brokers—is that owning is cheaper than renting especially since interest payments and local property tax payments are deductible expenses when figuring both your federal and state income tax liabilities. These brokers neglect to tell you that landlords also can deduct interest payments and property tax payments when they compute their income tax liabilities. Competition among landlords means that the savings from these tax benefits are passed on to the tenants in the form of lower monthly rents, so the tax-deductibility issue is a wash. Moreover, landlords have tax advantages not available to homeowners, since they can deduct the costs of repairs and painting and can depreciate their properties. Again, com-petition among landlords means that a large part of these tax advantages are passed on to tenants in the form of lower rents. (If this weren't the case, then the rate of return to landlords would be relatively high, and the number of landlords and the number of their properties would ex-pand, which would induce a decline in rents.)

Homeowners have one major tax advantage that landlords do not: the Internal Revenue Service does not tax the implicit rental value of the home. Assume, for example, that you could rent your home for $2,000 a month or $24,000 a year—and that $2,000 a month is a fair rental value. Your home provides you with $24,000 of rental services. Some costs are associated with owning the home, so that the net income after payment of these costs is less than the revenues. Assume the income is $10,000, which is not taxed; if you're in the 35 percent tax bracket, this tax advantage saves you $3,500 a year. The value of this tax advantage probably is smaller than the amount that the landlord can deduct each year for depreciation and maintenance expenses.

An additional advantage of owning is a nonpecuniary one: you're in charge. You don't need anyone's permission to paint the bathroom a lascivious red or to put a mirror on the ceiling in the master bedroom. You can attach new built-in cabinets to the walls with the hope that you may capture some of the increase in the value of the property when you move. But the flip side of being in charge is that you have to deal with the plumbers and the electricians; you may be required to devote a lot of effort to managing the property and aren't compensated for this time.

The rent-or-buy choice encounters one more modest complication that involves the U.S. income tax system and the difference in the tax rates on ordinary income and on capital gains income. If you own and realize a capital gain on the sale of the house, that gain may not be taxed and may never be taxed. (Capital gains on owner-occupied homes are discussed in Chapter 7.)

One aspect of the rent-or-buy choice is easier than the GE-or-GM choice, and that involves the estimation of the rental services that the house will provide. In the GE-or-GM choice, you need to estimate the increases in the dividends that both GE and GM would pay. You know the rent that the landlord intends to charge and it's a safe assumption—at least a safe initial assumption—that this payment amount and the value of the implicit rental payments if you buy are similar.

Now assume you decide to buy a home. You will need to estimate the value of the rental services that the home will provide (which is the counterpart of estimating the dividends paid by GE) by determining how much you would pay to rent a comparable home; assume that the estimate is $2,000 a month, or $24,000 a year (see Table 4.1). You will also need to estimate the market value or price of the home five and ten years from now; the price appreciation is comparable to estimating the increases in the price of GE stock.

Now assume that you have money to buy the same home for $200,000. If you rent, you can use the $200,000 to buy GE stock; assume that the combination of the dividends and the price appreciation means that the average annual rate of return on the stock is 6 percent, or $12,000 a year. Your rental payments of $24,000 a year will exceed the projected income on the stocks by $12,000 a year. If instead you buy the house, then you as the homeowner will have to pay the taxes, insurance, and maintenance. You will secure a capital gain from increases in the market value of the house, which in this example is assumed to be at

Table 4.1
The Rent-or-Buy Choice

	The Rental Choice	The Purchase Choice
"Cash out"		
Rent	−$24,000	no value
Operating costs	no value	−$6,000
Value of implicit rental services	no value	$24,000
"Cash in"		
Income on bonds/stocks	$12,000	no value
Increase in value of house	no value	6,000
Net	−$12,000	$24,000

Source: Author.

the rate of 2 percent a year, or $6,000 a year. You also benefit from the rental services the house provides. The conclusion is unambiguous: you are better off financially if you buy.

The buy-and-own choice is more attractive financially because the landlord has set the monthly rent so the rate of return on the $200,000 invested in the home is 9 percent (which is the difference between the landlord's rental income of $24,000 and the operating costs of $6,000 that the landlord incurs). This landlord did not include the anticipated gain from the increase in the value of the property in setting the rent. If the rent had been reduced to reflect the anticipated increase in the market value of the property of $6,000 a year, the annual rent would have declined to $18,000 and the monthly rent would have declined to $1,500 and the net cost of the rental choice would have been −$4,000.

You can structure the rent-or-buy decision when you view a particular house or apartment. Remember that the outcome of this decision is very sensitive to the assumptions you'll make about the rates of return on stocks and your estimate of the annual increase in the market value of the home. The higher the projected rate of return on stocks, the stronger the case for renting; the higher the projected rate of increase in the market value of the home, the stronger the case for owning. You can also adjust the values to reflect after-tax values. Finally, you could adjust the values to reflect "leverage": for example, you might assume that the buyer made a $50,000 down payment at the time the home was purchased and borrowed the remaining $150,000. (Buyers of homes can obtain greater leverage than buyers of stocks, and the interest rate on the mortgages usually is lower than the interest rate on margin loans on stocks. This difference is discussed in Chapter 9.)

To sum up: whether renting or owning is less expensive depends on two central assumptions. One is the rate of return if you rent and use the funds to buy bonds or stocks or some combination of bonds and stocks that you would otherwise have used to buy the property. The other is the rate of increase in the value of your property. If bonds or stocks are cheap and real estate is expensive, then the prospective rate of increase in bond or stock prices is likely to be high relative to the prospective rate of increase in home prices. And vice versa.

Taxes and the Rent-or-Buy Decision

Several features of the federal income tax affect the rent-or-buy decision. The first $500,000 of the capital gain on owner-occupied homes is not subject to the capital gains tax, provided that the owner has lived in this home for two of the last five years. Someone obsessed with avoiding income taxes might own three homes and rent two of these properties; this landlord would move into one of the rental properties after owning it for three years. The landlord would live in the home for two years and then sell the property, move into another home that had been rented for three years, and buy one more home that would be rented for the next three years. Each year the landlord would take a depreciation charge on the rented properties to reduce taxable income. Note that depreciation reduces the basis or cost when the landlord estimates the gain from selling the home. None of the capital gain on the increase in the market value of the home relative to the tax basis would be taxable as long as this gain was less than $500,000. This strategy would lead to tax savings of $100,000 every other year.

Interest payments on the amount of the mortgages in excess of $1 million on first and second homes are tax deductible—but not on third homes. Interest payments on personal loans (as opposed to business loans) other than home mortgages and funds borrowed to finance the purchase of securities are not deductible from taxable income.

Home ownership has been a great investment in many regions in the United States over the last thirty years. Prices have increased more rapidly than household income. You might conclude that residential real estate will continue to be the great investment. The ratio of home prices to household income cannot increase indefinitely. Houses must remain affordable. A "limit theorem" applies: at some stage house prices can increase no more rapidly than household incomes. The insight from the historical data is that house prices will decline or remain flat in nominal terms and the consumer price level and real personal income will increase until the traditional relationship is established once again.

Cartels and Real Estate

Title insurance is sold largely by lawyers who act as agents for one of the title insurance companies. The lawyer checks county records to ensure that there are no liens or encumbrances on the property that would interfere with the lender taking over the property if the borrower fails to make the timely monthly mortgage payments. The lawyer works as the agent for a title company and is paid a large share of the premium that you pay for the title insurance policy; the payment to the lawyer is partly a sales commission and partly a reimbursement for the time committed to researching the records on property ownership. The amount of payment to the lawyer per hour spent researching the title might be higher than the lawyer's regular hourly rate. Your lender is likely to require that you buy a title insurance policy, but see if you can shop around to find one that is less costly than the others.

The real estate commissions to brokers who sell homes are generally between 5 and 7 percent. When you select a real estate broker, you are asked to sign a contract indicating the amount that you will pay the broker as a percentage of the sales price. Assume that the commission is 6 percent. Usually the listing broker gets 3 percent and the selling broker gets 3 percent. The listing broker will incur advertising and related costs and wants compensation.

Some real estate brokers will compete for your listing by suggesting that they will be able to sell your home at a high price; they are appealing to your greed. Try to get real estate brokers to compete with each other for your listing. If business is tough and they're hungry, you may be able to find someone to take a lower commission. The idea that you should pay the broker who gets the listing as much as you pay the broker who sells the house seems to defy common sense. You might offer to pay for the marketing costs in exchange for a lower real estate commission.

The real estate broker may ask for an "exclusive." Once you've given the listing to a real estate broker, other brokers will try to sell the house since they may know the individuals who would like a house similar to yours. If the housing market is hot, you may receive offers higher than your asking price. Otherwise you may have to decide whether to reduce your asking price and begin a negotiation or to hold firm. At this stage different brokers are competing to sell your house. Some brokers may suggest that you accept a price below the asking price; they want the commission income from the sale. One study observed that when real estate brokers sell their own homes, they keep their own homes on the market longer than when they sell other people's homes.

As home prices increased in 2005 and 2006, rental incomes declined relative to market prices. The rents received by some landlords were less than the sum of their payments for interest and other costs, but they were happy because the prices were increasing at the rate of 15 to 20 percent a year. Some investors continued to buy properties in anticipation that prices would increase further; property prices were increasing more rapidly than rents, in part because of these speculative purchases. Eventually, the increases in property prices slowed, and then some landlords became distress sellers because their rents were too low relative to the payments they had to make for interest and maintenance.

In the long run there is an "equilibrium relationship" between rental rates and house prices. If interest rates decline, then house prices increase relative to rental rates. But house prices increase only because someone is willing to pay more for the property; if a large number of individuals conclude that house prices are very high relative to rental rates, they will continue to rent and house prices will increase less rapidly.

Investing When Asset Values Are Skewed

Remember Eloise, the young girl in the 1950s children's books who lived in a room at the top of the famous Plaza Hotel in New York? Well, if Eloise were a flesh-and-blood character instead of a fictional one, she'd have been evicted. An entrepreneur with a sharp pencil calculated that the Plaza would be more valuable as several hundred condominium apartments; the hotel closed in 2005 for extensive renovations. That developer's back-of-the-envelope calculation was that the hotel room rates would have to be increased by 40 to 50 percent if the use of the property as a hotel were to be as profitable as the conversion of the property into apartments.

The conversion of hotel properties and apartment properties into condominium apartments was one aspect of the boom in U.S. house prices in the 2004–2006 period. The surge in house prices skews the rent-or-buy decision. If the ratio of home prices to GDP is more than 20 or 25 percent higher than its long-term average, then you might be better off renting for a few years. Use the money that you otherwise would have spent to buy a house to buy bonds or stocks or some other security, and allow your financial wealth to accumulate until house prices have declined significantly.

The Menu of Mortgages

It would be great to win the lottery so you would have enough cash to pay for your first home. Most first-time homebuyers borrow 80 percent or more of the money needed to pay for their purchase; some have borrowed more than 90 percent. In 2005, 43 percent of first-time homebuyers made no down payment. A mortgage is a pledge of the property being acquired to the lender as collateral for the loan. If the borrower does not adhere to the loan repayment schedule, the lender can acquire ownership of the pledged property. The laws in California and Florida and a few other states stipulate that mortgage loans are nonrecourse—if a borrower defaults and the remaining balance due on the mortgage loan is larger than the amount that the lender receives when the property is sold, the lender cannot chase the borrower for the difference. But in most states, mortgage loans are recourse loans, and the lenders can chase the borrowers into bankruptcy court if the balance due on the loan is larger than the amount received when the home is sold.

Housing and Mortgage Calculators

The housing market is one of the largest in the country in terms of the value of sales in an average year. There are lots of mortgage calculators that enable you to compare the monthly payment on mortgages with different maturities and different interest rates. See "The Mortgage Professor's Web Site" (http://www.mtgprofessor.com) or search the Internet for "mortgage calculator."

The principal features of a mortgage are the amount of the loan, the ratio of the mortgage loan to the value of the house (and hence implicitly the ratio of the down payment to the purchase price or value of the house), the maturity of the loan, the interest rate, and whether the interest rate is fixed or periodically adjusted according to changes in a reference interest rate. A principal distinction is between mortgages with a fixed or set interest rate and adjustable-rate mortgages that feature increases and decreases in the interest rates as money becomes tight or easy. Another feature of a mortgage is whether the lender recovers the administrative costs associated with issuing the mortgage by increasing the interest rate or by "points"—in effect increasing the size of the loan relative to the amount of cash distributed to the borrower.

Fannie Mae, Freddie Mac, and Government-Sponsored Enterprises

Fannie Mae, Freddie Mac, and the Federal Home Loan Banks own the credit risk attached to more than 50 percent of U.S. home mortgages. Fannie and Freddie were chartered by the U.S. Congress (they are known as government-sponsored enterprises, or GSEs). Fannie and Freddie obtained the money to buy mortgages by issuing bonds in the U.S. capital market. Many buyers of these bonds believed that these firms were "too big to fail," and their bonds were judged almost as free of default risk as the bonds issued by the U.S. Treasury. Because these bonds had a superior credit rating, the interest rates on the mortgages that these firms might buy were significantly lower than interest rates on other mortgages. Fannie and Freddie were taken over by the U.S. Treasury in 2008 because of losses on the mortgages in their portfolios.

Mortgages come in two sizes, "conventional conforming" and "jumbo." The distinction—and the dollar value of the boundary between these two sizes—is that Fannie Mae (more formally the Federal National Mortgage Association) and Freddie Mac (more formally the Federal Home Loan Mortgage Corporation) were prohibited from buying mortgages larger than a stipulated amount by the Federal Housing Finance Board. This ceiling is adjusted annually to reflect changes in the median house price. The ceiling had been $421,000 until 2008 and was increased to $729,000 in some parts of the country during the financial crisis to provide support to the market for larger and more expensive homes. Fewer than 20 percent of all mortgages are in the jumbo group.

Private Mortgage Insurance

The biggest challenge for first-time homebuyers is accumulating the money for a down payment. Lenders require that borrowers pay a minimum of 20 percent down of the appraised value of the home so that the mortgage can be sold readily in the secondary market. Private mortgage insurance (PMI) was developed as a "gap filler" that would enable home buyers whose incomes qualified them to buy a more expensive home to compensate for lack of the cash to meet the 20 percent threshold. The insurance protects the lenders against loss if the borrower defaults and ensures that the mortgage can be readily sold in the secondary market. The borrower pays an insurance premium, which often is packaged with the monthly mortgage payment. The monthly premium on the PMI varies with the amount of the borrower's down payment relative to the amount associated with a 20 percent down payment; a borrower who pays 10 percent down pays a lower insurance premium than a borrower who pays 5 percent down. The amount of the monthly insurance premium is based on the total amount of the mortgage (and not just that part of the mortgage in excess of 80 percent of the property's market value). When the borrowers' equity increases to 20 percent of the appraised market value, the borrower can drop the PMI policy.

Prior to the Great Depression, the typical home mortgage was a five-year, interest-payment-only loan; at the end of five years, the borrower would effectively take out another five-year mortgage loan to get the cash to repay the maturing loan. The borrowers had a "rollover risk": their ability to repay the mortgage on the maturity date depended on their ability to get another five-year mortgage. (A mortgage with a large principal payment due on the maturity date is known as a balloon loan.) Many borrowers whose mortgages were maturing during the Great Depression could not get the mortgages renewed because the banks that they had borrowed from had failed and were closed, and some of these borrowers were forced into bankruptcy.

A bright entrepreneur developed the idea of an "amortizing mortgage"; the amount borrowed would be repaid in full over thirty years, and hence there would be no need to refinance the loan at the maturity date. The inspiration for the thirty-year maturity was railroad bonds. The monthly debt service payment is constant over the life of the mortgage; in the first several years, more than 95 percent of the monthly debt service payment is for interest. Month by month, the interest payment component of the fixed monthly debt service payment decreases, and the principal-reducing component increases.

The annual and hence the monthly payments on a thirty-year fully amortizing mortgage would be slightly more than 3 percent higher than the monthly payment on an interest-only mortgage. If the interest rate on the mortgage were 6 percent and the mortgage were for $100,000, the monthly payment on the interest-only mortgage would be $500 (or $6,000 a year), and the monthly payment on the amortizing mortgage would be $515 (or $6,180 a year). Fixed interest rate mortgages are available for other maturities, including fifteen years and ten years.

Adjustable rate mortgages (ARMs) combine a long maturity, say, thirty years, and a short-term interest rate; in some cases, the interest rates are reset every year, and in others, every third year or every fifth year. The interest rates are reset on the anniversary dates so that a fixed margin is maintained with a benchmark interest rate. ARMs usually have a limit on the maximum change in the interest rate each time the rate is reset, and there may be a second ceiling on the maximum change in the interest rate during the term of the mortgage.

Interest-only mortgages may be at a fixed interest rate or at an adjustable interest rate. The key feature of these mortgages is that the principal—the amount owed—is constant.

Several facts about the pattern of interest rates bear on your choice of the terms of a mortgage. Short-term interest rates are lower than long-term interest rates most of the time. Both short-term and long-term interest rates vary over the business cycle; as the economy develops slack, both short-term interest rates and long-term interest rates decline, and the decline in short-term interest rates is larger than the decline in long-term interest rates. As the economy expands, interest rates increase, and short-term interest rates increase more rapidly than long-term interest rates. At the peak of the expansion, short-term interest rates can be as high as or modestly higher than long-term interest rates. Interest rates are especially sensitive to changes in the anticipated inflation rate; changes in the interest rates due to changes in the anticipated inflation rate can moderate or even dominate the changes due to altered business conditions.

You're likely to have two conflicting objectives when you choose a mortgage. One is to minimize your monthly debt-servicing payment—the monthly cash payment that you make to the lender. The second is to minimize your net interest payments. The difference between these two statements is that in the former case the monthly payment includes a payment to reduce your indebtedness. The conflict between these objectives is illustrated by comparing the monthly payment on a fixed interest rate fifteen-year mortgage with the monthly payment on a fixed interest rate thirty-year mortgage. The interest rate on the fifteen-year fixed interest rate mortgage can be as much as 0.5 percent a year below the interest rate on the thirty-year fixed interest rate mortgage; the relationship between these two interest rates varies over the business cycle. Thus, if the face value of the mortgage is $100,000, the interest payment on the first year of a fifteen-year mortgage might be $5,500, and the interest payment on the thirty-year mortgage might be $6,000. The first-year amortization payment on the shorter-term mortgage would be $6,666, and the comparable payment on the thirty-year would be $3,333.

When choosing the terms of a mortgage, your primary objective should be to minimize your after-tax interest costs over the life of the mortgage. Your secondary objective should be to minimize the large swings in your monthly debt service payments. Mortgages that enable you to minimize your monthly payments may have higher interest rates.

One way to minimize your after-tax interest costs is to choose a one-year ARM. When interest rates increase, your monthly interest payment will increase. Nevertheless, your monthly interest payment is likely to be lower than the interest payments you would have made if you had had either a fifteen-year mortgage or a thirty-year mortgage.

You could create your own interest payment reserve account with the savings in interest payments. For example, if your mortgage is for $100,000 and the interest rate on the one-year ARM is 3.5 percent and the interest rate on the thirty-year fixed interest rate mortgage is 6 percent, you will save $2,500 in the first year if you take the ARM. Allocate most or all of this amount to a special savings account. Year by year, allocate the amount that you save from taking the ARM to this account. If the interest rate on the ARM increases above 6 percent, take the cash from your special savings account that represents the excess of the amount due over the $6,000 that you would have paid if you had taken the thirty-year fixed interest rate mortgage. Alternatively, you could apply the difference between the interest payment that you would have made if you had taken the fixed interest rate at 6 percent and the interest rate that you actually pay to reduce the amount owed on the mortgage.

The primary argument for preferring a fixed interest rate mortgage is that you believe that the inflation rate is going to increase with the consequence that both short-term and long-term interest rates will increase, and this increase will dominate the savings you might have made if you had taken the one-year ARM. Individuals in this group don't like the uncertainty associated with a one-year or three-year ARM. Many borrowers are not comfortable with the prospect that the monthly interest payment on an ARM might increase, and so they prefer a fixed interest rate.

The monthly payment on a fifteen-year fully amortizing $100,000 mortgage would be about 15 percent higher than the monthly payment on a thirty-year mortgage with the same interest rate. The exact amount of the difference depends on the interest rate on the fifteen-year mortgage. Often the interest rate on the fifteen-year mortgage has been 0.5 percent lower than the interest rate on the thirty-year mortgage, in this case, say, 5.5 percent. The monthly payment on a fifteen-year mortgage would be 10 to 15 percent larger than the monthly payment on a thirty-year mortgage; part of the money for the more rapid pay-off comes from the lower interest rate on the shorter-term mortgage.

Compare the interest rate and the monthly payment on a fifteen-year fixed interest rate mortgage with the interest rate and the monthly payment on a thirty-year fixed interest rate mortgage. Your monthly payment on the fifteen-year mortgage will be larger because you will be repaying the principal in half the time. The larger monthly cash payment may be a stretch for your budget, but think of the accelerated repayment as a form of "forced saving" and the lower interest rate as a subsidy to your saving.

Now compare an ARM and the fixed interest rate on a fifteen-year mortgage loan. The interest rate on the ARM is likely to be lower than the interest rate of the fixed interest rate fifteen-year loan, and the difference between the two interest rates will depend on whether the economy is operating at or close to full employment or whether there is a lot of slack in the economy.

When to Refinance Your Mortgage

The transaction costs of refinancing your mortgage are likely to be about 1 percent or a bit more of the outstanding balance on the mortgage. The implication is that you can profitably refinance whenever the interest rate on the new mortgage is at least 1.25 percent below the interest rate on the outstanding mortgage. Don't necessarily rush to refinance, because mortgage interest rates may decline further.

When interest rates are cyclically high relative to trend, consider an ARM; if interest rates are increasing, consider a three-year ARM. But if interest rates have been decreasing, choose the one-year ARM. Your bet is that interest rates will decline further, and in that case it would be costly to be locked into a fixed interest rate mortgage. Conversely, if interest rates are exceptionally low relative to the long-term average value, consider a fixed interest rate long-term mortgage to capture a low interest rate for the life of the loan.

Points or No Points

Generally, the lenders set the interest rates and points so that they are indifferent between whether you choose the mortgage with or without points provided that you hold the mortgage at least four years. If you hold the mortgage for a shorter period, then the lower interest rate is likely to be less costly; if you hold the mortgage for a longer period, then the payment of points is likely to be the lower-cost choice.

Your third decision when you borrow is how you will reimburse the lender for the one-time administrative costs the lender incurs when it arranges the loan. You might pay these costs up-front through "points," or they may be "buried" in the interest rate. The "points" might be 1 percent of the value of the mortgage or 1.5 percent of the value of the mortgage; these points are like a wedge between the face value of the mortgage and the amount of cash you receive when you borrow. Assume you take out a $100,000 mortgage. If the points are 1 percent of the face value of the loan, the seller receives a check for $99,000. You may be offered a choice between a mortgage with points set at 1 percent and a mortgage without points with a slightly higher interest rate.

How Big a Mortgage?

Assume you've won the lottery and are cash rich. Should you repay the mortgage? You'll "earn" the interest rate on the mortgage—actually you'll earn the after-tax interest rate on the mortgage, since you will no longer have the tax deduction from the interest payments. Assume that the interest rate on the mortgage is 5.5 percent and that you're in the 40 percent marginal tax bracket as a result of the combination of the federal and state income taxes; then the after-tax interest rate is 3.3 percent. If you can invest in tax-free bonds that pay 4.5 percent, then you're ahead by 1.2 percent a year. The trade-off involves the comparison between the after-tax interest cost of the mortgage and the after-tax rate of return on the securities you might have held if you hadn't paid down the mortgage.

ACTIONABLES

1. When you contemplate a move, ask yourself how long you intend to live in the new location. If it seems unlikely that you will live in that new location for more than three or four years, be reluctant

to buy, because the transaction costs associated with the purchase and the sale will raise your annual housing expense.

2. When you contemplate buying a home, project your income for the next four or five years. Calculate your average annual income, and be reluctant to buy if the purchase price is significantly higher than three times your projected average income.

3. When you buy, borrow from family to obtain the funds so that you can pay 20 percent down. A second mortgage at an interest rate slightly higher than the interest rate on the first mortgage is preferable to private mortgage insurance.

4. When you are searching for a mortgage, first seek the lowest possible interest rate. One approach is to take a fifteen- or thirty-year ARM with an interest rate that is adjustable once a year. Your lifetime interest payments will be minimized with this approach.

5. If the variability of the interest rate on a one-year ARM is unsettling, consider a three-year ARM if the interest rate on the three-year ARM is only modestly higher than on the one-year ARM.

6. If the variability of the interest rate on ARMs is unsettling, consider a fifteen-year fixed interest rate mortgage; the interest rate is likely to be lower than on the thirty-year fixed interest rate mortgage. The monthly cash payment will be larger.

7. If interest rates are extremely high relative to trend, take a one-year ARM; your strategy is that you will refinance when interest rates decline.

8. As the equity in your home increases, arrange a home equity line. Use the line as your primary source of liquidity.

9. Periodically compare interest rates on newly available mortgages with the interest rates on your current mortgage. Consider refinancing when the interest rate that you might pay on a new mortgage is at least 1.25 percent below the interest rate on your current mortgage. Develop a friendly relationship with a mortgage broker and ask him to keep you informed of the mortgage interest rate. Don't rush to refinance—you want to refinance when the spread between the interest rate you currently pay and the interest rate you would pay if you refinance is sufficiently large so that the reduction in your interest payments is twice as large as the one-time refinancing costs.

10. Don't be bamboozled into fully paying off your mortgage. Your strategy should be to borrow on short term and invest at long term.

11. Points—consider the trade-off between a mortgage with points and one without—you want to be able amortize the points, essentially a fixed cost, over at least four years.

12. When selling your home, don't be shy about negotiating the commission with the broker. Consider using a discount broker.

13. If you have rental properties and will be required to pay large capital gains on the difference between the market price of the properties at the time of sale and your tax basis, consider living in the house for several years.

14. Before you buy a timeshare, scout the market in secondhand timeshares; usually there are ads in *USA Today*.

15. When you go into the second home market in resort communities, be very cautious of the sharks with real estate licenses.

16. Be skeptical when the seller suggests that the rental income will cover your mortgage.

5   How Much Insurance Should Noah Have Carried on His Ark?

When God told Noah to build an ark because of the coming flood, Noah was perplexed—he had never built an ark. And there was no one to go to for advice, since no one had ever built an ark. There were no design standards for a large structure that had to accommodate many diverse travelers. What if the ark developed a leak? Who would reimburse the cost of repairs? Noah wondered whether he should buy liability insurance. Noah also was apprehensive that the ark might damage someone's property since he had no navigation experience; he thought it would be prudent to buy collision insurance. And then there was the question of whether some of the passengers might find their accommodations uncomfortable and might sue because the living experience on the ark differed from the advertisements.

Noah couldn't find anyone who would sell insurance against these risks; there was no Allstate, GEICO, State Farm, Hartford Group, or Lloyd's. Insurance requires that a firm buy the risk of losses that others want to sell—but generally the buyers would want to be able to buy a large number of similar risks on the assumption that only a few would lead to losses. No one had any data for estimating the likelihood of the events that kept Noah up all night. Noah had no choice—he had to self-insure because he could not sell the risks to others.

Noah's quandary is typical of many. When should you buy insurance and when should you self-insure? Each year Americans write checks totaling hundreds of billions of dollars to insurance companies and their agents to buy policies that will compensate for losses due to death, floods, fires, auto accidents, theft, lawsuits, credit card fraud, and the failures of automotive power trains, ovens and microwaves, garage doors, and toasters. (Policies to reimburse the losses due to the "premature" failure of products are called warranties or extended warranties). If individuals can't or won't buy insurance to compensate for the loss associated with a particular risk, they self-insure by default—usually without thinking about it.

If you can buy insurance to reimburse part or all of the losses associated with different risks, the central question is when to self-insure and when to buy insurance. In effect, the purchase of insurance is the "sale of the risk of a loss" to someone willing to buy and carry the risk. Whether you should self-insure depends on both the significance of any possible loss to your income and wealth, and the true cost of the insurance.

You may be "required" to buy several different types of insurance. If you have a mortgage, the lender almost certainly will require that you have a homeowners' policy and a title insurance policy to protect the value of the loan. Your state government may require that you carry auto liability insurance to provide for payment to others should you be at fault in an accident. Otherwise most Americans take an incremental approach to the purchase of insurance. Some individuals buy individual policies because of some unique events on their calendar. A brochure in the mail suggests the need for insurance against credit card fraud. The premium seems modest, and why not? You're at the Avis counter at Logan Airport to pick up a car, and the agent suggests collision insurance; you've heard about the habits of drivers in Greater Boston, and the insurance is a few bucks and seems cheap—a good deal. Your travel agent suggests you buy a travel insurance policy in case an untoward event prevents you from taking the cruise that you have already paid for. When you're checking out at the appliance store, you're almost always asked whether you want an extended warranty.

An alternative approach is to decide how much you plan to spend on insurance each year—over and above the amounts required by mortgage lenders and the state motor vehicle departments. Once you've decided on this amount, the next step is to determine the cost-effectiveness of different types of insurance. Are you spending the appropriate amounts on life insurance, disability insurance, and homeowners insurance?

When you consider whether to buy these kinds of insurance, you need to weigh the trade-off between two variables. One is the impact of an accident or mishap on your financial well-being and the well-being of your dependents, and the second is the true cost of each type of insurance.

The True Cost of Different Types of Insurance Policies

Ask ten of your friends, "How much does your auto insurance cost each year?" It's a safe bet that virtually all of them will answer by telling you the amount of the semiannual or annual premiums. Your friends misunderstand the question. They confuse the "premium" with the "cost." The premium is the payment to the company. The cost is the difference between the amounts that the buyers of the insurance as a group pay the company that sells the insurance and the amounts that this company pays in the settlement of losses.

There's an apocryphal but illustrative story on this distinction. A clever entrepreneur in Chicago designed a cancer insurance policy that had a $5 monthly premium and so much fine print that none of the insured was ever successful in receiving any money from the company to reimburse their losses. The $5 premium was low so that the company could convince customers, "You can't afford not to have it." But the cost was actually extremely high, because the company never made any payments in settlement of losses.

Indeed, it's axiomatic that the lower the premium, the higher the cost; low premiums are like penny stocks, "sucker bait" designed to attract the gullible. Individuals often fall into the trap of spending $40 or $80 for a policy because "it isn't an awful lot of money." Maybe not to you, but it's a lot of money to the companies that sell tens of thousands of these policies; they have designed these policies so the premium is low.

Some airports once had machines that sold insurance policies against loss of life due to air crashes. The buyers paid $3 for a policy that would pay $1 million if the airplane had an unplanned abrupt landing. The buyers filled out a short form when they bought the policy in which they identified themselves as the insured and designated the beneficiary of the policy. They dropped one copy of the form in a slot in the machine before boarding their flight, and mailed another copy to a relative or a friend.

This policy seemed cheap because the premium was less than the price of a pack of cigarettes. But whether the $3 premium was cheap or expensive depends on the frequency of crashes that would lead the insurance company to pay $1 million to the beneficiaries of the insured. In many years there were no crashes, so the insurance company kept the hundreds of thousands of $3 premiums that it collected. When a crash occurred, the company would pay $1 million to the designated beneficiaries of each of the insured. Measuring the true cost of this type of insurance requires a comparison between the amounts the company collected in premiums over the years with the amount the company paid in settlement of losses.

Take an extreme case. If the amount of money paid by the insurance company manager in the settlement of claims is more or less equal to the cash received from those paying the premiums and the investment income on the cash reserves built up in the previous years, then the cost of the insurance is zero. This outcome seems unlikely by design unless the Salvation Army or the Sisters of Mercy manages the insurance company—or unless the company mistakenly set the premiums too low relative to the likelihood of losses and the amounts of these losses. In a few cases, insurance companies have paid out more in the settlement of losses on a particular type of risk than they have collected in premiums, and in these instances the buyers of the insurance are subsidized—inadvertently—by the insurance companies. (Property and casualty companies took extremely large losses on the policies that they had sold in Florida and nearby states because of damage due to hurricanes. Some of these companies went bankrupt.) You might say the insurance is free. (The companies use the profits from selling other types of insurance to subsidize these losses.)

The true cost of insurance is the percentage difference between the cash payments from the manager to the insured in the settlement of losses and cash payments to the manager in the form of premiums collected and investment income on the cash reserves built up over the years. When the ratio of the amount paid in settlement of claims to the amount collected from premiums is low, the insurance is expensive.

Ballpark estimates of the "true cost" of different types of insurance policies are not readily available. The companies that sell credit card insurance, identity theft insurance, travel insurance, burial insurance, and extended warranties are reluctant to reveal the true costs because their sales would decline sharply if the buyers knew the scope of the rip-offs. When someone tries to sell you one of these policies, ask two questions. "How much money does your firm take in each year in premiums?" and "How much money does your firm pay out each year in the settlement of claims?"

If the loss is unambiguous, the cost of the insurance is relatively low; the manager doesn't have to spend much money verifying the loss. The loss of life almost always is unambiguous; the death certificate provided by the medical authorities is sufficient proof for the company (although if the loss of life occurs within a year or two after the policy was purchased, the company might spend some money to determine if the death was self-inflicted). One reason that the cost of auto liability insurance is so much higher than the cost of life insurance is that company managers incur substantial costs to determine both the legitimacy of claims and the amount of the losses. Some scoundrels made a good living—at least for a short while—duping the managers of auto insurance companies to pay for their inability to work because of "whiplash injury" incurred in auto collisions. The Russian mafia in the Brighton Beach neighborhood of Brooklyn bilked insurance companies out of tens of millions of dollars as a result of "injuries" incurred in staged "auto accidents."

Americans spend too much money to buy insurance against nickel-and-dime losses and not enough money to buy life insurance—and disability insurance—on the breadwinners in their families. You've seen the ads with the smiling four-month-old child and the suggestion that a life insurance policy should be purchased on the child's life. These policies are costly because the payment in the settlement of losses is low relative to the premium revenues. The premiums paid for these policies are not an efficient use of the limited funds available to buy insurance. Indeed, this type of insurance is largely a waste of money; the sellers are taking advantage of the sentimentality of the buyers.

A risk is the likelihood that an unanticipated event—or an event that is possible but unlikely—might lead to personal injury or death or a financial loss. The risk is low when the probability that an event might occur is less than one in a thousand; the risk is high when the likelihood of this event is one in ten or one in fifteen. The risk of death from Russian roulette is high, one in six.

The probable loss is the product of the likelihood of a loss and the amount of the loss if the event should occur. In some cases the amount of the loss is modest. When you rent a car from Hertz or Avis and decide not to take the collision insurance, you're on the hook for a maximum of

$500—in the grand scheme of things, not a lot of money. (Hertz, Avis, et al. have one premium across most cities regardless of the time of year; these insurances are less costly on those winter days when the roads are snowy and icy because the probability of an accident is so much higher.) The risks that should be insured are those where the probable loss is large and could lead to a significant decline in your standard of living—or in the standards of living of those who depend on you—because of a decline in the family's assets or income.

Life is risky. You can slip on a banana peel and on ice and on mixtures of oil and water. Airplanes fall from the sky, fortunately much less frequently than in the past. Lightning causes fires. Rivers overflow and basements get flooded. Forty thousand people a year are killed in auto accidents, and hundreds of thousands are injured. Your automobile may break down, or you may hit the proverbial telephone pole. Cavities develop in teeth. Some elderly individuals are affected by Alzheimer's or Parkinson's disease or some other incurable debilitating illness.

The likelihood of any one of these events occurring in a year or even in a five-year period is low. In some cases the loss is modest and in others it is very high. A fire in your home or the death of the breadwinner can be devastating. Several of these events can reduce your income or net worth significantly or—if you are a breadwinner and die early—the income and net worth of your survivors.

The Design of Insurance Policies

The principle of insurance is that a large group of individuals pay cash every month or every quarter or every year to a manager who has agreed to pay up to a specified amount of cash to any member of this group that incurs a loss because of a specified event—a death or an auto accident or a fire or a plane crash or a flood or a heavy rainstorm on a day of a major outdoor event like a tennis match.

The cash payments to the manager are the premiums. The dollar amount of the cash payments—say, $100,000—from the manager to the insured or to the beneficiaries of the insured in the payment for losses due to death is specified in the life insurance policies. With many types of policies, including homeowners and auto insurance, the amounts of the payments in compensation for the losses depend on the amounts of the losses. Those who have incurred losses may be required to obtain several estimates of the losses. Often the insurance policy provides for an upper limit on the amount that will be paid in the settlement of a loss and may pay only a fixed proportion of the loss, say, 75 percent. This type of payment feature is known as co-insurance; the insured self-insure the remaining loss. Moreover, the manager may pay the insured only if the loss exceeds a specified amount, so the individuals self-insure for small losses in a feature known as the deductible.

A manager has two objectives when designing an insurance policy. The premiums must be sufficiently low so that individuals will buy the policy; if the premiums are high, many of the potential customers may buy insurance from competitors, or they may self-insure. The premiums must be high enough so that the cash coming in each month and each year will be sufficient to pay all legitimate claims. Often the manager builds up a "reserve" to protect the company from the exceptionally large losses in excess of premiums that can be sustained in a particular year or several years.

The manager keeps the premiums low by being selective about whom the company insures. The manager is reluctant to sell life insurance policies to those who have a history of heart problems and to sell auto insurance policies to young male drivers. (However, some managers specialize in selling policies to young male drivers and to individuals in other high-risk groups. The premiums for these riskier groups accordingly are high.)

From time to time, an insurance company may go bankrupt—in retrospect the premiums were too low or the manager was not sufficiently discriminating between "good" and "poor" risks. (A number of individuals who sold insurance at Lloyd's in London were forced into bankruptcy because the losses in settlement of claims for premature death because of inhalation of asbestos were much larger than the premiums collected; their reserves were too small.) To reduce the likelihood of bankruptcy, the manager often insures several different kinds of risks; rather than specialize in selling fire insurance or flood insurance, the manager sells both in a "package" policy on the assumption that large payments to those with losses from fires would be unlikely to occur at the same time as large payments to those with losses from floods. Each manager insures only a very few houses in the same neighborhood; the manager wants geographic diversification.

Each buyer of insurance hunts for bargains. But the premium payments are only one side of the bargain. The other side involves the amounts that the manager pays in the settlement of losses.

The Principles That Should Guide the Purchase of Insurance

There probably are as many types of insurance policies as there are types of losses. Once an imaginative entrepreneur has identified a potential loss that might occur because of an otherwise unfortunate event, he determines whether a profit could be made by selling an insurance policy that would compensate the insured against losses from this event.

Your first question is when to self-insure and when to buy insurance. If you self-insure, you save the cash that would otherwise be used to pay the premiums for the insurance—but then you are exposed to a financial loss in the event of an accident.

Self-insure when any loss would be small relative to your income and net worth and the cost of insurance is high, and buy insurance when the loss would be large relative to your income and net worth and cost of the insurance is low. It is not a good use of your money to insure against small losses, especially since the true cost of this type of insurance coverage is likely to be very high. If you're at the airport and have the choice between the $3 flight insurance policy and $3 of lottery tickets, buy the lottery tickets—the price is the same and if your number comes up, you collect the money.

For example, auto rental companies sell insurance that will compensate against losses if the vehicle is damaged—the premium often is $20 or $25 a day for a policy that would reimburse the first $500 of damage; they also sell a personal liability policy, and they sell a personal injury policy. These insurances are costly; the amounts that these companies pay in the settlement of losses are low relative to the amount they collect in premiums. The Hertz and Avis insurance businesses almost certainly are much more profitable than the auto rental business since there is virtually no price competition in the sale of these insurances. It's as if the rental of the auto at a very competitive price is the bait that induces a nontrivial number of renters to buy one or several of these insurances. Hertz and Avis haven't figured out how to sell the insurance without renting autos.

To the extent possible, self-insure against small losses and buy insurance policies that have the largest possible deductibles. It's costly for insurance companies to reimburse relatively small losses because the administrative expenses involved in determining the legitimacy of these losses are likely to be high, and the premiums must be set high enough to pay for these expenses. Continually ask for larger deductibles as your capacity to adjust to large losses increases. Search out firms that offer higher deductibles.

Only buy insurance if its cost is reasonably low—that is, if the amount of cash the companies pay out in settlement of claims is large relative to the premiums collected by the company. Insurance against loss due to credit card fraud or loss of luggage or of an overnight stay if travel plans are disrupted is very expensive. Never buy these policies. Yes, these policies may offer some "peace of mind," but think of the peace of mind that you will have acquired because you have saved thousands of dollars over the years if you continually self-insure against these low-likelihood events and small losses.

Be selective in the choice of companies from whom you buy insurance— you want to deal only with companies that are reluctant to insure those who are likely to incur losses. The less discriminating the company is in the selection of risks to be insured, the higher the premiums it charges. Consider the TV commercials that offer $10,000 life insurance policies without any medical exam. Those individuals who have been denied insurance elsewhere because of their irregular heartbeats buy these policies because they wouldn't be sold a policy if they were required to pass a medical exam. If you have an irregular heartbeat, buy one or several of these policies; otherwise, avoid them.

If you have dependents, you will need life insurance and disability insurance so that your dependents can maintain their standard of living in the event of a sharp decline in your income. If you own a home, you'll need a homeowners policy to compensate for exceptionally large losses due to hurricanes, floods, and heavy snows (remember, ask for the highest deductibles). If you own a car, you'll need liability insurance and you may need collision and comprehensive insurance if the value of the car is high relative to your income. But if you drive an el wrecko, skip the collision and comprehensive insurance. You may conclude that you'll need a policy that would compensate against large legal costs in case you're sued because someone slipped on the sidewalk in front of your home. The basic types of policies that most individuals need include life, disability, homeowners, and automobile and personal liability insurance. Most other types of insurance are excessively costly.

Life Insurance: The Gap Filler for Dependents

Life insurance is a gap filler—its primary purpose is to enable dependent survivors to maintain their standard of living should the proverbial train hit their "breadwinner." There are tens of millions of life insurance policies now in force in the United States. Many of these are group life insurance policies, usually available as a benefit from employers to many or all of those on their payrolls. Often the employer provides a modest subsidy to help pay part of the insurance premium; the employer might pay the premium associated with the purchase of the first $12,000 or $25,000 of life insurance. Employees can buy additional life insurance up to some multiple of their salaries and the premiums for these policies are withheld from their monthly salary checks.

Some group life insurance is sold to members of an organization, who may or may not choose to buy the insurance. Usually the organizations that arrange for the sale of these policies do not subsidize the purchase.

One advantage of group life insurance is that the premiums may be low because selling costs are lower than for individual life insurance policies. Moreover, medical exams usually are not required for those who buy group life insurance, although at times the insured individuals may have to sign statements declaring that they have not been denied a life insurance policy in the previous two years.

Some group life insurance policies provide that the insurance premium each member of the group pays is the same regardless of age (and hence mortality expectancy). In contrast, other group life policies provide for age-related insurance premiums; older individuals pay somewhat higher premiums. Fraternal groups often sell these age-related policies.

Disability Insurance: The Forgotten "Twin" to Life Insurance

If you lose your ability to remain employed because of a medical problem or an accident, earned income will decline sharply, and there will be a gap to fill. Twenty percent of Americans will lose more than ninety days of employment at some stage during their careers as a result of an illness or accident. Often their income will stop. A small number will become permanently unemployable; others may only be employable at lower annual incomes.

The family's savings or living standard may decline or debt may increase, perhaps sharply. Moreover, although the personal circumstances may be less traumatic than an early or premature death, the financial circumstances may be even more difficult for the family because of the costs of maintenance of the disabled breadwinner.

One source of income for disabled Americans is benefit payments from the U.S. Social Security Administration, which totaled $99 billion in 2008. These payments continue until individuals are eligible to receive traditional Social Security retirement benefits.

The monthly check from Social Security to the disabled is not likely to be large enough to maintain the family's standard of living. Disability insurance from private firms can fill the gap. The amount of disability insurance that each family needs changes over time and varies with the age of the breadwinner and the ages of the children; the amount of disability insurance needed can be estimated much like the estimate of the necessary amount of life insurance.

Groucho Marx once quipped that he would never join a club that would accept him as a member. If the premiums charged for each individual participating in the group purchase are the same regardless of the age or health of those about to be insured, the insurance is going to be expensive for the younger and healthier members of the group, who are subsidizing the older and less healthy ones.

Is group life insurance a "good buy"? It depends on whether the premiums are higher or lower than those of an individual life insurance policy that would pay the same benefit.

Who Owns AARP?

AARP has more than 12 million members, more than any other voluntary association. Membership is open to anyone over age 50. Annual membership costs are modest. AARP lobbies on behalf of seniors, publishes a monthly magazine, and obtains discounts for its members at hotels and auto rental facilities.

AARP also offers "Guaranteed Acceptance Life" insurance policies through New York Life. AARP has similar arrangements with other companies for auto insurance and motorcycle insurance. The older the insured are at the time they buy a policy, the higher the premiums. Consider some of the sentences in the marketing literature. "AARP members ages 50 to 80, and spouses ages 45 to 80, cannot be turned down. No doctor's visit or health questions are needed." "To guarantee acceptance without medical underwriting, the premium includes an extra mortality risk charge." "Benefits are limited to 125% of the premiums paid during the first two years of the policy." "Benefits will not be paid if death results from suicide in the first two years of the policy." This type of policy may be useful for those who would be "turned down" (really a wonderful way to say rejected), but the policy almost certainly is much too expensive relative to the alternatives for those who would not be turned down.

Is AARP the advocate of its members or of the companies that want to sell insurance policies to its members?

How Much Life Insurance Do You Need?

The most important use of life insurance is to enable the survivors of breadwinners to maintain their standard of living should the breadwinner die. In effect, the cash payment that the survivors of the insured would receive after the death of the insured would be used to "buy an annuity" that in turn would provide monthly checks to the survivors to enable them to maintain their standard of living as long as they remain dependent. The likelihood is high that the surviving dependents would receive a monthly check from the Survivors Benefits component of the U.S. Social Security program. (See Chapter 13 for a discussion of Social Security benefits and how to access the Social Security Administration's Web site.) Moreover, the breadwinner may have had a defined-contribution pension plan, and the accumulated savings in this plan are likely to become available to the dependent survivors. There may also be a payment to the survivors under a defined-benefit pension plan.

Life insurance "professionals" often suggest that the amount of insurance needed is six times the insured person's annual income. This rule of thumb may help sell life insurance, but it's a meaningless estimate for most individuals. This rule doesn't account for the number of dependents and their ages, the employment skills of the surviving spouse, and the accumulated savings and pension benefits of the breadwinner.

Some individuals, for example, single individuals without a dependent parent or sibling, do not need any life insurance. Similarly, a couple without dependent children, parents, or siblings has no need for life insurance as long as both spouses are employed or employable. Retired individuals are no longer breadwinners, and hence they rarely need life insurance, especially if the sum of the funds available each month from Social Security, employment-related pensions, and the income of accumulated assets is adequate to maintain the standard of living of the survivor. Note that monthly payments under Social Security and under a defined-benefit plan may decline when the retired breadwinner dies. (One possible exception is that there might be a need for insurance if the pension payments would decline sharply if the former breadwinner dies.)

Four factors influence the optimal amount of life insurance for breadwinners with dependents. The greater the number of dependents, the larger the amount of life insurance needed. The younger the dependents and hence the greater the number of years before each becomes self-supporting, the larger the amount of life insurance needed. The higher the income of the breadwinner, the greater the amount of insurance needed. The amount of life insurance needed also is larger, the smaller the value of assets in the estate.

Consider James Bond. Bond has no need for life insurance as long as he is single and has no dependents. When he is married, he also has no need for life insurance as long as Mrs. Bond is an active member of the labor force. When the first child arrives, Bond needs life insurance so that his wife and child can maintain their standard of living; Mrs. Bond is reluctant to enter the labor force because she wants to stay home to care for James Jr. When the second child arrives, the amount of life insurance that is needed increases.

Distinguish the financial needs of the dependent survivors from the sources of funds to pay for these needs. One approach to estimating these financial needs is to extend the replacement ratio discussed in Chapter 12 to the money needs of the dependent survivors. Assume that Mrs. Bond and the children will need 75 percent of Bond's income to maintain their living standard until the children leave school or college and enter the labor force. For example, if Bond's income is $60,000 a year, the survivors would need $45,000 a year. As the first child enters the labor force, the amount needed by the dependent survivors is assumed to decline by ten percentage points to 65 percent or to $39,000 a year. After the second child has gone to college, the amount needed by the surviving spouse declines another ten percentage points, or to $33,000 a year.

Assume Bond is 35 years old when he first realizes that he will need life insurance. Mrs. Bond and the children then will need $45,000 a year for the next fifteen years before the older child will cease to be dependent, and then $39,000 for the next three years until the younger child ceases to be dependent, and then $33,000 for the next twelve years until Mrs. Bond becomes eligible for full Social Security benefits at age 65.

Now consider the sources of funds for the survivors. The U.S. Social Security program provides a monthly benefit to the survivors of breadwinners who have been covered by the Social Security program; the amount of the payment depends on the taxable earnings of the breadwinner and the number of the dependents. If the breadwinner had paid the maximum taxable earnings for twenty years, then the annual payment would be $12,000 for one child, a second $12,000 for a spouse, and a maximum annual payment of $30,000 if there are two or more children. Earlier it was assumed that Mrs. Bond and the children initially would need $45,000 a year, and so the survivors' benefits initially will provide two-thirds of the family's needs. These payments continue until the children reach age 18 or, if they are in college, age 21.

If Bond had an employment-related pension, its value would be transferred to Mrs. Bond and the children. Similarly the family may have some accumulated savings. This difference could be readily adjusted to reflect the cash that might be available from the pension benefit and the accumulated savings of the breadwinner's family.

Once the "gap" has been estimated on a year-by-year basis, the next step is to determine the price of the annuity that would be required to produce the money that the dependent survivors would need each year. The amount of required life insurance matches the price of this annuity— in effect, the proceeds of the life insurance policy would be used to buy the annuity.

James Bond needs life insurance to fill the gap that remains after the estimates of the family's needs to maintain its standard of living and the three sources of funds. Think of this gap as a series of annual payments that will be made to the dependent survivors. The amount of life insurance

Table 5.1

Estimating Life Insurance Needs

	Annual (1)	Total (2)	Present Value at the Interest Rate of:		
			4% (3)	5% (4)	6% (5)
Years 1–30	$5,000	$150,000	$86,000	$76,000	$69,000
Years 1–18	7,000	126,000	92,000	81,000	75,000
Years 1–10	8,000	80,000	53,000	51,000	49,000
Total		$356,000	$231,000	$208,000	$193,000

Source: Author.

that Bond needs declines as he becomes older in part because the children will be dependent for a smaller number of years and in part because the values of both pension and the accumulated savings will be larger.

Let's keep it simple. Assume that the gap based on the difference between the needs of the survivors based on the replacement ratio and the funds available from other sources is $15,000 a year for the next ten years, $12,000 a year for the next eight years, and $5,000 a year for the subsequent twelve years. This sentence can be reformulated to read that $5,000 is needed for the next thirty years plus $7,000 additionally for the next eighteen years plus $8,000 for the next ten years; see column 1 in Table 5.1. The sum of these values is $356,000; see column 2. The price of the annuity that would pay these values depends on the prevailing interest rates at the time that the annuity is purchased; the higher the interest rate, the lower the price of the annuity. If the interest rate is 4 percent, then the price of the annuity would be $231,000 (see column 3); if the interest rate is 6 percent, then the price of the annuity would be $193,000.

Life Insurance: Term versus Permanent Life

Every insurance company has a pricing policy to help it determine the premium to charge those who want to buy a life insurance policy. Assume 10,000 men at age 20 decide to buy an identical one-year $100,000 life insurance policy. Also assume that the mortality tables indicate that the probability of death of a 20-year-old man during the next twelve months is 0.5 percent. The "fair value" for the premium would be $500 if the insurance company selling the policies could operate without incurring any costs or if its operating costs were subsidized. The manager of the insurance company would set a $500 premium and collect $5 million in premiums ($500 × 10,000). The expectation is that fifty individuals in this cohort would die in the ensuing year, and the company would pay $100,000 to the beneficiaries of each of these individuals.

Note the two simplifying assumptions in this example. One is that the company doesn't have any operating costs, and the other is that the manager has perfect foresight about the number of individuals who would die each year.

The premium set by the manager would have to be somewhat higher than the amount inferred from the mortality data to cover the costs of selling the policies, collecting the premiums, investing the premium receipts for a short period, and distributing the proceeds to the beneficiaries of the deceased. Moreover, the manager might build a "cushion" or a safety margin into the premium to protect the company against bankruptcy should a surprisingly large number in the age cohort die during the same year.

The firms that sell life insurance policies set the annual premiums on the basis of anticipated mortality, which increases with age. The older individuals are when they purchase the policy, the higher the premium. One approach to the design of an insurance policy that is reflected in a "term policy" is to increase the premium each year. The competing approach used in "permanent life (PL) policies," sometimes known as "whole life policies" or "cash value (CV) policies," is that the premium is "fixed forever"—or at least until the individual reaches age 90 or 95 or 100. A third approach—actually a variant of the PL policy—is that the insured makes a one-time payment, which would be the discounted present value of the premium payments under the second approach.

There are a lot of variants of the term policy, which differ depending on whether the premium is increased every year or every fifth year or every tenth year. Renewable term policies can be extended at the end of the fixed term of five or ten or twenty years, usually up to age 70, without a medical exam; the annual premium increases on the renewable dates. A convertible term policy can be exchanged for a PL policy without a medical exam. The face value of a decreasing term insurance policy declines, although the annual premium remains constant.

Similarly, there are fifty-seven different names for PL policies, including whole life and universal life. These distinctions are like the different brands of vodka—distinctions without much of a difference. If the premium is more or less fixed, it's a PL policy.

A term policy is a term policy, period. A PL policy, in contrast, contains an embedded term policy and a dedicated savings program. Part of the annual premium that is paid to buy a PL policy is used to buy a decreasing term policy, and the rest of the premium—actually the much larger part of the premium—is added to a dedicated account planned savings program. The insurance company uses the money in your planned savings program to buy bonds, mortgages, or occasionally stocks, and the investment income is added to your accumulated savings. Each year, the value of the account in this planned savings program also increases from the combination of that part of the annual premium in excess of the amount that is required "to buy" the decreasing term policy.

At some date, the PL policy is "fully paid up"—the insured no longer makes an annual premium payment. The policy might be fully paid up when the insured reaches age 80 or 99; in some so-called endowment policies, the policy is "fully paid up" when the insured reaches age 65. When the policy is fully paid up, the investment income on the PL is sufficiently large to pay the premium for the declining term insurance component of the policy. The insured may borrow against the CV of the policy, or may ask to receive the cash; in that case the insurance policy would no longer be effective. When the CV is invested in stocks, the policy is known as a "variable life insurance policy."

The changing values of the two components of a PL policy are illustrated in Figure 5.1. The $100,000 value of the policy is measured on the vertical axis. During the first year, part of the premium is used to "buy a decreasing term insurance policy"; however, most of the premium payment is allocated to the planned savings program. During each successive year the value in the planned savings program increases, both because of the investment income in the previously accumulated savings and because part of each year's premium is allocated to the planned savings program. Hence the amount of term insurance that is purchased each year decreases (and at an increasing rate) because the value of the planned savings program is increasing at an increasing rate.

Comparisons between the premiums on a term policy and the premiums on a PL policy are shown in Table 5.2, for policies purchased at age 25—similar comparisons could be made for any age. Bob Hope (line 1) buys a $100,000 five-year level premium term life insurance policy at age 25, and the annual premium is $121 for the first five years, $123 for the second five years, $125 for the third five years, $141 for the fourth five

Figure 5.1
Components of a Permanent Life Insurance Policy

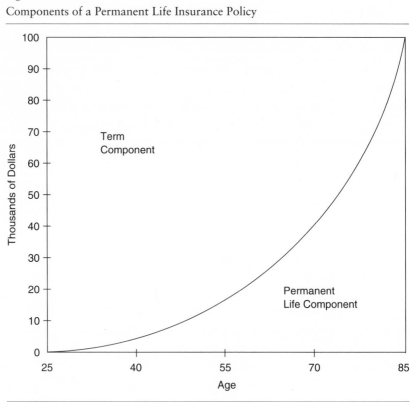

Source: Author.

years, and so on. Bing Crosby (line 2) buys a $100,000 PL policy at the same age and pays a premium of $438 for the next seventy-four years. The premium paid by Bing initially is more than three and half times higher than the premium paid by Bob; this difference declines every time Bob renews the policy, but it is only when Bob renews the policy at age 65 that the premium that he pays is higher than the $438 premium that Bing is paying.

Line 3 shows the cumulative savings that Bob has made from buying the term policy. The assumption is that Bob puts the money saved under the mattress and hence no interest is earned on this money. If Bob were slightly more ambitious, he could put the money in the bank and earn the going rate of interest.

Line 4 shows the CV attached to Bing's PL policy at the end of every fifth year. The CV increases continuously, but it is only at the end of the twentieth year that the CV is larger than the cumulative amount that Bob has saved by purchasing the term policy. This crossover probably occurred at the end of the sixteenth year, since the excess of the CV over Bob's cumulative savings is very large in the twentieth year.

The assumption implicit in line five is that Bob has moved the money from under the mattress and has found a safe and secure investment on which he earns 3 percent a year after tax.

The biggest "surprise" in Table 5.2 is that for the first fifteen or so years, Bing's CV is less than the cumulative savings that Bob has made by

Table 5.2

Comparison of Costs of Term and Permanent Life Insurance

	Annual Premiums per $100,000 for Males Bob Hope and Bing Crosby's Ages								
	Initial Age								
	25	30	35	40	45	50	55	60	65
Premium									
1. Term (Bob)	121	123	125	141	181	217	265	389	629
2. Cash value (Bing)	438	438	438	438	438	438	438	438	438
Savings									
3. Cumulative savings (Bob)		1,585	3,160	4,725	6,210	7,495	8,600	9,465	9,710
4. Cash value (Bing)		815	2,348	4,418	7,438	11,130	15,584	20,882	27,827
5. Line 3 + 3% interest		1,712	3,711	6,014	8,595	11,336	14,245	17,455	20,342

	Initial Age					
	40	45	50	55	60	65
1. Term (Bob)	141	181	207	255	379	629
2. Permanent life (Bing)	808	808	808	808	808	808
3. Cumulative savings (Bob)	3,335	6,470	9,475	12,240	14,385	15,280
4. Cash value	2,496	5,803	9,984	15,625	22,169	29,363

Source: Author.

buying the term policy. One of the sales pitches that the life insurance companies make is that their investment income is not taxable, so they have a big tax advantage. What is the economic significance of this result that the CV is smaller than the cumulative savings that Bob has made? It is highly unlikely that they have had a negative rate of return—and that is evident because over a period of fifteen years and longer, the rate of return is positive.

One explanation for the low implicit rate of return on the PL policy is that the insurance companies incur higher costs in selling a PL policy than a term policy. Another explanation is that buyers of term policies are much more sensitive to small differences in price than the buyers of PL policies.

But something strange is in the data. Either the interest rate that the insurance company is crediting to Bing's policy is low or the costs associated with the sale and management of the PL policy are high. (The likelihood that the mortality experience is higher for the buyers of the PL policy is low.)

Let's continue with the race. When Bob is age 40, the premium he pays on his term policy increases to $141. The excess of the amount that Bing pays over the amount that Bob pays has declined to $307. The product of $307 and five years is $1,535. The cumulative amount that Bob has saved is $6,240—before any imputation of interest. The CV of Bing's policy has surged to $7,438. Now Bing is ahead—but by how much depends on the interest rate that Bob can earn on the money that he didn't use to buy a PL policy.

The premium on Bob's term life policy increases again when he reaches age 60, which is the seventh increase. Still, the premium is significantly below the premium that Bing is paying. It is not until Bob renews the policy for the eighth time, at age 65, that the premium that he pays has increased over the premium that Bing pays. This type of comparison can be made at different starting ages—30, 40, and so on. The results will tend to be similar.

If, instead, both Bob and Bing had purchased these policies when they were age 30, the premium paid by Bing would be five times that paid by Bob. Note that the $389 annual premium that Bob pays on his term policy at age 60 is still slightly less than the $438 premium that Bing has been paying on his CV policy since age 25. Note that the premium that Bob pays on the term policy has increased to $629 at age 65.

Assume that Bing and Bob had first bought these policies when they were age 40. Bob's premium on the term policy would have been $207, and Bing's premium on the PL policy would have been $808. The increase in the premium on the PL policy reflects that the CV must build up to $100,000 over sixty years rather than over seventy-five, and hence the annual contribution to the savings program is larger.

When Bing buys a PL policy, in effect he is buying a package of a decreasing term insurance policy and a planned savings program that leads to the buildup of the CV. Assume that Bing bought the PL policy at age 25. Five years later the CV for this policy is $815, by age 35 the CV has increased to $2,348, and at age 65 it has increased to $27,020. If Bing lives to be 100, the CV becomes equal to the face value of the policy. At that stage, actually just before that stage, the value of the decreasing term insurance policy is a smidgen above a nickel.

Note that the annual premium paid by Bing of $438 at age 25 exceeds the $121 premium Bob paid by $317 a year, which is allocated to the accumulating CV. The product of $317 for five years amounts to $1,585 even before any investment income on the accumulating CV; at the interest rate of 5.3 percent, the CV should be approaching $2,000. Yet the CV at the end of the fifth year was $815. What happened? Who knows? The generous interpretation is that the insurer has higher management expenses for the PL policy.

You can readily replicate the savings plan embedded in the PL policy by saving and investing on your own the difference between the excess of the premium on the PL policy over the premium on the term insurance policy with the same face value. One advantage of this "do it yourself" approach is that you do not pay the selling costs and the administrative costs associated with having an insurance company manage a "contractual savings plan."

Some of the sellers of life insurance policies may seek to convince you to buy a PL policy. They will suggest—correctly—that the investment income earned by the life insurance company on the accumulating CV is not subject to income tax, whereas investment income on the funds that you invest directly would be taxable—unless you invest these funds in an IRA or 401(k) or some other tax-advantaged account or buy the tax-free bonds issued by state and local governments. Another advantage of such a policy is that you might not follow through with your planned savings program and so you will spend rather than invest the difference between the premiums on the two policies.

A PL policy is advantageous if you want a package of a term policy and a contractual savings plan. Think of the contractual payments plan as prepayment of insurance premiums when you're in your twenties and thirties of the insurance you might want in your fifties. If James Bond were asked at age 25 to pay part of the insurance premium for the insurance policy on his Aston Martin thirty years down the road, he would conclude that the person who made the suggestion is nuts. In effect that's what happens with a PL policy.

Note that when Bing is age 65 the CV of his policy is $27,000. The likelihood that Bing will need insurance when he is in his sixties or seventies is trivially low. In effect the individuals who buy a PL policy today are spending a large amount of the money that is embedded in their premium payment to prepay the premiums for the insurance that they will need to buy tomorrow. For example, consider that James Bond at age 25 buys an endowment policy that requires premium payments for the next thirty years. When Bond reaches age 55, the policy will be fully paid up and no further premiums will be necessary. Thereafter all of the cash necessary to pay the premium on the term component of the PL policy will be provided by the investment income on the accumulated CV of the policy. The CV of the policy continues to increase because the investment income is larger than the premium payment.

The Rate of Return "Built into" Whole Life Insurance Policies

The sellers of PL insurance policies set the annual premiums on the basis of their estimates of the mortality data and the rates of return that they will be able to earn when they invest that part of your premium that is not used to buy term insurance. These firms take on a longevity risk because the existing data on mortality are not likely to provide a perfect forecast of how long individuals now in their twenties, thirties, and forties will live, in large part because of the success of the health care professions in prolonging life. These firms also take on an investment risk, because they cannot know the rates of return that they will be able to earn on that part of the premium payments that will be used to build up the CVs of the millions of whole life policies. The higher the rate of return built into the policies, the lower the annual premium payment associated with a PL policy of a given amount.

If the sellers underestimate the increase in longevity, then they might bankrupt the company because the payout on their annuity contracts will prove larger than anticipated. If they overestimate the rates of return, they may bankrupt the company because the CVs will build up less rapidly than anticipated.

The sellers protect themselves against these two risks by building a "fudge factor" into the policy. That is, the premiums are set higher than the sellers think will be necessary to protect themselves against the low probability of exceptionally long life spans and exceptionally low rates of return. The sellers provide dividends, but these dividends are not guaranteed.

A Strategy for Buying Life Insurance

For most individuals, the gap that must be filled by life insurance changes over the life cycle. One approach is to buy a large renewable decreasing term insurance policy each time a new dependent arrives, either a ten-year or a twenty-year decreasing term. The year-by-year decline in the amount of insurance would more or less correspond with the decline in the price of the annuity that would be brought on by the policy's proceeds. For example, John Doe might buy a $200,000 twenty-year decreasing term insurance policy when his first child is born; as each year passes, the amount of the policy would decline by $10,000, and at the end of the twentieth year the policy would no longer be in force. The assumption is that the child becomes self-supporting at age 20. When the second child arrives, another $200,000 twenty-year renewable term insurance policy would be purchased.

The alternative to the purchase of a decreasing term policy is to buy a renewable five- or ten-year level premium policy. And the alternative to buying a traditional renewable term insurance policy and decreasing the amount of the insurance at successive renewable dates is to buy a decreasing term insurance policy. Both reduce the amount of the insurance to correspond with the decline in the years of dependency of the children and spouse of the breadwinner. The advantage of the traditional term policy is that you have the ability to determine how rapidly the face value of the policy declines.

You are presented with a series of choices. The first is whether to participate in a group policy or to buy an individual policy, and the second is whether to buy a term policy or a PL policy. The choice between the group policy and the individual policy should be based on cost. The likelihood is high that if there are several dependents, individual policies will be necessary to supplement the group life policy.

The implication is that one or several term insurance policies are preferable to a PL policy for two reasons. The first is that cash outlay per $1,000 of insurance is much smaller, so that a policy with a much higher face value can be purchased with the same number of dollars. To the extent that the dollars available from the family budget to buy insurance are limited, the first dollars spent always should be used to buy term insurance until the gap is fully filled.

Which Life Insurance Company?

There are more than 500 life insurance companies in the United States. These companies sell the same standard vanilla types of term policies and PL policies; some may sell some company-specific policies. Innovation is quickly rewarded by imitation.

These companies are evaluated by four different rating agencies with respect to their "safety and soundness"—the adequacy of their capital relative to the potential liabilities.

The relationship between the credit rating of each company and the premium charged by each company for the standard $100,000 twenty-year term life insurance policy for a 30-year-old man differs significantly. Companies with lower credit ratings charge lower premiums.

Because the policies are more or less identical, the intuition is that the premiums should be identical. But they are not—there are modest differences in the premiums. The policies are identical, but the prices are not identical. The problem in making these comparisons is that the dividends are not known.

In general, the higher the credit rating of the company, the higher the premiums for the standard policy, which leads to the question of whether you should buy a policy sold by one of the less highly rated companies. Are you at risk?

Yes, insurance companies go financially bust. But when they do, the industry becomes a mutual protection society and takes over the policies of the failed companies. The rationale is the industry wants to protect its "good name."

ACTIONABLES

1. Develop a list of the various insurance policies that you own and the amounts of premiums that you have paid in each of the last several years.

2. Develop a list of the largest risks that your family and you are exposed to and the probable loss under each risk.

3. Estimate the living costs of the family members if the income of the breadwinner suddenly declines, either because of the death of the breadwinner or because of a debilitating illness or injury.

4. Estimate the family's cash inflow from the survivors benefit program of the Social Security Program.

5. Estimate the income that the survivors will have from other sources.

6. Review the life insurance policies to determine whether together with the values you have sufficient insurance to provide an adequate standard of living to the survivors.

7. Determine the possible reduction in annual payments for life insurance if additional term insurance is purchased.

8. Review your insurance policies to determine whether you have adequate disability insurance coverage.

9. Review your homeowners' policy to determine whether coverage is adequate. Determine the reduction in the annual premium from raising the deductible.

10. Every second or third year, get a quote on the premium from some other company that sells homeowners policies.

11. Determine whether your liability against lawsuits is covered.

6   The Most Expensive U.S. Colleges Are the Best Bargains

The purchase of a college education is an investment in human capital—in the student's ability to analyze, to communicate, to persuade, to problem solve, and to lead. Only a small fraction of students and parents view the choice of a college as an investment decision, similar to the choice between buying bonds and buying stocks, or the choice between houses in different neighborhoods. Many families spend more time debating the merits of mid-priced automobiles than they do the impact of attending Omega U. rather than Alpha U. on the lifetime incomes of Sally and of Johnny.

For four to six years, the incomes of the high school graduates who immediately start work are much higher than the incomes of their classmates who chose the college option. Once the college students receive their bachelor's degrees and begin to work, they more than catch up, in that their higher incomes more than compensate for the absence of income when they were studying. The annual earnings of college graduates are more than 30 percent higher than the annual earnings of high school graduates. Moreover, the lifetime earnings of college graduates exceed those of high school graduates by an even larger amount because college graduates have fewer extended periods of unemployment and because they remain actively employed for a longer period; they have fewer on-the-job accidents that lead to early retirement. In part the high rate of return reflects that a college degree is a necessary ticket to pass through the narrow gates to high-income professions, including medicine, dentistry, and law.

The all-in costs of four years of full-time attendance at a college range from $100,000 to $250,000 or more. Tuition and fees for four years are $8,000 to $10,000 at some community colleges to $150,000 or more at the most expensive private colleges. The forgone income while attending college for four years amounts to $50,000 to $100,000. The cost of room and board should be added to the total if it exceeds the amounts the individuals would have spent on lodging and food had they not attended college. The all-in costs of attending one of the more expensive colleges for four years exceed the price of the median U.S. home. You can do the math when a family has two or more siblings.

Each year, 3 million young Americans start a four-year college program that will lead to a bachelor of arts or a bachelor of science or a comparable degree. Hundreds of thousands drop out after a year or two because "something is wrong" or at least not quite right—the college they selected was inappropriate for their interests, preferences, and level of preparation. Dropping out is costly, both financially and psychologically. The incomes of those who complete only two years of college are only slightly higher than those who entered the labor force immediately after high school. Hence the rates of return on the investment in the third and fourth years of college are extremely high.

For many students and families, the choice of a college primarily involves noneconomic issues, including "breaking away" from the family or the tradition of attending the same college that other family members were at, the search for a "prestige brand," conformity with the plans of high school peers, and the desire for "one's own space" rather than as an investment in human capital. America is an upwardly mobile country and the educational ambitions and achievements of many students are high, often exceeding those of their parents—which can be difficult for both groups. The objectives of parents often differ from those of their children—and both often find it difficult to articulate these differences. Some parents are interested in the bragging rights attached to having a child at a selective and prestigious college—or the same college that they attended.

Ask most Americans why they want their children to go to college, and most will say that they want their children to "have a better life"—to have more opportunities and to become culturally enriched. Press further, and they might say that they want their children to have more satisfying careers or to earn higher incomes. The American dream is to get ahead, both materially and in the larger sense of personal achievement.

Many students are eager for the high incomes associated with success as lawyers, doctors, and business executives. Other ambitious students are interested in careers in the military, religious organizations, government service, or environmental activism; helping other individuals and contributing to their communities are more important than a high income. But even these students want to be able to pay their bills, save for retirement, and become attractive candidates to employers in their chosen fields.

Hundreds of articles and books have been written on the choice of a college, including annual issues of *U.S. News and World Report*. These articles and books contain much helpful information on the costs, especially out-of-pocket payments, for tuition and living expenses; they also provide information on scholarships and other types of financial aid. But they offer little information on the investment aspects of the college experience—how colleges can be compared in terms of the value that each is likely to add to the student's lifetime income. If a family chooses wisely, the prospective rate of return can be 40 or 50 percent or more on the family's tuition payments.

The paradox is that even though a large part of the college experience is about upward mobility, getting ahead, and the Horatio Alger sentiments about success, relatively little attention has been given to estimating the increase in lifetime incomes associated with attendance at different colleges. You're going to have to sort through the relative importance of the financial aspects of the college experience. One way to proceed is to identify the group of colleges whose attributes provide the best match with the student's interests and personality and then help identify which of these colleges is likely to lead to the largest increase in lifetime earnings relative to the tuition and fees.

This chapter has a singular thrust. Assume that tomorrow's mail contained a ticket "Good for four years of all-in educational expenses at the college of your choice. This ticket does not guarantee admission, but it does guarantee that all costs will be covered if you are admitted." How should you choose which college to attend?

The Higher Education Industry

The choice of a college is complex because there are so many differences in the features and attributes and strengths of the firms that sell a four-year bachelor's degree. Some colleges are parts of large universities, and others are freestanding four-year institutions. Other variables include the total enrollment and the size of the freshman class, the average number of students in each classroom in the freshman year and in the senior year, the ratio of faculty to students, the proportion of faculty who have advanced degrees, the endowment of the college and the endowment per undergraduate student, the existence of an "honors" program or a "fast track" for high achievers, whether the college is in a large city with many cultural advantages or in a small town that offers close proximity to nature, religious affiliations (if any), whether golf is a year-long sport, whether "big-time" athletics are an important part of the college culture, and the college's reputation—as a party school or a nerd's haven. Does the college have a chapter of the Phi Beta Kappa national honor society? Fewer than 200 do.

The U.S. higher education industry is large and diverse. More than 4,000 firms with plants—usually known as campuses but increasingly office buildings—are based in all fifty states; many of these firms have teaching facilities in separate cities, and a few have programs in foreign countries. Like firms in the beverage industry or the automobile rental business, each competes with a large number of other firms on both price and product and in its marketing programs. Similarly to professional baseball, in which the major leagues span the country and three or four different minor leagues compete within each of the regions, each group of colleges has a different market. Thirty or forty colleges compete for students globally or nationally; their admissions officers make recruiting trips to high schools across the country in search of talented students, and they mail lavish brochures to high school juniors and seniors. Other colleges focus on their regional markets, and the community colleges target local markets.

Each college sells promises to young Americans and their parents. "If you graduate from Old State, you'll find it a cinch to get into medical school." "If you complete our program of study, you'll be able to think systematically and critically about a number of important social and political problems." "Our placement record in the accounting profession is second to none." "We have the third-ranked chemistry department in the country." "Our graduates have the highest success ratio in law school applications." "Your classmates will be one of the most important networks in your professional life." "More of our entering freshmen complete their course of study in four years than at any other comparable college." Most of these statements are variants on the theme of "We can help you get ahead," which is a proxy for increases in your human capital.

Each college strives to increase its market share—or at least its share of the brightest and most ambitious students. All the firms—including the community colleges and state universities—want to improve the quality of their educational product, attract more talented faculty, offer more and varied programs, and feature more up-to-date classrooms, computing facilities, and laboratories. Each also has a budget and a limited amount of money to spend. The promises are made because the college president has allotted 525 seats for the incoming freshman class; a smaller enrollment will crimp revenues and delay improvements in programs and in facilities.

Colleges can be grouped on the basis of selectivity in admissions. Usually there are three or four ranks—extremely selective, highly selective, selective, and open admissions. Selectivity also can be measured by the ratio of the number of applicants relative to the number admitted to the freshman class. Deans of admissions "massage" these data so that the college will appear to be more selective and thereby draw a larger number of applicants. These deans also want a "high yield." That is, they want an exceptionally large number of admitted candidates to matriculate; a low yield ratio might suggest that many applicants view the college as less desirable than one of its competitors. Admissions personnel may want a strong indication that students will accept before admitting them—and they may deny admission to those students who they think will go to some other college as a way to increase their yield. (Since many high school seniors apply to five, ten, or more colleges and are admitted to several, the yield ratios at many colleges are bound to be low.) The colleges that have both the largest number of applicants relative to the number of seats and the highest yields are in the "highly selective" group.

A rule of thumb is that 2 or 3 percent of any population can be considered outstanding—which suggests that there are one hundred outstanding colleges, plus or minus twenty or thirty. This outstanding group encompasses the Ivy League of venerable and rich universities, including Harvard, Yale, and Princeton in the northeast. Stanford University and Cal Tech are peers to the Ivies, better endowed than most. Big Ten schools such as the University of Michigan, the University of Illinois, and the University of Wisconsin are great state universities with brilliant schools of agriculture, engineering, forestry, and liberal arts. The Pacific Coast Conference includes the University of California at Berkeley, the University of California at Los Angeles, the University of Southern California, and the University of Washington. The Atlantic Coast conference includes the University of Virginia and the University of North Carolina; both are top-ranked research institutions. There are a large number of quality small colleges; the "potted-Ivies" include Amherst, Wesleyan, Williams, Bowdoin, and Middlebury. The Massachusetts Institute of Technology, California Institute of Technology, Carnegie-Mellon University, Rensselaer Polytechnic Institute, and Georgia Tech have outstanding programs in science and engineering. Johns Hopkins University, the University of Chicago, and Washington University in St. Louis are top-quality research institutions with stellar undergraduate programs.

The universe of higher education is summarized in Table 6.1. About one-fifth of colleges in the United States—the for-profits—are in the educational business "for the money." That's great—an entrepreneur has decided to risk personal capital in the belief that a profit can be made from delivering a product that is superior to those available from the nonprofit colleges—or at least a different product. The for-profits have a clear view of their markets and their objectives—and they aren't burdened by sports programs and chapels, nor are they in the hotel business. Many of the for-profits target older students; many specialize in part-time programs that are applications oriented. The University of Phoenix is the largest, with facilities in thirty-five cities. Some of the for-profits are accredited, but most are not.

Like the for-profits, community colleges are nonresidential and offer few of the nonacademic activities that private and state colleges do,

Table 6.1
The Universe of American Colleges

	Community	Public Four-Year	Private	For-Profit
Number	1,101	612	1,676	808
Undergraduates	5.7 million	4.8 million	2.2 million	0.4 million
Average tuition	$1,735	$4,081	$18,273	$11,043
Annual cost	$5,000–$8,000	$7,000–$25,000	$12,000–$80,000	$8,000–$10,000
Graduation rate	7%	47%	62%	1%

Source: Data from Business Week, April 28, 2003.

although some have athletic teams. Many students are employed full time and attend classes in the evening or on the weekends. Tuition is low and much of the money for the educational costs comes from the taxpayers.

Public four-year colleges often are parts of large university systems, which include ten or fifteen professional schools, and perhaps an extension program that offers nondegree programs for adults. Some of the financing for the undergraduate program comes from the state government—and this subsidy per student is much higher in some states than in others. In many states a relatively small proportion of the total revenues of these colleges comes from the state government. The University of Wisconsin is one of the largest and most prestigious; about 18 percent of its revenues come from the state government, and the rest comes from the endowment, gifts, government contracts, and the tuitions of out-of-state students. State governments may also help with capital costs of buildings, libraries, and laboratories.

The differences in tuition among these four major types of colleges are large. If college-bound high school students and their parents believed that the product offered by the costly schools were not significantly superior to that offered by community and state colleges, there would be a lot of empty classrooms in Cambridge, New Haven, and Palo Alto.

The Value Added by Higher Education

If a randomly selected group of 1,000 individuals were offered the choice between a Cadillac and a Chevrolet at the same price, more than 95 percent would select the Cadillac. The ride is quieter and more comfortable, the cabin is roomier, and there are more amenities and safety features. If it costs no more than a Chevy, the Cadillac is a bargain. Virtually everyone "knows" that the Cadillac's features dominate those of the Chevy. A few would choose the Chevy because of its higher gas mileage or because it would more easily fit in their garage.

If 1,000 high school seniors were offered the choice of any U.S. college at the same price, a high proportion of the students would pick Harvard or Yale or Cal Tech or Rice or another of the hundred or so outstanding colleges. These students—at least most of them—"know" that attendance at one of the outstanding colleges would be a bargain if the price were more or less the same as that charged by Central City Community College or Middle State University and their peers. A few students would not choose one of these highly selective colleges, perhaps because they are too far from home, or their friends wouldn't approve, or they wouldn't feel comfortable in the competitive environment, or their parents went to Middle State, or their football teams are third rate.

Only a small proportion of the 3 million high school seniors apply to one of the highly selective or selective colleges. Some seniors have chosen not to go to college, and others have concluded that they don't have the smarts or the preparation for one of the more demanding programs. But a large number are put off by the costs and the resulting financial burden on their parents.

Return to the choice between the Cadillac and the Chevy and raise the price of the Cadillac by 10 percent. Most who selected the Caddy when its price was the same as the Chevy's would choose the Caddy again because they believe it still is a bargain. Some, however, will be diverted to the Chevy because they can't afford the Caddy. Raise the price of the Cadillac by 20 percent, and a smaller number, most of whom still believe that they are getting a bargain, would buy it.

Now consider the choice between a group of highly selective colleges and a group that includes Central City and Middle State. Raise the tuition at any of the colleges in the first group relative to those in the second by 10 percent, and many of those who picked one of the more selective colleges in the first group when the two groups cost the same will continue to prefer one of the highly selective colleges; they're a bargain even when tuition is 10 percent higher.

And why would these outstanding colleges be such a bargain? Well, what would be the value added in the form of the increase in the individual's lifetime income by attending one college rather than another? The value added by a college is based on the increases in the lifetime earnings of its graduates. Tuition and the other costs of attendance can be thought of as the "financial input" and value added as the "financial output."

A model of this calculation is provided by the annual rankings of U.S. business schools by *Business Week* and other publications, which use the difference between the starting salaries of the new graduates from each of these schools and their salaries before they began the program as a measure of value added. Often the starting salaries of those who have just received the MBA degrees are more than twice their salaries before they entered the program.

John Doe and Jack Doe are identical twins. John enters the labor force immediately after high school and his lifetime earnings are $850,000 over forty-seven years of active employment. Jack Doe attends a public four-year college and enters the active labor force four years after John; he retires two years after John. His lifetime earnings are $1,450,000. The value added by the college experience to Jack's lifetime income is $600,000. Much of the difference is due to income earned when the twins were in their late forties and their fifties; Jack's annual income increased at three times the rate of John's. The cost to Jack of the four years of college was $120,000; $50,000 in out-of-pocket costs for tuition, fees, and books, and $70,000 in forgone income. Dividing $600,000 by $120,000 (the cost of the four-year education); the rate of return is 500 percent. The increase in lifetime earnings is $480,000 after adjusting for the costs of the four years of college; this increase averages slightly over $10,000 a year.

A Chevy is a great $20,000 car, and Central City Community College and Middle State University are great teaching institutions with some excellent faculty and relatively low tuitions. But Central City and Middle State have less money to spend on education—tuition is low and the grants from the city and county governments are modest.

In the automobile market, the implication is that the value of different automobiles in terms of safety, reliability, and comfort is related to their costs of production. The counterpart proposition in the higher education market is that the value of the educational experience at different colleges is related to the cost that each college incurs in providing educational services; the higher this cost, the more valuable the educational experience. There are exceptions in both markets; in some cases the educational values are very high relative to the cost and in other cases high costs are is associated with inferior products.

Tuition and the Cost of Education

The cliché "You get what you pay for" may be true in the markets for automobiles and fresh fruit, but it certainly is not valid in the market for higher education. The cost of education in virtually every college is higher—and in many cases much higher—than the posted tuition. (There are two major exceptions: one is that the posted tuition in the "for-profits" approximates the cost of education, and the other is that the tuition charged out-of-state students by virtually every state university is higher than the cost of education; out-of-state students are a "profit center.") Students in the most selective colleges are subsidized because the cost of education per student is higher than the tuition, so they get more than they pay for; similarly, in-state students in state and community colleges also are subsidized.

A second unique feature of the market for higher education is that sellers engage in price discrimination, more so than in most other industries. Tuition is the advertised basic price set by each college. Colleges post their tuitions in their announcements and on their Web sites and then have an arcane set of policies to determine which students will pay full price and which will pay lower prices. A few students receive cash stipends that subsidize their living costs. Many of these scholarships are based on the financial needs of the students.

Discounting by the colleges that are highly selective is designed to raise the quality and diversity of the student body. Discounting by the colleges that are not selective is intended to fill more of the classroom seats because the president has decided it is financially more rewarding for the college to charge three-quarters tuition or half tuition to selected students to meet the enrollment targets. (This practice is called "yield management" by the airlines.)

Tuition and Tuition Revenues

A lament since the early 1990s is that tuition has been increasing more rapidly than the consumer price level and that colleges are "getting rich." Multiply the posted tuition by the number of students in the entering class in several colleges for each of the last fifteen years to obtain an annual dollar value for "projected tuition revenue" for each of these colleges—an uncomplicated calculation because the data on both the number of students and the tuition are readily available. Then compare "actual tuition revenue"—the cash that each college collects—with the projected tuition revenue. You'll find that in most colleges, actual tuition revenue has increased less rapidly than the posted tuition revenue and only slightly more rapidly than the consumer price level. The counterpart of the increase in the posted tuition has been an increase in scholarship aid; a higher proportion of students receive scholarships and the scholarships are larger. Price discrimination has become more extensive.

Table 6.2
College Revenues and the Cost of Education

Revenue Sources	Cost of Education
Tuition	Faculty salaries
Income from endowment	Libraries, laboratories
Private gifts	Computing facilities
Government subsidies	Athletic facilities
"Building rents"	"Building rents"

Source: Author.

Tuition is a major revenue source that helps pay for the cost of education; the other revenue sources are in the left column in Table 6.2. Endowment income is an important source of revenue in about 100 colleges. Each college has a formula for deciding how much money to take from its endowment each year to help pay for annual operating expenses and to use for scholarships. The endowment tends to increase as a result of new gifts and each year's investment income and to decrease because of withdrawal of funds for operating expenses and scholarships.

The benefits of the endowment income in the freestanding four-year colleges flow directly and primarily to the undergraduates. Identifying the beneficiaries of the endowment income in large universities is complex. Harvard is the wealthiest American university—its endowment is the sum of the endowments of each of its professional schools as well as of the Faculty of Arts and Sciences. The endowment of the Harvard Divinity School may help its students get closer to God, but the direct benefit to the undergraduates in Harvard College is small. Many members of the Faculty of Arts and Sciences teach both undergraduate and graduate students; determining how much of the endowment income of this faculty directly benefits the undergraduates is difficult.

Some of the annual gifts to a college help pay annual operating expenditures, and some are used to increase the endowment. The buildings and other facilities owned by the college provide useful services; if they were not owned, they would be rented, and the college would make monthly or annual rental payments.

Now for the costs. Faculty salaries are a major cost. Colleges compete intensely for faculty—and business firms and governments and scientific laboratories compete for the same highly educated individuals. Other education costs include the expenses of libraries, laboratories, and computing facilities, as well as the "rent" of the buildings and grounds.

The cost of education per student in most public four-year colleges and perhaps 200 of the private colleges is significantly higher than tuition revenue per student. The income from the endowment, funding from state legislatures, and gifts "subsidize" the students at state colleges, just as funds from city and county governments subsidize students at community colleges.

These subsidies vary widely among the 3,400 colleges—and even within the undergraduate colleges of some of the state universities. Many of these universities have honors programs for undergraduates who are deemed high achievers; class sizes in these programs are significantly smaller than in other undergraduate programs, and talented teachers and researchers are encouraged to teach the high achievers. The cost of education per student in these select programs often is several times higher than the costs for other undergraduates in the same university.

Enrollments at these institutions differ sharply: Columbia, Cornell, and Pennsylvania are large universities with more than 20,000 students, and Amherst, Bates, and Bowdoin have fewer than 2,000 students. Fewer than half of the enrolled students at Duke, Columbia, and most of the other universities are undergraduates. This presents an apples-and-oranges problem when determining how much of the endowment and annual gifts at the large universities subsidizes the undergraduates.

University and college endowments and endowments per student are shown in Table 6.3. The policies that these institutions follow in taking money from the endowment for current operating expenses differ; the formula is likely to be a variant on "take 4 (or 4.5 or 5) percent of the average value of the endowment for the last three (or four or five) years" from the endowment to cover current operating costs. Remember that some of these institutions are universities with five or ten or more professional schools and perhaps a hospital, and others have only undergraduates. Some of the income from the endowment is dedicated to undergraduate scholarships, perhaps for individuals from a particular geographic area.

The estimate for endowment income per student at ten of these colleges is in the same ballpark as tuition per student. Moreover, the average

Table 6.3

College Endowments, Student Enrollments, and Endowment per Student

College	Endowment (billions)	Student Enrollment	Endowment per Student (thousands)
Princeton University	$16.353	7,334	$2,230
Yale University	23.614	11,454	2,062
Harvard University	36.260	19,955	1,817
Pomona College	1.794	1,522	1,179
Amherst College	1.706	1,720	992
Stanford University	17.214	17,362	991
Massachusetts Institute of Technology	10.069	10,220	985
Swarthmore College	1.414	1,491	947
Williams College	1.911	2,046	934
Grinnell College	1.472	1,654	890
Rice University	4.610	5,243	879
Wellesley College	1.611	2,274	709
Dartmouth College	3.721	5,849	636
Bowdoin College	0.831	1,716	485
Smith College	1.366	2,829	483
University of Chicago	6.632	14,658	453
Washington University, St. Louis	5.429	13,588	399
Bryn Mawr College	0.689	1,790	385
Duke University	5.473	14,316	382
Northwestern University	7.135	19,005	375
Hamilton College	0.670	1,873	358
Middlebury College	0.885	2,500	354
Brown University	2.747	8,167	336
Carleton College	0.648	2,005	323
Colby College	0.600	1,867	322
Mount Holyoke College	0.663	2,204	301
Columbia University	7.147	24,298	294
Oberlin College	0.743	2,774	268
Cornell University	5.385	20,561	262
University of Pennsylvania	6.233	24,107	258
Wesleyan University	0.652	2,817	231
Colorado College	0.451	2,075	222
University of Rochester	1.722	9,420	183
Trinity College	0.413	2,502	165
Bates College	0.267	1,660	161

(continued)

Table 6.3 (*continued*)

College	Endowment (billions)	Student Enrollment	Endowment per Student (thousands)
Tufts University	1.492	9,789	153
Johns Hopkins University	2.685	19,980	134
Connecticut College	0.214	1,991	107
Barnard College	0.216	2,346	92
Georgetown University	1.059	15,318	69

Source: Data from Council for Aid to Education, 2008 Voluntary Support of Education, http://www .cae.org.

of the endowment income per student at the ten institutions that are at the top of this list is six times the average of the endowment income per student at the colleges that are toward the bottom of the list. One implication is that colleges that are at the top of the list will have more scholar- ships, and another is that they are likely to have "richer" programs. The endowments of the colleges that are in the second group of twenty seems large in absolute dollars, but the average of the endowment income per student in this group is in the same ballpark as the subsidy per student at many of the state colleges shown in Table 6.3.

Grants from the federal government are an important source of revenue for research universities, and part of the overhead from these grants benefits undergraduates because part of the institution's overhead is paid for from these grants and less is charged to the undergraduates.

Consider several patterns in the data that relate prestige of individual colleges, student applications, tuition, and the cost of education. Prestige is elusive, but it is more closely related to the accomplishments of the faculty—their professional achievements and their standing within their academic disciplines—than to the accomplishments of the college's football team. Generally, the higher the endowment per student, the greater the prestige. These selective colleges "buy" current professorial academic stars and potential stars. The faculty has Nobel laureates and members of learned societies. The faculty members at these colleges are more likely to be in the news about developments in science and business, and to be called on by the national media to provide authoritative statements on new cancer research discoveries, surges in the oil price, and the gerrymandering of electoral districts in various states. They also serve on advisory committees to national and state governments.

The second pattern is that the greater the prestige, the higher the tuition. (A few colleges have used their endowment income to keep tuition low for all students—which means that all their students are subsidized, including those from wealthy families.) Most colleges with high endowments appear to have taken the view that "we are giving something very valuable away, and it would be silly to make large gifts to families that are very wealthy and can easily afford to pay the tuition." A relatively small share of the student body may pay full tuition. Some of the colleges in the great state universities have tuitions for out-of-state students that are in the same ballpark as the tuition charged by the highly selective private colleges. (Note that the reverse is not true: high tuition is not always associated with a high ranking on the prestige hit parade.)

The greater the prestige, the larger the number of applicants relative to the number of seats for the entering freshman class. Tens of thousands of graduating high school seniors want to be associated with a "prestige brand." Some of these students also may realize that if they are admitted they will benefit from the large subsidy provided by the endowment and the gifts (there appears to be no other industry where wealthy buyers receive such large subsidies for the amount that they spend).

Another pattern is that the colleges with the largest endowments also do the most extensive discounting of tuition. Harvard, Yale, Princeton, and their peers could fill all the seats in their freshman classes without discounting their tuitions; indeed, they could raise tuition steeply and still fill all the seats—although they would be less selective in their choice of students. Their revenues would be higher, and they could use the additional income to raise faculty salaries and build more indoor tennis courts and skating rinks and to increase the faculty-student ratio.

Their rationale for discounting tuition is to increase the quality and diversity of the student body. The tuition has been set at a seemingly high level for applicants from upper-middle-income families; even though most of these students pay full tuition, they still benefit from the large subsidies from endowment income and annual gifts. It is as if the president and the board of trustees of each institution had asked, "Should we charge a high tuition and extend a large number of scholarships, or should we charge a lower tuition and make fewer scholarships available?"

Consider the view of each of these prestigious colleges and its choice of which of the many applicants to admit. The presidents and trustees know that the applicants who are admitted will benefit from a large subsidy. The presidents, trustees, and faculty at these colleges want "payback" on these subsidies—although they are almost certainly too genteel to mention this view to the *New York Times*. It's as if the college administrators are trustees who manage sequential intergenerational transfers. Some of the payback will be financial. Some will be reflected prestige: Georgetown University benefited greatly because President Clinton had been an undergraduate. Yale benefited because both Presidents Bush matriculated there. The president, trustees, faculty, and staff of these colleges are keenly interested in their rankings within their peer groups. They want high achievers in part because some of these women and men are likely to be important donors in the future and to add to the luster of the institution. Legacy admits—the admission of daughters and sons of alumni—are rationalized because the total lifetime revenues from these families allow the college to provide more scholarship aid to less-affluent families.

Value Added and the Cost of Education

Higher education is similar to most other industries in that the higher the cost, the greater the value added. The value added by each college is best measured by the cost of education per student. Colleges with the largest endowment incomes per student are more selective in their choice of faculty, seeking candidates who are likelier to be more productive scholars as well as distinguished teachers. Moreover, these colleges attract a higher proportion of the ambitious, achievement-oriented students, who are likely to be competitive in their pursuit of higher grades, perhaps because they anticipate applying to professional schools and graduate schools.

State Universities: Subsidies, Tuition, and the Cost of Education

The cost of education per undergraduate at the University of North Carolina and the University of Michigan is two to three times higher than at some other state universities. The subsidies per student provided by some state governments are three to four times higher than those provided by other state governments. Tuition for in-state students is somewhat less variable than the subsidies from state governments. The tuition charged out-of-state students always exceeds the cost of education. (Imagine the

Table 6.4

Public Universities, Tuition, In State and Out of State (data in thousands of dollars per full-time equivalent)

	Tuition and Fees	
	In State	Out of State
North Carolina, Chapel Hill	$4.6	$21.8
Michigan	9.8	16.3
Maryland	7.8	14.6
Iowa	5.6	13.8
Nebraska	5.5	13.4
Pittsburgh	7.5	11.4
Wisconsin	6.3	12.6
Rutgers	9.2	9.4
Illinois	8.6	9.7
Virginia	7.4	10.7
Iowa State	5.6	12.2
Florida	3.1	14.7
Washington	5.6	11.9
Purdue	6.5	10.7
Indiana	7.1	10.0
Ohio State	8.1	8.8
Penn State	4.9	4.9
Missouri	7.5	8.7
SUNY–Stony Brook	5.6	9.8
Texas	6.9	8.1
Michigan State	6.9	6.9
SUNY–Buffalo	6.1	8.7
Texas A&M	6.4	7.5
Kansas	5.4	8.2
Oregon	4.6	4.6
Colorado	3.1	3.1

Source: Data compiled by the University of Virginia from a November 2005 query to all public members of the American Association of Universities.

flak if the president of a state university said that tuition charged residents of other states was less than the cost of education.)

Tuition for out-of-state students at a few state universities is significantly higher than the cost of education (see Table 6.4); in effect, as mentioned, the out-of-state students are a "profit center" that subsidizes the

in-state students. The states that tax the out-of-state students have a relatively low subsidy per in-state student.

The Choice of the College and the Increase in Lifetime Earnings

Many parents, students, and guidance counselors will not be comfortable
with the proposition that the best proxy for the value added at each college is the cost of education per student. Some may feel that this approach
is too elitist (although others may believe that the approach reflects that
there is a U.S. meritocracy). Some will respond that students can obtain
great educations at Central Community and Middle State and their peers;
many graduates of these colleges are great success stories and testament
to the openness of American society and the talents and ambitions of their
graduates. The counterpart to this view is that many of the promising
young women and men who were admitted to the most prestigious colleges somehow failed to fulfill their promise after they graduated—and
some did not graduate. These exceptions do not refute the key proposition that a good proxy for the increase in the lifetime income is the cost of
education—the higher the cost, the greater the increase in lifetime income.
Not all colleges with high tuitions are a bargain, but nearly all the colleges
that are bargains have high tuitions because they provide large subsidies
to all of their undergraduates. The differences in lifetime value added per
student are many times larger than the differences in tuition.

Every high school senior implicitly considers three groups: the in-
state public colleges, including the community colleges that are often
their "feeders"; private colleges; and out-of-state colleges. (The U.S. service academies—West Point, Annapolis, the Air Force Academy, and the
Coast Guard Academy—are a fourth set. These are quality institutions
with an emphasis on engineering; graduates are committed to stay in
the service for two or four years as a trade-off for the otherwise free
education.)

Every American high school senior starts on the great golden road
toward a college education with a significant birthright subsidy from the
state legislature, available to every resident admitted to one of the state's
public colleges. This subsidy from the taxpayers ranges from $3,000 a
year in some states to $20,000 in others. Moreover, in-state students also

are subsidized by tax on out-of-state students; this in-state subsidy can be as much as $7,000 a year.

High school seniors who forgo the in-state subsidy have two main choices. One is to attend an out-of-state public college, and the other is to select a private college. In the former case, the student will be "taxed" because tuition for out-of-state students is higher than the cost of education (a few states have mutual assistance arrangements whereby students from nearby states are not charged out-of-state tuition).

A highly stylized view of the three choices is illustrated in Table 6.5. The assumption is that the cost of education per undergraduate is identical in the three groups—a useful starting point but far-fetched. A student who attends the in-state public college pays $9,000 in tuition a year to buy a $22,000 education. A student who decides on either a public out-of-state college or a private college forgoes an annual subsidy of $13,000 a year. A student who goes to an out-of-state public college pays $26,000 to buy a $22,000 education.

Why should any student forgo the large subsidy available at the in-state college and pay the tax to attend a similar out-of-state college? There are two principal reasons. One is that some other college might offer an even larger subsidy in the form of a partial or full tuition scholarship. Consider Scott Fitzgerald from St. Paul, Minnesota. If Scott attends the University of Minnesota, he will pay the in-state tuition of $6,000 and benefit from the subsidy for in-state students of $12,000. Each dollar that Scott pays for tuition "buys" three dollars' worth of education. If instead Scott attends the University of Wisconsin or the University of Michigan, he forgoes the in-state subsidy and pays the out-of-state tuition

Table 6.5
A Stylized View of the Choice of a College

| | Type of Institution | | |
	In-State Public	Private	Out-of-State Public
Cost of education	$22,000	$22,000	$22,000
Subsidy	12,000	3,000	0
Tuition	9,000	19,000	26,000
Tax	−1,000	0	4,000

Source: Author.

and tax. If the University of Wisconsin or the University of Michigan were to offer Scott a scholarship of $14,000 or more, Wisconsin and Michigan would be financially competitive choices.

Scott might apply to Princeton because of its brand name. If Princeton offered Scott a full tuition scholarship, his choice would be easy. The cost of education per student at Princeton is much higher than at Minnesota—and because of the scholarship, Scott does not pay tuition at Princeton.

Assume that the University of Minnesota matches the Princeton package and offers Scott a full-tuition scholarship. Scott's choice is easy because the cost of education is so much higher at Princeton and the value added is much greater. (Note that this is the Chevy-Caddy choice when both cars cost the same.)

Now complicate the choice. Assume that Princeton would charge Scott a higher tuition than Minnesota would charge. Scott might conclude that he would be better off at Princeton because the anticipated difference in his lifetime earnings is so much greater than the difference in tuition. This comparison is a twin to the question of how much more you would pay for the Caddy than the Chevy. This choice is complex and uncertain, since the higher cost is reasonably certain and occurs in the next several years, and the increase in lifetime income will occur over the next thirty to forty years.

Assume that Princeton offers Scott a partial scholarship; his tuition payment at Princeton after the scholarship would be $5,000 per year. The cost of education per student at Princeton is three times the cost of education at Minnesota, say, $75,000 to $22,000. (Remember that this is an analogy, and the numbers are ballpark estimates. Substitute your own values in the comparison.) If Scott chooses to spend $5,000 more a year on tuition, he can "buy" $45,000 more of education each year—which seems like the proverbial no-brainer.

This calculation can be modified by increasing the amount that Scott might have to pay if he were to go to a college other than Princeton. The tuition would be higher and the cost of education lower than at Princeton.

Few individuals would leave a $50,000 income tax refund on the dining room table. Many of these same individuals have little hesitation in forgoing the in-state subsidy to attend an out-of-state public college that is in the same peer group as the in-state institution in terms of value added.

The logic is straightforward. The higher the cost of education per student, the greater the value added; the greater the value added, the larger the increase in lifetime earnings. The cumulative increase in Scott's lifetime earnings might be in the range of $500,000 to $1 million over a forty-year period—say, from $12,500 to $25,000 a year.

ACTIONABLES

1. Establish a section 529 account in your child's name on his or her first birthday. Establish a section 529 account for each of your grandchildren.

2. Transfer funds to these accounts whenever you have a bonus— and whenever you splurge on a vacation for yourself.

3. About 20 percent of U.S. state universities are world class. If you live in a state where one of these universities is located and have children who might want to attend it, be reluctant to move to a state that has a university where the public university is less competitive. If you have the opportunity to move to a state with a great university, remember to include the value of the university in your calculation of whether to move.

4. Seek to measure the value of the in-state subsidy that your state provides for its university and colleges. Write the president of your state university and ask him for information on the in-state subsidy; also ask for information on the tax on out-of-state students. And ask for comparable information on public colleges and universities in nearby states.

5. Impress on your child the value of the in-state subsidy.

6. If your child indicates an interest in attending an out-of-state public university that taxes out-of-state students, just say *no*. That's stupid. Refuse to pay.

7. If your child indicates an interest in attending an out-of-state university that is not significantly superior to the in-state university, point out that forgoing the in-state subsidy is extremely costly to family finances.

7   Minimizing the Bites of the Tax Collectors

In 1969 the U.S. Congress passed the Alternative Minimum Tax (AMT) to ensure that all the millionaire "fat cats" in the United States would have to pay federal income tax even though thousands had avoided paying any tax because they had large deductions from taxable incomes. In 2005 several hundred Americans with annual incomes over $1 million did not pay any federal income tax, despite the AMT. Most of the incomes of these millionaires consisted of the tax-exempt interest earned on the bonds of state and local governments. The federal government and the state governments have an understanding about taxable turf that goes back 200 years—the Feds won't tax the interest income on state and local government bonds, and the state governments won't tax the interest income on U.S. Treasury bonds.

These millionaires arbitraged the differences in the tax rates applied to different types of income. "Arbitrage" is a French word that means to profit from the differences in prices of the same or nearly identical goods in different locations. Individuals arbitrage the differences in national tax systems when they shop in the duty-free stores in airports. Individuals arbitrage the differences in prices of tickets to the movie theaters by attending the matinees rather than the evening showings; ticket prices generally are lower in the afternoons. Residents of Virginia and Maryland who live near the District of Columbia arbitrage state sales and alcohol taxes by purchasing their booze in the nation's capital, which has lower tax rates on alcohol. Similarly, residents of Vermont, Massachusetts, and Maine who live near New Hampshire arbitrage the difference in state sales taxes by shopping in the Granite State. A relatively high percentage of the state liquor stores in New Hampshire are located on highways one to two miles from one of the neighboring states. You can mimic their transactions by increasing the amount of your investment income that is subject to low tax rates—or is not taxed at all. Not earthshaking, but cost effective—and legal.

The interaction of the federal and state tax systems provides you with numerous arbitrage opportunities to increase your after-tax income. Most of the states have income taxes, and the marginal tax rates range up to 10 percent; you can move your domicile to one of the states that doesn't have a state income tax. New Hampshire claims it doesn't have an income tax—but the "Live Free or Die" state taxes dividends and interest income, so the claim can be viewed as hollow or dented. States differ in their tax treatment of estates. Payments to state tax authorities are a deduction from the federal income tax.

You can arbitrage time by moving funds into a dedicated retirement or educational account or a health savings account; your taxable income declines (except for the movement of funds into a Roth retirement account). Moreover, the recognition of income on specified assets in these accounts can be deferred to years when your marginal income tax rate is likely to be lower than the rate in the current year.

You can arbitrage the federal income tax treatment of different types of income (Table 7.1 lists the tax rates applied to different types of income). "Total income" includes wages and salaries, interest and dividends and capital gains, money received from individual retirement accounts (IRAs) and other annuities, Social Security and unemployment benefits, business income, and alimony. "Adjusted gross income" may be smaller than total income because of contributions to IRAs, moving expenses, and alimony payments. "Taxable income" is smaller than adjusted gross income because of deductions; taxpayers can take a standard deduction, or they can itemize their deductions. Itemizing deductions is worthwhile if their value is greater than 5 or 6 percent of your adjusted gross income. (If you're on the borderline between taking the standard deduction and itemizing, consider an eany-meany approach—to the

Table 7.1

Federal Tax Rates on Different Types of Income

Type of Income	Effective Tax Rates
Ordinary income—wages, salary, dividends, interest	Up to 35%
Capital gains income	15%
Interest income on state and local bonds	0%
Investment income of life insurance companies	0%
Investment income of IRAs, Keoghs, SRAs, and SEPs	0%
Proceeds of life insurance policies	0%
Distributions—Roth IRAs	0%
Distributions—educational IRAs	0%

Source: Data from J. K. Lasser's Your Income Tax 2010 (New York: John Wiley and Sons, 2010).

extent possible, shift deductions to the even-numbered years; take the standard deduction in the odd-numbered years and the itemized deductions in the even-numbered years.)

Payments that you have made for medical expenses, taxes to state and local governments, interest payments on mortgages on first homes and second homes, charitable contributions, and casualty losses are deductions from adjusted gross income and hence reduce the amount of the tax. In some cases these deductions apply only if they exceed a specified percentage of your taxable income. For example, only those medical expenses that exceed 7.5 percent of your taxable income are deductible. Casualty losses that exceed 2 percent of your taxable income are deductible. Interest payments on mortgages on your first and second homes in excess of $1 million are not deductible—which means that up to $2 million in interest payments is deductible. Charitable contributions in excess of 50 percent of your income generally are not deductible, although that part of those contributions that is not deductible during one year can be carried forward and deducted in the next tax year.

Health Savings Accounts Provide an Arbitrage Opportunity

In 2003 the U.S. Congress authorized the establishment of health savings accounts (HSAs, sometimes known as Medical Savings Accounts) in the effort to control health care costs. The model was that of the individual retirement accounts (IRAs); funds transferred to a health savings account would reduce taxable income on a dollar-for-dollar basis—even if you did not itemize your deductions—up to a specified ceiling. Hence the transfer of money to one of these accounts would be an end-run around the stipulation that medical expenses were tax deductible if they exceeded 7.5 percent of taxable income.

The money in your HSA account can be used to pay medical expenses. Money can accumulate without limits in your HSA. Moreover, the interest income on the money in an HSA is not taxable. Distributions from your account to pay appropriate medical services are not taxable. Contributions to your account by your employer are not taxable income. The HSA account is portable; you can continue to own the account if you change employers or leave the active labor force.

Two conditions have to be satisfied before you can establish an HSA. One is that you have a high-deductible health insurance policy; the idea was that modest health care expenditures would be paid for with money that had been parked in the HSA. The second is that you did not have a health care insurance policy, either one purchased by an employer or one personally. Moreover, if you are enrolled in Medicare, you do not qualify for an HSA. But you can continue to own the funds in your HSA that had accumulated before you enrolled in Medicare.

In 2009 the upper limit to the annual contribution to the HSA was $3,000 for an individual and $6,000 for a family. The amount of money that could be transferred to the HSA each year was directly linked to the value of the deductible in the major medical policy; the higher this deductible, the larger the amount of tax-free dollars that could be transferred.

Two preliminary points. First, on objectives. Your objective should be to increase your after-tax income, never to minimize your tax payments. At times minimizing income tax payments and maximizing after-tax income are identical. But not always. Consider: are you better off if you own a tax-exempt bond issued by the State of Delaware that pays a 5 percent annual interest rate, or a U.S. Treasury bond that pays 6 percent in interest? True, you minimize your federal income tax liability and your income tax payments if you own the tax-exempt bond. But assume your marginal federal income tax rate is 15 percent; you pay a tax of $0.15 on each additional $1.00 of taxable income. Your income of $60 a year on the taxable bond would be subject to a tax payment of $9; your after-tax interest income would be $51—slightly more than the nontaxable income of $50 on the tax-exempt bond.

Second, the distinction between "tax deductions" and "tax credits" is key. A "tax deduction" reduces taxable income on a dollar-for-dollar basis, and a "tax credit" reduces tax liability and tax payments on a dollar-for-dollar basis. The principal tax deductions include medical payments, interest payments, payments of state and local taxes, and charitable contributions. If your marginal federal income tax rate is 25 percent, a $1 tax credit reduces your tax payments by $1 and is as valuable in maximizing your after-tax income as $4 of tax deductions would be. Congress loves to establish tax credits. There was a tax credit of up to $8,000 for first-time home buyers, and there are various credits for expenditures that conserve energy.

One take-away from Table 7.1 is that the tax on $1.00 of income can vary from 0 percent to 35 percent depending on the source of income. Your objective is to shift income from a high tax source to a lower tax source. These shifts may be direct, which would involve increasing capital gains income or interest income on state and local bonds by changing the composition of securities you own. An indirect shift would involve increasing the deductions that reduce taxable income. For example, you might borrow some money, and the interest payments would be a deduction that would reduce taxable income.

You can arbitrage between taxable and nontaxable securities. You can arbitrage—within limits—by acquiring the bonds of the states and localities if their before-tax rate of return is higher than the after-tax rate of return on the bonds of the U.S. government and of corporations.

If you have a high marginal income tax rate, you're better off buying bonds of state and local governments. If you have low marginal income tax rates, you're better off buying the taxable bonds because the higher interest income is larger than the increase in the tax payments.

You can arbitrage the difference between the federal tax rate on capital gains and the tax rate on interest income by selling securities that pay high dividends and buying the securities that reward stockholders by the repurchase of shares—which should lead to increases in their prices.

Moreover, you won't be obliged to pay the tax until you sell the shares and realize the capital gain, and you may be able to take advantage of much of the gain without paying the tax. More on this detail later.

When you're in your fifties and sixties, your focus should be to maximize your own after-tax income. As you move along the life cycle into your seventies, you may want to maximize the after-tax income of your family on an intragenerational basis if you think you will bequeath wealth to your children and grandchildren.

The U.S. government has established several programs to encourage you to save for your retirement through dedicated accounts offered by plan sponsors, including banks, mutual funds, and insurance companies. (The details of these various tax-advantaged accounts are discussed in Chapter 14.) Similarly, several programs encourage saving for the future educational expenses of your children and grandchildren. The common feature of all these accounts is that interest income, dividends, and capital gains on the securities are not taxed when the income is earned. The funds distributed from these accounts usually are taxable income if the funds transferred to establish these accounts reduce your taxable income.

You may conclude that you do not have the funds to take full advantage of these accounts. Consider a home equity loan or an increase in your mortgage; the income in these accounts is not taxed, and the interest payments are tax deductible.

Maximize the use of tax-advantaged accounts to grow your wealth; remember that the transfer reduces taxable income. If your marginal income tax rate is 40 percent, 35 percent at the federal level and 5 percent at the state level, the transfer of $1,000 to one of these accounts reduces your income tax payments by $400. If your annual purchases of bonds and stocks are larger than the amount that you can transfer to these tax-advantaged accounts, then invest for interest income and dividends in the tax-advantaged accounts and invest for capital gains in non-tax-advantaged accounts.

Similarly, you can use a home equity loan or increase your home mortgage to get the money to buy tax-exempt bonds issued by state and local governments; your interest income on these bonds is not taxed, and the interest payments on the borrowed money are a deduction from taxable income. (However, capital gains on these bonds are taxable, and some states tax the interest income received by state residents on the interest income of bonds issued by other state and local governments.)

Assume, for example, that the interest rate on the mortgage is 6.5 percent and that your marginal income tax rate is 35 percent; the after-tax interest rate is 4.5 percent. If the interest rate on the state and local bonds is 5.5 percent, then you have earned one percentage point from your arbitrage of the differences in the tax rates. If your home mortgage is $100,000, you've increased your after-tax income by $1,000 a year—an increase that will compound to more than $20,000 in fifteen years.

Tax-exempt bonds are most attractive to individuals who have high marginal tax brackets. Individuals with low marginal tax rates are likely to have a higher after-tax rate of return on a taxable corporate bond in the same risk class. The crossover marginal tax rate between these two options usually is between 20 and 25 percent. If your tax rate is higher than 25 percent, the tax-exempt bonds are more attractive; if your marginal tax rate is below 20 percent, the after-tax income on taxable corporate bonds will be higher. If your marginal income tax rate is between 20 and 25 percent, then the bond with the higher after-tax interest rate depends on the scope of the difference between the two interest rates.

For many individuals the tax rate on long-term capital gains (gains on securities owned for more than a year) is a bit less than 50 percent of the tax rate on ordinary income. Capital losses on securities and other assets can be offset against capital gains on a dollar-for-dollar basis. Moreover, up to $3,000 in capital losses each year can be offset against ordinary income, and these capital losses can be carried forward for five years.

If your capital losses are much larger than the amount that can be offset against ordinary income, tilt your stock purchases toward firms that distribute their earnings through repurchases of stock. These repurchases induce increases in the prices of their shares and should produce capital gains that won't be taxable because they are offset by the capital losses that you had earlier. Warren Buffett got rich—or at least richer—by figuring out how to fully exploit recognized capital losses to reduce tax payments on capital gains.

You might use a home equity loan or increase your mortgage and use the cash to buy shares in firms that as a matter of policy buy back their shares rather than pay dividends. Assume—to facilitate the comparison—that the dollar amount of the increase in your mortgage interest payments is equal to the dollar amount of the capital gain on the shares that you purchased with the borrowed money. The interest payments on home mortgages are tax deductible and reduce your tax payments by the product of the amount of the payment and your marginal income tax rate, and the capital gains on the shares increase your tax payments by the product of the amount of the gains and the capital gains tax rate.

You can also borrow from your broker to get the cash to buy the shares of firms that repurchase their shares. There is a $10,000 limitation on the amount of investment interest payments in excess of investment income. (Broker loans can be an expensive source of borrowed money because the interest rates often seem high unless you have negotiated a low interest rate on the loan.)

Capital gains from the sale of an owner-occupied home are not taxed, provided a new, more expensive home is purchased within eighteen months. Up to $500,000 of the capital gains on the sale of an owner-occupied home is not taxed, provided the individual is age 55 or older and the house has been the primary residence for three of the last five years.

Consider buying an apartment or a house as an investment; each year you will be able to reduce your taxable income because you will be able to depreciate the property over twenty-five years. Then move into this property three years before you intend to sell it. Assume that the unrealized capital gain is $150,000, in large part because of depreciation. All of this gain is nontaxable, provided that you can satisfy the IRS that the property was your primary residence for the last three years. Otherwise, you have to pay a capital gains tax of $30,000 when you sell the house.

To Pay or Not to Pay: The Capital Gains Tax

One of the most serious mistakes that investors make is that they hold onto securities and other assets because they fear having to pay a capital gains tax. This tax eventually must be paid, except in one of several circumstances: if the securities are to be given to a charity or transferred to your estate on death. The tax basis of value of assets—houses, securities, rare books, paintings, and other assets—transferred to an estate on death is the then-market value rather than the initial purchase price; the individuals who inherit this property pay no capital gains tax on the excess of the market value over the cost. The term is that "the basis is stepped up." You might be reluctant to sell the property and realize the capital gains now because you believe that the capital gains tax rate will be reduced in the future. But you could be unpleasantly surprised. Uncle Sam is your silent, uncomplaining, but always avaricious partner.

The choice (unless one of the three scenarios above is applicable) is between paying the tax this year or at some other time. Assume you have a large unrealized capital gain. Now assume you sell half of the shares in the account, pay the tax, and reinvest the funds in the same stock. In effect, you now have two different portfolios of the same stock. Time passes. The price of the stock increases.

You now decide to sell both sets of shares. You will have a large capital gain on the first group of shares and a smaller capital gain on the second group. Now compare after-tax values of the two portfolios. The first portfolio is more valuable—but the difference between the values of the two portfolios is modest. And if the stock price had declined modestly, you would have been better off if you had sold the stock and paid the capital gains tax on the sale.

Tax Arbitrage: Gifting Appreciated Assets

Americans are generous in their contributions to charities, and in part because both the federal and state tax systems encourage such gifts by treating those to qualified charities as tax deductions. You can arbitrage the tax system by giving securities and other assets with unrealized capital gains to charities. In effect, never give cash for contributions greater than $50. Because you receive a tax deduction equal to the market value of the securities, you are, in effect, avoiding paying the capital gains tax, and part of the deduction you receive is for what otherwise would have been the capital gains tax payment.

The unrealized capital gains on securities and other assets given to a university, hospital, or other charity are not taxed, and there is a deduction from current income of the full market value of the gift. For example, assume you own stock with a current market value of $1,500; your tax basis is $600, and hence you have an unrealized capital gain of $900. If you sell the stock, you will pay the capital gains tax on the realized gain of $900. If the capital gains tax rate is 20 percent, your tax payment will be $180 and your after-tax proceeds will be $1,320. Assume instead that you had given the stock to a charity. You receive a tax deduction of $1,500 that reduces your taxable income by the same amount, and your tax payment declines by $450 if your marginal tax rate is 30 percent.

You may conclude that $50 or $100 of securities with unrealized gains is a nuisance to charities. You can instead give these securities to one of the large mutual fund families that have charitable gift accounts; you receive an immediate tax deduction for the year in which you make the gift. The mutual fund will sell the security and invest the funds in a money market account or in some other type of account, according to your instructions. You then instruct the mutual fund to write checks to the charities of your choice—and you can continue making these gifts as long as you have a positive balance in this account. (Some of these charitable gift funds have a policy of not writing a check for less than $250. If you're in the habit of making a gift to the ABC Community Center of $50 a year, then you can inform the center that you will arrange that they receive a payment of $250 every fifth year.)

The Pesky AMT

The AMT (Alternative Minimum Tax) has become a nuisance of the first order. There are two ways to determine taxable deductions: the traditional approach, which involves summing medical payments above a threshold, state and local tax payments, interest payments, and contributions, and the AMT approach. The law requires you to calculate your income tax liability both ways and pay the higher tax.

Because of the AMT, your marginal income tax rate may be higher than you think—probably by three percentage points.

Differential Tax Rates: Parents and Children

If you're saving for the college educations of your children and grandchildren, open Section 529 accounts in their names. The investment income in these accounts is not taxable. Funds withdrawn from the accounts for tuition, room and board, books, and other educational expenses are not taxed.

You can also use Educational IRAs to save for future college expenses. Again, the investment income on the funds in these dedicated accounts is not taxable, and neither are the funds withdrawn. Moreover, the income tax rates applied to the investment income of your children often is lower than your income tax rate. The major difference between Section 529 accounts and Educational IRAs is that the annual contribution limit to the Educational IRAs is $1,000, and the states set maximum values for Section 529 accounts, usually in the range of $150,000 to $250,000.

A charitable remainder unitrust is like the deferred payment annuity except that you are paid the lesser of a specified proportion of the trust assets or the actual net income earned by the trust. The payment to you is variable and can be pegged to inflation. The securities to be held in the tax-advantaged accounts should be somewhat less risky than those in the regular accounts, since capital losses in these accounts cannot be offset against earned income. During your retirement, retain funds in the tax-advantaged accounts for the longest possible period subject to the requirement about minimum annual distributions.

Finally, remember that the federal tax system always is "in play." The George W. Bush administration reduced tax rates in the first three years it was in power, but the kicker was that in 2011 rates would revert to their level in 2000. And the Obama administration has a large fiscal deficit and almost certainly will propose increases in some tax rates to reduce the projected deficits.

ACTIONABLES

1. Determine if you have maximized the opportunities to use tax-advantaged accounts.

2. Borrow and use cash to buy tax-exempt securities.

3. Borrow and use the funds to buy conservative growth stocks. The payment of interest reduces taxable ordinary income, and the sale of the growth stocks leads to a capital gain that is taxable at a significantly lower rate.

4. When buying growth stocks, prefer those companies that reward their shareholders through "buy-backs" of their stocks rather than through cash dividends.

5. Establish Section 529 accounts for your children's educational expenses.

6. Give assets to children and grandchildren if their marginal tax rates are below your tax rate.

7. Give appreciated assets to charities using a two-tiered approach: if the amount is large, say, above $500, give directly to the charity. For smaller gifts, establish a charitable gift account at Fidelity,

Vanguard, or one of the other mutual fund families by transferring appreciated assets to these accounts.

8. If you own assets with a very low cost relative to their current market price, consider holding these assets so they will be transferred to your estate on your death. The basis will be stepped up and the beneficiaries of the estate will avoid a capital gains tax payment.

8   Bernie Madoff: Mugger, Con, or Scam Artist?

Robert Redford and Paul Newman starred in the movie *The Sting*, based on the novel by David S. Ward. The sting is an exercise in "mugging" a bookie—the "mark"—who takes bets on horse races. Redford and Newman—the "sharks"—place a large bet on a horse that they know already has won a race. The bookie accepts the bet because he doesn't know that the race is over; the sharks have manipulated the clocks in his office so they run slow. The success of the sharks depends on their success in withholding or suppressing information.

    Bernie Madoff was a shark who had 4,000 of his "closest friends" as marks. Month after month, Bernie provided monthly statements to these clients that indicated the value of their accounts was increasing at the rate of 10 to 12 percent a year, regardless of whether stock prices were increasing or decreasing or going sideways. Bernie's secret was that he was using a "split strike price strategy." Investors clamored to invest with Bernie; they needed an "in" to get him to take their money. Some newspaper accounts reported that $50 billion had been invested with Bernie, others that the total was $64 billion. Bernie Madoff was the "grandchild" of Carlos Ponzi, probably the most famous banker in American history after Alexander Hamilton. Ponzi now is immortalized in the term "Ponzi scheme." Ponzi ran a small, unregulated deposit-taking institution in Boston in the early 1920s. He promised to pay interest at the rate of 45 percent a year on his IOUs. Ponzi suggested that he was able to pay this very high interest rate because of the profits from arbitraging "international postal reply coupons." In the years immediately after World War I, the British pound, the French franc, the Italian lira, and the other European currencies had depreciated. Ponzi said he bought these currencies with the U.S. dollar, and then he used these foreign currencies to buy international postal reply coupons denominated in one of the European currencies, which he then had shipped to the United States and exchanged at their face value for the U.S. dollar.

Apparently Ponzi purchased only several hundred dollars' worth of postal reply coupons. Ponzi's story of the profits from arbitraging international postal reply coupons is the father of Bernie Madoff's split strike price strategy. Every manager of a Ponzi scheme has a story of why he or she can consistently pay rates of return that are much higher than those paid by traditional bankers.

Ponzi used the money received from the sale of deposits on Tuesday to pay the interest to those who had purchased deposits on Monday. Most of those who made their deposits on Monday were happy to keep their money with Ponzi because the interest rate was so high—and hence the amount of cash that Ponzi initially needed to meet these withdrawals was modest.

As the value of their deposits increased, more and more individuals asked for some of their money. Ponzi needed enough new cash from the sale of deposits on Wednesday to finance these cash withdrawals by those who had purchased deposits on Monday and Tuesday. As the cash withdrawals increased, Ponzi was obliged to raise the interest rates that he would pay on new deposits. The scheme collapsed when the inflow of new cash was smaller than the withdrawal of cash.

The fraud in every Ponzi scheme is that there is no underlying economic activity that leads to the high rates of return. Instead, the cash paid to those who were among the first to buy deposits is obtained from those who bought their deposits at later dates. The scheme continues until the manager runs out of cash. In the meantime the manager lives high—Madoff had a penthouse in Manhattan, a mansion in Palm Springs, a villa in the south of France, a yacht, and partial ownership of two jet aircraft.

Ponzi schemes proliferate. When the promised interest rate is several times higher than the market interest rate, there is a strong presumption that a Ponzi scheme is at work; it's extremely likely that the only way the promoter can obtain the cash to pay the funds to the existing depositors or investors is from new investors. The promoter has to expand the geographic market in order to stay in business.

Bernie Madoff is at the top of two hit parades. One is the dollar value of his Ponzi scheme, and the other is the length of time that his scheme flourished, which appears to have been somewhere between fifteen and twenty years.

Where did the money come from? Bernie had a number of "feeder funds"—essentially touts that were hustling for Bernie. One was Fairfield Greenwich, which placed more than half of the money that had been entrusted to it by clients with Madoff. Ezra Merkin, who had formerly been head of GMAC, the financial arm of GM, managed a hedge fund that invested half of its assets with Madoff. Merkin received a finder's fee for bringing money to Madoff. The attorney general of New York State said that Merkin had told his clients that Madoff was A-OK—and Merkin said that he had lost some of his own money when Madoff collapsed.

Ponzi schemes flourish as long as the inflow of money from new depositors is larger than the outflow from other depositors who are withdrawing funds. But when prices of stocks and real estate began to decline, the cash withdrawals increased and became larger than cash inflows, and Madoff's collapse was inevitable.

When Madoff admitted there was a fraud, there was less than $300 million in the accounts. What happened to the money? The difference between the $50 billion or the $64 billion that Madoff supposedly owed his clients and the $300 million in his bank account was immense. Consider the range of answers: high living, trading losses, payments to the feeders, and transfers to secret accounts in offshore banks. If a high standard of living is $25 millon a year, then the total costs might have been $300 million or $400 million. And Bernie almost certainly paid income tax on the funds withdrawn from the company. A small dent in the $50 billion plus.

Trading losses. Maybe. But the press reported that Bernie never traded. So the trading losses were minimal.

Payments to the feeders. The feeders served two purposes, bringing in the money and dealing with the clients, so Madoff had little face-to-face contact with the clients. The feeders were paid "one and ten percent." Assume that Willie Sutton is the feeder, and he brings $10 million to Madoff. Willie immediately receives a $1 million check (that's the "one"), so Bernie had only $9 million to invest. But then Madoff was obliged to pay the feeders 10 percent of any gain in excess of a benchmark. Assume that the benchmark is the U.S. Treasury bill rate, which averaged 4 percent. Assume also that Madoff reported that he earned 11 percent on his investments. Madoff was obliged to pay the feeder 0.7 percent on the gains.

But wait: there's more. In year 2 the feeder gets the same "one and ten percent"; it's as if he has brought in new money. And the feeder gets the same 10 percent of any gains over the benchmark. Year by year, the feeder gets paid.

Press accounts suggest that the feeders lost a lot of money when Madoff folded. Madoff probably had an agreement with the feeders that they had to keep a significant proportion of their revenues with him for five years, sort of a lockup.

There are a lot of Bernie Madoffs out there. Most do not start with a plan to rip off their friends. They make a bad investment, they're under water, and their choice is to fess up and take the heat or to fudge the data and hope that the next bet might be a winner.

There are four striking insights from the Madoff story. The first is that a nontrivial number of investors lost virtually all of their financial wealth; they were too dumb or too stupid or too greedy to diversify their wealth among two or three investment advisors. All their eggs—or what they thought were eggs—were in one basket. In the end, the eggs in the basket were hollow shells. The second is that the investors did not take the precaution of ensuring that there were checks and balances and an independent auditor for their investments; they failed to ask who was verifying the data on the financial reports. (The Enron saga is that some of the independent auditors had been co-opted to participate in the con.) The third is that it is risky to trust your friends. Con men always play the friendship game. The fourth is that any financial advisor that says the exceptionally high or exceptionally consistent returns result from a "secret formula" probably is engaged in falsification.

A lot of sharks are likely to tag you as a mark as you move along the life cycle. Some of the muggings will be involuntary or inadvertent; you might be physically assaulted, or someone may get hold of one of your credit card numbers and charge items to your account. Someone may figure out how to access your bank account; the sharks will print phony checks with your name and then copy your signature. Someone may call your broker with a request that money be wired from your account to another of "your accounts" in a nearby state or a distant country; the sharks will structure this second account so they can readily withdraw the money. You may be overcharged when your car is towed from a place that you weren't supposed to park. Someone may pick your pocketbook or wallet while you're in a crowd leaving an athletic event. A roofer or a chimney repair man or a tree surgeon may fail to deliver on the promised work after you have made a sizeable deposit and you have to decide whether the cost of the legal remedies is worthwhile; the mode of operation of the promise breaker may be to commit modest frauds that invite few lawsuits.

Seniors are more likely to be mugged than juniors. Police forces have special units that deal with theft of property from seniors because seniors are often the victims of the muggers; they are less capable of resisting the physical assault than they would have been thirty and forty years earlier. Some of the mugging will be advertent, perhaps because you dropped your skepticism or because of your greed.

The market system is based on trust; it is one reason the system is a reasonably efficient and low-cost way of producing goods and services. Caveat emptor, but most buyers trust the sellers when they say there is a one-year warranty or a money-back guarantee. Scamsters prosper by taking advantage of our trust. The scams almost always involve a payment of cash from you (the mark) to the shark today in exchange for the shark's promise to pay you much more cash tomorrow. The shark is extremely adept at making promises. The shark is skillful in appealing to your greed and in lulling your skepticism. The shark may sell you penny stocks or nickel stocks or ten-dollar stocks.

The Pigeon Drop and Its Cousins

The "Pigeon Drop" involves "newly found money" that doesn't appear to belong to anyone; it's as if a pigeon dropped the money from the sky. Someone—a total stranger—approaches you and states that he or she has just found $4,500 in a large brown shopping bag—you are invited to see the $100 bills in the bag. What should be done with the money? There is no sign or indication about who the rightful owner is. The shark offers to share the money with you. But first the shark wants some evidence of your "good faith," a demonstration that you are a person of good will and someone who can be trusted. The shark asks you to place some of your own money in the bag. You agree. The shark accompanies you to the bank while you withdraw $2,000, which you place in the shopping bag. Then the shark asks you to hold the shopping bag with the money while he or she takes care of a sudden need to go to the toilet. The shark doesn't return, but initially you're not uncomfortable; you have the bag with the money. Eventually you become curious and open the shopping bag—which has toilet paper rather than the money.

Consider the following e-mail dated July 9, 2006.

From: Mr. Arthur Edelmarr
London, England
Fax Number + 44 87 1256 4913

First of all, I would like to apologize to you, should my e-mail in any way invade your personal privacy. I hope you can bear with me and understand that the urgency of the matter at hand compelled me to write you this very important e-mail in my search for a very reliable person, who can assist me in this very urgent business matter. I am Mr. Arthur Edelmarr an external auditor of a well known bank here in the United Kingdom.

In one of our periodic auditings I discovered a dormant account with a current holding balance of £5,000,000 (Five Million British Pounds) which has not been operated for the past seven years. From my investigations and confirmations, the owner of this account, was a foreigner by the name of Mr. Richard Burson, who died in plane crash on 31st October 1999 abroad EGYPTIAN AIRLINE 990 and since then nobody has done anything as regards the claiming of this money because he has no family members who are aware of the existence of either the account or the funds.

I have secretly discussed this matter with a top senior official of the federal Ministry of Finance here and we have agreed to find a reliable foreign partner to deal with us although due to his position he did not want to take active part but as soon as you follow my instructions everything will be successful because we will be working hand in hand with him.

We thus propose to do business with you, in order for you to stand as the next of kin of these funds from the deceased and after due legal processes have been followed the funds will be released to your account without delay and we will use it for investment abroad. Everything will be done following due legal processes, so you have nothing to worry about.

I depend on you to TREAT AS STRICTLY CONFIDENTIAL every matter relating to this transfer process until after you have received this money and confirmed the receipt to me. This is because I do not want to lose my current job with the bank or implicate the finance minister. I would also like you to know that the whole wire transfer process will NOT take more than 7 to 9 banking days.

At the conclusion of this transfer, you will be given 40% of the total amount, 60% will be for me.

This transaction is totally free of risk and troubles. If you require any further clarification, kindly feel free to inform me and include your phone number, so that I can promptly get in touch and we get to know each other better.

I look forward to your earliest response, so that I can inform you about the necessary steps that will be taken to actualize this transaction.

Do keep in touch.

Best regards,

Mr. Arthur C. Edelmarr.

Arthur is not a native Brit—indeed, Arthur doesn't exist. A Brit would have used the term Her Majesty's Treasury rather than the federal Ministry of Finance. Arthur is probably from Nigeria.

If you reply, "Arthur" will ask you to forward some money because of costs that he is incurring in registering you as the next of kin with the Home Office in London—part of the British government. The amount will be modest. Once you send the money, Arthur is likely to mention that his friend in the federal Ministry of Finance wants some money up front; Arthur is prepared to pay 60 percent of the amount since he will receive 60 percent of the money in the dormant account. If you send the money, you will learn that your share of the money will be wired to your account in two or three days; you're likely to be asked for the wiring instructions. Then, whoops: something else will happen that will delay the transfer, perhaps some sort of tax payment or a legal fee. The amounts that Arthur will ask for will increase. You will face the dilemma of whether to continue to send more money to "protect your investment" or to drop out.

If you threaten to go to the police or some other authority to get your money back, Arthur will indicate you are vulnerable to prosecution because you have claimed—falsely—that you are related to the recently deceased Mr. Richard Burson.

Arthur's e-mail is known as a "Nigerian 419" from the section of the Nigerian penal code that deals with promises of this type. The letters and e-mails come from Uganda, Togo, Sierra Leone, and other African nations.

The money is always a large amount. The money never has a rightful owner; perhaps like Burson, the owner was killed in a plane crash or the owner gathered the funds illegally and now can't touch the money because of fear of prosecution.

The 419 account scams are a serial version of the Pigeon Drop. You are asked for a series of payments as you get closer and closer to the money. The money is always just slightly out of your reach and you will be strung along in the attempt to get you to forward more and more money. The con continues until you're broke or exhausted.

Before the advent of e-mail, the sharks in Lagos would approach the marks with imposing letters, perhaps from the wife of a recently deceased finance minister. Now the costs of e-mail are much lower.

Often you are promised future cash; in the meantime you have to provide cash with an application fee to qualify for the cash. Your child may be offered a scholarship; however, there is a $125 application fee. Or you may be promised assistance with a low-interest-rate loan; however, there is a $150 application fee. These application fees seem modest relative to the cash that you are promised. You send in the application fee. The cash that you are promised never arrives.

On July 3, 2008, the mail contained a check for $9.25 made out to the author. The following sentence was printed on the back of the check: "By cashing this check I agree to a thirty-day trial offer in Everyday Values. I understand that my membership will be automatically extended for an additional eleven months and the $139.99 annual membership fee will be automatically billed to my card on file with _____ for a membership in Everyday Values unless I cancel my membership by calling 1-877-880-1825 before the end of the trial period."

A tepid corporate version of the Pigeon Drop.

Chain Letters, Pyramid Clubs, and Multilevel Marketing Schemes

The chain letter scam involves a request that you send $10 to a name at the top of the letter and copy the letter after moving the person in the number 2 position to the number 1 position, the person in the number 3 position to the number 2 position, the person in the number 4 position to the number 3 position, and the person in the number 5 position to the number 4 position, adding your name in the number 5 position. Send the letter to five of your friends and ask each to send $10 to the person in the number 1 position and repeat the process. If each recipient of the letter follows the instruction, then within a month you will receive $62,500.

Chain letters are great for the individuals who start the scam and who insert their own name in the top position. They will have sent out thousands of letters at the cost of postage. If the letters are sent out by regular U.S. mail and the positive response rate is 5 percent, they are still ahead. With e-mail, the cost of sending the letters has become trivially low.

A pyramid club is a multilayered marketing version of a chain letter. The scam is that you are asked to purchase an inventory of products that you will sell; the products might be vitamins or health supplements or x. Your purchase of these products entitles you to recruit sales personnel who will also sell the product; you are promised a share of their revenues. You are encouraged to recruit individuals who will be successful in hiring others to sell the same product, and you are promised a share of their revenues. If you hire five individuals and each of these five hires five individuals, then you will receive revenues based on the sales of thirty individuals. These chain letters and pyramid clubs rely on the greater fool theory of financial markets that there is an infinite number of individuals who will sign up and provide cash to the early entrants.

Penny Stocks

Penny stocks are a specialty of "boiler rooms," so called because of the high-pressured sales tactics used to sell "hot stocks." The sharks have figured out that you're much more likely to part with $15,000 to buy 100,000 shares of a stock that trades for $0.15 a share than you would be to part with $15,000 to buy 1,000 shares of a $15.00 stock. The sharks always point out two features. The first is that the price per share was low, almost always less than $0.50 per share, and the second is that the percentage increase in the share price had been very large in the previous several weeks. The fellow—these sharks are almost always men—at the other end of the conversation chats about some new discovery that is not yet well known. The shark wants you to be the first to know.

The price action in the penny stocks results because brother Peter buys shares from brother Paul on the odd days of the month and then Paul buys the shares on the even days of the month. After they have sold $1 or

$2 million worth of stock, both Peter and Paul stop buying, and the price falls off a cliff.

Currently the boiler rooms operate over the Internet. You'll receive an e-mail about a "hot stock" whose price is very low—$1.00 a share and never above $2.00; the percentage increase in the price in the last several weeks has been rapid, and the prospect is that the price is going to double and perhaps triple in three months.

There is only one reason why a total stranger would share this information with you, and that is that he intends to con you after appealing to your greed.

Charity Scams

Americans are generous to charities, and the tax law encourages contributions to charities. Some scamsters masquerade behind the façade of a charity, often seeking to raise money for disabled veterans or for the policemen or for the firemen. The solicitation often is over the phone, and frequently the caller will immediately use your first name.

One of your major concerns should be how much of each $1.00 that you might donate to the charity goes to the beneficiary of the charity and how much goes to those who called you on the phone and their bosses. Ask three questions politely: would you please send the annual report, what proportion of each $1.00 collected goes to the charity, and what is the percentage commission of each $1.00 collected that goes to the telephone solicitor?

How Much Is a U.S. Government $2 Bill Worth?

The *New York Times* of August 22, 2009, carried a full-page ad with the headline "Release of U.S. Govern't $2 bills in full color and gilded with 22k Gold leaf begins now." The gist of the ad is that "*Today* for 48 hours only" you can buy "four Estate Wallets each one stuffed with a crisp $2 bill that has been color-enhanced and gilded with 22-karat Gold Leaf for just $72 per Vault Pak plus shipping. There is a strict limit of 10 Vault Paks per household." So $72 plus shipping will buy you four $2 bills plus some packaging.

Why would anyone pay $72 plus for four $2 bills?

The ad is typical of those involving buffalo nickels, Morgan silver dollars, and other items. Usually there is a discovery of a sudden cache, the amount is limited, and the sotto voce message is that the value of these collectibles will increase over time. Various "mints" specialize in the production of "collectibles." One theme is that the number of these units is limited. From time to time, you'll receive ads offering to sell some rare or uncirculated buffalo nickels. Or the offer will be for some uncirculated Morgan dollars that have just been discovered in a vault in the underbasement of the U.S. Treasury. Or the coins may be Spanish thalers just recovered from 300 feet of water in the Caribbean, from a sunken boat that has not been disturbed for 300 years. It seems like there is an infinite supply of Morgan silver dollars or buffalo nickels and other "rare" coins.

There are two elements to the hustle. One is rarity; there is a small, finite amount that will soon be exhausted. The other is that the price is about to increase.

White-Collar Muggings

Sharks sometimes known as brokers always want to sell blue sky. They mention the high rates of return on new inventions, a new fuel system for cars that will double the mileage, the discovery of a new gas field or the next Microsoft or Dell, or a new formula for producing a rubber-like substance so that the tires on a car will last longer than the car itself. Their supply of promises is virtually unlimited when your money is in view.

Henry Blodgett was a stock market analyst with Merrill Lynch during the dot-com bubble of the late 1990s. He had graduated from Yale. Blodgett's "skill" was his willingness to identify price targets for some stocks that Merrill had underwritten. These targets were much higher than the current price. Stock prices were increasing, and so Blodgett appeared to have exceptional foresight. Blodgett was well paid by Merrill, with an income many times higher than that of the president of Yale, because Blodgett's reports generated lots of business for Merrill. Blodgett's masters at Merrill must have known that his recommendations were a con—even if they were good for business. On several occasions Blodgett sent e-mails to friends disparaging the stocks that he was recommending.

Blodgett earned a lot of money from Merrill. Merrill earned a lot of money from Blodgett. Guess where the money came from. Was Merrill engaged in white-collar mugging?

Two lessons. Diversify, to reduce the harm if you're about to be mugged by Merrill or Ponzi or Madoff. And your "best friends" may turn out to be the muggers.

Part II INVESTMENT DECISIONS

9   The Merrill Lynch Hustle:
Can You Trust the Brokers?

As your savings accumulate, you need to decide how to invest your money. Should you buy bonds or stocks or both bonds and stocks, and if so, in what proportions? Should you purchase bonds and stocks directly, or should you instead buy mutual funds that hold bonds and stocks? And there are more decisions: Which bonds and stocks? Which mutual funds? Should you follow a buy-and-hold strategy, or should you trade bonds and stocks, and if so, how frequently?

The thrust of this chapter is the historic rates of return on bonds and on stocks and the prospective rates of return on both types of securities. Wall Street hypes that the real rate of return on stocks (that is, the rate of return adjusted for the increases in the consumer price level) has been 7 percent. That assertion—let's call it the conventional wisdom—is highly unlikely, but it's the sort of preposterous claim that helps brokerage firms sell stocks. There is an immense amount of data on the rates of return on bonds and on stocks. Some of those data are summarized and presented in this chapter. You can't make wise and safe investment decisions unless you understand the data. If you understand the data, you'll know when the brokers for the firms that sell stocks and mutual funds are trying to take advantage of you, and you'll then have to decide whether they are charlatans or knaves. There's a pervasive belief that the laws of financial gravity do not apply to stocks, which simply isn't true; U.S. stock prices are tethered to U.S. corporate profits, and the growth of U.S. corporate profits is closely linked to the growth of U.S. gross domestic product (GDP).

Much of the conventional wisdom about the rates of return on bonds and stocks exaggerates the rate of return on stocks over the rate of return on bonds. Not surprisingly, that information comes from those who sell securities; they know that if they sell you bonds, you'll sit on them for a long time and that if they sell you stocks, you'll get itchy and trade more often—and that's better for their commissions. Moreover, the old saw that "stocks are a great inflation hedge" is wrong or misleading and probably both wrong and misleading; when the inflation rate accelerates, bond prices and stock prices both decline. Finally, the management fees and the associated transaction costs often can be so high when you buy actively managed mutual funds that you need to understand that the fees and costs charged by most mutual funds drive a massive wedge between the rates of return on bonds and on stocks and those that you would receive as an owner of shares in mutual funds—but that's the story of the next chapter.

The Investment Decision Ladder

Your investment decisions are arrayed in a four-step ladder in Table 9.1.

Decision 1. First you must decide between bonds and stocks as a group and Treasury bills, certificates of deposits, and other short-term money market investments. The prices of both bonds and stocks vary sharply, but there is virtually no price risk with U.S. Treasury bills and other short-term securities. Moreover, U.S. Treasury bills are not sensitive to credit or default risk—the U.S. government will never go bankrupt, because the U.S. Treasury can always get the cash to pay the holders of maturing bonds and bills by borrowing from the Federal Reserve banks. (You then should be concerned with inflation risk, the decline in the pur-

Table 9.1
The Investment Decision Ladder

Decision 1	Bonds versus stocks versus Treasury bills (near-cash)
Decision 2	Direct ownership versus mutual funds
Decision 3	Which bonds? Which stocks? Which mutual funds?
Decision 4	"Picking" versus "Timing"

Source: Author.

chasing power of your interest income and the principal of your bonds.) Most U.S. bank deposits of up to $100,000 are guaranteed by the U.S. government; the limit to the insurance was raised to $250,000 until June 30, 2009, and this ceiling was extended as a way to enhance investor confidence in response to the 2008 financial crisis.

The bond issues of various U.S. government-sponsored enterprises (GSEs)—the Federal National Mortgage Association (Fannie Mae), the Federal Home Loan Mortgage Corporation (Freddie Mac), the Student National Loan Association (Sallie Mae), and the Federal Home Loan Banks—were not formally guaranteed by the U.S. Treasury, but they were generally believed to be "too big to fail." That belief was tested in September 2008, when both Fannie and Freddie were taken over by the U.S. Treasury. The investors who owned the common shares and the preferred shares lost all their money, and the owners of their bonds in effect then had a U.S. Treasury security. Deposits in money market accounts offered by brokerage firms, mutual funds, and other financial institutions initially were not guaranteed by the U.S. government, and the value of money market deposits could decline below their face value (the cliché was "break the buck") if the firm that issued it incurred large loan losses and was unable or unwilling to obtain the money from another source to offset these losses—but these deposits were brought under the U.S. government's deposit guarantee umbrella to prevent the cascading of the financial crisis. There are minor choices on the menu as well. You can buy gold, silver, and other commodities—and you can buy financial securities whose prices are closely linked to the prices of these commodities. You can buy real estate, and you can buy foreign bonds and foreign stocks.

Decision 2. Now you must determine whether to invest your funds directly or instead to invest through mutual funds or to hire a professional money manager or a financial advisor. There are 10,000 U.S. mutual funds, more than four times the number of firms listed on the New York Stock Exchange. Many of the brokerage firms and investment banks, such as Merrill Lynch and Charles Schwab, have established mutual funds to obtain the fees and other income from managing these funds.

To begin, develop a "template" for your portfolio of securities: the ideal composition of bonds, stocks, and other securities. Figure 11.3 shows a sample diversified portfolio, a template that you can follow and modify. Most individuals approach the purchase of bonds and stocks in an opportunistic way; their portfolios reflect a number of incremental decisions.

Be sure to consider the diversification of your wealth among bonds and stocks and other assets as you develop your portfolio. (Moreover, limit your holdings of the shares of the firm that is your employer—when Enron and Lehman Brothers failed, many of those who lost their jobs also lost a substantial part of their wealth.) Fortunes are made (and lost) by specialization; fortunes are conserved by diversification.

Decision 3. Which, among the thousands of bonds, stocks, and mutual funds, should you select? When considering bonds, you must weigh the credit risk of the governments and the corporate borrowers and you must also determine whether the interest payments on the bonds are taxed by the U.S. Treasury and by the various states. The interest payments on bonds issued by the U.S. Treasury are subject to federal income tax, but the interest payments on bonds issued by state and local governments are not, although these "municipal bonds" are subject to a credit risk that is not attached to ownership of U.S. Treasury securities. Corporate bonds, both the bonds that have been given ratings by Moody's, Standard & Poor's, and Fitch Ratings, as well as the "junk bonds"—those with a credit rating of BBB or below and those without a credit rating—are subject to credit risk. The riskier the bond, the higher the interest rate. You'll need to decide whether the additional interest income is worthwhile in terms of the risk of loss if the borrower goes bankrupt. You also must select the maturity of the bonds. You might buy U.S. Treasury bonds that are guaranteed to compensate you for increases in the consumer price level, known as Treasury Inflation-Protected Securities (TIPS). You might buy convertible corporate bonds that can be exchanged for stock. Similarly, you can choose among 10,000 U.S. stocks—and perhaps as many foreign stocks. Should you buy "growth stocks" or "value stocks"? Should you buy stocks of very large, medium-sized, or smaller firms ("large cap," "medium cap," and "small cap," respectively)?

Decision 4. Once you've chosen your initial portfolio, you must decide whether you will be a "timer" or a "picker." Timers believe that there are cyclical variations in the prices of bonds and stocks and that exceptional returns can be made by buying low and selling high, and the pickers believe that "all the information is in the price," so pickers tend to follow a buy-and-hold strategy.

Your position on the life cycle—whether you are in your thirties, fifties, or sixties—should affect your choice between bonds and stocks. Bonds are less risky than stocks—their prices vary less than the prices of stocks from one month to the next and from one year to the next. If you've just retired or are about to retire, you may take a more conservative approach and increase the proportion of bonds in your portfolio. The nostrum that "the proportion of bonds in your portfolio should be equal to your age" doesn't hold true, because you are likely to live twenty or more years after you retire; moreover, you may hope to bequest wealth to children and other family members and to charities.

How Are Stocks Doing?

How are stocks doing? The answer depends on the stock price index that you consult. The indexes differ in terms of both the number of firms that are included and the weight of individual firms in the construction of the index. First consider the annual rates of return based on the selected stock price indexes (see Table 9.2).

Several of these indexes, including the Dow Jones, the S&P 500, and the Russell 2000, always include the same number of stocks; the number of stocks included in several of the other indexes changes over time. Some indexes are inclusive: all the stocks in the Dow are included in the S&P 500, all the stocks in the S&P 500 are included in the Russell 2000, and all the stocks in the Russell 2000 are included in the Wilshire 5000. None of the stocks included in the NASDAQ index is included in the New York Stock Exchange, and none of the stocks included in the New York Stock Exchange is included in the NASDAQ index. Note that several of these indexes include foreign stocks as well as domestic stocks.

The Dow Jones industrial average is the oldest index and probably the most famous. Each of the thirty stocks included in the index has the same weight in computing the changes in the value of the index from one day to the next. The NASDAQ index includes stocks that are traded in the over-the-counter market (as opposed to the stocks that are traded on the New York Stock Exchange). Many of the firms in industries associated with the newer technologies, including Microsoft, Dell, Intel, and Cisco, are traded on the NASDAQ. The S&P 500 includes 500 large firms (although not necessarily the 500 largest firms) selected from across most industries; the stocks of these firms are widely held. The market value of each firm determines its weight in the S&P 500 index, and changes in the market values of the stocks of individual firms from one day to the next lead to changes in their weights in the index. Two

Table 9.2
Annual Rates of Return, Selected Stock Price Indexes

	1997	1998	1999	2000	2001	2002	2003	2004	2005	2006	2007	2008
American Stock Exchange	17.4	0.6	27.3	2.4	−5.6	−2.7	42.4	22.2	22.6	16.9	17.2	−42.0
Dow Jones Industrials	24.9	18.2	27.3	−4.7	−5.4	−15.0	28.3	5.6	1.7	19.0	8.9	−31.9
NASDAQ Composite Index	21.6	39.6	85.6	−39.3	−21.1	−31.5	50.0	8.6	1.4	9.5	9.8	−40.5
NYSE Composite Index	30.3	16.6	9.1	1.0	−10.2	−19.8	29.3	12.2	7.0	17.9	6.6	−40.9
Russell 2000 Index	20.5	−3.4	19.6	−4.2	1.0	−21.6	45.4	17.0	3.3	17.0	−2.7	−34.8
S&P 500 Composite	33.4	28.6	21.0	−9.1	−11.9	−22.1	28.7	10.9	4.9	15.8	5.5	−37.0
Wilshire 5000	21.3	23.4	23.6	−10.9	−11.0	−20.9	31.6	12.5	6.4	15.8	5.6	−37.2

Source: Data from ATIVO Research, Chicago.

values often are reported for the S&P 500 index. One is without dividends, and the other adjusts for the reinvestment of the cash received from dividends to buy each of the stocks in the index in proportion to its weight in the index.

An Overview of Stock Prices between 1950 and 2008

The average annual nominal and real rates of U.S. economic growth together with the nominal and real rates of return on bonds and stocks for holding periods of different lengths—five, ten, twenty, twenty-five, and fifty years—are shown in Table 9.3. The nominal rates of return on U.S. Treasury bonds were computed from a bond wealth index, and the nominal rates of return on stocks were derived from a stock wealth index based on the S&P 500 index. (The methods used to construct these indexes and their limitations are discussed later in this chapter.)

Table 9.3
U.S. GDP Growth Rate and Real Rates of Return on Bonds and on Stocks

	GDP Growth		Bond Returns		Stock Returns	
	Nominal	Real	Nominal	Real	Nominal	Real
Five years						
12/1950 to 12/1955	7.1%	4.5%	0.7%	−0.8%	24.6%	22.8%
12/1955 to 12/1960	4.9%	2.5%	0.3%	−1.8%	8.4%	6.2%
12/1960 to 12/1965	6.4%	5.0%	1.4%	0.1%	13.5%	12.0%
12/1965 to 12/1970	7.6%	3.4%	0.6%	−3.8%	2.9%	−1.5%
12/1970 to 12/1975	9.5%	2.7%	2.9%	−3.8%	3.2%	−3.5%
12/1975 to 12/1980	11.2%	3.7%	0.5%	−8.0%	13.7%	4.1%
12/1980 to 12/1985	8.6%	3.2%	17.5%	12.1%	14.4%	9.1%
12/1985 to 12/1990	6.6%	3.3%	11.2%	6.8%	13.3%	8.8%
12/1990 to 12/1995	5.0%	2.5%	13.0%	9.9%	16.6%	13.4%
12/1995 to 12/2000	5.8%	4.1%	7.7%	5.0%	18.5%	15.6%
12/2000 to 12/2005	4.8%	2.3%	7.3%	4.6%	0.5%	−2.0%
12/2005 to 12/2008	7.2%	3.0%	25.4%	21.4%	−14.1%	−16.8%
Ten years						
12/1955 to 12/1965	5.7%	3.7%	0.8%	−0.9%	10.9%	9.0%
12/1965 to 12/1975	8.6%	3.1%	1.7%	−3.8%	3.1%	−2.5%

(*continued*)

Table 9.3 (*continued*)

	GDP Growth		Bond Returns		Stock Returns	
	Nominal	*Real*	*Nominal*	*Real*	*Nominal*	*Real*
12/1975 to 12/1985	9.9%	3.5%	8.7%	1.6%	14.0%	6.6%
12/1985 to 12/1995	5.8%	2.9%	12.1%	8.3%	14.9%	11.1%
12/1995 to 12/2008	5.6%	3.1%	10.3%	7.4%	4.9%	2.1%
Twenty years (overlapping)						
12/1955 to 12/1975	7.1%	3.4%	1.3%	−2.3%	6.9%	3.1%
12/1965 to 12/1985	9.3%	3.3%	5.2%	−1.1%	8.4%	1.9%
12/1975 to 12/1995	7.8%	3.2%	10.4%	4.9%	14.5%	8.8%
12/1985 to 12/2008	5.7%	3.0%	11.1%	7.8%	9.3%	6.1%
Twenty-five years						
12/1955 to 12/1980	7.9%	3.4%	1.1%	−3.5%	8.2%	3.3%
12/1980 to 12/2008	6.2%	3.1%	12.3%	8.6%	10.3%	6.7%
Fifty years						
12/1955 to 12/2008	7.0%	3.2%	6.8%	2.6%	9.3%	5.0%

Source: Data from ATIVO Research, Chicago.

Are Stocks Cheap or Expensive?

The traditional answer to the question of whether stocks are cheap or expensive is based on whether the price-earnings ratio is low or high relative to its long-run average value; this ratio relates the market prices of the stocks to earnings per share. (The value for earnings might be those for the current quarter or year or the anticipated earnings for the next twelve months or the earnings for the most recent quarter.) The price-earnings ratio is the reciprocal of the "earnings yield," which has the value of earnings for the group of firms as the numerator in the fraction and their aggregate stock price as the denominator. The earnings yield on stocks often is compared with the earnings yield on bonds, which is the ratio of the sum of the interest coupon and the anticipated price change to the date that the bonds mature to the current price of bonds. For example, if the interest coupon on the bond is 6 percent, and the price of the bond is $925 and the bond matures in ten years, then the annual yield to maturity is the sum of the $60 annual interest payment and the anticipated annual increase in the price of the bond of $7.50 for a total annual income of $67.50 divided by the $925 price of the bond, or 7.30 percent. In the long run, the price-earnings ratio for the S&P 500 firms has averaged between sixteen and seventeen. Assume that this ratio has averaged sixteen and one-half; then the earnings yield on stocks is 100/16.5 or about 6.06 percent. If at any moment the current value for this ratio is lower (say, twelve or thirteen) than its average value, some observers conclude that stocks are cheap; if the current value is higher than the average value, they conclude that stocks are expensive.

Another approach to the same question is to look at the anticipated rate of return on stocks. Stocks are cheap if the anticipated rate of return on a portfolio of stocks is high and expensive if it is low. If investors anticipate that stock prices will continue to increase at the annual rate of 10 or 12 percent a year, stocks might be cheap even though the price-earnings ratio is higher than its long-run average. The anticipated rate of return on stocks cannot be measured in an objective way, since in an uncertain world there is no unambiguous yardstick.

The real rates of return on bonds were negative in the 1950s, 1960s, and 1970s, and then positive in the next two decades. The negative real rates of return on bonds in the 1950s resulted from both a decline in the price of bonds as the ceiling on long-term interest rates that had been adopted at the beginning of World War II and had been set at a low level was removed and from an increase in the U.S. consumer price level. The negative real rates of return on bonds in the 1960s and 1970s resulted from the more rapid increases in the consumer price level than in the bond wealth index. Bond prices declined sharply in the 1970s as the increase in the U.S. inflation rate led to higher U.S. interest rates. In contrast, the U.S. inflation rate declined in the 1980s and 1990s, and bond prices increased.

The Dow Jones Industrial Average and the S&P 500 index for the period from 1950 to 2008 are shown in Figure 9.1. This fifty-eight-year period breaks into four subperiods: a significant upward trend in both stock price indexes from 1950 to 1968, the large variability of these indexes around a flat trend between 1968 and 1982, the dramatic surge in

Figure 9.1
A Stylized View of U.S. Stock Prices

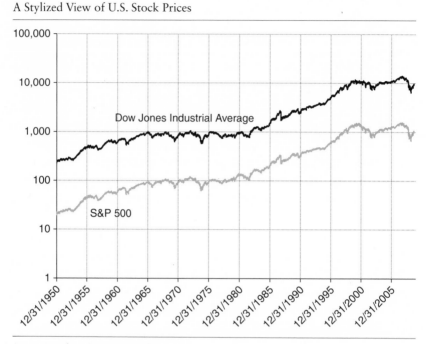

Source: Data from ATIVO Research, Chicago.

both indexes from 1982 to 2000, and then a slight downward trend to 2008, with a lot of movement above and below this trend between 2000 and 2008. At the end of 2008, the Dow Jones index was at the level that it had first reached in 1997.

The first of these periods is sometimes called the "Eisenhower bull market." In 1968 the major stock price indexes were more than three times higher than in 1950. Stock prices declined by more than 5 percent in only one year during this period. One explanation offered for this trend increase is that stock prices were unusually low in the second half of the 1940s because many investors were expecting a sharp recession after World War II (apparently because a sharp recession had followed World War I). The 1950s and 1960s were decades of remarkable economic growth in the United States and most other industrial countries. American household savings had rapidly increased during World War II because there was full employment with lots of overtime pay and modest opportunity to spend because of shortages. Spending surged after the end of the war, and the U.S. economy prospered. Corporate profits increased significantly more rapidly than U.S. GDP, and stock prices increased significantly more rapidly than corporate profits as investors became increasingly optimistic.

The United States experienced its largest inflation ever in the 1970s; the U.S. consumer price level in 1982 was more than three times higher than in 1968. Interest rates on U.S. dollar securities surged—as they always do when the inflation rate accelerates. Interest rates on U.S. Treasury bills increased even more rapidly than on U.S. bonds. U.S. stock prices were volatile; in 1973 and again in 1974 the Dow Jones index of stock prices declined by more than 25 percent. The prices of U.S. stocks decreased as the prices of bonds declined. The inflation of the 1970s led investors to shift wealth from financial securities to "hard assets"—gold and other commodities, real estate, and collectibles including stamps, paintings, and antique furniture. The decline in the price-earnings ratio from eighteen at the end of 1968 to less than nine at the end of 1979 indicated the increasing pessimism of investors.

The period from 1982 to 2000 (sometimes known as "The Great Moderation") was marked by a gradual decline in the U.S. inflation rate. Prices of U.S. dollar bonds increased. The Dow Jones index fell by more than 5 percent in only one year. During many years in the 1980s and 1990s, the price of U.S. bonds and the price of stocks increased together; as investors became more optimistic that the U.S. inflation rate would decline, they became more enthusiastic buyers of both bonds and stocks.

The period between 2000 and 2008 was marked by a slight downward trend in stock prices, which declined by 40 percent between 2000 and 2003 as the dot-com bubble imploded. Stock prices then trended up and then declined sharply in 2008 in response to the accelerating financial crisis.

The Bubble in the Price of Baseball Cards—and Stocks

A bubble is a nonsustainable increase in the price of a particular asset. For a while, asset prices increase because of the increase in their earning power or because of a decline in interest rates. Then a small but increasing number of investors buy the asset to profit from anticipated increases in its price. Investors continue their purchases because they believe that they will be able to sell the asset at an even higher price in the near future.

You may have heard the quip "I was all set to go to college until my mother threw out my baseball cards." For a while, individuals were buying baseball cards because their prices were increasing. And their prices were increasing because individuals were buying the cards. The rate of return on cards was derived from changes in their prices. The rationale for the purchases—at least one rationale—was that there was only one Ty Cobb card and only one Roger Hornsby card, and they weren't making any more. True, but there was no limit to the number of firms that could produce baseball, hockey, and basketball cards, nor was there any limit to the number of cards that each firm might produce. New collectors often were attracted to the more recently produced cards because they were less expensive. Their purchases of the newly produced cards reduced the demand for cards whose prices had been increasing at a rapid rate.

Some analysts are reluctant to accept the view that there are bubbles in the price of assets, because that implies that investors are not rational. These analysts contend that the price increases can be explained in terms of the "fundamentals." The empiricists say bubbles were evident in the real estate and stock markets in Japan, Finland, Norway, and Sweden in the second half of the 1980s, in U.S. stocks in the second half of the 1990s, and in U.S. residential real estate in Florida and Nevada and Arizona between 2004 and 2006. They assert that there is no way that the high levels of these asset prices could be rationalized in terms of the economic fundamentals—and that the subsequent declines resulted from the implosions of the bubbles. Investors were buying real estate and stocks because their prices were increasing rather than because of the earning power of these assets—and their prices were increasing because investors were buying these assets.

In Japan in the 1980s, real estate prices increased by a factor of five. Investors obtained bank loans to pay for their real estate purchases. These investors were becoming wealthier at a rapid rate since the rate of increase in real estate prices was much higher than the interest rate on the money borrowed to finance the purchase of real estate. These investors—at least many of them—borrowed even more money to buy even more real estate. Since the supply of real estate increased slowly, the major impact of their purchases was to induce further increases in real estate prices. Because prices were rising rapidly relative to GDP and to rents, the interest payments on recent loans were larger than the rental income. But not to worry; the funds to pay the interest on the outstanding loans could be obtained from new loans. The bubble in the real estate prices pulled up the prices of stocks, in part because many of the companies listed on the Tokyo Stock Exchange are property companies and construction companies. The bubble was pricked at the beginning of 1990, and in 2008 stock prices in Tokyo were less than one-third of the 1989 level.

The Facts of Life about the Rates of Return on Bonds and on Stocks

One of the key factors in your choice among securities is the rates of return that you might expect to earn on both bonds and stocks in the next five, ten, and twenty years. Although the rates of return in coming years are likely to differ from those in the 1980s and 1990s, the data on the rates of return on bonds and on stocks in the previous decades provide the basis for projecting rates of return. In the long run the rates of return on bonds and on stocks are related to the growth of the U.S. economy; the more rapid the rate of growth, the more rapid the increase in corporate profits, and the higher the rates of return on stocks. Similarly, the more rapid the rate of economic growth, the more money that firms are likely to borrow to finance their new investments and the higher the interest rate on bonds.

The continuity in the real rates of U.S. economic growth from one decade to the next is much greater than the continuity in the real rates of return on bonds and on stocks from decade to decade. It's as if there are waves of optimism and of pessimism about the future of the U.S. economy that have magnified impacts on the prices of both bonds and stocks—but especially on the prices of stocks.

You might think that computing the historic rate of return on bonds and stocks would be as straightforward as measuring the height of the Empire State Building or the length of the U.S. Navy aircraft carrier *George Bush*. In fact, it is impossible to devise measures of the changes in the prices of bonds and stocks that do not involve some arbitrary assumptions about the allocation of the interest income on bonds and of the dividend income on stocks. Moreover, the introduction of new firms in the stock price indexes to replace firms that are no longer in the index complicates the measurement of the rates of return.

The rates of return on bonds are calculated from a "bond wealth index"; the rates of return on stocks are calculated from a "stock wealth index." These indexes are useful benchmarks, but both have shortcomings.

The Bond Wealth Index and the Stock Wealth Index

One of the perennial questions is how much money you would have made if you had invested in bonds compared with how much you'd have made if you had invested in stocks. The excess of the rate of return on stocks over that on bonds is known as the "equity risk premium." The bond wealth index and the stock wealth index have been constructed to answer this question.

The bond wealth index is based on the data on the interest payments and prices of U.S. Treasury bonds, almost always the bond with the longest maturity. Once, that was the thirty-year bond; after the U.S. Treasury stopped issuing thirty-year bonds, the twenty-year bond replaced it in the bond wealth index. Start on a particular date, buy $10,000 of these bonds, and every time you receive an interest payment, use the money to buy more bonds at the market prices of bonds on that day. The value of the bond market wealth changes partly because of cyclical fluctuations in the market price of bonds and partly from the use of all of the interest income to buy more bonds.

At a terminal date, the increase in the value of the bond wealth index from the starting date is divided by the increase in the consumer price level during the same period; the result is the increase in the real value of the bond wealth index. Determine the average annual rate of return on bonds as the geometric mean of this increase in the bond wealth index. (The geometric mean is a way to adjust for the compounding of interest.) For example, assume that the bond wealth index increased from 100 to 175 in nominal terms and that the consumer price level increased from 100 to 135 during the same period. The 175 is divided by the 135 to obtain the increase in the real value of the bond wealth index of 129.6—say, 130. If this increase occurs over five years, then the average annual real rate of increase is 6 percent, based on the arithmetic mean; if the more appropriate geometric mean is used, the average annual real rate of increase is 5.5 percent.

The stock wealth index is constructed following a similar procedure. At the beginning of any period, assume you had bought $10,000 of the stocks that are included in the S&P 500 index in the same proportions that each is represented in the index. The changes in the value of this index are a proxy for the changes in the price of stocks. The value of the purchase is set at 100 as an index number. All of the money received as dividends on the stocks is used to buy more stocks at the prevailing price of each stock in proportion to each stock's weight in the index. The value of the stock market wealth index changes because of changes in the price of stocks and because of the purchase of more stocks with dividends received on existing holdings of stocks. At a terminal date, divide the value of the increase in the stock wealth index by the increase in the consumer price level from the initial date to the terminal date. Then compute the average annual rate of return as a geometric mean of the increase in the stock wealth index.

One of the basic propositions in finance is "In the long run, the rates of return in the financial markets reflect the rates of return in the markets in which goods and services are produced." (If this proposition weren't true, we wouldn't have to work; we could simply trade stocks with each other at prices that might increase by 15, 20, or 30 percent a year and become increasingly wealthy as stock prices eventually kissed the sky. From time to time, we would sell a few stocks to get the money to pay for our living expenses, although it's not clear who would produce the goods and services we would want to consume.) During the 1980s and 1990s, the rates of return to the owners of both U.S. bonds and stocks were substantially higher than the rate of U.S. economic growth and of corporate profits. In the 1980s, the real rate of return on stocks was three times the real rate of growth of U.S. GDP, and in the 1990s this real rate was four times the real rate of U.S. economic growth. U.S. stock prices were increasing rapidly relative to U.S. corporate profits—the price-earnings ratio was increasing.

The conventional wisdom that the real rate of return on bonds has been about 4 percent assumes that all of the interest income on bonds is immediately reinvested. In fact, less than 50 percent of the interest income on bonds is reinvested. Universities, hospitals, and religious groups that own bonds use part of their interest income to pay some of their current operating expenses. Similarly, many retirees use some of the interest income on their bonds to pay part of their monthly living costs. If the bond wealth index had been computed using data on the amount of interest income that was actually used to buy more bonds, the increase in the index would have been much less rapid than the increase based on the assumption that all of the interest income was reinvested, and the rate of return to the holders of bonds would have been lower—probably about half as high. Thus the bond wealth index measures what could have happened if individual investors as a group had used all of their interest income to buy more bonds at the prevailing prices and if their purchases did not otherwise affect any of the observed values, but it does not measure what actually happened.

An alternative approach to measuring the rate of return on bonds is to divide the annual interest payments on the bonds by the annual inflation rate year after year and then to average the sum of these changes in the real rate of return on bonds. The real rate of return on bonds averages 3 percent, more or less commensurate with the real rate of U.S. economic growth, perhaps slightly higher.

The nominal rate of return on stocks shown in Table 9.3 is based on a stock wealth index constructed by assuming that all the cash that stockholders received as dividends was used immediately to buy the stocks included in the S&P 500 index at current market prices and in proportion to the weight of each stock in the S&P 500 index. Then the change in the price of stocks was divided by the increase in the consumer price level to obtain the real rate of change in the price of stocks. Then the average annual real rate of return was computed as the geometric mean of the change in the price of stocks.

The stock wealth index assumes that all dividend income was immediately reinvested. In fact, less than 50 percent of the dividends is reinvested. Assume a "new" stock wealth index is constructed based on the amount of the dividend income that was actually reinvested. The real rate of return on stocks would have been about half of the real rate of return that was calculated on the assumption that all of the dividend income was immediately used to buy more stocks.

Moreover, the use of the stock wealth index to suggest the real rate of return to the owners of stocks encounters two measurement problems that do not have a counterpart in the bond wealth index. One is the survivorship bias, which leads to an upward estimate of the rate of return to stockholders. The identity of the firms included in the S&P 500 index changes continually; firms drop out because they go bankrupt or are acquired by some other firms—usually the firms that are acquired have been less successful than the acquiring firms. In recent decades, between twenty and forty new firms have been added to the S&P 500 index; the profits of the firms that are added to the index almost always have been increasing somewhat more rapidly than the profits of the firms that are already in the index.

This survivorship bias means that the reported average annual rate of return on the stocks in the S&P 500 index is 0.2 percent to 0.4 percent higher than the average rate of return on stocks as a group. Hence the rates of return that investors would have earned if they continually held the stocks that they initially acquired would have been lower than the rates of return inferred from the stock wealth index.

The Survivorship Bias and the Changing Membership of the Dow Jones Industrial Average

The Dow Jones stock price index has been composed of thirty firms since 1928. The thirty firms that were in the index in 1950 are noted in Table 9.4. Five of these firms, including AT&T, DuPont, and Procter and Gamble, are still in the index, although several have new names: Standard Oil (N.J.) became Exxon and is now ExxonMobil, and United Aircraft became United Technologies. More than two-thirds of the firms that were in the index in 1950 are defunct; Chrysler became part of Daimler-Benz and then was sold to a private equity firm. The Texas Company (Texaco) is part of Standard Oil of California (now Chevron), and Sears was acquired by Kmart. Firms that were in the index in 1950 that subsequently

Table 9.4
Dow Jones Industrial Membership, 1950

Allied Can*	General Electric	Procter & Gamble
Allied Chemical*	General Foods*	Sears, Roebuck & Company*
American Smelting*	General Motors	Standard Oil (New Jersey)
American Tobacco B*	Goodyear Tire*	Standard Oil of Califonria
AT&T	International Harvester*	Texas Corporation*
Bethlehem Steel*	International Nickel*	Union Carbide*
Chrysler*	Johns-Manville*	United Aircraft
Corn Products Refining*	Loews*	U.S. Steel*
Dupont	National Distillers*	Westinghouse*
Eastman Kodak*	National Steel*	Woolworth*

Note: *means the firm was not in the Dow Jones index in 2009.

Source: Data from ATIVO Research, Chicago.

went bankrupt include Bethlehem Steel, National Steel, and Johns Manville. The other dropouts from the index weren't able to keep up, and hence were acquired by more successful firms—usually at low stock prices. GM went bankrupt in 2009.

The firms that have replaced the Dow Jones dropouts were chosen because they were large and successful and would provide the index with diversification across industries. Moreover, these firms were younger and growing more rapidly than the firms that were dropped; in the previous five or ten years the stock prices of the firms that were added to the index increased more rapidly than the stock prices of the firms that were dropped. This pattern of replacement of tired old firms by younger and more vigorous firms leads to an upward bias in the rates of return on the stock price indexes that might amount to 0.2 percent and 0.3 percent a year. All stock price indexes are subject to this bias.

Now for a quiz. The value of the Dow Jones Industrial Average at the beginning of 1950 was 199; its value at the end of 2008 was 7,800, thirty-four times higher. The average annual rate of increase in this index was over 8 percent. If your grandparents had given you $30,000 in 1950 so you could buy $1,000 of the stock of each of the firms then in the Dow, how much would that portfolio of Dow stocks have been worth at the end of 2008? You would have had exceptional gains in the five firms that remained in the Dow over this extended period, and you would have had traumatic losses in the twenty-four firms that failed to survive.

The traditional measure of the increase in stockholder wealth neglects that each year corporate America issues more shares—and hence more ownership claims on profits. One reason that firms issue more shares is that they want to raise cash to finance their expansion. Hence the measurement of the rate of return to stockholders based on the increase in the market value of stocks should adjust for the cash that the shareholders have provided to the firms when they purchased more shares. This adjustment would reduce the rate of return that the shareholders have earned by two percentage points.

Firms also issue more shares when the options that have been awarded to top executives and managers as a form of incentive compensation are used to buy more shares. At that time the outsiders or public stockholders are being "diluted"—their share of the ownership of the firm and their proportionate claim on its future profits and dividends decline, which means that the rates of return that the public shareholders earn increase less rapidly than the rates of return on stocks as a group.

You need to decide whether the rates of return that you might earn on bonds and on stocks in the next several decades will be comparable to the rates of return in the 1980s and 1990s. Many on Wall Street say so; many on Main Street hope so. Both groups are likely to be disappointed.

One view on Wall Street is that the rates of return on stocks in the next ten to twenty years will be exceptionally high because there is "a new American economy"—the rate of economic growth will be higher because of new technologies or reduced regulation or a new entrepreneurial spirit, and hence the corporate profits will grow more rapidly.

The Gertrude Stein view—that in the long run the average is the average is the average—is that the rates of return on both bonds and stocks between 2010 and 2020 won't match those of the 1980s and 1990s. Those who advance this view believe that in the long run the average rate of return on U.S. stocks reflects the growth of the U.S. economy and the growth of corporate profits. Because rates of return on bonds and on stocks were much above average in the 1980s and the 1990s, they are likely to be below average for an extended period—a "reversion to the mean" view—although this extended period began in 2000.

Real Rates of Return versus Nominal Rates of Return

There is a lot of chatter from the firms that want to sell stocks and mutual funds that stock prices have increased at the rate of 8 percent, 9 percent, or even 11 percent a year. Often proponents of this view will try to persuade you of how rapidly your financial wealth will increase if you invest with a particular mutual fund. The 8 percent estimate is a "blue sky estimate"; no attention is given to how much of the 8 percent rate of return is due to the increase in the consumer price level. Hence it is critically important to measure the rates of return on bonds and stocks in "real terms"—after adjustment for the increases in the U.S. consumer price level. (Remember to focus on the real after-tax rates of return.)

The single most important factor determining the rate of return to owners of stocks is the rate of growth of U.S. corporate profits. U.S. GDP and corporate profit data are first available for the year 1929; corporate profits then were 8 percent of U.S. GDP. In 2008 corporate profits were 10.5 percent of U.S. GDP; this ratio had peaked at 12.7 percent in 2006.

The average annual value of this ratio between 1929 and 2008 was 8 percent. This ratio has varied over the economic cycle; it has declined to 3 percent during a few recessions and has reached 12 percent toward the end of economic expansions. In the last seventy years, nominal GDP has increased at the rate of 6.7 percent a year, and nominal corporate profits have increased at 6.6 percent a year. The U.S. inflation rate (GDP deflator) averaged 3.1 percent a year, so the real rate of increase in corporate profits averaged 3.5 percent—just slightly higher than the real rate of growth of the U.S. economy and consistent with the view that the profit share of GDP is more or less a constant in the long run.

If in the long run the U.S. economy grows at 3 percent a year in real terms, the "invisible hand" will ensure that corporate profits will increase at the same rate. (If corporate profits increased more rapidly than U.S. GDP, then at the extreme the dollar value of corporate profits would be larger than the dollar value of U.S. GDP. That's a very unlikely outcome.) The rate of return to stockholders, then, is the sum of the dividend rate, which is the ratio of cash dividends to GDP, and the rate of growth of the U.S. economy.

For many decades the dividend rate was about 4 percent; in the last few years it has declined to 2 percent, in part because a smaller proportion of firms pay dividends and in part because an increasing number of firms return cash to their stockholders through share repurchases (note that these firms were helping their shareholders engage in tax arbitrage by this change in the form of cash payment to the shareholders) since the tax rate on the capital gains was below the tax rate on dividend income. If the dividend rate remains at 2 percent and the U.S. economy grows at the rate of 3 percent a year in real terms, then the total return to the stockholders would be 5 percent, the sum of these two values—and the real rate of return on stocks would exceed the real rate of return on bonds by two percentage points. Once an adjustment is made for the survivorship bias and dilution of the public shareholders, the excess of the rate of return on stocks over the rate of return on bonds to the public shareholders shrinks dramatically.

The difference between the projected rate of return that stockholders earned using counterfactual assumptions and the actual amount they earned given the rate of reinvestment of dividends might seem small— about two to three percentage points a year. But these small values accumulate and exaggerate the excess of the rate of return on stocks over the rate of return on bonds.

In the long run, the two most important factors that determine the income of stockholders are the rate of growth of corporate earnings and the price-earnings ratio. In a period longer than fifteen or twenty years, changes in the price-earnings ratio are too small to have a major impact on the rate of return to stockholders. For example, if this ratio increases from sixteen to twenty-four over a fifteen-year period, the rate of return to stockholders would increase from 6 percent to 6.4 percent. Thus over any long period the rate of return to stockholders primarily depends on the rate of growth of corporate earnings and the dividend yield.

There are no free lunches in the financial markets. Corporate profits and the U.S. economy have grown at the same rate. If the U.S. economy continues to grow at the real rate of 3 percent a year, corporate profits are likely to increase at about the same rate. Stock prices would increase at the same rate if the number of shares remained unchanged, and the rate of return to stockholders would be between 5 and 6 percent a year. If firms were to continue to buy back their shares to distribute cash to shareholders, stock prices would increase more rapidly because the share repurchases would lead to more rapid increases in earnings per share than in earnings and the real rate of return would be somewhat higher.

Wall Street promotes the view that the real rate of return on stocks will be 7 percent a year after adjusting for inflation to help sell stocks. You would be poorly advised to invest your wealth on this assumption. When a broker calls with the pitch that the real rate of return on stocks will average 7 percent, ask whether corporate profits can increase significantly more rapidly than the GDP in the long run and whether the price of stocks can increase relative to corporate earnings. If the broker answers yes to either question, ask to see the data. If the broker answers yes to both questions, look for another broker.

Transaction Costs and Measurement Bias

Virtually all efforts to measure the rates of return on bonds and stocks assume that their investors incur no transaction costs when they buy bonds and stocks. That's fine as an exercise. You won't be as fortunate as an investor; in the real world, Merrill Lynch and Charles Schwab and Fidelity want to be paid when you ask them to buy and sell bonds and stocks. Transaction costs are of two types. There are the formal fees, and then there is your share of the bid-ask spread. These costs are likely to be in the range of one-quarter to one-half of the dollar value of the transactions.

The Bursting of the 1990s U.S. Stock Price Bubble

Alan Greenspan, former chairman of the Board of Governors of the Federal Reserve, first used the term "irrational exuberance" in December 1996. The Dow Jones was then at 6,600 and the NASDAQ was at 1,300. The market value of the stocks listed on the NASDAQ was 11 percent of the market value of those listed on the New York Stock Exchange; the "new economy" firms such as Microsoft and Cisco were traded on the NASDAQ, and the "old economy" firms such as Boeing, General Electric, and General Motors were traded on the New York Stock Exchange.

Three years later, the Dow peaked at 11,750 and the NASDAQ peaked at 5,555; the market value of the NASDAQ stocks was 40 percent of the market value of the stocks on the New York Stock Exchange. The percentage increase in the price of the NASDAQ stocks was twice that of the stocks traded on the New York Stock Exchange, but the increase in the market value of the stocks traded on the New York Stock Exchange was larger than the increase in the market value of NASDAQ stocks.

Greenspan is very knowledgeable about financial data and very cautious. It seems unlikely that he would have made his cautionary statement if he thought that U.S. stocks were overvalued by less than 15 or 20 percent. Stock prices increased by 70 percent from December 1996 to the peak in the spring of 2000.

U.S. stock prices declined in 2000, 2001, and 2002; the peak-to-trough decline in stock market wealth was 40 percent, and the peak-to-trough decline in the NASDAQ index was more than 80 percent. U.S. GDP in 2008 was 20 percent higher than in 2000. The ratio of the market value of stocks to GDP now is lower than at their peak, but still slightly higher than in December 1996. Moreover, corporate earnings in 2008 were only slightly higher than in 1997.

The high rate of return on U.S. stocks in the 1990s resulted from the surge in the price-earnings ratio to forty-one—about two and a half times its long-run average value—during a decade when the ratio of corporate profits to U.S. GDP increased by 40 percent, from 7.5 percent to 10.5 percent.

The correlation between the changes in the profit share of GDP and changes in the price-earnings ratio has been strong and positive since the late 1920s. When the profit share of GDP increased, the price-earnings ratio increased—this was true in the 1920s, in the 1950s and 1960s, and for a third time in the 1980s and 1990s. When the profit share of GDP declined, the price-earnings ratio declined, and the rates of return to stockholders were low.

The Rates of Return on Bonds and Stocks over Increasingly Long Holding Periods

Consider a series of annual "races" between the rate of return on bonds derived from the bond wealth index and the rate of return on stocks derived from the stock wealth index. During seventeen of the last fifty-five years, the annual rate of return on bonds has been higher than the annual rate of return on stocks (see Table 9.5). The winning percentage on bonds was 36 percent.

Now progressively increase the length of the holding period, first from one year to two; the winning percentage on bonds declines to 24 percent. When the holding period is increased to three years, the winning percentage on bonds declines to 19 percent. As the holding period is lengthened further, the winning percentage on bonds declines.

There have been two extended periods when the rate of return on bonds was higher than the rate of return on stocks (see Table 9.6). Each of these periods began when stock prices fell sharply. The first period began in 1929; it was not until 1949 that the increase in the stock wealth index "caught up" with the increase in the bond wealth index. The second

Table 9.5
Bonds versus Stocks (annual data from 1950 to 2008)

Holding Period (Years)	Stocks Outperform Bonds	Bonds Outperform Stocks	Stocks' Winning Percentage
1	37	21	64
2	41	16	72
3	42	14	75
5	41	13	76
10	41	8	84
15	43	1	98

Source: Data from ATIVO Research, Chicago.

Table 9.6

Periods When Bonds Outperformed Stocks

	Cumulative Wealth	
Period	Stocks	Bonds
1928–	100	100
1939	219	263
1968–	100	100
1977	128	176
2000–	100	100
2008	76	224

Source: Data from ATIVO Research, Chicago.

Table 9.7

Bull and Bear Markets, 1901–2000

	Bull Markets	Bear Markets
Number of years	66	34
Percentage of years	66	34
Mean return/year	23.4%	–9.6%
Standard deviation	2.2	11.9
High return	253.4%	6.1%
Low return	14.2%	–64.3%

Note: Bull markets are characterized by annual stock market returns greater than those on Treasury bills; bear markets are characterized by annual stock market returns lower than those on Treasury bills.

Source: Data from ATIVO Research, Chicago.

period began in 1967; it was not until 1978 that the stock wealth index increased to match the increase in the bond wealth index on the 1967 base. As you can see, the rate of return on a portfolio of stocks is higher in the long run but not in a large number of one-year, two-year, and three-year holding periods.

The frequency of bull and bear markets is shown in Table 9.7. (In case you've forgotten, stock prices increase in bull markets and decline in bear markets.) The annual percentage increase in the price of U.S. stocks in the bull market years has been two and a half times larger than the annual percentage decline in the bear market years. (One reason for the secular increase in stock prices has been the increase in the consumer price level by a factor of nineteen from 1900 to 2000; in the long run, increases in the consumer price level lead to increases in corporate profits that in turn lead to increases in stock prices.)

A brief summary of the data in the last few pages may be useful. Stock prices do not rise continuously from one year to the next; rather, in the long run stock prices have declined one year out of three. When stock prices declined, the annual rate of return on bonds usually has exceeded the annual rate of return on stocks. Moreover, the average annual change in the prices of stocks when they decline is larger than the average annual change when they increase—but stocks gain value in the long run because stock prices increase in about two-thirds of the years.

Timing versus Picking, or Risk and Return in Financial Markets

One widely held view is "that you can't time the market." Many of those who share this view are known as "pickers" who buy and hold bonds and stocks for the long run. Some of the aficionados of the "efficient market persuasion" believe that "all the information is in the price" and hence there are no patterns in the data. Investors who follow the adage "Buy low and sell high" believe that you *can* time the market and there are patterns in the changes in the prices of bonds and of stocks. Those who share this view implicitly believe that there is a "reversion to the mean" process for both bonds and stocks. Bond prices vary around an average value so that in the long run the real rate of return on bonds is a bit more than 3 percent. Similarly, stock prices vary around an average value— although the mean value is around a rising trend because stock prices increase as corporate earnings increase.

For example, in 1966 and 1967 the timers took the view that stock prices were too high relative to their long-run trend value given current corporate earnings and the prospects for the continued growth in earnings. The price-earnings ratio was 17.7. Timers would have sold their stocks. In the early 1980s, in contrast, the timers concluded that stock prices were too low relative to their long-run trend value, and they would have begun to buy stocks.

Pickers take the view that there is no way of knowing whether the next price movement will be toward or away from the mean. Pickers buy stocks that they are going to hold for a lifetime—or at least for a very long time.

The debate between pickers and timers is long-standing. The timers believe that when stock prices differ from their long-run average value (perhaps as judged relative to the historic value of the price-earnings ratio) by more than 25 or 35 percent, the stock prices are more likely to revert toward their average value than they are to move further away from this value. The timers suggest that they don't have to forecast the peaks and troughs with perfect accuracy to earn a higher rate of return than the rate they would from the buy-and-hold strategy.

A busy day on the New York Stock Exchange involves the purchase of several hundred million shares of stock—seemingly a very large number. The number of shares outstanding is enormous. In the course of a year, each share is traded a bit more than one time. Many shares are not traded (because these shares are owned by the buy-and-hold investors, some of whom are reluctant to sell and pay capital gains taxes), and others are traded many times a year. Each day less than 0.5 percent of the total of outstanding shares is traded. Hence the sharp variations in stock prices result from the transactions of investors who own a small fraction of the total shares outstanding.

The values of the S&P 500 index, the price-earnings ratio, the interest rate on Treasury bonds, and the profit share of U.S. GDP from 1950 to the present are shown in Figure 9.2. Most of the variations in stock prices can be attributed to variations in the price-earnings ratio, which was 11.0 in 1950 and 27.0 in 1999. A timer might say that whenever the price-earnings ratio is 25 or 35 percent above the average value, stocks should be sold and bonds purchased. Conversely, whenever the price-earnings ratio is 25 or 35 percent below its average value, stocks should be purchased. There are numerous variants on this rule.

Assume you were clairvoyant and on every New Year's Eve you could foresee whether it would be more rewarding to be in stocks or bonds for the coming year. You would then use all of your financial wealth to buy either bonds or stocks, which you would hold until the following January.

The column on the left in Table 9.8 shows the cumulative increase in wealth from investing in stocks; the changes in wealth reflect the reinvestment of dividends and the changes in the price of stocks. The second column shows the cumulative increase in wealth from investing in bonds; the change in wealth reflects the reinvestment of the interest income on the bonds and the changes in the market price of the bonds during the holding period. The third column shows the cumulative increase in

Figure 9.2
A Sixty-Year View of Stock Prices

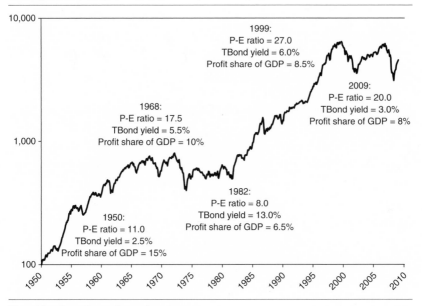

Note: P-E ratio = price-earnings ratio.

Source: Data from ATIVO Research, Chicago.

Table 9.8
Wealth Indexes with Perfect Foresight

Year	S&P 500	Bonds	Annual Decisions	Monthly Decisions
1950	100	100	100	100
1955	300	103	300	402
1960	449	105	662	1,496
1965	844	112	1,484	4,536
1970	976	116	2,304	11,780
1975	1,143	134	4,433	38,620
1980	2,170	137	8,549	137,225
1985	4,256	307	23,676	616,936
1990	7,961	523	51,617	2,559,462
1995	17,136	963	124,536	8,546,988
2000	40,099	1,397	367,620	41,767,247
2005	41,197	1,990	645,879	165,523,032
2008	30,391	3,130	1,098,453	418,481,062

Source: Data from ATIVO Research, Chicago.

wealth with perfect foresight; at the beginning of each year, you as the clairvoyant investor choose either stocks or bonds on the basis of which will have the higher rate of return in the next twelve months. The fourth column is similar to the third, except that now you choose either stocks or bonds on the basis of which will have the higher rate of return in the next month.

Clearly, the rate of return on clairvoyance is very high on a yearly basis and massively high on a monthly basis. Moreover, there is a great deal of randomness in the month-to-month changes in stock and bond prices. Even though there has been a powerful long-run upward trend in stock prices, these prices often decline from one year to the next and from one month to the next. Any investor who could determine when to be out of the stock market during the years and the months in which stock prices declined would secure a much higher rate of return than investors who follow the buy-and-hold strategy.

The investors who make fortunes in the market are not pickers. If they were and the real rates of return were 7 percent, they would double their money every ten years. They amassed their fortunes because their rates of return have been much higher than 7 percent.

Since the rate of return from owning stocks has been higher than that from owning bonds, the question is why more investors don't own stocks. Why would anyone own bonds? The investors who buy bonds for the long run are concerned that stocks are too risky—that the variability of the year-to-year rate of return on stocks has been higher than the variability of the year-to-year rate of return on bonds.

There are several different approaches to measuring the risk of holding individual bonds and stocks. One is to measure the range of the price movement of each security from one date to another; the larger the range of the movement, the larger the variation in the rate of return, and hence the greater the risk. Similarly, the risks of portfolios with different proportions of bonds and stocks can be measured by comparing the period-to-period changes in the value of each portfolio or the range of the change in the wealth of each portfolio over an extended period.

Stocks are riskier than bonds. And bonds are riskier than Treasury bills and other near-cash financial instruments with short-term maturity. The higher rate of return on stocks than on bonds and on bonds than on bills and other near-cash instruments compensates investors for the greater risk.

The strategy of the "timers"—the investors who shift between stocks and bonds or between stocks and bonds on the one hand and cash on the other—might be considered riskier if they get the timing wrong and less risky if they get it right. The timers might devise a strategy of moving into stocks when their prices seem low relative to their long-run trend value and out of stocks when their prices are high relative to their long-run trend value. They won't get the timing absolutely correct, but the question is whether the strategy increases their return and reduces the variability in their net worth relative to the buy-and-hold strategy.

Looking Ahead: Stock Prices and Corporate Earnings

In the long run, the rate of return on stocks has been higher than the rate of return on bonds by an amount that approximates the dividend rate. The real rate of return on bonds approximates the real rate of growth of the economy. The rate of growth of corporate earnings approximates the rate of growth of the economy in real terms. When the dividend rate was 4 percent, the rate of return to stockholders was 7 percent; now that the dividend rate is 2 percent, the rate of return to stockholders is in the range of 5 to 6 percent after adjusting for the increases in the cost of living.

One of the dominant features of U.S. financial history for the twentieth century was the increase in the consumer price level; the purchasing power of $1.00 in 1900 was a bit more than $0.05 in 2000. The increase in the consumer price level was episodic rather than continuous and steady. The first episode occurred during World War I; the U.S. price level increased by 35 percent from 1900 to 1935. The U.S. price level increased by 60 percent between 1935 and 1965, during and after World War II. The most dramatic episode was in the last third of the century, when the price level increased by 300 percent. The inflation rate of the 1970s was the highest ever in peacetime in the twentieth century, and the last of three periods of remarkable surges in the U.S. inflation rate. Despite the conventional wisdom that common stocks are a good inflation hedge, stock prices did not increase as the inflation rate accelerated; rather, stock prices increased after the inflation rate and interest rates began to decline. The financial history of the twentieth century shows that periods of financial stability and of remarkably high rates of return on bonds and stocks follow periods of instability. These periods of instability occur because of market developments that were not anticipated. And the policies adopted to move toward greater economic stability may lead to sharp declines in bond and stock prices.

There have been three distinct periods since 1950 in terms of stock prices. From the early 1950s to the late 1960s, stock prices increased sharply. From the late 1960s to the early 1980s, stock prices varied extensively around a more or less flat trend. From the early 1980s until 2000, stock prices increased even more sharply than in the first period—the most rapid increase in U.S. history. The hallmark of the 1970s was the acceleration in the U.S. inflation rate and the surge in interest rates on U.S. dollar securities to the highest level ever in peacetime.

One reason that the rate of return on stocks was so high in the 1980s and 1990s is that the share of corporate profits in national income increased from the lower end of its historic range to the upper end. The implication is that the rate of growth of corporate earnings is likely to slow (otherwise the share of corporate profits to GDP would increase to levels not previously achieved) and hence the rate of return to stockholders is likely to be lower.

Moreover, because stock prices increased so sharply in the 1990s, the ratio of dividends to stock prices fell much below its long-run average value. If the dividend rate continues at 2 percent rather than 4 percent, the historic return to stockholders can be maintained only if stock prices increase at a more rapid rate than in the past. The implication is that the rate of U.S. economic growth must increase or that profit share of U.S. growth must increase.

You're going to have to decide on the anticipated rates of return that you might earn on stocks in the next several decades. These rates of return and the amount you need to save for a comfortable retirement have a symbiotic relationship: the higher the rates of return, the smaller the amount of the annual saving necessary to achieve your lodestone value (noted on pages 285–286 of Chapter 14.)

ACTIONABLES

1. Why are stock prices so variable?
2. Why are stocks riskier than bonds?
3. How valid is the statement "Inflation is good for stocks"?
4. Why do stock prices increase in the long run?

5. What is the conventional wisdom about the real rate of return on bonds and the real rate of return on stocks?

6. Why is the conventional wisdom about the real rate of return on bonds misleading?

7. Why is the conventional wisdom about the real rate of return on stocks misleading?

8. What is the "survivorship bias," and how does it affect the measured rate of return on stocks? What are the implications of changes in the membership of the Dow Jones index and the S&P 500 index for the measurement of the long-run rate of return on stocks?

9. Why did stock prices increase so rapidly in the 1950s and most of the 1960s?

10. Why were stock prices in 1981 not very different from stock prices in 1967?

11. What is a stock price bubble?

12. What is the distinction between the "timers" and the "pickers"?

13. How high are transaction costs for bonds and for stocks? What is the ratio of transaction costs to average annual rates of return?

10   Why Are There 10,000 Mutual Funds in America and Only Two and a Half Automobile Firms?

In 2008 Americans paid more than $200 billion to the firms that own and manage mutual funds for selection of bonds and stocks, record keeping, and other services associated with the management of more than $14 billion invested in mutual fund shares. Most of this money was paid because the buyers of mutual funds were convinced that the managers of these funds had above-average skills in selecting bonds and stocks. This view was based on advertisements like the one reproduced in Table 10.1, which appeared in 2006. The top sets of rows show the performance of the fund, and the bottom several rows show the benchmarks—the average rates of return for the investments of the same asset class. Advertisements of this type are selective; the sponsors show you their winners. And when markets are down, as they were sharply in 2008, ads of this type appear far less frequently.

One of the standard lines in advertisements of this type is "Past Performance Is No Guarantee of Future Results." When you see this type of ad, ask whether the managers of these funds have above-average skills or whether they are involved in an elaborate con.

Remember the coin-tossing experiment from high school math class? First you're asked, what is the probability that a fair coin toss will come up "heads"? The answer is ½, or 50 percent. Next, what's the probability that the outcome of two successive coin tosses will be two heads in a row? It's the product of ½ and ½: ¼, or 25 percent. Now, what is the

Table 10.1
Mutual Fund Performance Record

	1 Year	5 Years	10 Years
T. Rowe Price Growth Stock Fund	16.21%	5.53%	9.86%
Lipper Large-Cap Growth Fund Average	14.24%	0.93%	6.53%
T. Rowe Price Spectrum Growth Fund	19.17%	8.62%	9.36%
Lipper Multi-Cap Core Funds Average	14.56%	5.03%	8.79%
T. Rowe Price Value Fund	13.62%	7.54%	11.28%
Lipper Multi-Cap Value Funds Average	12.99%	7.45%	9.66%

Source: Data from *Money* magazine, August 2006.

probability that five coin tosses will result in five heads in a row? The answer is $\frac{1}{2} \times \frac{1}{2} \times \frac{1}{2} \times \frac{1}{2} \times \frac{1}{2}$: $\frac{1}{64}$, or 1.56 percent. And finally, what is the probability that someone who has correctly forecast the coin toss on five successive throws will be able to forecast the outcome of the toss on the sixth throw? The answer is 50 percent—the coin has no memory.

What is the likelihood that T. Rowe Price or Fidelity or Janus would pay for an ad that showed that some of the funds under their management had below-average rates of return? What is the likelihood that these firms would sponsor ads that showed the annual results of all of their funds under management? The answers are self-evident.

A hole in one in golf is a marvelous achievement. Consider the odds of sinking a hole in one. How many individuals from a group of 100,000 who have played a round of golf are likely to hit the ball into the cup with one stroke? The data show that a pro on the golf tour has a one-in-3,700 chance. Assume the pro plays thirty-six holes a day on each of 100 days a year, and then the odds are that the pro will have one hole in one during the year. The likelihood of a hole in one for an amateur golfer is one in 12,700. Because so many millions play golf once or twice a week, several thousand will sink a hole in one in the course of a year. If a professional golfer has a one-in-3,700 chance of hitting a hole in one, and 3,700 golfers are in the same "tournament," it's a fair bet that one of the group will hit a hole in one—but it is impossible to identify this person beforehand.

Bill Clinton's success in achieving a hole in one has little predictive ability on the likelihood that he might achieve a second hole in one in the next month or the next year. Tiger Woods, arguably the best golfer of his generation, hit his first hole in one when he was six. He may hit two or three holes in one in the course of a season's play.

Now consider the success of the forecasts of changes in prices of bonds and of stocks of the thousands of analysts on Wall Street and State Street and LaSalle Street and Montgomery Street. The data indicate that stock prices increase in two years out of three (see Table 10.6). If Simple Simon forecasted that stock prices would increase year after year after year, he would be right two-thirds of the time. Since there are a large number of forecasters, many are likely to be successful—that is, they have above-average returns—in predicting changes in prices of bonds and of stocks several years in a row—but so does Simple Simon.

The key question is whether the success of an individual forecaster has a higher probability than could be explained by chance. Some forecasters exhibit above-average skills; year after year, the portfolios they manage have been in the top 10 or 15 percent as measured by their annual rates of return. Dozens of individuals have gotten fabulously rich from their forecasts of changes in the prices of bonds and of stocks. Still, if thousands of individuals are forecasting changes in prices, then by chance some of them will be successful for several years in a row. Does a record of successful forecasts for five successive years have any predictive power for the sixth year? Remember the results of the coin-tossing experiment.

An impressive track record in forecasting changes in the prices of bonds and of stocks is the key to the success of individual mutual funds as businesses. Understanding the significance of these records is important for helping you decide when to allocate some of your accumulated savings to purchase mutual funds and which mutual funds you should buy—and which funds you should avoid because the odds are high that they will be costly to your financial health.

When you first consider the purchase of mutual funds, you have a choice similar to the one you encounter when you buy vodka or chicken or toilet paper or fifty other products—you can buy the low-cost generic or you can buy the higher-cost branded funds. The first mutual fund— then named Massachusetts Investors Trust—was established in 1923 to reduce the costs that individual investors incurred in their efforts to develop diversified portfolios of bonds and of stocks. Initially there were no competitors and no performance record, and the sales pitch probably highlighted the cost-savings approach to diversification. As the more firms developed mutual funds, the cousins of the Madison Avenue geniuses that hustle toothpastes and breakfast cereals realized that a lot of money could be made by stressing the superior forecasting skills of individual financial managers in picking bonds and stocks.

In the 1950s and the 1960s the only way that Americans could own diversified portfolios of securities was to buy actively managed mutual funds; there were no generics. A remarkable innovation in the 1970s was the development of "index funds," which are diversified portfolios of bonds or of stocks or of a mix of both that are designed to mimic the performance of a given bond or a given stock index. These funds have two objectives. One is to select bonds and stocks so the rates of return on the portfolio replicate those of a particular index, and the other is to minimize the selection costs. Investors can buy diversified portfolios of bonds and stocks without being required to buy the services of financial managers that promote themselves as geniuses in selecting bonds and stocks. The "exchange-traded funds" (ETFs) that were first developed in the 1990s are a variant of index funds and generic—the selection occurs when you decide which generic to buy.

The U.S. Mutual Fund Industry

Every mutual fund has an owner. The Massachusetts Investors Trust was renamed Massachusetts Financial Services and then MFS. Sun Life, a Canadian insurance company, acquired the firm in the early 1970s. Some mutual fund owners, including Morgan Stanley and Merrill Lynch, acquired by Bank of America in the 2008 financial crisis, are parts of financial conglomerates. Others, including Fidelity, are owned by the entrepreneurs who founded them or by their families. Several firms that specialize in owning mutual funds are publicly owned, including Janus and T. Rowe Price; the shares in these firms are traded on the NASDAQ. Several firms that own "generic" mutual funds are "co-ops" and owned by individuals who own the shares in the mutual funds; Teachers Insurance and Annuity Association–College Retirement Equities Fund (TIAA-CREF) and Vanguard are in this group.

Types of Mutual Funds

Mutual funds can be grouped in several different ways: by the types of securities they acquire, by their investment strategies, and by their approach toward issuing more shares. Bond funds buy bonds, stock funds buy stocks, and hybrid funds (sometimes called balanced funds) buy both bonds and stocks. Money market funds acquire short-term liquid securities like Treasury bills and commercial paper—the short-term IOUs of major firms. Some of these funds acquire foreign bonds, and some acquire foreign stocks. Some specialize in acquiring bonds or stocks issued in a particular country or geographic region or even a particular state.

A major distinction is between actively managed funds that seek above-average rates of return from their choice of securities and passively managed or index funds that seek average rates of return by mimicking the composition of a particular index. Index funds own the shares of each of the firms that constitute the index in proportion to the ratio of the market value of each firm to the aggregate market value of all the firms included in that index.

Closed-end mutual funds have a fixed number of shares outstanding; in contrast, the number of shares issued by open-end funds varies daily in response to changes in investor demand. The owners of a new closed-end fund might sell 10 million shares at $10 each and raise $100 million. After deducting the underwriting and other costs of raising this money, the managers of this fund would have $92 million, which they would use to buy the shares in a narrow or a wide range of industries. The shares in this closed-end fund may be actively traded, perhaps on the New York Stock Exchange or the NASDAQ. At the end of each day or each week, the managers report the net asset value per share, which they obtain by dividing the total market value of all of the shares that the fund owns by the 10 million shares outstanding. The market price of the shares and the net asset value per share often differ, at times by as much as 25 percent; usually the market value is below the net asset value, but infrequently the market price has been slightly higher than net asset value. You pay the usual transaction costs to the stockbrokers when you buy and sell shares in closed-end funds, and the firms that own the funds pay themselves a management fee before they pay dividends to the shareholders. From time to time, the managers may distribute rights to buy additional shares to each of the shareholders in the closed-end funds.

Open-end funds increase the number of shares outstanding if investors wish to buy more shares in the fund and reduce the number of shares outstanding if investors wish to redeem some of their shares; these new sales and redemption occur at the net asset value per share plus any sales or redemption fees. If you wish to buy $5,000 worth of shares of Alpha-

Omega fund, the managers divide $5,000 by the net asset value per share at the end of the previous day's trading day and any sales charges to determine the number of shares you have purchased. In contrast, if you wish to redeem 100 shares in the fund, the managers multiply the net asset value per share by 100 and send you a check after adjusting for any redemption fees and other charges. About two-thirds of open-end funds have sales charges, or "loads."

From time to time, some closed-end funds with stellar performance records have been converted to open-end funds as the owners seek to capitalize on their performance.

ETFs are like index funds in that they take a passive approach to the selection of bonds, stocks, and commodities, and they are like open-end funds in that the number of shares outstanding increases or decreases in response to changes in the demand for the shares. Whenever the market price of each share increases relative to the net asset value by more than 0.25 percent or 0.50 percent, some investment firms issue more shares in the ETF and use the money collected from the sale of these shares to buy more of the outstanding stocks. ETFs are like stocks in that they are traded continuously throughout the day.

A few firms own a family of more than one hundred mutual funds; others own more than fifty funds. Ten firms own and manage the mutual funds that hold 50 percent of the money under management, and ten more firms manage an additional 25 percent.

One direct impact of the sharp increases in the prices of bonds and of stocks in the 1980s and the 1990s was that the revenues of the firms that own mutual funds surged, as a result of much higher valuations; the indirect effect was that millions of Americans bought mutual funds for the first time because annual rates of return were high, consistently above 10 percent. Moreover, interest rates on bank deposits were declining as the inflation rate fell. Finally, thousands of firms adopted defined-contribution pension plans; now more than 40 million Americans have a 401(k) pension plan or a 403(b) pension plan, and virtually all the money in these plans has been used to buy mutual funds.

Managing other people's money has been very profitable, with rates of return higher than those earned by General Electric (GE), General Mills, and other stalwarts of the U.S. economy. GE Capital, the financial subsidiary of GE, owns and manages nearly fifty mutual funds; it's a safe bet that the rate of return on GE's investment in mutual funds is much higher than its rates of return on the production of light bulbs and washing machines.

Individuals who have established a record as successful brokers or investors can establish a new mutual fund—and the first of what might be many funds—with an investment of several hundred thousand dollars.

A mutual fund family brings out new funds because there are economies of scale and scope in marketing and distribution of a large number of funds at the same time. As assets under management within a family increase, revenues increase more rapidly than costs and profits grow rapidly, much like selling a few more seats on an airplane on a flight from New York to Tokyo. Each mutual fund family wants more "shelf space" and so brings out new funds that may be modest variants on the ones that it already has, more or less like the firm that owned Smirnoff vodka brought out Smirnoff Silver, Smirnoff Black, Smirnoff Orange, Smirnoff Citrus, Smirnoff Watermelon, and other versions of plain old Smirnoff.

Moreover, the mutual fund families are responsive to investor demands. Some investors want funds that concentrate on specific industries—energy, biotechnology, telecommunications, and others. Some investors want funds that own the shares of firms headquartered in a country or region—South Korea, Mexico, Asia, and Africa. Many investors want tax-exempt bonds issued by their state government or by one of the local governments in their state; residents of New York do not pay state income tax on the interest income on bonds issued by New York State and by city and county governments therein; similarly, these residents do not pay income tax on the dividends of the mutual funds that own these bonds.

Finally, T. Rowe Price, Fidelity, MFS, Jason, and other firms establish new funds in the hope that several will develop superior performance records and that their market price per share will soar. The firms know that small funds on average outperform larger funds; that is, they have higher annual rates of return. The managers of a new fund have several years to establish a superior performance record. During this period, relatively little attention is given to selling shares in these newly established funds. Instead, the goal is to build a "track record" in the form of rapid increases in net asset values per share. After two or three years, the managers of the funds that have established impressive performance records are backed with large marketing budgets, and the newly established funds that have had mediocre performance are merged out of existence. The larger the number of new mutual funds that a family establishes, the higher the likelihood that it will have several "winners" with above-average performance for two or three years.

One reason why the newly established funds outperform in the first two or three years is that they are not likely to sell many of the securities that they have purchased, and so their transaction costs will be smaller than those of older and larger funds.

Some inferences about the profitability of the mutual fund industry can be drawn from the data on publicly owned companies like Janus and T. Rowe Price. The rate of return on capital of these firms is in the range of 20 to 30 percent, three or four times higher than the rates of return on capital for most American industries, including biotech and semiconductors. Moreover, the annual salaries of the top officers and of the managers of the large funds can exceed $10 million to $20 million a year. The ease of entry into the industry may suggest that the industry is competitive, but entry has not led to a significant decline in the rates of return on capital to a competitive level. The inference is that the fees charged by the owners of mutual funds are much higher than they would be if the industry conformed to the textbook model of a perfectly competitive industry. Most of the buyers of mutual funds are not significantly motivated by the level of fees in the choice of funds.

The Performance of Mutual Funds

The rates of return for different types of mutual funds grouped by market capitalization, value or growth investment style, and industry for 2004–2008, along with the average annual rates of return for that five-year period, are shown in Table 10.2. Then the total returns during bull periods and bear periods are summarized. The rows at the bottom of the table under the heading Index Comparisons show the same values for four different types of index benchmarks. For the five-year period, the average annual return on the Dow was 2 percent and the average annual return on the S&P 500 was 0.6 percent; the lower return on the S&P 500 reflected the sharp decline in the prices of some NASDAQ stocks as the late 1990s stock price bubble imploded.

The five-year period from 2004 to 2008 was not glorious for the performance of stock funds. If the period of observation had been extended to the ten-year period from 1999 to 2008, the performance results would

Table 10.2

Mutual Fund Performance by Selected Categories

	Annual Returns (%)					Total Return (%)		
	2008	2007	2006	2005	2004	5-Year	Bull	Bear
Stock Funds								
Large-Cap	−38.6	8.5	13.0	6.5	11.6	−2.4	109.4	−41.5
Mid-Cap	−40.3	10.0	13.2	10.2	16.4	−1.4	143.7	−43.4
Small-Cap	−39.3	2.5	14.5	7.0	16.8	−2.4	145.1	−43.5
Value Style	−35.0	0.3	17.3	6.6	16.5	−1.2	123.1	−38.8
Growth Style	−42.3	14.3	9.8	8.1	12.1	−2.8	129.9	−45.1
Index Comparisons								
Dow Jones	−31.9	8.9	19.1	1.7	5.3	−1.1	54.5	−23.7
S&P 500	−37.0	5.5	15.8	4.9	10.9	−2.2	64.7	−41.4
S&P MidCap 400	−36.5	7.7	10.0	12.3	16.2	−0.3	103.2	−16.5
S&P SmallCap 600	−31.1	−0.3	15.1	7.7	22.7	0.9	121.2	−10.2
Bond Funds								
Long Gov't	30.7	10.4	−0.1	8.5	9.0	10.8	21.6	37.5
Intermediate Gov't	9.6	7.8	3.4	2.1	3.2	5.1	15.7	12.6
ML HighYield Bond	−21.5	2.4	9.7	2.1	9.4	0.7	51.3	−22.6
Index	22.7	9.7	2.1	6.6	8.0	9.6	8.7	40.0

Source: Data from American Association of Individual Investors, *The Individual Investor's Guide to the Top Mutual Funds*, 28th ed. (Chicago: American Association of Individual Investors, 2009), p. 69.

have been slightly less unimpressive; stock prices increased in 1999 and then decreased in the next three years. Most investors would have had a higher rate of return on certificates of deposit during this ten-year period than on their shares in mutual funds that owned stocks. During the five-year period that ended in 2008, the performance of bond funds was more impressive than the performance of the stock funds.

One of the insights from the last five, ten, and fifteen years is that large swings in the prices of stocks mean there are high risks to being into a fund whose investment strategy gives modest weight to the volatility of stock prices.

Decisions and More Decisions

You need to consider three nested investment decisions before you make a commitment to buy one or several mutual funds. First, "Should

I select the bonds and stocks on my own, or instead should I buy shares in one or several mutual funds and let professional asset managers choose for me?" Second, "If I choose to buy mutual funds, should I buy an index fund, or instead should I buy an actively managed fund that promises superior returns?" Third, "Which index funds or which actively managed funds should I buy?" These three decisions are not exclusively either/or; you can buy some bonds and stocks on your own, and you can buy both index funds and actively managed funds.

If you buy bonds and stocks on your own, you will save the fees that would otherwise go to mutual fund firms. Can you develop a diversified portfolio of bonds and of stocks at lower cost than if you bought shares in a mutual fund that promises superior performance? A modest variant of the question is "How much of my accumulated savings should I invest in mutual funds—and how much on my own?"

If you decide to invest through mutual funds, then you will need to choose among the thousands of funds. You might rely on a financial advisor—who might be a broker or a "certified financial planner" or the trust department of a bank—to make these decisions in a managed account, and even then you will need to choose among dozens of firms and individuals that want to manage your money.

You may have acquired shares in one or several mutual funds because you participate in a defined-contribution pension plan associated with your job. Part of your monthly salary is deducted from your check as your contribution to your pension. Your employer may also make a payment to your pension account. Your employer probably offers you the option of having your contributions forwarded to one or several of the mutual fund families. You then need to choose both the firm and from the menu of funds owned by one of these complexes. If your money goes to a bond or a stock fund, you'll have to select the fund.

Firms that manage 401(k) plans charge fees based on the value of the assets in each individual's account. These fees come directly from your account, although in some cases the employers pay these fees—probably from money that they would otherwise have paid you. It's unlikely that your employer has given you the chance to direct your contributions to firms that charge the lowest fees in the industry or to firms whose funds have been star performers. It's a good bet that you don't know how much you're paying in management fees each year.

You have a similar set of decisions about the allocation of your personal savings in other tax-advantaged accounts—individual retirement accounts (IRAs), Simplified Employment Pensions (sometimes known as SEP-IRAs), and Keogh plans. A truncated list of these funds takes up more than two pages in the *Wall Street Journal.* Your choices are the same—between bond funds and stock funds, and then among lots of bond funds and stock funds.

You can create your own "personal mutual fund" with the money in your tax-advantaged account; you can "self-direct" the investment of your money provided the assets are held in a dedicated account available from registered financial institutions like brokerage firms, banks, and insurance companies. No sales fees, no management fees, no marketing fees, and no miscellaneous charges. A large number of financial institutions offer these accounts; they follow your instructions to buy and sell individual bonds and stocks. You'll pay a modest account maintenance fee, probably in the range of $25 to $50 a year, and you'll have to pay the transaction costs when you buy and sell bonds and stocks.

In the long run, the rates of return that mutual funds earn as a group reflect the growth of the U.S. economy and the increases in corporate earnings. Some actively managed mutual funds achieve above-average rates of return for several years in a row, but it's inevitable that other participants in the financial markets must then have below-average returns. That's what an average means.

Consider the Triple Crown in horse racing as a metaphor for developing a portfolio with an above-average rate of return. Some of the most promising two-year-olds meet in the Kentucky Derby, the Preakness, and the Belmont. What is the likelihood that the winner of the Kentucky Derby also will win both the Preakness and the Belmont? Assume that the same ten horses run each of the three races. If the winner of each race is determined by a random process, the likelihood that the winner of the Derby will win the next two races is $\frac{1}{10} \times \frac{1}{10}$: $\frac{1}{100}$, or 1 percent. The likelihood that the same horse would win each of the three races is $\frac{1}{10}$ of 1 percent. Of course the winners are not randomly selected—some horses are stronger, some have more skillful jockeys. The data show that the winner of the Derby is more likely to win the Preakness and the Belmont than any of the other horses in the Derby, but the predictive power is slight. Similarly, how likely is it that a mutual fund with above-average performance one year will have an above-average performance the next year? The success of forecasters from one year to the next is an important factor in your decision about whether to choose an actively managed mutual fund or an index fund.

The Benefits of Using Mutual Funds—and the Costs

The major benefit of buying shares in a mutual fund is that you acquire a diversified portfolio of securities. The manager of the mutual fund reduces the risk that you might lose a large share of your wealth because you have most of your eggs in one basket—an individual bond or an individual stock. The rationale for diversification is that changes in the prices of the bonds and stocks in these different baskets are not likely to be sensitive to the same risks (unless you buy shares in a sector-specific fund, and even then its holdings would be diversified among a number of firms).

The second advantage of owning shares in a mutual fund is professional management. The manager of the mutual fund works full time with his or her own reputation on the line. Virtually all managers follow a disciplined approach to selecting a portfolio of bonds and of stocks.

In a good year, the manager of a large actively managed mutual fund earns a lot of money, probably more than the combined salaries of the presidents of the universities in any of the major college football conferences. Each manager has a strong interest in enhancing performance and recognizes that day by day, month by month, and quarter by quarter, his or her performance will be compared with the performance of other managers. As a minimum, each manager seeks to avoid mistakes that drag the realized rates of return on the funds under management significantly below those of their competitors. It's that simple, and it has two advantages: diversification and a commitment to follow a disciplined approach.

If you own shares in an actively managed mutual fund, you're likely to pay four or five different types of fees and costs. Some of these fees and costs are direct and can be measured, and others can only be estimated. Together these fees and costs drive a wedge between the rates of return on bonds and on stocks summarized in the previous chapter, and the rates of return that will add to your wealth. One distinction is between shareholder fees that are associated with the purchase or sale of mutual fund shares and the costs associated with the ownership of these shares. The regulatory authorities require that each fund publish a table

Table 10.3
Mutual Fund Fees

Shareholder fees (paid by the investor directly)	
Sales charge (load) on purchases and reinvested distributions	3.0%
Deferred sales charge (load) on redemptions	None
Annual operating expenses (paid from fund assets)	
Management fees	0.47%
Distribution (12b1) fees	0.21%
Other expenses	0.36%
Total annual fund operating expenses	1.04%

Source: Data from American Association of Individual Investors, *The Individual Investor's Guide to the Top Mutual Funds*, 28th ed. (Chicago: American Association of Individual Investors, 2009).

with the data about its fees and expenses, a version of which is reproduced in Table 10.3.

More than two-thirds of open-end funds charge sales fees or redemption fees, and a few charge both. These fees can range up to 8 percent of the amount of the purchase; many funds charge a fee of 6 percent. Some redemption fees are reduced the longer you remain invested with a particular fund or with a particular fund family. (The reason that many of the buyers of open-end funds pay the sales fees and/or redemption fees when they might buy other open-end funds and avoid these fees is that the sellers of these open end funds receive a commission. These sellers feel no fiduciary responsibility to minimize the costs that their clients incur, at least not when cost minimization would conflict with their own incomes.)

Owners of shares in mutual funds are charged a management fee that is a percentage of the fund's assets at the end of each quarter. The owners of the mutual funds are free to set the fees at any level that they like, presumably their view of what the traffic will bear. Index funds charge 0.20 percent to 0.40 percent a year, and actively managed funds charge 1.00 percent or even 1.50 percent a year. The fees are payable quarterly and are deducted from the value of each shareholder's account.

Many companies charge the owners of shares in the funds up to 0.50 percent a year of the value of their accounts for the so-called section 12b1 fee (the name derives from the section of the Investment Company Act of 1940 that applies to mutual funds). The fee allows the companies that own the mutual funds to recoup part or all of their marketing costs.

This arrangement was adopted in the early 1980s as a "temporary measure" on the rationale that the larger the number of shareholders in a fund, the lower its costs and hence the greater the benefit to the individuals who own mutual fund shares.

The surge in assets under management in the 1980s and 1990s might have led to a sharp decline in fees. Fees have declined modestly, and the inference is that costs and profits—or both costs and profits—have increased. The marketing fees could be included with management fees, but the owners of the funds want to keep the management fees low. If these marketing fees were included with the management fee, some individuals might ask why these fees were so high.

Mutual funds incur other expenses, including "fees paid to the fund's transfer agent for providing fund shareholder services, such as toll-free phone communications, computerized account services, Web site services, recordkeeping, printing, and mailing." Together the management fee, the section12b1 fee, and the other costs add to the annual operating expenses. Three other types of costs are harder to quantify because they are indirect, but they add to the yearly cost of owning mutual fund shares.

Mutual funds incur transaction costs when they buy and sell bonds and stocks. You might think that mutual funds can buy and sell securities at lower cost than you can because they buy and sell in much larger volumes at one time. The flip side of the large size of their purchases is that these purchases lead to increases in the price of the stock, and when the fund sells the stock, its sales depress the price. Large mutual funds aren't nimble. Their all-in costs of buying and selling the stocks of a particular company are higher than those that you would pay if you used a discount broker. These transaction costs cannot be readily measured across so many funds that differ significantly in their size and in the types of securities they acquire, but they could be as large as 0.25 percent or even 0.50 percent, especially when a large mutual fund wants to buy and sell shares in firms that are not among the 50 or 100 with the largest market capitalization.

Mutual funds may also incur a cost associated with "excessive" diversification. Once an investor or a fund owns fifteen or twenty well-chosen stocks of firms in different industries, the addition of stocks to this diversified portfolio can reduce the risk of the portfolio by a trivial amount. Yet many actively managed mutual funds often hold 40, 50, 60, 100, or more stocks—many more than they need to achieve the reduction in the risk of the portfolio from diversification.

One reason that actively managed funds hold so many different stocks is that the funds need to be ready to provide cash if investors wish to redeem their shares. In this sense, a mutual fund share is like a bank deposit, and the manager of the mutual fund has to be ready to provide cash to any owner of shares that decides it is time to sell the mutual fund shares. If there is a sudden demand for cash, the funds must sell stocks and the prices of these stocks will decline. Assume that a fund needs $10 million in cash; it might obtain the cash by selling the stocks of ten companies or alternatively of fifty companies. The smaller the number of companies whose stock is sold, the larger the number of shares of each of these companies that must be sold, and the stronger the downward pressure on the stock prices. Not good. The decision of the funds to hold shares in many different firms as a way to maintain liquidity is an indirect cost, since it blurs the focus in the stock selection process. (Note that this cost involves a comparison between investors who hold bonds and stocks directly and those who own shares in mutual funds.)

A second possible rationale for holding so many different shares is that the fund is hunting for a "winner"—a home run or "four bagger." Four baggers bring bragging rights. Most shares in most years will perform in an average way. Some will be above average; some will be below average. It's sort of like Harry Tout's visit to the Kentucky Derby: the larger the number of horses that Harry bets on in the Derby, the more likely he will have a winning bet. A winning bet in the financial markets is owning shares in a firm whose stock price triples in a year.

So much for stock selection. There is no way to measure the cost to owners of shares in mutual funds of excessive diversification. This cost hurts performance despite the occasional four baggers.

Many buyers of shares in mutual funds—except for those who own shares in tax-advantaged accounts—pay income taxes on the dividends that the funds distribute. Mutual funds distribute all of their dividend income, interest income, and capital gains so they won't have any income on which they would be obliged to pay income tax. When a mutual fund distributes dividend income, interest income, and capital gains to its shareholders, all of the shareholders—those that bought their shares eleven years ago and those that bought their shares eleven days ago—are credited with same share of the income.

For example, assume that Goldfinger bought 1,000 shares in ABC Mutual on December 1, at a price per share of $10. On December 15, the share price is $10 a share; ABC Mutual declares a dividend of $1 a share. ABC Mutual sends Goldfinger a check for $1,000; the U.S. Treasury is sent a 1099 form indicating that Goldfinger has been paid a dividend of $1,000. The dividend payment to Goldfinger is a return of a portion of the money that he used to buy the shares on December 1; the share price has not increased. If Goldfinger is in the top income tax bracket, he'll pay a tax of $0.35 a share on what in reality is the return of his capital rather than income. Not very efficient.

These costs—the management fees, the section 12b1 marketing fees, the other expenses, the transaction costs, the costs of excessive diversification, the tax inefficiency costs, and the sales charges—add up. If you invest through mutual funds, you'll pay between 1.5 and 2 percent a year of the value of your mutual fund shares to the firms that own these funds.

Assume that the U.S. economy grows at the rate of 3 percent a year and that the dividend rate is 2 percent and that the U.S. inflation rate is zero. Then the rate of return on stocks will average 5 to 6 percent a year in the long run. If you own shares in mutual funds, the costs incurred by these funds will take 30 to 40 percent of this return. The incomes of those who manage mutual funds are much, much higher than the Joe Blokes who own the shares in these funds.

Mutual Fund Fees and Your Wealth Accumulation

Assume that your objective is to accumulate $100,000 by the time you retire in your mid-sixties. The amount you'll need to save each month depends on the rate of return and the length of the investment period and average annual amount that you will pay the owners of the mutual fund company as management fees and other charges.

The top panel in Table 10.4 shows the future value of saving $1,000 a year for various holding periods—5 years, 10 years, 15 years, 20 years, 30 years—associated with each of the columns and several interest rates—4 percent, 5, percent, 6 percent, and 7 percent—noted in each of the rows. (Future values are discussed extensively in Chapter 14; see pages 281–286.) The first value in each cell indicates the value of accumulated savings at the end of the holding period associated with each of the interest rates. Thus if the holding period is thirty years and the rate of return is 7 percent, then the accumulated savings will total $94,461. The values

Table 10.4

The Cumulative Costs of Mutual Fund Fees

Pre-Fee Rate of Return	Holding Period, in Years				
	5	10	15	20	30
4%	$5,416	$12,006	$20,024	$29,778	$56,085
	(5,304)	(11,464)	(18,599)	(26,870)	(47,575)
5%	5,525	12,578	21,579	33,064	68,439
	(5,416)	(12,006)	(20,024)	(29,778)	(56,085)
6%	5,637	13,181	23,276	36,786	79,058
	(5,525)	(12,578)	(21,579)	(33,064)	(56,085)
7%	5,751	13,817	25,129	40,996	94,461
	(5,637)	(13,181)	(23,277)	(36,786)	(79,058)

Note: Cumulative costs of these fees is shown by the difference between the first row (without the parentheses) and the second row (with the parentheses) for each of the pre-fee rates of return.

Source: Author.

in parentheses in each cell indicate how much of the accumulated savings is retained by the investor if the total fees to the firm that owns and manages the mutual fund is 1 percent a year. The difference between the two values in each cell is the amount of the cumulative dollar payment to the firm that owns the mutual fund. These differences are small for the five-year holding period, less than 0.2 percent. When the holding period is thirty years, the percentage difference between the two values is in the range of 15 percent. The increase in this wedge is the power of compound interest. If the aggregate fees are 1.5 percent, then the difference is more than 25 percent.

The longer the investment period, the larger the payment to the owner of the mutual fund company as a percentage of the increase in your wealth. If you save $100 a month for forty years and the rate of return is 6 percent a year before the payment of the 2 percent annual fee, then the payment to the owner of the mutual fund company is $105,000 and your future value is $160,000. Yet you've carried all the investment risk. The nickels you pay to the owner of the mutual fund company add up—especially for the owners who collect millions of nickels. That's why J. P. Morgan once quipped, "Where are the customers' yachts?"

A Horse Race: Passive Index Funds and Actively Managed Funds

The development of index funds means you can buy "professional" diversification without also having to buy "professional" security selection. The costs of index funds are much smaller than the costs of actively managed funds, in part because they spend relatively little on marketing and investment research and because their transaction costs are much smaller since they trade much less often. Moreover, salaries are lower. Vanguard, one of the major firms that produce index funds, advertises that its costs are one-sixth those of actively managed funds.

In contrast, actively managed funds seek above-average returns by some combination of "picking" and "timing." They spend money—in some cases a lot of money—on investment research, and their transaction costs are higher, often much higher, because they buy and sell shares more frequently. Their "promise" is that they can achieve above-average rates of return and that the margin of their superior performance will more than compensate the owners of the shares in the mutual fund for these higher costs. (They would be out of business if they said otherwise.) The all-in costs of an actively managed mutual fund may be five, six, or even eight times those of a passively managed fund.

Advocates for index funds make two points. The first is that stock price movements are random in the short run, and hence some actively managed mutual funds will realize increases in net asset value per share higher than those of index funds. The second is that the margin of superior performance of the actively managed funds over the index funds will not be large enough in the long run to overcome the disadvantage of higher costs.

The defenders of actively managed funds point to the track records of several of these funds. Since there are more than 10,000 funds, some actively managed funds will achieve rates of return higher than those achieved by the index funds—at least for a few years. The first question is whether the successes of these funds for an extended period reflect managerial skill or chance; the second is whether these highly successful funds can be identified in advance.

There is a survivorship bias in this observation, of course. Many newly established funds that did not achieve above-average returns have been closed. In the 1990s about 400 mutual funds were shuttered, and it's a safe bet that few if any of these funds had an above-average performance.

The funds that have gone kaput are not included in the calculation of the average rates of return for mutual funds as a group, although their inclusion probably would not have made a significant difference because they generally were small.

One empirical finding is that the above-average performance of a mutual fund in year 1 has no value in forecasting whether the fund will be an above-average performer in year 2. Some funds bounce frequently between below-average and above-average performances. Still, a few funds have had remarkable success in achieving above-average rates of return year after year.

Hedge Funds

Hedge funds differ from mutual funds in that they are lightly regulated private partnerships. Initially a hedge fund would take a long position in one group of stocks and a short position of about the same market value in another group of stocks; in this way the portfolio would be "market neutral." The idea was to profit from changes in the prices of the stocks due to the firm effects and to neutralize the impact of changes in the prices of stocks as a group. Now the term has been broadened to include financial firms that are virtually unregulated; these firms invest in a wide variety of securities and assets. Hedge funds differ from traditional mutual funds in that they open their books to receive money from investors once or twice a year. Usually these investors must demonstrate that they have net worth of at least $1 million. The hedge funds often borrow money to use with money received from investors. Most of the hedge funds are not hedged in the traditional sense; they seek to profit from large changes in the prices of securities. Usually, investors pay an annual fee of 2 percent and a performance fee of 20 percent of the profits.

The most famous of U.S. hedge funds was Long Term Capital Management (LTCM). Two Nobel laureates were among its owners and senior executives. The public version of the investment philosophy was that the fund would take large and nearly offsetting positions in similar securities. For example, LTCM would buy U.S. Treasury bonds with a twenty-nine-year maturity and sell—go short—a comparable amount of the thirty-year U.S. Treasury bond, for the thirty-year bond was much more liquid than the twenty-nine-year bond and so the interest rate was lower. In 1998 the correlations became much less strong, and LTCM was on its way to bankruptcy before the Federal Reserve forced its major lenders to make equity investments in the firm.

The most successful mutual fund in the 1980s and 1990s was Fidelity's Magellan, which was managed by Peter Lynch from 1977 to 1990. Magellan was established in 1963. Assets under management increased from $20 million to $13 billion when Lynch managed Magellan. The average annual increase in net asset value of each share was 29 percent. Investors who held shares in Magellan were ecstatic. The money poured in. Lynch had to decide where to invest the money. Eventually Magellan owned shares in more than 700 firms.

There are three partially overlapping views about Magellan's success. One is that Lynch was a genius; he had "hot hands," to use the term applied to jockeys who have had a run of winners at the racetrack. An alternative view is that since there are several thousand mutual funds, a handful will have "runs" and achieve above-average returns for an extended number of years. A third view is that once Lynch had achieved an enviable track record either because of his hot hands or chance and as his success became known, the money poured into Magellan, and he promoted his own track record by purchasing more of the shares that Magellan already owned, which induced further increases in the prices of these shares.

Peter Lynch may have been a genius, or he may have been the fellow who was able to achieve ten heads in a row. His winning streak attracted performance-oriented hot money, and so he had lots of cash to invest at a time when the prices of stocks were continually hitting new highs. His continued purchases of the stocks in Magellan's portfolio contributed to the increase in Magellan's net asset value, and his success as a stock picker attracted copy cats that tried to mimic his stock selections—and that led to further increases in the prices of these same stocks.

Peter Lynch's successor as one of the top mutual fund managers was William Miller of Legg Mason. *Forbes* reported, "His Legg Mason Value Fund outperformed the S&P 500 every single year for a decade and half through 2005, an astonishing streak regularly cited as evidence that a smart fund manager can consistently beat the market. Customers flocked to this hot hand. Assets in the fund climbed to $12 billion, which led to management fees of $200 million a year for Legg Mason" (*Forbes*, April 13, 2009, p. 44). The *Forbes* story continues that the average return on the fund since its beginning in 1983 was 11.1 percent compared with the average return on the S&P 500 of 10.9 percent (see Table 10.5). But when an adjustment is made to reflect that much of the money came to the Legg Mason Value Fund in recent years, its performance was 5.4 percent compared with the performance of an index fund of 5.8 percent.

Consumer Reports has published two articles that highlighted the success of an approach that it had developed to select winners among the mutual funds. One of the lead articles in the February 2007 issue of *Consumer Reports* was titled "60 Funds You Can Count On." The article noted that investors needed "more information than annualized returns. . . . Our goal was to shift focus from how *much* a Fund beat its benchmark stock index to how *often* it beat that index. "We are happy to report that the system worked pretty well" (*Consumer Reports*, February 2007, p. 18; emphasis in original.) Thus far *Consumer Reports* has not published any article indicating how well its "system" worked.

The Legg Mason Value Fund beat its benchmark for fifteen years. Its losses in the next several years dominated the earlier gains.

Table 10.5
Performance of Selected Actively Managed Funds, 1999–2009

	10-Year Annualized Total Return	Assets, 2/28/99 (billions)	Assets, 2/28/09 (billions)	Annual Expenses per $100
Fidelity Contrafund	1.3%	$40	$42	$0.89
AmerFundsInCoAmerA	−0.1%	49	44	0.54
AmerFundsWashMutualInvsA	−0.8%	51	38	0.58
Vanguard WindsorII Fund-Inv	−1.1%	31	23	0.32
PutnamFundfor Growth&IncomeA	−4.2%	38	3	1.00
Janus Fund	−4.5%	27	6	0.88
AmerCenturyUltraFund-Inv	−4.8%	32	4	0.99
Fidelity Magellan Fund	−5.2%	89	17	0.73
Fidelity Growth&Income	−7.2%	48	5	0.68
Fidelity Adviors Growth Opportu	−7.7%	28	1	1.27
Vanguard 500 Index Fund-Inv	−3.5%	78	61	0.16

Source: Data from *Forbes* magazine, April 13, 2009, p. 44.

Life Cycle Funds

In the last few years the mutual fund families have begun to market life cycle funds. The idea is straightforward: when you're retired and perhaps drawing down your wealth to help maintain your standard of living, you need a more conservative portfolio than when you're still in the active labor force. These life cycle funds often are targeted to the year of your planned retirement.

The shortcoming of this rationale for the selection of bonds and stocks is that individuals will consume some of their financial wealth for twenty or twenty-five years after they retire. And many will want to bequeath some financial wealth to their children and grandchildren.

Magellan: An Index Fund in Drag

Magellan was the largest U.S. mutual fund in the late 1990s. As assets under management increased, Magellan's purchases of stocks induced increases in its prices, and its transaction costs increased relative to its assets under management. Magellan found it more and more difficult to maintain its margin of performance relative to the stock price indexes and to smaller actively managed funds.

As Magellan became larger, the overlap between the stocks in its portfolio and the stocks in the portfolio of an index fund based on the S&P 500 index increased. All the S&P 500 stocks owned by Magellan would be owned by the index fund, but Magellan did not own all of the stocks that were in this index. Magellan owned shares in more than 200 firms that were not in the S&P 500 index.

Consider the overlap between Magellan's portfolio and the portfolio of an index fund based on the S&P 500 (hereafter Alpha) illustrated in Figure 10.1. Assume initially that the two portfolios have the same market values. Each of the solid bars in the figure represents shares in a different firm owned by Alpha, and the height of each solid bar indicates the market value of the shares in each of these firms in Alpha's portfolio. The stock with the highest market value in Alpha's portfolio (and hence the highest market value in the index) is shown on the left, the stock with the next highest value is the second from the left, and so on. Since there are 500 stocks in the index and Alpha owns shares in each of these firms,

Figure 10.1
Overlap between Alpha Index Fund and Magellan

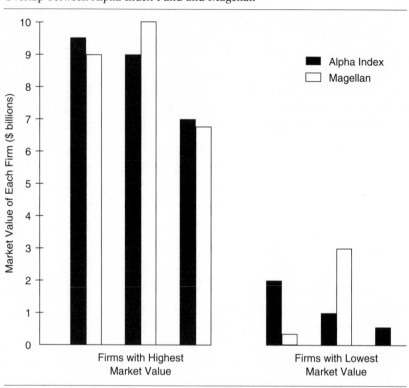

Source: Author.

there are 500 bars. Eighty percent or so of the market value of the index fund is likely to be represented by the fifty firms with the highest market values, and 90 percent of the market value of the index will be represented by the 100 firms with the highest market values.

Overlap between Alpha Index Fund and Magellan

The market value of each of the same stocks owned by Magellan is represented by the hollow bar that is attached to each of the solid bars. Magellan owns relatively more of some of these stocks than Alpha and relatively less of others. Magellan does not own some of the stocks that Alpha owns, and hence some of the solid bars are not "married" to a hollow bar, and some of the stocks that Magellan owns are not owned by

Alpha, so in that case the hollow bar is not married to a solid bar. The overlap between the shares owned by the index fund and the shares owned by Magellan is likely to be extensive, since the holdings of Magellan are concentrated in the sixty or eighty firms with the highest market values—and most of the holdings of Alpha are in these same firms.

Magellan's portfolio can be deconstructed into two components. There is an embedded index fund, which can be considered the passive component; the remainder is the active component. The active component of Magellan's portfolio—and this is based on the logic of the comparison—is likely to be no more than 20 to 30 percent of the market value of its portfolio.

If Magellan is to have a higher rate of return than Alpha, it must occur because the rate of return on the 25 percent of its actively managed fund is significantly higher than the rate of return on the embedded index fund to compensate for its higher costs. Moreover, if the shareholders in Magellan are to achieve more rapid increases in the net asset value than the shareholders in Alpha, then the rate of return on the active component of the Magellan portfolio must be sufficiently high to compensate for Magellan's higher costs.

Assume that total costs of the Alpha index fund are 0.25 percent of assets under management and total costs of Magellan are 0.75 percent and that the embedded index fund in Magellan is three-fourths of its portfolio. The rate of return on the active component of Magellan's portfolio must be three percentage points higher than on the embedded index fund if the Magellan shareholders are to achieve the same rate of return as the Alpha shareholders.

Every large actively managed mutual fund contains an embedded index fund. The larger this embedded index fund, the less likely that the actively managed fund will outperform an index fund by enough to warrant its higher costs. If you want to own a mutual fund that is broadly representative of the economy, buy an index fund. Avoid buying any large actively managed fund.

Fidelity obviously recognizes that Magellan is an "index fund in drag"—and that its costs and fees are significantly higher than those for index funds based on the S&P 500. Many people who own shares in Magellan do so because they are lethargic; they could increase their rate of return by switching to an index fund or to one of the smaller Fidelity funds. Fidelity keeps Magellan alive because it gets a lot of milk from a dead cow.

If you buy shares in an actively managed mutual fund, you are participating in a gigantic lottery that on average has a lower rate of return than if you had invested in an index fund. Each year some owners of shares in the actively managed funds win the lottery because their fund achieves above-average rates of return and by more than enough to compensate for their higher costs. A smaller number of investors will have above-average returns for two years or three years running, or in a handful of cases, for an even longer string of years.

These aged actively managed funds with glorious histories are cash cows that are kept around because they are very, very profitable. The polite term for those who own shares in these funds is that they are detached. Less polite terms include lazy and ignorant. Loyalty to an older fund can be costly to your financial health.

Thomas Malthus's "Closet" Index Fund

Thomas Malthus is a serious investor who has learned and relearned the importance of diversification. Malthus holds shares in six different mutual funds—one based on large firms, another based on mid-cap firms, a third based on small-cap firms, a fourth focused on the energy industry, a fifth concentrated on biotech, and a sixth that emphasizes consumer goods.

The more specialized each of these mutual funds is, the higher its management fees. In fact, the overlap between Malthus's holdings of the different mutual funds and an index fund is extensive, perhaps as much as 80 percent. Malthus would be better off by first buying shares in a broad index fund and then supplementing ownership of shares in this fund with shares in one or two index funds that focus on an industrial sector or a geographic region. He would pay much lower management fees.

Closed-End Funds versus Open-End Funds

The market value of closed-end mutual funds is about 5 percent of the market value of open-end funds. Many of the open-end funds have close cousins among the closed-end funds.

If you've decided that you want a mutual fund that specializes in owning stocks of firms in the financial industry or the stocks of bank, or one that specializes in owning the stocks of firms headquartered in Southeast Asia, then a comparison of a closed-end fund and its open-end cousin will be instructive—and perhaps profitable.

There are two principal advantages to owning a closed-end fund. One is that the market price of the closed-end fund may be at a discount of 5 or 10 percent of its net asset value; if the discount is 10 percent, then each $90 purchase of the shares of the closed-end fund will buy you $100 worth of assets. (Recognize the risk that the discount may be larger on the date that you decide to sell this position.) The other is that the all-in management fees of the closed-end fund are likely to be lower than that of the open-end cousin, in part because there are no marketing costs and in part because there is less attention to using a boost in performance as a way to sell more shares. Moreover, the closed-end funds are not tax-inefficient.

When Staying with a Mutual Fund
Can Be Costly to Your Financial Health

The feature of the mutual fund industry (remember the advertisement that was reproduced as Table 10.1) is that "hot hands"—a superior track record—attracts "hot money"—investor funds that move from one fund to another in the belief that an asset manager can repeat the superior performance. Some of the asset managers will repeat; others won't. More of the hot money will flow to those that do. The investors that move the money don't know of the outcome of the coin-tossing experiment or aren't convinced. As the "hot hands" managers bring in more and more money, maintaining the performance becomes more difficult. The managers are happy; their incomes are soaring. As the funds increase in size, they become more nearly alike. In some cases, their performance may lag that of the index funds because the securities have ceased being in favor.

Minimizing the Costs of Becoming Diversified

Diversification is of key importance in conservatively managing your financial wealth. Five basic approaches toward diversification and their features are summarized in Table 10.6. But it's not that you need to rely on only one of these approaches; you could use each of the five and initially

Table 10.6
Five Basic Approaches to Diversified Portfolios

| | DIY | ETFs | Index Funds | Actively Managed Funds | |
				Closed-End	Open-End
Shareholder fees	No	No	No	No	Probably
Management fees	No	Yes	Yes	Yes	Yes
12b1 fees	No	No	No	No	Yes
Other fees	No	No	No	No	Yes
Transaction costs	Yes	Yes	Yes	Yes	Yes
Excess diversification	No	No	No	No	Perhaps
Tax inefficient	No	No	No	No	Perhaps
Summary	.50	.50			

Note: DIY = Do It Yourself; ETFs = Exchange-traded funds.

Source: Author.

allocate 20 percent of your financial wealth to each one. Or you could initially allocate 50 percent of your financial wealth to one of the five, say, the index fund approach, and 20 percent to one of the others, perhaps an ETF, and 10 percent to the other three. As the years pass, you can alter the proportions as you become more comfortable and confident about your ability to one of the approaches. Column 1 is a do-it-yourself (DIY). Column 2 involves purchasing an ETF. Column 3 involves purchasing an index fund. Column 4 involves purchasing an actively managed closed-end stock fund, and column 5 an actively managed open-end fund.

You are going to have to make asset allocation decisions with each of the columns, and the number of decisions will be larger if you follow the DIY approach. You could follow a buy-and-hold strategy for each approach.

The costs associated with each column differ, increasing as you move from left to right. You will pay management fees in columns 2, 3, and 4, although the management costs in column 4 generally will be higher and perhaps much higher than with the other options. The management costs associated with column 3 might be trivially higher than in column 2, but the transaction costs in column 2 will be modestly higher than in column 3. You would not incur any sales fees in columns 1 and 2; you might in columns 3 and 4. If your funds are in the $20,000 to $30,000 range, you can obtain a diversified portfolio on your own. Transaction costs have declined sharply with the advent of discount brokers.

You want to hold a diversified portfolio of securities to reduce the likelihood of a significant decline in your wealth because the price of one of these securities declines sharply. If you own a number of different securities, it's unlikely that the prices of many of these assets would decline at the same time. If in contrast you own only one type of asset—say, you own only real estate and mutual funds that own real estate—then you might suffer a significant divot in your wealth if real estate prices decline.

If you are a typical middle-class American, you already have a diversified "portfolio" of assets and securities. You probably own a home (two-thirds of Americans do), and a large part of your net worth is in real estate. The odds are high that you have an employment-related pension. Nineteen out of twenty Americans can expect a check from Social Security (and many of the remaining 5 percent will have a pension from the U.S. government or from one of the states or local governments); you might have to pay $300,000 to buy an annuity that would provide you with a monthly check comparable to the one that you receive from Social Security or from some other government source.

One low-cost way to become diversified is to buy a clutch of closed-end funds. Another is to buy the shares of GE, which owns businesses in more than ten different industries, including a wide array of financial services, aircraft engines, appliances, medical equipment, chemicals, plastics, and broadcasting. Similarly, you could buy shares in Berkshire Hathaway, which owns large positions in Coca-Cola, the *Washington Post*, and numerous other industries, especially insurance firms. Deutsche Bank owns shares in many German and foreign firms. When you buy shares in several of these diversified firms, you've become a mutual fund manager. Pay yourself the management fee.

The usual test of how well diversified a portfolio of stocks is involves the variability of the value of a portfolio relative to one of the major stock price indexes. If the value of your portfolio is perfectly correlated with changes in a stock price index, then the changes in the value of your portfolio would vary on a one-for-one basis with the change in the stock price index.

The folklore is that if you own nine or ten well-chosen stocks, more or less one from each industry, you can achieve 95 percent of the diversification you would have if you owned an index fund. Now that conventional wisdom has been amended, and the number of securities you would need has increased from eighteen to twenty.

If you want more diversification, scan the portfolios of five or ten large mutual funds. You'll note that they own shares in many of the same major companies—General Electric, Citicorp, AIG, Coca-Cola, McDonald's, AIG, IBM, Pfizer, Merck, ExxonMobil, Home Depot, and others. The relative amounts of these stocks in their portfolios differ. Still, it's almost as if the managers asked, how much of each of these stocks would we hold if we wanted to mimic the holdings of a mutual fund? And should we overweight or underweight a particular stock? These are the same stocks that will be at the core of an index fund based on the S&P 500 or the S&P 100. You can easily mimic their portfolios.

ACTIONABLES

1. Establish one or several accounts in different index funds—perhaps a stock index fund and a bond index fund—before you buy any other type of mutual fund.

2. Structure a "horse race" between the performance of these index funds and the performance of other investments with mutual funds and personally managed investments.

3. Try to determine how risk averse you are.

4. Once you've decided to move beyond a market-wide index fund, consider purchasing shares in index funds dedicated to individual industries.

5. Compare the management costs of mutual funds and trading volumes in any index fund. If the trading volumes are higher than the average, do not hold the fund. It's not likely to be a high performer.

6. Do not hold shares in any mutual fund that has been a below-average performer for more than two years in a row.

7. Consider individual firms like GE and Berkshire Hathaway as indirect ways to buy mutual funds in drag.

8. Consider closed-end funds as an alternative to open-end funds. Buy these closed-end funds only if they can be purchased at a discount of 8 or 10 percent below their net asset value.

9. Avoid purchasing more than three performance-oriented funds. The more different types of mutual funds you purchase, the more nearly you have constructed a "closet" index fund.

10. Recognize the impact of year-by-year management costs that you might pay on the rate at which your savings accumulate.

11   If You Won $100,000 in the Lottery, How Should You Invest the Money?

One of the stock answers to the question "How do you make a small fortune in the futures markets?" is "Start with a large fortune." The professionals who are permanent fixtures in the market tease amateurs with the prospect of exceedingly high returns to bring in new outsiders eager to get rich. A large part of what happens in financial markets is that the small investors who are saving for their retirement are set up so that the insiders can get the money to buy the fuel for their yachts.

Over the last 100 years or so, a slew of financial regulations have been adopted to protect individual households from financial losses. Some argue that regulation is unnecessary because each individual's concern with his or her own reputation for credibility is so overwhelming that no one would have an incentive to mislead—and that individual investors would be more skeptical in the absence of regulation. The abuses in the last several decades identified with junk bonds, savings and loan companies, Enron, and subprime mortgages suggest that self-regulation is hollow and won't protect the innocent and the unwary—and frankly, the ignorant. The trusting are scammed more often than the skeptical. Time after time, the arrangements implode and tens of thousands of small household savers lose a large part of their wealth. Cynics would suggest that the new regulations have been adopted to keep the small savers in the game. Your choices about how to allocate your accumulated savings between bonds and stocks are based on firms' statements about their profits and the prospect of their future earnings. The price-earnings ratio (often referred to as the P-E) is the most cited measure of corporate performance. The price of each stock is determined in the marketplace, and the closing prices of the stocks of the larger firms are published every day in many of the country's newspapers. Earnings, on the other hand, are decided upon in a dark closet as top management massages revenues and costs and dips into reserves in an effort to produce a value for earnings that shows steady growth, perhaps at a rate modestly higher than the rate of growth of U.S. gross domestic product (GDP). "Earnings management" is a complex and delicate issue. The business schools do not offer courses in earnings management. Senior financial officers do not meet in Boca Raton or Palm Springs to participate in seminars on the topic offered by the leading accounting firms—or even the lagging accounting firms. Wall Street analysts want guidance about corporate earnings so they can issue reports on whether the stock will "outperform" or "underperform" the market; each analyst wants to enhance his or her reputation for providing accurate forecasts. Many of the large corporate firms are "covered" by analysts from fifteen or twenty different investment banks and brokerage firms, so the analysts compete with each other. Once they publish their forecasts, corporate managers are "captive" to them. If actual earnings come in below forecasts, investors will dump the stock. If actual earnings appear likely to come in above the forecasts, then the conservative approach is to "save the good earnings" for a rainy day by delaying the recognition of some receipts or by speeding some payments. Often the managers want to ensure that reported earnings for the quarter are one or two pennies higher than the estimates of the Wall Street analysts. A conservative estimate is that half of the firms in the S&P 500 have played the game, though it's illegal to do so.

The manipulation of reported earnings by publicly traded firms is one of the lesser forms of mischief practiced on those saving for retirement. During the bubble years of the late 1990s, Merrill Lynch and Morgan Stanley and the other investment banks used shills and hucksters to hype stocks, especially of the dot-com and telecom companies. Henry Blodgett of Merrill Lynch is the poster child of misrepresentation. His genius was that he was happy to set "price targets" for firms, especially for firms that were clients of Merrill Lynch's investment banking activities. Merrill's bankers could then point to their track record of securing high prices when potential clients were seeking to sell stock for the first time. Merrill could say, "We've got 15,000 brokers spread all over the world who will help create a demand for your stock with their clients." Blodgett indicated that the price target for the Fountain of Youth—a made-up name in this context—would be $400 a share in three to six months. Investors bought the stock, and the price got to $400. A nice call. Stock prices were increasing in the late 1990s because there was a bubble, and Blodgett was a cheerleader for the bubble—at least in public. His downfall was triggered by someone who reported that he was making highly critical statements to some of his Merrill colleagues about the firms that he was praising to the investing public.

The Enron financial debacle revealed that there are insiders inside the insiders, more or less like one of those Russian dolls. Enron started as a regulated gas pipeline company and transformed itself into an unregulated financial intermediary that traded natural gas, petroleum, electricity, and broadband frequencies. Professional investors loved the Enron story. Investment banks benefited greatly from helping Enron raise the cash for its new businesses. The mutual funds loved Enron because its revenues and profits—sorry, its reported profits—were growing at a nice pace, and the stock price increased rapidly. Enron became the darling of the financial press for the way it was transforming both itself and the electric power industry; economists of the free-market persuasion asserted that Enron did more to deregulate the electric power industry than any other firm in the country. *Fortune* magazine called Enron one of the United States' most successful firms. (It is to *Fortune*'s credit that two of its writers were the first to uncover and blow the whistle publicly on the Enron scam.)

The price of Enron shares went from $7 in 1990 to $20 in 1995 to $95 in 2000. Enron employees who owned a lot of Enron stock in their 401(k) plans became wealthy. Quarter by quarter, Enron reported higher profits. Enron's new trading activities and investments in major hard assets required lots of capital; the firm sold bonds to the public and borrowed from banks. Sometime around 1997 or 1998, Enron hit a borrowing limit, so it began to move some of its loans from its own balance sheet into private partnerships. The private partnerships would borrow in their own names and use the cash to buy bonds and other IOUs issued by Enron. (The private partnerships were considered "independent entities" as long as 3 percent of the shares in the partnerships were owned by non-related individuals. In the Enron case, the 3 percent were owned by Enron officials.)

Within three months, toward the end of 2001, Enron collapsed and filed for bankruptcy—the largest bankruptcy ever of a public company until MCI-WorldCom tumbled into bankruptcy a few months later. Enron turned out to have been the proverbial house of cards. In mid-November 2001, two weeks before Enron marched into bankruptcy court, most Wall Street stock market analysts still ranked Enron as a "buy," and some said a "strong buy," even though the stock price had declined to $20.

These Wall Street analysts are professionals—and you're an amateur. The analysts are paid to estimate the profit prospects of the companies they cover; some of the analysts were skilled in detecting corporate deception and still failed to recognize that the greater hustlers were alive and well in Houston.

One of your continuing concerns should be, "Whom can I trust?" The related question is, "Which information is trustworthy?" If you're like most individuals, you're puzzled about how to get started with a systematic approach toward investing. There's a bewildering amount of information to digest and assemble before you can make the decisions that could dramatically improve (or, sadly, subtract from) your quality of life in retirement.

This chapter is designed to help you get started in managing your savings on your path to retirement. The first lesson is that the greed in the corporate universe and in the financial services sector has been extensive, and a significant number of the people whom you would like to trust will abuse your good faith by providing incomplete and misleading information. The second lesson is to reread the first lesson. Most of the chapter centers on developing a diversified portfolio. One of the concluding sections deals with investment styles—value investing, the efficient market approach, momentum investing, and several others.

Assume that you won the lottery and have $10,000 or $50,000 or $100,000 to invest. How should you organize a portfolio of bonds and stocks? After you've decided on how to invest the prize money, you can return to reality and focus on developing a more systematic approach to the management of your own savings as they accumulate.

Getting Started

The odds are high that you buy stocks and perhaps bonds with relatively little concern about the impact of each purchase on the return and the risk of your portfolio of bonds and of stocks and of real estate. Someone

Figure 11.1

The Investment Decision-Tree Template

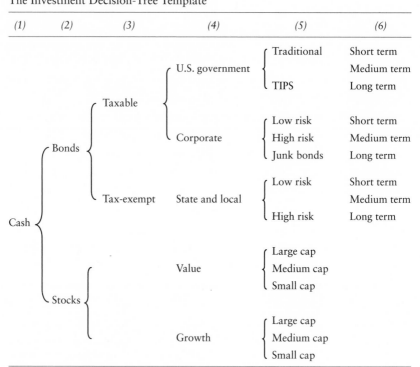

(1)	(2)	(3)	(4)	(5)	(6)

Note: TIPS = Treasury Inflation-Protected Securities.

Source: Author.

has suggested that the future is in "plastics"—or maybe it's biotech or high-tech or even low-tech or Atlantic City casinos or the local bank. A lot of individuals buy the stocks on the basis of these "tips." And a stable of brokers and touts make their living by providing these tips.

The alternative approach involves developing a template or a model of an "ideal portfolio," assigning target proportions of the prize money that you will use to buy bonds and stocks, and then determining some of the characteristics of individual bonds and stocks. Once you've developed the template, you will select individual bonds and stocks that fit it.

Consider Figure 11.1 as a framework for organizing the template. The move from the left toward the right on a column-by-column basis provides the basis for organizing your portfolio. Your lottery prize money is the cash in column 1; move to column 2 and first decide how much of the prize money should be used to buy bonds and how much to buy stocks.

Once you've made that allocation, move to column 3 and now make the allocation of the bond component between taxable bonds (those of the federal government and private firms) and tax-exempt bonds issued by state and local governments. Similarly allocate the amount of the prize money that you will use to buy stocks between those in the value group and those in the growth group. Then move to column 4 and choose between the riskless bonds of the U.S. Treasury and corporate bonds. Once you've decided on the amount to be allocated to U.S. Treasury bonds, choose between traditional bonds and Treasury Inflation-Protected Securities (TIPS). Finally, choose among the maturity of the bonds: short term, medium term, and long term.

Remember, at this stage you're developing the guidelines for a diversified portfolio; it's premature to select individual bonds and stocks before you complete the template. Moreover, you needn't choose to allocate part of the prize money to one of the groups simply because it's a box on the decision tree; you may conclude that junk bonds are for others.

The percentages of your wealth in bonds and in stocks primarily should reflect your psychological response to the decline in wealth when interest rates increase or some other event causes the prices of bonds and stocks to decline. If you've experienced a substantial decline in financial wealth, you understand; if not, know that it's an experience millions of individuals have found depressing or even terrifying. You want to ensure that the susceptibility of your portfolio to a decline significantly larger than one you think you can handle without great pain is low. If you're in doubt, start with a portfolio that is mostly bonds until you observe how your psyche is affected by a decline in the value of your portfolio of 10 or 15 percent.

One approach is to develop a "bonds-only" portfolio; you anticipate that the real value of your bond portfolio will increase at an annual average rate of 3 percent if you buy U.S. Treasury bonds and at a slightly more rapid rate if you buy bonds issued by the government-sponsored enterprises (GSEs) and the private firms with the highest credit ratings. You recognize that in the long run the rate of return on a stocks-only portfolio would be higher, but you've concluded that the higher anticipated rate of return is not worth the increase in risk or the variability of your net worth from one month or year to the next and the value of a good night's sleep.

At this stage it is important to think systematically about risk, so please follow the discussion in the following box.

Risk and Uncertainty and Your Financial Wealth

Risk is one of those ambiguous terms that has different meanings for different individuals—and several meanings for the same individual. Professional financial analysts are concerned with several risks, especially market risk—the risk of changes in the price of the stocks and bonds. Risk and uncertainty seem related; in a world of certainty, all outcomes would be known and horse races, boxing matches, and the World Series would be boring. Risk is the probability of an event from a distribution of possible outcomes; for example, the risk of a home fire or an auto accident can be estimated from large databases. In contrast, uncertainty involves far-out, one-off events much like the flooding of New Orleans after Katrina, so it is impossible to estimate the probability of such events because they are so infrequent.

Financial analysts measure the variability of the prices of different assets relative to the average value for these assets. The risk attached to a bond or a stock is measured by the range of movement in its price relative to the price of a "riskless security." U.S. Treasury bonds are viewed as riskless because the government always can get the cash to repay the principal by going to the Federal Reserve—hence no credit risk is attached to owning these bonds, although they are subject to market risk. The risk of other bonds and of stocks is measured as the ratio of the variability in their price relative to the variability in the price of government bonds (the risk of different types of bonds and of stocks was summarized in Table 9.2). Junk bonds are riskier than U.S. Treasury bonds because their prices vary by a much larger amount; when the economy is in recession, the prices of junk bonds are low because the likelihood that some borrowers might default is high.

Similarly, the variability in the price of stocks is measured by the variability of their prices: the greater the variability, the riskier the stock. Growth stocks are riskier than value stocks. Small-cap stocks are riskier than large-cap stocks.

Most investors have a more direct or institutional, less quantitative approach. Many ask, "What's the likelihood that I will lose most or all of my money?" If in 1998 or 1999 most financial analysts had been asked, "What is the risk attached to owning shares in Enron or MCI-WorldCom or Tyco?" the answer would have been something like "About average for rapid growth firms." These investors are forward looking and concerned with episodic events, not the averages for the last several years that are used by financial managers.

Individuals planning for retirement should be concerned with three different aspects of the risk of the portfolios that they are acquiring. One is the trade-off between risk and return; the rate of return on their portfolios is likely to be higher the more willing they are to hold a somewhat riskier portfolio. Thus a portfolio of stocks is riskier than a portfolio of bonds. Risk could be associated with a decline in the purchasing power of the securities in their portfolios if they had to sell all their stocks and bonds at the same time. The much more likely case is that these individuals' bonds and stocks might be high on some of these sale dates and low on others. The statement that "it all averages out in the long run" would be a slight exaggeration, since there is some probability that prices might be below trend when the bonds and stocks are first sold. Virtually all of these measures are in nominal terms; they measure the variability of the price of the security in terms of cash, but individuals should instead be concerned with the purchasing power of their bonds and stocks in terms of the traditional bundles of goods and services.

Investors are concerned with several different risks. One more or less identical with that of the financial analysts is the price risk, the variability of the price of the security. A second risk is implicitly identified with junk bonds and Enron and Lehman and Countrywide Financial and Washington Mutual: what is the likelihood that a firm will default, that the shares in the firm will become virtually worthless and that the bondholders will incur large losses? A third risk is that of inflation: what is the likelihood of a decline in the purchasing power of the interest or dividend income because of significant increases in the consumer price level?

Three of the major risks associated with owning the securities are noted in Table 11.1. These risks can be evaluated in the short run and in the long run, and they can be evaluated for individual securities and for portfolios of securities.

First note that the risk is inherent in the ownership of securities. If you think you've found a security that isn't subject to one of these three risks, think again—in effect you are paying someone else to own the risk, and the security offered by that institution may be subject to a credit risk. Financial analysts treat the U.S. Treasury bonds as riskless, because the likelihood of default risk is trivially small, but these bonds are subject to large price risks

Table 11.1

The Risks of Different Securities

	Credit Risk	Inflation Risk	Price Risk
Bank deposits	No	Yes	No/Yes
Treasury bills	No	Yes	No
Treasury bonds	No	Yes	Yes
TIPS	No	No	Yes
Tax-free state bonds	Yes	Yes	Yes
Corporate bonds	Yes	Yes	Yes
Junk bonds	Yes	Yes	Yes
Value stocks	Yes	Yes	Yes
Growth stocks	Yes	Yes	Yes
Small-cap stocks	Yes	Yes	Yes
Mutual funds	Yes	Yes	Yes

Note: TIPS = Treasury Inflation-Protected Securities.

Source: Author.

and to inflation risks. Bank deposits, at least those covered by the U.S. government's deposit insurance, are not subject to credit risk and to the price risk. The banks that sell these deposits pay a premium to the government for the deposit insurance; congressmen debate whether the premiums are too high or too low. (Actually, they are both: they are too high for conservatively managed banks and too low for badly managed banks.) But these deposits are subject to inflation risk, and the real rate of return on these deposits is a nickel north of zero in the long run. And if you pay income tax on your interest income, the after-tax real rate of return often is negative.

Note the price risk: stock prices and bond prices vary extensively, and they have a lot of price risk. You might think there is no price risk with certificates of deposits, but the variation in interest rates over time is a price risk.

Consider the cumulative aggregate losses to Americans from the ownership of each type of securities in the long run or the very long run. In the long run, the price risk washes out; that is, the price increases and the price decreases are offsetting. Similarly, the price risk in stocks in the very long run is modest, since the data show that the price-earnings ratio averages about sixteen, and the price trend is upward as the economy grows and corporate earnings increase. The credit risk is large on high-risk bonds and individual stocks.

In the long run, the losses from inflation risk are much greater than those from the credit risk. And despite the cliché that stocks are an inflation hedge, the losses can be large as the inflation rate is accelerating. But once the inflation rate declines, interest rates are likely to decline and stock prices are likely to increase, as in the 1980s.

The implication of the institutional approach is that you are likely to find a portfolio of stocks more rewarding than of any other asset class, although if the price variability is too large in the short and medium runs, you might add some bonds to your portfolio to reduce the changes in your net worth. The primary reason you should slight the price risk is that it is smaller, the longer the period of observation. You will be drawing down your wealth over twenty or thirty years when you are in retirement.

Bonds are less risky than stocks (junk bonds are riskier than some stocks, and hence this statement is about bonds as a group rather than about individual bonds). The period-to-period changes in the prices of bonds are smaller than the comparable changes in the prices of stocks, in part because at the specified maturity dates the borrowers are required to purchase the bonds at their face value (or else they will be bankrupt) and in part because the borrowers are required to pay interest on a quarterly or semiannual basis.

The alternative approach is a "stocks-only" portfolio on the rationale that the increase in the rate of return of 1 to 2 percent a year over the bonds-only portfolio amounts to big bucks over twenty and thirty years. You believe that these changes in the market value of a stock portfolio from one month to the next and one year to the next "average out" in the long run and so the risk of a significant decline in your financial wealth from periodic declines in the value of stocks is low.

Individuals differ in their psychology and their tolerance for changes in the value of their accumulated savings. Bravura is not the name of the game. It is silly and uncomfortable to mimic the portfolio of someone who has a higher tolerance for risk.

One reason that there are both bonds and stocks on the menu is that corporations have realized that there are significant differences among investors, and they can reduce their own financing costs by recognizing and catering to these differences. Over time, the proportion of bonds and stocks that particular individuals want may change, partly because of changes in their financial circumstances and partly because of changes in the way they foresee market developments.

A third portfolio includes both bonds and stocks; its rationale is that the inclusion of stocks increases the rate of return above that on the bonds-only portfolio with a smaller increase in the risk associated with a stocks-only portfolio. Sort of a compromise—the bonds component of this portfolio reduces the risk of large downside losses, and the stocks component provides more upside potential than the bonds-only portfolio.

Once you've decided to include both bonds and stocks in your portfolio, you must determine their proportions in the portfolio. There's no scientific way to make this choice; some individuals will be more comfortable with a relatively high proportion of bonds, others with a much lower proportion. Moreover, individuals may change their views about the ideal proportions as they become more comfortable and more knowledgeable; you might increase the share of stocks in your portfolio as your accumulated savings increase.

The third portfolio raises a basic choice that centers on the "picker-timer" distinction. Should you hold the proportion of bonds and stocks more or less fixed, following a buy-and-hold approach, or should you instead alter these proportions in response to changes in the business cycle and the relative prices of bonds and stocks? Assume that initially you decide to allocate 50 percent of the prize money to buy bonds and 50 percent to buy stocks; as the economy expands, the market value for the stock component of your portfolio will more or less automatically increase. Should you rebalance your portfolio and sell stocks to return to the initial allocation?

The "picker-timer" distinction also applies to the bonds-only and stocks-only portfolios. The strategy of the pickers is "to buy and hold"—in the case of bonds until the maturity date and in the case of stocks until the end of time. One approach to this third portfolio is to hold more or less constant shares of both bonds and stocks. Changes in the relative prices of bonds and stocks would lead to changes in the market value of bonds in the portfolio relative to the value of the stocks, which would be the passive outcome of the changes in the relative prices of bonds and stocks rather than the result of purchases and sales of bonds and stocks. You would not actively rebalance the amounts of bonds and stocks in your portfolio in response to these price changes.

Figure 11.2
The Investment Decision Cube

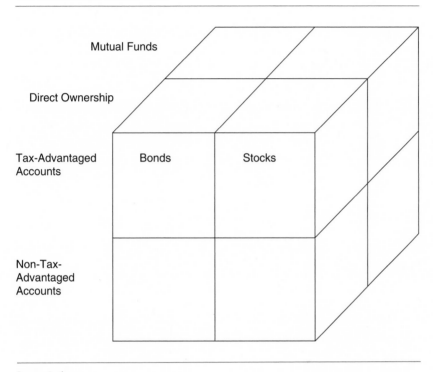

Mutual Funds

Direct Ownership

Tax-Advantaged
Accounts

Bonds   Stocks

Non-Tax-
Advantaged
Accounts

Source: Author.

In contrast, the timers would alter the proportions of bonds and stocks in their portfolios in anticipation of the changes in their prices. They would sell stocks and buy bonds toward the end of the business expansion; stock prices would then be high and bond prices low. They would sell bonds and buy stocks toward the end of recessions; stock prices then would be low and bond prices would be high. The timers would have to decide on the proportion of their portfolios that would be managed in this way.

Now introduce two more aspects of your portfolio choices: one is whether to own bonds and stocks directly or instead to buy mutual funds that own bonds and stocks, and the second is to distinguish between the securities you hold in your tax-advantaged accounts and those that you hold in non-tax-advantaged. (In a technical or legal sense you have two different portfolios, but conceptually you should integrate the securities in these portfolios.) Note the cube in Figure 11.2. The left column in the front of the cube is the bonds column, and the right column is the stocks column. The top row in the front of the cube is for tax-advantaged accounts, and the bottom row is for non-tax-advantaged accounts. Now note the depth dimension: the front half of the cube represents investment on your own, and the back half of the cube represents investment through mutual funds.

You'll have to make three choices at more or less the same time when you decide to buy securities: should you buy bonds or stocks, should you buy these securities in your tax-advantaged account or in an ordinary account, and should you buy these securities directly or should you use mutual funds?

You have eight basic choices:

1. Bonds, non-tax advantaged, direct ownership
2. Bonds, non-tax advantaged, mutual funds
3. Bonds, tax advantaged, direct ownership
4. Bonds, tax advantaged, mutual funds
5. Stocks, non-tax advantaged, direct ownership
6. Stocks, non-tax advantaged, mutual funds
7. Stocks, tax advantaged, direct ownership
8. Stocks, tax advantaged, mutual funds

Moreover, the mutual funds choice can be segmented into passively managed index funds and actively managed funds.

Remember that lottery prize money? Allocate as much of the prize money to the tax-advantaged accounts as you can. The more comfortable you are in your ability to achieve a diversified portfolio on your own, the smaller your need for mutual funds.

The Menu of Bonds

Now consider the extensive menu of bonds, initially from the point of view of completing the upper part of the template. (The next few pages are irrelevant if you decide to hold only stocks in your portfolio.) One way to group bonds is by the major types of borrowers. A further distinction is between tax-exempt and taxable bonds. Another grouping is the liquidity of the markets in which bonds are bought and sold (the more liquid the market, the smaller the transaction costs). A further distinction centers on the maturity of individual bonds.

An alternative approach to grouping bonds is based on their sensitivity to three major types of risks: credit risk, inflation risk, and price risk. Credit risk is the ability of the borrower to pay the interest on a scheduled basis; one or several of the credit rating agencies may downgrade the ranking of the bond, and its price may decline even if the borrower continues to pay the interest on a timely basis. The various credit rating agencies including Standard & Poor's and Moody's rank bonds using somewhat similar scorecards. Borrowers pay these firms because they want a high rating to reduce their interest payments.

The inflation risk is the likelihood that the purchasing power of the interest income and the principal repayment will decline as the U.S. price level increases, so that the real rate of return attached to owning the bond would decline below the nominal rate or, as in the 1950s, 1960s, and 1970s, become negative. (Note that many of those that owned bonds had to pay income tax on the interest income even though the real rate of return on the bonds was negative; both the pretax real rates of return and the after-tax real rates of return were negative and the real rates of return were negative by a larger amount.)

The price risk is that the market price of the bonds might decline in a rising interest rate environment. All bonds are subject to this risk. The prices of outstanding bonds decline so that the nominal rate of return on the previously issued bonds will be comparable to the higher nominal rates of return on newly issued bonds. The owners of the outstanding bonds then incur losses (which are realized only if they sell the bonds), and the holding period returns could be negative if the annualized rate of price decline is larger than the interest payments—as it was in the 1970s. At times a U.S. Treasury bond that will mature in twenty-five years—and then be exchanged for $1,000 on the maturity date—has sold for as little as $700 because the interest rates on these previously issued bonds were so much lower than the interest rates on newly issued bonds. The relationship is symmetric; if interest rates on newly issued bonds decline, the prices of outstanding bonds increase.

The losses due to the inflation risk and the price risk may occur together, since an increase in the anticipated U.S. inflation rate leads to an increase in the interest rate on newly issued bonds and hence the prices of outstanding bonds decline. If the anticipated inflation rate should decline, this price movement will be reversed. Eventually the price of the bond will return to $1,000 on the date that the bond matures.

When you buy a bond, you're buying a bundle of risks—and the question is whether these risks are overpriced or underpriced. One of your concerns should be whether the sensitivity of the bond to one or several of these risks is likely to increase, which would lead to a decline in the market price of the bond.

Three patterns are evident in the changes in bond prices. One is that interest rates on long-term bonds almost always are higher than interest rates on shorter-term bonds; the term is that the "interest rate yield curve is positively sloped." The second is that the interest rates on both short-term and long-term bonds increase over the economic cycle as economic activity expands relative to the productive capacity. (The interest rate yield curve is negatively sloped about 10 percent of the time, and at the peak of the business cycle when the Federal Reserve seeks to restrict the growth of credit.) Moreover, interest rates on short-term securities increase relative to interest rates on longer-term securities, and interest rates on riskier securities increase relative to those on less risky securities as the economy expands.

Glossary of Bond Market Terms

Agency issues   Bonds sold by government-sponsored agencies like the Federal National Mortgage Association ("Fannie Mae") and the Student Loan Group ("Sallie Mae").

Basis point   One one-hundredth of 1 percent in the interest rate on the bond. Twenty-five basis points equates to one-fourth of 1 percent.

Callable bonds   Bonds that can be redeemed by the borrower before the maturity date.

Call date   The first date at which the bonds can be called.

Convertible bonds   Corporate bonds that can be exchanged for a fixed number of shares at a specified exchange price after a particular date. Convertibles have some of the features of a bond in that the interest rate is guaranteed. They have the upside potential of a stock. Firms issue convertible bonds because the interest rates are lower than on a traditional bond. This "hybrid" security provides investors with the "best of both worlds" because there is the potential for large capital gains that would occur if the firms' stock prices increased, and the interest rates on the bonds means that the capital loss associated with the decline in the prices of the bonds is smaller than the capital losses that would occur with the stocks of the same firms.

Coupon The interest rate attached to the bond, as in the quarterly or semiannual interest payment.

Credit risk The likelihood or sensitivity that the borrower will default.

Duration The "average maturity" of both the interest payments and the principal repayment attached to the bond.

Inflation-protected bonds In 1997 the U.S. Treasury began to issue Treasury Inflation-Protected Securities (TIPS). The semiannual interest rates and the principal are adjusted upward to reflect increases in the consumer price level, and they would be adjusted downward if the consumer price level were to decline. The U.S. Treasury introduced this new security to reduce its borrowing costs in the belief that the "inflation premium" embedded in the interest rates of traditional bonds was too high. TIPS by definition are not subject to the inflation risk. Moreover, because the bond is an obligation of the U.S. Treasury, there is no credit risk. Finally, the price risk that is generally associated with bonds is smaller than with traditional bonds because of the periodic adjustment of the interest rate to changes in the consumer price level, though there remains a price risk associated with the cyclical movements in interest rates.

Inflation risk The likelihood or sensitivity that the consumer price level will increase more rapidly than anticipated at the time the bond was initially purchased.

"Junk bonds" A colloquial term for high-risk bonds, those that are judged too risky to be ranked as investment grade by the credit rating agencies. Junk bonds should be viewed as stocks with high dividends. "Fallen angels" are bonds that once had a credit rating but are no longer rated because the risk of default has increased. The term "high-yield bonds" is a euphemism for junk bonds.

Liquidity risk The likelihood or sensitivity that the terms on which bonds can be bought and sold change, which leads to changes in the costs of buying and selling bonds.

Maturity The number of years until the borrower redeems the bond at its face value.

Price risk The sensitivity of the price of the bond to changes in interest rates. The variability of the price of bonds that mature in the distant future is greater than the sensitivity of bonds that mature in the near future. The variability in the price of bonds that have a high credit-risk rating is lower than the variability of bonds that have a low credit-risk rating.

Tax-exempt bonds The interest income on bonds issued by state and local governments and their various subdivisions, such as school districts and toll highways and public power systems, is not subject to federal income tax.

Yield to maturity The average interest rate on the bond until the maturity date, which includes both the change in the price of the bond as well as the periodic interest payments.

Zero-coupon bonds Bonds that provide for the payment of interest income to the bondholder solely through the increase in their prices as they approach their maturity date. Borrowers were attracted to issuing zeros because they did not have to be concerned immediately with generating the cash to pay the interest. The investors were attracted because initially the interest income would be taxed at the rate on capital gains rather than the much higher rate on ordinary income (this feature of the zeros was terminated, and the owners were taxed as if they had received a cash interest payment). Another attractive feature was that the interest rate on the interest income could be locked in at the high prevailing interest rates. Zero-coupon bonds are subject to modestly larger price risks than traditional bonds, and as a result their yield to maturity generally is higher than the yield to maturity of a traditional coupon bond. The difference in these yields generally has been below fifty basis points—less than one-half of 1 percent. Their greater risk reflects that their average maturity is substantially longer, since a traditional bond pays interest twice a year. Since the timers seek the capital gain from the price appreciation of the bond, zeros offer the potential for a larger price gain—and loss— for a given change in the interest rate.

Relatively few government borrowers have defaulted, but many corporations have. Hurricane Katrina sharply eroded the tax base in New Orleans and nearby areas, and the owners of the bonds issued by the city and other local borrowing districts took a large loss.

The credit risk of the "agency issues" or bonds issued by entities chartered by the U.S. government—the GSEs, including the Federal National Mortgage Association ("Fannie Mae"), the Federal Home Loan Mortgage Corporation ("Freddie Mac"), the Federal Home Loan Bank system, the Government National Mortgage Association ("Ginnie Mae"), and the Student Loan Marketing Association ("Sallie Mae")—is uncertain. These firms are quasi-governmental; their charters provided some advantages in raising money in the capital market. Each firm is a private corporation, and the shares it issues (with the exception of the Tennessee Valley Authority) are traded alongside thousands of other firms. Fannie Mae and Freddie Mac went bust in the housing downturn, and their shares are no longer traded. These firms sell bonds to get the cash to buy home mortgages and student loans; the bonds are not backed by the "full faith and credit" of the U.S. government—at least not formally. But when push came to shove, the U.S. Treasury took measures so that the owners of Fannie and Freddie bonds did not incur a loss. The interest rates on these bonds often have been one-quarter of 1 percent to one-half of 1 percent higher than the interest rates on U.S. Treasury securities of the same maturity.

If one of the GSEs incurred large losses because of defaults on the mortgage loans that it owns, investors would become skeptical of its ability to redeem its bonds on their maturity dates, and the interest rates on the outstanding bonds would increase, perhaps higher than the interest rates that they would be earning on their loans. Many U.S. Congress members would lean on the U.S. Treasury to "bail out" the GSE with a loan or a loan guarantee because of the adverse impacts of a default on the housing market and on home building firms. Because of the likelihood that the U.S. Treasury would prevent a default, the investors are betting on a political risk.

The spread between the interest rates on TIPS and the interest rates on traditional U.S. Treasury bonds reflects investors' assessment of inflation risk. When investors believe that the inflation risk is high, TIPS are very attractive. If you think that the inflation rate is likely to average 3 percent a year and the interest rate on the traditional bond is 6 percent but the interest rate on the TIPS is 2 percent, you might decide to buy the traditional bond because the additional interest income of four percentage points would more than compensate for the anticipated inflation rate and the risk that the inflation rate could be higher. At the same time, other investors might decide that the additional four percentage points are too small.

One of the major empirical issues is whether the additional interest income associated with bonds that do not have the highest credit rating is sufficient to compensate for the losses that investors incur when the governments and firms that have issued these bonds go bankrupt. The initial argument for junk bonds in the 1980s was that the interest rates were exceptionally high relative to the losses incurred by holders of these bonds when the bonds tanked. Then there were large losses on junk bonds that overwhelmed the higher interest income that the owners of these bonds had previously earned.

The interest rates on TIPS can be considered as the benchmark, since they have no credit risk and no inflation risk, and consequently there is a smaller price risk. Investors can use TIPS as the basis for asking a series of pairwise comparison questions: "Is the additional interest income on a traditional U.S. Treasury bond worthwhile in terms of the inflation risk and the somewhat greater price risk?"and "Is a tax-exempt bond with the highest credit rating more attractive than a traditional U.S. Treasury bond with the same maturity?"

Initially the tests of the relationship between higher interest rates and default rates on junk bonds in the 1980s led to the conclusion that the buyers of junk bonds earned an "excess return"—that the additional interest income was more than the losses due to the occasional defaults. The massive defaults on the junk bonds in the early 1990s led to a sharp reversal in the relationship, and it became apparent that the buyers of the junk bonds had been "underpaid."

The same type of comparison can be made with the highly rated bonds. There may be a financial shock in the future greater than that experienced at any other time in the last fifty years, and some of the bonds not previously in default may be thrown into default.

Consider the following analogy. ABC Inc. sells flood protection insurance to the residents of New Orleans. Each resident pays an annual insurance premium of $100. For many, many years there are no floods; ABC Inc. builds up a large reserve against the losses that it will incur when the flood occurs. The residents want a reduction in their insurance premium because they believe they are being overcharged. Then a once-in-a-century flood occurs; the damage is massive, and the claims for losses are much larger than the reserves that ABC Inc. has built up. The company goes bankrupt. In retrospect it appears as if the premiums were too low, and the company should have been adding to its reserves year after year so that when a massive flood occurred, it would have had enough cash on hand to cope with the losses. Lots of other examples would make the same point: if an event that leads to very large losses occurs very infrequently, measuring the appropriate risk premium is extremely difficult.

Junk bonds have some of the characteristics of stocks. As long as the borrowers are able to pay the interest, the prices of these bonds are not likely to vary a great deal. Once there appeared a significant likelihood that the borrower might not be able to pay the interest on a timely basis, the prices of the junk bonds declined sharply, and in the post-bankruptcy corporate reorganization the bonds were exchanged for stock.

About the only time that interest rates on short-term bonds are higher than those on long-term bonds is when the Federal Reserve has been following a tough anti-inflationary monetary policy. The interest rate yield curve became inverted at the end of 2005; the previous episode when interest rates on short-term bonds were higher than interest rates on long-term bonds was in 1980 and 1981.

The Menu of Stocks

The menu of stocks is simpler than the menu of bonds because there are fewer legal distinctions among different types of stocks. There are thousands of stocks, and the companies differ by industry, history, and other characteristics, and yet the institutional features of the market are less complex—although the analysis of the firms that issue the stocks can be more complex because the array of risks is much greater. One significant institutional distinction involves the country where the firm is headquartered and incorporated; British Petroleum is headquartered in London, and yet it might be considered almost as American as ExxonMobil because more of its profits are earned in the United States than in Britain.

When you buy shares in a company, you become a partial owner of the firm. Your objective is to share in the "profits" of the company. Good news for the company is likely to be reflected in increases in the company's stock price and increases in your wealth as an owner of shares in the firm. As an owner of a company you can hope to be rewarded in two ways: the firm pays a dividend, and the stock price increases. You may also receive cash from the firm if it decides to purchase some of its outstanding shares and you sell your shares to the company.

On a busy day, investors trade more than 10,000 different stocks. More than 2,000 stocks are listed on the New York Stock Exchange; hundreds of other stocks are listed on the various regional exchanges in Boston, Chicago, and San Francisco and other cities; and 6,000 or 7,000 stocks are traded on the NASDAQ. You can buy several hundred foreign stocks that are listed on the New York Stock Exchange (the technical term is "cross-listed")—great companies like British Petroleum, Nestlé, Sony, Toyota, hundreds of smaller companies you have never heard of, and a few you never want to hear about.

Depository receipts representing the stock in several hundred large foreign firms can be purchased on the New York Stock Exchange; U.S. banks have bought the shares in these foreign companies and have issued the depository receipts that represent claims to a specified number of shares of each of these foreign firms. You also can buy the shares in these foreign firms directly, although you'll first have to buy the foreign currency.

Glossary of Stock Market Terms

Dividend earnings ratio   The ratio of the dividend per share to the share price.

Earnings-price ratio   The reciprocal of the price-earnings ratio.

Growth stocks   The stocks of companies whose anticipated earnings are expected to increase at an above-average rate.

Market capitalization   The total market value of all the company's shares, which is the product of the number of shares and the market price of the share.

Price-earnings ratio   The ratio of the price of the firm's shares to its annual or quarterly earnings.

Stock split   An increase in the number of shares effected by providing every shareholder with the same percentage increase in the number of shares.

Value stocks   The stocks of companies whose anticipated earnings are expected to increase at an average rate.

Stocks can be grouped in many different ways. A traditional grouping is between value stocks and growth stocks; the basis of this distinction is the anticipated rate of growth of sales of the company. Another grouping is by industry (energy, motors, housing, real estate, construction, banks, nonbank finance, biotech, information technology). Stocks can be grouped according to the country where the firms are headquartered, or they can be grouped according to the countries that account for most of their profits.

Return to the distinction between value stocks and growth stocks. Traditionally, value stocks are those of firms with established businesses that are able to "grow their profits" about as rapidly as the economy grows or slightly more rapidly. These firms usually are in humdrum, long-established businesses, often selling directly to consumers. Consumer demand increases at a steady pace, more or less at the rate of growth of U.S. GDP. The anticipation is that the earnings of companies that produce the goods and services that satisfy these traditional needs will increase at a comparable pace.

In contrast, the firms identified with growth stocks have developed a new good or service, and the anticipation is that for five or ten years their sales and profits will increase at a much more rapid rate than the growth of the economy.

In the 1920s General Motors, Ford, and Chrysler were growth stocks; many American families were buying their first cars, and hence auto sales and production were increasing more rapidly than the U.S. rate of economic growth. The profits of many of these firms were growing rapidly, and the auto companies were "capturing profits" from other American companies.

By the 1960s most American families already owned an automobile; the rate of growth of demand for autos had declined sharply and was only slightly more rapid than the rate of growth of the U.S. economy. The rate of growth of profits of the auto firms had declined sharply. The stocks of the auto firms had drifted into the value group—at least the stocks of those auto firms that had not become bankrupt.

The history of the stocks of automobile firms is typical of the stocks of companies in many other industries. When a company is considered a growth stock, investors pay a high price for its shares; the Wall Street buzz is that the firm's price-earnings ratio (the ratio of the price of a share of its stock to earnings per share) is high. As the anticipated rate of growth of earnings increases, the prices of the firms' shares increase, and the shareholders in these firms participate in large capital gains. At a later stage—perhaps twenty or thirty years later—these firms metamorphose into value firms; the rates of growth of corporate earnings slow, perhaps sharply, and the stock prices and the price-earnings ratios decline.

The price-earnings ratios for growth stocks often can be three to four times the ratio for value stocks.

Price-Earnings Ratios and the Growth Rate

One rule of thumb for investors involves the relationship between the growth rate of the firm and of its profits and its price-earnings ratio. Is the stock of a firm with a price-earnings ratio of twenty-five cheap or expensive? The dividend yield of this stock is likely to be low; for all practical purposes, it's zero. Whether the stock is expensive depends on the rate of growth of the firm's earnings and the opportunity yield that investors can earn on bonds and value stocks; if the yield on value stocks is 8 percent, then the earnings of the companies associated with the growth stock must increase at a rate in excess of 9 or 10 percent a year if the rate of return on the growth stock is to be more attractive than the rate of return on the value stock.

At some stage it is inevitable that growth stocks morph into value stocks. As more and more investors realize that this transition is inevitable, the prices of the individual growth stocks will decline. A debate exists about whether the rates of return on growth stocks are higher or lower than the rates of return on value stocks. Since many value stocks were initially growth stocks, the answer depends on when the reclassification of the stocks of individual firms from growth to value occurs. If the reclassification occurs soon after the growth rate slows, then the rates of return on growth stocks will be high and the rates of return on value stocks will be low.

One of the stylized facts is that the rate of return to the owners of stocks of small firms is higher than the rate of return to the owners of stocks in the large firms. The story is that the rate of growth of sales and profits of small firms—of the small firms that survive—has been larger than that of established large firms. Often the small firms are in new industries—those identified with new products and new processes for supplying some of the basic needs. This conclusion is subject to a large survivorship bias, since the rates of return on the small firms that did not survive almost certainly were negative, and if their returns were netted against those of the survivors, then the rate of return on the stocks of small firms would decline.

From time to time, the structure of a particular industry and the number of firms in the industry change sharply, perhaps because of changes in the regulatory framework or because of changes in technology. Banking and financial services, telecommunications, electrical generation and distribution, and airlines all have had rapid change. Mergers have been extensive. The rate of return from owning the stocks of the firms that are to be acquired—usually smaller firms—can be high.

Organizing Your Portfolio of Bonds and Stocks

Now that you've scanned the menu of bonds and stocks, you're going to have to fill in the details for the template. Figure 11.3 is virtually the same as Figure 11.1. The difference is that there are empty boxes next to each major heading. Your task is to fill in the values of the empty boxes in each column so they sum to 100 percent. The allocation of your funds in each column primarily will reflect your preferred trade-off between risk and return.

You'll note that as you move from column 2 to column 3, there are more boxes because there is greater detail. It's all important, but as you move to the right, the distinctions are smaller; in effect, the securities are closer substitutes for each other.

If you're puzzled, uncertain, or apprehensive, don't be too concerned. Be conservative—start with a relatively high proportion committed to bonds and a relatively high proportion committed to bonds that have high credit ratings. At this stage, don't worry about the distinction between tax-advantaged accounts and when the use of mutual funds is likely to be cost effective.

Once you've completed your assignment and have the target values for a top-down portfolio, your next step will be to see how closely the financial wealth that you have accumulated over the years matches the target values in Figure 11.3. In effect, sketch a comparable figure and initially leave the values in parentheses in the columns empty, and then estimate the values of the bonds and of the stocks that you own.

The sample diversified portfolio won't place you at the top of the get-rich-quick hit parade—more than half of your financial wealth is in bonds, and value stocks constitute the larger part of the stock portfolio. This type of portfolio would have weathered the storms of 2008 and 2009 reasonably comfortably.

Figure 11.3

A Sample Diversified Portfolio

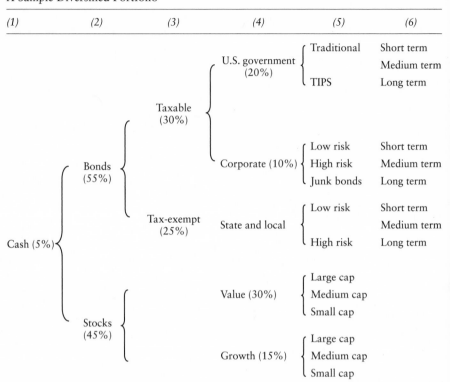

Note: TIPS = Treasury Inflation-Protected Securities.

Source: Author.

Make an inventory of your "assets" in the widest possible context. You need to decide those components of your wealth that have bond-like features and those are more nearly like stocks; set up a bond column and a stock column. As you approach the date of retirement, include your anticipated Social Security benefit, which is like a bond with an automatic adjustment for increases in the U.S. price level; the value of your monthly benefit will increase year by year as the price level increases. Include the value of your defined-benefit pension plan. You will have to determine whether the monthly benefit will increase as the inflation rate increases. If the monthly check will not increase, then put this plan in the bond column. If you own your home and other real estate, include these assets in the stock column. The odds are high that the market value of your home will increase as the price level increases, at least in the long run if not on a year-to-year basis. Include the value of the defined-contribution plan in your portfolio, and segment the bond and the stock components of these accounts.

The likelihood that there is a close fit between the values in the template and your own wealth is low. The next step is to figure out which securities you should keep and which you should sell because they don't conform to the template. Develop a plan to conform the shares of bonds and stocks in your portfolio to the template that you have developed over a two- or three-year period. One way to get greater conformity is to use the increases in your financial wealth to achieve your target values. If you're short bonds, then use some of the money you save each month to buy more bonds.

Managing the Bond Component of Your Portfolio

Once you have decided on the size of the bond component of your portfolio, you have three principal decisions. The first is the timing of the purchase of the bonds, the second is the bonds to be purchased and their maturity, and the third is the timing of the sale. If you are a picker, the third decision may be irrelevant, since your strategy may be to hold bonds until they mature. The timers would follow the maximum of buy low and sell high; they would buy bonds toward the peak of an economic expansion, when interest rates are relatively high and hence bond prices are low, and sell the bonds during recessions when bond prices are high and interest rates are low. Similarly, they would tend to buy somewhat riskier bonds because of their greater price variability.

You can be both a timer and a picker with different components of your bond portfolio; for example, you might conclude that you want 40 percent of the bond component to be in the timer group and 60 percent in the picker group. The basic decisions involve the selection of bonds to buy and the maturities of the bonds, and especially the credit risk attached to them.

You can buy bonds through your neighborhood stockbroker. You can also buy U.S. Treasury bonds and notes and bills from one of the twelve regional Federal Reserve Banks and avoid paying a broker's transaction costs. Similarly, on the maturity date, you can present your U.S. Treasury securities to one of the Fed offices for payment and avoid any transaction costs.

If you intend to be a timer, the choice of securities is straightforward: buy long-term U.S. Treasury bonds, especially the most liquid of these bonds and hence the bond that can be bought and sold with the lowest transaction costs. You anticipate that the major component of the return from your ownership of bonds will be from the increase in their price; you will be purchasing bonds at or toward the peak of economic expansion when their prices will be low because interest rates are high, and you'll hold the bonds for two or three years toward the bottom of a recession when interest rates are low and bond prices are high. You will also earn interest income during this period. Because of the frequency of transactions, you will want to own the most liquid bonds to minimize transaction costs. Buy traditional long-term U.S. Treasury bonds.

To the extent that you are going to be a picker, stay with the bonds that have among the highest credit ratings. Start with TIPS; your real rate of return is guaranteed. TIPS provide a useful benchmark or reference point, since there is no credit risk and no inflation risk and modest price risk. Once you have identified the interest rate—the yield to maturity on TIPS—and the yield on a traditional Treasury bond with the same maturity, you will need to decide whether the higher yield is worthwhile in terms of the inflation risk and the price risk and the tax implications.

You might earn a slightly higher interest rate if you buy bonds that are not at the top of the hit parade in terms of the credit rating, but part of the increased payment to you would be for the probable loss when and if the credit rating attached to these bonds declines. Let the pros and the mutual fund managers buy the riskier bonds.

One of your first bond purchase decisions involves the choice between taxable and nontaxable bonds—say, between traditional U.S. Treasury securities and the most highly rated tax-exempt bonds. Remember that tax-exempt bonds are far less liquid than Treasuries, so buy them only if you intend to hold them to maturity. Your concern should be whether the after-tax rate of return on the tax-exempt bonds is higher than on the Treasuries. Two factors are important in this comparison. One is the spread in interest rates between the two types of bonds, and the other is your marginal tax rate. The higher your marginal income tax rate, the more likely that the after-tax return on the tax-exempt bonds will be higher; the larger the spread in the interest rates between the two kinds of bonds, the more likely the after-tax return on the taxable bonds will be higher.

Developing a Laddered Maturity Structure of Bonds

You might "ladder the portfolio" of the bonds you buy to take advantage of the pattern that interest rates on longer-term bonds are higher than on bonds with shorter maturities. Once you have decided whether tax-exempt bonds are preferable to taxable bonds, you might divide your "bond budget" into four or five different segments by maturity. For example, you might commit one-fifth of this amount to buying a bond with a three-year term to maturity, another fifth to buying a bond with a term to maturity of six years, another fifth to buying bonds with a term to maturity of nine years, and so on. In this case the longest maturity would be fifteen years, and the average maturity would be seven and a half years.

When one of these bonds matures, you'd use the cash you receive from the borrower to buy another bond with a fifteen-year maturity. Once you have the ladder established, your interest income would be that on fifteen-year bonds even though the average maturity of the portfolio of bonds would be seven and a half years. There is no magic here—both the number of steps in the ladder or segments and the maturity are arbitrary. Find your own comfort level and stick with it.

Once you're comfortable with TIPS in your portfolio, you then can ask, "Is it worth the thirty or forty additional basis points of interest income to acquire U.S. Treasury bonds with their greater inflation and price risks?" The next question is, "Is it worth another thirty or forty basis points of interest income to acquire the bonds of Fannie Mae and Freddie Mac and other government-sponsored enterprises?" Their bonds are not inflation-adjusted. If inflation-adjusted bonds are attractive, you can move from TIPS to an inflation-adjusted corporate bond; you would then be increasing your exposure to credit risk.

First decide on the degree of credit risk that you're willing to accept. If you go from AAA to A bonds, you may be able to increase your rate of return by 0.5 percent a year on average relative to the rate of return on a U.S. Treasury bond of the same maturity. The rates of return on these bonds with a credit rating that's less than AAA increase relative to those on the least risky bonds during economic contractions, since the likelihood of default is higher during these periods.

If you're in a low marginal income tax bracket, then the after-tax rate of return on the corporate bond is likely to be higher than the interest rate on a tax-exempt bond. The additional return on top-rated corporate bonds ranges from 1 to 2 percent higher than the interest rate on U.S. Treasury bonds with the same maturity. In contrast, if you're in a very high marginal tax bracket, then the rate of return on the tax-exempt is likely to be higher. The "crossover point" between these two approaches generally is marginal tax rates in the range of 20 to 25 percent.

Your last decision is whether to buy the bonds directly or instead to buy shares in a bond mutual fund and allow the managers of the fund to make the investment decisions. If you follow the timer strategy, there is no reason to buy a mutual fund to deal with the credit risk, since you'll be buying U.S. Treasuries. Similarly, if you concentrate on TIPS, there is no need to buy a mutual fund.

You might consider a bond mutual fund if you're buying bonds other than those of top credit quality. The larger the risk attached to the bonds, the stronger the case for buying these bonds through a mutual fund, which will provide you with a share of a diversified portfolio of bonds and the use of a professional manager to select bonds. Remember that the owners of an actively managed bond mutual fund will take 30 or 40 percent of the increase in the rate of return on the higher-risk bonds; they get paid first regardless of whether you make or lose money.

The mutual fund route is likely to be more attractive the riskier the bonds that you decide to buy. You don't need a mutual fund to buy U.S. Treasury securities, and you don't need a mutual fund to buy the highest-grade corporate bonds or tax-exempts if you plan to hold them until they mature. In contrast, if you are reaching for the high rates of return on junk bonds, then diversification and selection provided by a mutual fund should be attractive. Remember that the increase in the average annual rate of return if you buy junk bonds might be three percentage points or 300 basis points and that you will be paying the mutual fund manager about one-third of this amount. The mutual fund manager always wins, whether you win or lose.

Even though you are not a timer, the implication of these cyclical changes in both the height of interest rates and the difference between short-term interest rates and long-term interest rates is that you might want to buy long-term bonds when the economy is at or near the peak of the boom and interest rates are high relative to their long-run trend.

Choosing the Stocks for Your Portfolio

The four basic decisions about the selection of stocks for your portfolio include the scope of diversification, the choice between value stocks and growth stocks, the choice among large-cap, medium-cap, and small-cap stocks, and whether to buy stocks directly or to buy shares in a mutual fund that acquires stocks.

First, a note about buying and selling stocks. You have three main avenues for these transactions: the traditional "wire houses" like Merrill Lynch and Wachovia Securities, discount brokers like Charles Schwab and Fidelity, and Internet firms like Datek. The cost differences are significant.

The closest stock market counterpart to the purchase of U.S. Treasury bonds is the purchase of the value stocks of firms that consistently produce growth in profits to match the growth of the economy—as long as these stocks are not too expensive relative to their earnings. These firms are likely to make multiple repeat sales to consumers year after year; the product might be toothpaste or beer or tires or bread or perhaps even insurance. These firms are marketing geniuses, and most are generous with their dividends.

If your portfolio template was that you would allocate $12,000 of the prize money to stocks, you might begin by buying about the same U.S. dollar amounts of ten or twelve value stocks from different industries. Choose the stalwarts of the U.S. economy—Procter and Gamble, General Electric, and Johnson and Johnson. You might buy one of the energy companies, including ExxonMobil and Chevron, but you're making a bet on changes in the price of energy. You might buy one of the large banks or financial institutions, but then you're getting exposed to large financial risks. These value stocks are well-established firms, and you don't need to pay a mutual fund to select the shares for you.

Be sure to diversify your purchases of value stocks among firms that are identified with eight or ten different industries. Begin by purchasing shares in one of the top firms in each of these industries; try to ensure that the market value of each of these firms is no greater than 15 percent of the total market value of the stocks in your portfolio.

Since you're buying stocks for the long run, the difference in the transaction costs is not likely to have a significant impact on your total return.

Managing the Growth of Your Accumulated Savings

Thus far the allocation of the lottery prize money has been the metaphor for your choices among bonds and stocks. In the real world, your savings will accumulate, perhaps at the rate of $100 or $200 or $300 a month. You've already decided on the shares of the monthly increase to allocate to bonds and to stocks and how extensively you will seek to time the market.

The amounts you save each month are likely to be too small to buy individual bonds and stocks without paying transaction costs that although low in dollar amount are high in percentage terms. Mutual funds and especially index funds can be very useful. Establish four index funds: a bond index fund for your tax-advantaged account, another bond index fund for your non-tax-advantaged account, a stock index fund for your tax-advantaged account, and another for your non-tax-advantaged account.

Each month allocate the cash that is available among these accounts. Then as you accumulate $3,000 or $4,000 in one of these accounts, withdraw the money and invest directly on your own. Your tax-advantaged bond account will have two components. One will be the index fund that receives the new cash each month, and the other is the group of bonds that you will have acquired directly. When you receive interest payments on these bonds, you will move the cash into the index fund and allow the balance in this account to accumulate until there is enough cash to buy a group of bonds.

Similarly, your tax-advantaged stock account will include both the stock index fund and the stocks that you own directly. Each month, part of the cash that you are setting aside will be allocated to the stock index fund; similarly, the dividend income that you receive on the stocks that you own directly in the tax-advantaged account will be allocated to the stock index fund. When the amount in the stock index fund accumulates so you can buy 100 shares of a particular stock, withdraw the money from the stock index fund.

The Andy Warhol Theory of Corporate Growth and Survival

Andy Warhol's quip that everyone is famous for fifteen minutes is likely to outlast his Marilyn Monroe portrait and perhaps even his Campbell's Soup Can series. His famous quote is the basis for the statement that "every firm is a leader for 15 or 20 years." Remember the Pennsylvania Railroad and the New York Central? For a long time Sears Roebuck was one of the leading retailers in the United States with its famous brands such as Kenmore appliances and Craftsman tools and Elgin bicycles. Schwinn was once the dominant quality bicycle manufacturer. Or consider Zenith in household electronics. Pan Am was one of the great international airlines. The corporate cemetery is full of once-great American firms that couldn't keep up their momentum for more than a generation.

A few firms—IBM, Hewlett-Packard, Xerox—have interesting second acts. But the number is small. When the growth rate slows, the firm more or less automatically "ages"; the average age of its labor force and of its productive equipment is likely to increase. Its costs are likely to increase relative to those of younger competitors. Firms fall behind because they can't maintain their share of profits—part of a much longer story. The significance of this life cycle view of the corporate universe is that a buy-and-hold strategy can be costly if you lose sight of the changes in the competitive marketplace.

The low-cost alternative to acquiring a diversified portfolio of stocks on your own is to buy shares in an index fund based on the S&P 500 index or some other broad market index. Or you might allocate part of your funds that you've decided to allocate to the stock component of your portfolio to an index fund for the growth component while you buy value stocks on your own.

After you become comfortable with value stocks, experiment slowly with growth stocks. You can buy growth stocks on your own; remember that they are riskier because each of these stocks eventually will molt into a value stock, and the perception that that change will occur often is associated with a sharp decline in the value of the stock. You want your portfolio to be diversified, but there is the risk that if you hold too many stocks your focus and attention will be blurred.

How Much Is a Financial Advisor Worth?

Distinguish two sets of decisions:one is a set of decisions about which bonds and stocks to buy and sell, and the other is the set of purchase and sale decisions. Often the two decisions are part of a package; an investment banker from Morgan Stanley or a broker from Merrill Lynch calls with a suggestion that you buy a particular bond or stock. The information and the transactions are packaged in a bundle. That's unfortunate—you want to be in a position to buy information at low cost and to minimize the costs of the security transactions.

The practice among the financial advisors is to charge a fee of 1 percent for steering you into mutual funds. The financial advisors sometimes will have a "box-like" diagram, with anticipated return on one dimension of the box and risk on the other. You will be asked whether you prefer high returns and high risk or lower returns and lower risk.

It's a pseudo science, probably designed to make you feel grateful that you're not being overcharged. It's pseudo because it assumes that the performance of the funds during the next year or two will be like that in the last year or two.

If you want to use a financial advisor, fine—but negotiate an hourly rate. Probably an hourly rate comparable to the rate that you pay your dentist.

Choose among the funds that are keyed to each of these indexes on the basis of their costs and fees and the turnover in their portfolios. Generally, the higher the frequency of turnover, the lower the rate of return.

You might buy shares in a small-cap fund or a medium-cap fund that specializes in growth stocks. Invest a relatively modest portion of the amount you have committed to stocks to these performance-oriented funds, and choose among them on the basis of management fees. Indeed, there are no significant advantages to you of having $10,000 or $20,000 invested in one mutual fund rather than spread around several different funds.

Develop a scorecard so you can readily track the rates of return on the index fund, the actively managed funds, and your own choices. If one or several of the performance-oriented funds deliver superior rates of return, then allocate a relatively larger amount of your financial wealth to this fund. But move money gradually from one year to the next, because there's a great deal of randomness in the performance of these funds from quarter to quarter. Minimize the frequency of your transactions; otherwise you'll increase the wealth of Merrill Lynch and Charles Schwab more rapidly than your own. Try to limit your turnover to 20 percent a year.

Continually compare the anticipated return on each of the stocks in the portfolio with the yield to maturity of the bond issued by the same firm. The bond offers a guaranteed interest rate (at least until the firm goes bankrupt) and a smaller price risk. The ratio of the dividend on the stock to the price of the stock is likely to be below the interest rate on the bond, and probably by a very large amount. The stock offers greater upside potential, but the stock price might fall sharply while the variations in the price of the bond are much smaller because the bond is "anchored" to its face value on its maturity date.

This is the way the world works.

In the long run, investment success involves identifying the firms that are able to increase their earnings at a consistent rate for an extended period. As the skills of the managers of these firms become more widely recognized, the prices of the shares of these companies are likely to increase relative to their earnings. At some stage the price-earnings ratios of these companies will become extraordinarily high relative to the rate of growth of their earnings. More and more investors will buy the shares of these companies because the share prices have been rising; these investors aren't really interested in the rate of growth of the firms' earnings.

Don't be greedy.

Investment Mantras, Silver Bullets, and Wise Guys

You can buy books about "systems" for leaving the racetrack at the end of the day with more money than you had before the first race. You can buy books about "systems" for beating the blackjack dealers in Las Vegas and Atlantic City, although you may be asked to leave the casinos if you are suspected of being a card counter. You can buy lots of books—good books, thoughtful books—about the systems that will enable you to achieve an above-average rate of return in the bond and stock markets. You can buy books that will summarize the investment success of stars like Warren Buffett, whose acuity as a stock picker at Berkshire Hathaway helped him amass the second-largest personal fortune in the United States.

The piles of money that can be made in the stock market are so large that there is an ongoing search for a formulaic approach that would provide above-average returns. (Remember that two events affect the rate of return on stocks in the long run: one is the increase in market values that reflects both the growth of the economy and the increase in corporate profits, and the other is the redistribution of wealth to those who are quick to anticipate changes in bond prices and stock prices from those who are less swift.) Investors are continually hunting for a silver bullet—a formula for selecting bonds and stocks that will lead to above-average returns. The personal finance shelves in our bookstores are replete with these stories of how "I beat the averages." It's as if each of the authors—all right, most of the authors—were in the top 5 percent in terms of realized rates of return. Having achieved financial success, the authors want the world to know that they are smart. The implication is that those who lose to the benchmarks aren't especially smart.

One view—the efficient market view—is that it's all a waste of time, that at each and every moment stock prices and bond prices fully reflect all available information about prospective market developments. The cliché is that no one leaves $100 bills on the table; if the prospective rates of return on one or several stocks are high, investors rush to take advantage of the anticipated high returns.

Charles Dow developed a technical approach to forecasting changes in stock prices (this is the same Dow who is memorialized in the Dow Jones index). This approach focused on changes in stock prices and the relation between the pattern of these changes and volume of stocks traded. If both the trading volume and prices increased at the same time, that was a bullish sign, a buy signal. In the nineteenth century, after the invention of the telegraph, the practice was known as tape watching; more recently it has been known as "momentum trading." The cliché is "The trend is my friend."

Dow looked at stock prices as the output of a process. The contrast with Dow's mechanical or technical approach was the fundamental approach associated with Benjamin Graham and his very, very rich student, Warren Buffett. The value investors focus on the growth of the earnings of the firms.

Another mechanical view is the "odd lot index." An odd lot is smaller than 100 shares. Wealthy investors buy stocks in round lots of 100 or 200 or more. Purchases and sales of stocks in lesser amounts are by smaller investors. Smaller investors are believed to "always get it wrong." Hence an investor could always make money by undertaking a pattern of transactions that is the mirror image of those of the small investors.

A third mechanical approach centers on "insider trading." Insiders—the top corporate managers—are presumed to know more about their firms' prospects than the general public. If the insiders are buying, it must be because they anticipate that some good news will become available that will lead to increases in stock prices. The reverse is true if they are selling.

The contrarian view is less distinctive, but the implicit assumption is that there is a mean reversion process at work in the financial markets. Some factors lead to waves of optimism and then pessimism that lead stock prices to deviate from their long-run trend or even equilibrium values. The contrarians believe that you can make money by betting against the market.

The development of low-cost computing facilities in the 1960s led to a rapid increase in the data on stock price movements. The result was the "efficient market view" that there is no pattern in the movement in stock prices, that "all the information is in the price," and that the stock market adjusts immediately and fully to new information. This led to more extensive testing of movements in stock prices. The implicit assumption was that investors as a group were rational, even though individual investors were not.

One study or set of studies concluded that two-thirds of the returns to stockholders were from the market effect, another 20 percent from the industry effect, and the remaining 15 percent from the firm effect. The market effect clearly is a macro phenomenon. The firm effect is the return to stock picking.

The paradox is that if there were a silver bullet, it would be imitated either slowly or rapidly, and the high return associated with the bullet would be competed away.

The market is efficient in the short run even though there are patterns in the long run. One exception is that the market does not immediately adjust to all the new information, in that the flow of information is serial rather than random. There are long swings in the changes in the inflation rate and there are long swings in the interest rates. Similarly, there are long swings in the growth of the economy.

Your choices among bonds and stocks should recognize the key factors in the behavior of the economy and in the way the markets operate and the psychological biases. In the long run the rate of return on stocks will be in the range of 5 to 6 percent a year and reflect the profitability of American firms. The rates of return will be higher than this range in some years and lower in others.

Globalization—the integration of financial markets and the goods markets in many different countries as a result of declines in cost of communication and information storage—has two principal impacts. One is to increase the range of bonds and stocks that are available to you. The other is that competition among firms is more intense, as is evident in the impact of the Japanese, German, and Korean automobile firms on General Motors and Ford.

So many strategies, so much success, so much wealth creation—or so it seems. The investment strategies do not create wealth; rather, they capture it. The stock market is a positive sum game; as long as the U.S. economy grows and corporate profits increase, the rates of return for stockholders as a group will be positive. All participants can make money, but only half of the participants can be above average. Strategies that work produce exceptional returns until a group of copycats or imitators mimic those who took the initiative, so that the strategy ceases to produce exceptional returns.

One possible approach is to divide your financial wealth into three pots of about the same initial dollar value. The first pot would consist of bonds that would be purchased, initially with the intent to hold the bonds until maturity. The second pot would consist of a low-cost stock index fund. The third pot would consist of your "active trading account."

The Dreams of Riches and Mental Traps

The plethora of books and articles on personal finance suggests that there is a strong desire to get rich—quickly. Individual investors are reluctant to accept that getting rich involves either a great deal of luck or slow and continuous accumulation of savings. Books and articles about the bonds and stocks assume that investors are fully and completely and always rational and that each participant always is fully rational. Yet many observations about investors' behavior suggest that they are not always fully rational.

One mistake that investors make is that they have no strategy—or, alternatively, they have a mélange of strategies. A second mistake is that investors buy bonds and stocks, but especially stocks, without an "exit strategy"—a date and a price target for when they will sell the security. Purchasing bonds and stocks is not an "until death do us part" commitment. Instead, the purchase of a security always should be coupled with a locked-in target date for when the security will be sold. The timers will purchase bonds with the intent to sell them when the economy slows and interest rates decline and bond prices rise, or to hold the bonds until they mature. The purchase of a stock should be accompanied with a rationale for why the price of stock will increase. The story might be that earnings will increase more rapidly than expected. Or the story might be that the price will rise because interest rates will decline.

Investors tend to believe that tomorrow will be like today. There is a universal tendency to extrapolate the recent trend of stock price changes, especially when stock prices have been increasing. When the economy expands, investors become more optimistic and more confident and they forget or downplay the fact that the prices of stocks of individual firms are tethered to earnings of those firms and that in the long run stock prices can increase no more rapidly than earnings. Greed was evident in the stock market bubble of the late 1990s, and thousands of investors ended up as greater fools because they had lost sight of the forces that were moving stock prices upward. Some investors tend to hold out for the "last dollar" and to ignore the fact that when stock prices decline, they decline much more rapidly than they increase. Increases in the prices of stocks in one's portfolio lead to a lot of confidence in the ability to select stocks when the increases were a matter of luck. Remember that in the bubble years of the late 1990s, the price-earnings ratios were more than twice their long-run averages.

The innate belief that a mean reversion process operates in asset prices means that many investors are reluctant to sell securities whose prices have declined below their purchase prices until their prices again increase to the purchase prices. Investors are reluctant to recognize losses—as if the losses are not real because they are "paper" until they are realized. Some asset prices will increase after they have declined; some won't. If stock prices decline, there is no reason to believe that they will increase.

Tax factors often intrude on sales decisions. Investors are reluctant to sell because they may have to pay capital gains tax. The capital gains tax eventually must be paid, except when the owner dies and the securities are transferred to the estate. It is possible that the capital gains tax rate might be reduced—although paradoxically now that the rate has been reduced to 15 percent, Congress may be more reluctant to reduce the tax rate further.

ACTIONABLES

1. Try to determine how risk averse you are and then decide on the allocation of your wealth between bonds and stocks. If you're in doubt, assume that you've been instructed that two-thirds of your financial wealth should be invested in stocks and one-third in bonds, and then experiment to determine whether you would be more comfortable with some other allocation.

2. View your portfolio of financial securities in a "global context" and include various pensions; determine whether these pensions should be included with the bond or the stock component of your portfolio.

3. Develop an approach toward determining when stocks are too cheap and when they're too expensive in terms of the prospective rate of return. At the beginning of each year or some other anniversary date, estimate the rate of return on stocks and bonds during the next twelve to twenty-four months.

4. Allocate the bond component of your portfolio among five or six different bonds. Include a TIPS and a traditional U.S. Treasury security. Identify your marginal income tax rate, and determine whether the after-tax rate of return on corporate bonds is higher than the rate of return on tax-exempt bonds in the same risk class.

5. Decide on one of the following approaches to the allocation of the stock component of your financial portfolio.

   a. One hundred percent in an S&P 500 index fund.

   b. Fifty percent in an S&P 500 index fund and 50 percent in a specialized index fund.

   c. Thirty percent in an S&P 500 index fund, 30 percent in a specialized index fund, and 40 percent on your own.

6. Diversify your holdings of stocks among eight or ten different value stocks.

7. When you're offered tips and inside information, ask whether the suggested investment fits into your model portfolio.

8. At the beginning of each year or some other anniversary date, review the securities in your portfolio to determine how well they are meeting your objectives.

9. Choose tax-efficient funds. Sell the mutual funds the day before the dividend distribution date.

Part III

FINANCIAL PLANNING

DECISIONS

12   An Overview of Financial Planning

Nearly everyone's central question about financial planning is whether there will be enough money, month after month, during the retirement years to maintain the desired standard of living. The fear is that you will outlive your assets. You need to prepare for a future that might include a severe period of inflation, uncertain and highly variable rates of return on bonds and stocks, sharp dips in real estate prices, and escalating health care costs.

The test of a successful financial plan is whether the end of a regular salary check will have a baneful impact on your spending. You want to be sufficiently confident about your financial future so you won't be in the large majority that fears they will outlive their assets.

For most individuals in their twenties and thirties, the prospect of retiring is far over the horizon. Yet unless they begin to save systematically, they will encounter a seemingly insuperable problem when they eventually become concerned about the adequacy of sources of funds in retirement because they then will need a dramatic increase in their saving to compensate for the much shorter period when they will be saving. The choice is between starting early and saving a modest amount of your income or starting late and being obliged to save a much larger share to achieve the same target.

The money available to Americans as they move into the retirement cohorts in their sixties comes from four major sources. Each year Social Security benefits total $400 billion, about 40 percent of retirees' total receipts. Employment-related pensions provide another 20 percent. Personal saving accounts for another 20 percent. Finally, about 20 percent comes from employment. Some people remain at work after reaching the traditional retirement age of 65 because they like their jobs. But most of those over age 65 who continue to work do so because they need the money. It's a safe bet that few of these individuals thought much about financial planning until a year or two before they retired.

The earlier in your working life that you develop your first financial plan, the better; you will then have a rough check on whether your savings are accumulating at a brisk enough pace that you'll have enough money to maintain your standard of living when you retire.

You should ask yourself three basic questions when you're in your late twenties and thirties to ensure a comfortable retirement:

1. What is my income likely to be at the time of retirement?
2. How much am I likely to spend each year when I am in retirement to maintain a comfortable standard of living?
3. Where is the money going to come from—how much from Social Security, how much from pension plans, and how much from my accumulated personal savings?

When you're in your thirties or even your forties, retirement may seem to be something that your parents and your older neighbors should worry about. But these are the years when you must project your salary and other sources of income ten or twenty or more years into the future. No easy task. Your income might double between the time you're 40 and the date that you think you might retire even after adjustments for increases in the consumer price level. The increases in your income will result from inflation, productivity gains in the economy, and your upward movement on a career ladder. (Increases in income because of inflation aren't likely to help because living costs are likely to increase about as rapidly as your income.) Then you're going to have to estimate the sources of funds that will be available to pay for the goods and services you'll want to buy.

These long-term projections are useful ballpark exercises, but they aren't rocket science; you won't be graded on your accuracy. Don't be put off by the inevitable forecasting errors; you'll know more about your financial future at the end of the exercise than at the beginning.

One major worrisome uncertainty centers on the likelihood of changes in the U.S. inflation rate. How will such changes affect the purchasing power of your pensions and accumulated savings? The U.S. price level in 2000 was nearly twenty times the level in 1900. Increases in the price level were episodic rather than slow and steady. The first episode occurred during and after World War I, the second during and after World War II, and the third in the 1970s. The percentage decline in the purchasing power of the U.S. dollar was larger in the last episode than the combined percentage decline in the first and the second episodes. This pattern of increasingly severe inflations is not especially comforting for those who will retire in the next twenty to thirty years.

The inflation rate lifts most prices and wages, but not always by the same percentage; there are winners and losers, and often the losers have been the retired because all or most of their incomes are fixed. You want to ensure that increases in the U.S. inflation rate won't make a big hole in your finances—a topic discussed in chapters 13 and 14.

There are three primary ways to achieve consistency between your living standard when you're in the active labor force and the quality of your life in the postretirement years:

1. Achieve a higher rate of return on your accumulated savings in both the preretirement and retirement years.
2. Increase the amount you save each year while you're still employed.
3. Delay the date of retirement (or phase in to retirement gradually by shifting to part-time employment for a few years).

Achieving a higher rate of return on accumulated savings sounds like the proverbial free lunch. If you are now earning a rate of return of 1 or 2 percent a year on your accumulated savings, you should be able to increase your rate of return without a large increase in risk; you will need to acquire some less liquid investments and take on somewhat more maturity risk. If, in contrast, you're now earning a rate of return of 4 or 5 percent after adjusting for inflation, it's going to be difficult to increase your rate of return significantly. If you've been earning a significantly higher rate of return, you should be writing books about investments and financial planning.

The flip side of a higher rate of return on bonds and stocks that you might buy is that the firms that have issued them must earn exceptionally high rates of return on their investments. There are relatively few industries with persistently high rates of return; if the anticipated rates of return on particular investments are high, so are the risks.

Your basic question is whether you can achieve a significant increase in the rate of return without a commensurate increase in the riskiness of the securities in your portfolio. The riskier these securities, the greater the likelihood of financial loss.

Michael Milken's Promise of a Free Lunch

One of the "hot investments" of the late 1980s was "high-yield bonds," a euphemism for junk bonds. The basic idea and the promise were that the rates of return on speculative bonds were exceptionally high relative to the risk of default and the losses that would follow from defaults. Initially, many of these speculative bonds had been downgraded by the credit rating agencies and were known as "fallen angels"; the agencies downgraded them because the operating profits of the borrowers were low relative to their scheduled interest payments. Once these bonds were no longer investment grade, regulations required that insurance companies, pension funds, and banks sell any of these bonds that they owned. The prices of these bonds fell sharply and the rate of return on the bonds increased.

Michel Milken, one of the major traders for third-tier investment bank Drexel Burnham Lambert, claimed that these high-yield bonds were a bargain because the rates of return were exceptionally high relative to the risk of loss. Drexel began to issue lots of junk bonds to assist in corporate acquisitions and leveraged buy-outs. The buyers of the bonds were attracted by interest rates that were three or four percentage points higher than those on investment-grade bonds.

The major question was whether the firms that had issued these bonds were sufficiently profitable so they would have the money to pay the interest on the bonds. In fact, the term "bonds" was a bit of a misnomer because in effect these securities were "stocks with very high interest rates."

Milken provided financing for some individuals that enabled them to acquire control of savings and loan associations and of insurance companies; these firms then became ready and willing buyers of some of the new issues of junk bonds that were being underwritten by Drexel. These savings and loan associations offered high interest rates on their deposits, which increased at a rapid rate. Individuals were comfortable acquiring deposits in these federally insured savings and loan associations because the U.S. government's Federal Savings and Loan Insurance Corporation guaranteed them against a loss.

Milken had developed a "perpetual money-making machine." Americans were attracted to the deposits of the savings and loan associations controlled by Milken's buddies because of the combination of high interest rates and the government insurance of the deposits. As the deposits in the savings and loan associations increased, the managers of these savings and loan associations bought more of the high-yielding bonds issued by the firms that were controlled by Milken's other buddies. Drexel earned big bucks from underwriting and trading these bonds. Moreover, Drexel established some mutual funds that specialized in acquiring junk bonds underwritten by Milken.

Milken made hundreds of millions for himself and his partners and for some of those who profited from the acquisitions and buy-outs. But in the end, the junk bond market collapsed. The losses to the holders of these bonds were immense and dwarfed their previous gains from higher interest rates. More than a third of the firms whose junk bonds Drexel had brought to the market imploded. Many of the savings and loan associations that Milken had nurtured failed, and the U.S. government and the American taxpayers were on the hook for several tens of billions of dollars to bail them out. The junk bond episode proved to be a very expensive free lunch for most of those involved—especially for those who in their innocence or greed had believed the sales pitch. Milken went to jail for several years and paid a penalty of more than $500 million, but he remains one of the wealthiest people in the country.

Another way to achieve a higher rate of return is to acquire mutual funds with low costs and fees; the lower these fees, the more rapidly the value of your mutual fund shares will accumulate. You might be able to increase your annual rate of return by 1 to 1.5 percent if you buy low-cost index funds. Moreover, if you invest on your own rather than use a mutual fund, you can avoid these fees altogether; you might be able to increase your rate of return by several tenths of 1 percent.

Delaying the date of retirement is the default option. Each year's delay increases the money available to you in each of the years when you retire by 6 to 8 percent, primarily because the value of your accumulated savings will compound for one more year; if these savings are invested in bonds, then your total accumulated savings might increase by 4 or 5 percent a year for each additional year that you own the bonds. Moreover, you will contribute to your employment-related pension for one more year, which might add one to two percentage points to your accumulated savings. Finally, delaying your retirement by one year reduces the length of your retirement period by about a year, and so you can spend your capital at a slightly more rapid rate. When you're 70, your life expectancy is about twenty-five years; when you're 80, it's sixteen years. The later you begin to "eat your capital," the more rapidly you can eat your capital.

How much do you need to save? That depends on how well you want to live in your retirement years. The "replacement ratio" centers on the relation between your preretirement income and the money you will need in retirement to maintain a comparable living standard. First estimate the amount you will need each month to maintain your desired living standard, and then determine the capital sum that you will need when you retire to ensure that you will have the desired amount in each of the subsequent years.

The replacement ratio often is estimated at 65 to 75 percent of your current income. When you retire, some of your taxes and expenses will be lower. You won't pay Social Security taxes when you stop working; for many individuals that equates to 6 percent of their preretirement income. You won't have commuting and other employment-related expenses. You won't need to save for retirement. You'll buy fewer durable goods—automobiles and refrigerators and TV sets; similarly, your annual spending on new clothes and home decoration will be lower. You are less likely to have educational expenses and other costs associated with children. You may have fully paid off your home mortgage; if not, you may be able to refinance the mortgage so the monthly payment is lower—perhaps significantly lower. But you'll have more time to travel and to shop—and you might develop an expensive hobby.

Note two additional aspects of the replacement ratio. If you had a lot of employment-related travel while in the active labor force and you like to travel, you may spend an above-average amount on plane fares and hotels in the first several years after you retire—and all of that money will be your own.

Moreover, your year-by-year spending in retirement changes as you move along the life cycle. When you're in the 75- to 85-year-old age cohort, your annual expenditures on travel are likely to be lower than in the previous ten years. You'll also spend less on food and clothing.

A Cookbook Approach to the Replacement Ratio

The simplest approach to estimating the cash you will need in your early retirement years is to assume a value for the replacement ratio, either 65 or 75 percent. An alternative approach is to use the data from your current spending to estimate the amount you will need—but that assumes that you have these data or could construct them from the information in your checkbook, your income tax returns, and your credit card bills.

Use tables 12.1 and 12.2 to help you figure out how large your accumulated personal savings should be on the eve of retirement; the figures are identical except that the replacement ratio is 65 percent in Table 12.1 and 75 percent in Table 12.2. The columns in both figures are different values for your preretirement income.

You can use these figures when you're in your forties and fifties to help you understand your financial circumstances when you reach age 62, 65, or 70. The first step is to estimate your annual income at the time of retirement; then find the column that is closest to that income. Or you can create your own column, and then proceed from row 1 to row 2 and on to the subsequent rows.

Estimates of the income needed for several different values of preretirement income are shown in row 1 of tables 12.1 and 12.2. For example, assume that you project that your annual earned income on the eve of retirement will be $75,000. If your replacement ratio is 65 percent, you will need $48,750 (note this value is the cell in row 1 of the $75,000 column in Table 12.1) to maintain the same standard of living. If instead you estimate your replacement ratio will be 75 percent, you will need $56,250, which is the value in row 1 of the $75,000 column in Table 12.2.

The values in row 2 in both tables show the estimate of the annual benefits from Social Security for each of these levels of income for a married couple that begins to receive benefits at age 65. These values for each level of preretirement income are the same in tables 12.1 and 12.2. These values are the benefit payments for 2006 and were obtained from the benefits calculator on the Social Security Web site (http://www.ssa.gov). One assumption is that Humpty Dumpty was born on December 1, 1941, and will retire in November 2006, and a second assumption is that Humpty Dumpty is married and that the benefit to Mrs. Dumpty is 50 percent of the benefit to Humpty. (If instead both Mr. and Mrs. Dumpty had paid Social Security taxes and had approximately the same incomes for the

Table 12.1

Preretirement Income and Replacement Income (65 percent replacement ratio)

				Preretirement Income				
	$25,000	$40,000	$50,000	$75,000	$100,000	$125,000	$150,000
1. Replacement (65%)	16,250	26,000	32,500	48,750	65,000	81,250	97,500
2. Social Security	14,364	19,044	22,158	29,196	32,778	34,938	35,298
3. Defined-benefit pension	8,750	14,000	17,500	26,250	35,000	43,750	52,500
4A. Difference (1 − [2 + 3])	−6,864	−7,044	−7,158	−6,696	−2,778	2,562	9,702
4B. Difference (1 − 2)	1,886	6,956	10,342	19,554	32,222	46,312	62,202
5A. Price of an annuity	NM	NM	NM	NM	NM	30,744	127,525
5B. Price of an annuity	23,575	86,950	129,275	244,425	402,775	578,900	777,525
6A. Price of a perpetuity	NM	NM	NM	NM	NM	51,240	204,040
6B. Price of a perpetuity	37,720	139,120	206,840	391,080	644,440	926,240	1,244,040

Notes: The calculator on the Social Security Web site was used to determine the annual Social Security benefit for an individual who was born on December 1, 1941, and plans to retire in November 2006. The estimate of the monthly value was adjusted to an annual value and increased by 50 percent on the assumption that the worker had a spouse who had not qualified for Social Security benefits. The "A" rows are relevant for those with defined-benefit pensions; the "B" rows are relevant for those without defined-benefit pensions. NM = not meaningful.

Source: Author.

Table 12.2

Preretirement Income and Replacement Income (75 percent replacement ratio)

	Preretirement Income						
	$25,000	$40,000	$50,000	$75,000	$100,000	$125,000	$150,000
1. Replacement (75%)	18,750	30,000	37,500	56,250	75,000	93,750	112,500
2. Social Security	14,364	19,044	22,158	29,196	32,778	34,938	35,298
3. Defined-benefit pension	8,750	14,000	17,500	26,250	35,000	43,750	52,500
4A. Difference (1 − [2 + 3])	−4,364	−3,044	−2,158	804	7,222	15,062	24,702
4B. Difference (1 − 2)	4,386	10,956	15,342	27,054	42,222	58,812	77,202
5A. Price of an annuity	NM	NM	NM	10,050	90,275	188,275	296,525
5B. Price of an annuity	54,825	136,950	156,650	338,175	527,750	735,150	952,775
6A. Price of a perpetuity	NM	NM	NM	16,080	144,440	301,240	474,440
6B. Price of a perpetuity	87,720	219,120	308,640	541,080	844,440	1,176,240	1,524,440

Notes: The calculator on the Social Security Web site was used to determine the annual Social Security benefit for an individual who was born on December 1, 1941, and plans to retire in November 2006. The estimate of the monthly value was adjusted to an annual value and increased by 50 percent on the assumption that the worker had a spouse who had not qualified for Social Security benefits. The "A" rows are relevant for those without defined-benefit pensions; the "B" rows are relevant for those with defined-benefit pensions. NM = not meaningful.

Source: Author.

same number of years, the value of their combined Social Security benefits would be 33 percent higher than those shown in row 2.)

These estimates of Social Security benefits assume that you have had
an income comparable to the one in this column for thirty-five years and
have contributed to Social Security during each year. For each year less
than thirty-five, adjust this estimate downward by 3 percent.

If you want to retire at age 64, adjust the estimate of the Social Security benefit downward by 8.33 percent. (You'll learn a lot about Social
Security in the next chapter.)

The values shown in row 3 are estimates of income from defined-
benefit pensions and are assumed to be 35 percent of preretirement income for those who have this type of pension—obviously some individuals
will have larger pension incomes and many will have smaller ones. About
40 million Americans have defined-benefit pension plans, including most
government employees. A defined-benefit pension plan is like Social Security; the employer has guaranteed to provide you a monthly check based
on the number of years of employment and your average annual income
or perhaps your average annual income during the last three or five years
you were employed. (Defined-benefit plans are front-page news, as many
U.S. steel companies and airlines and auto parts companies have gone
bankrupt; the companies are no longer able to pay the pensions that they
promised. The responsibility for paying their pension benefits has been
taken over by the U.S. government's Pension Benefit Guaranty Corporation; see the discussion on this agency in Chapter 14.) The estimate of the
dollar value of these pensions is a "soft number" and an average for millions of retired individuals. Individuals who have served thirty years in the
U.S. armed forces receive a pension that is two-thirds of their highest pay.
Public school teachers might receive a benefit of 40 percent of their highest annual salary, although this percentage differs greatly among states
and cities. Most of those with relatively low annual incomes are not likely
to have a defined-benefit pension.

If you are associated with a firm that has a defined-benefit plan, you
should be able to obtain an estimate of your annual income in retirement
from the employee benefits or human resources office.

Increasingly, U.S. firms are shifting to defined-contribution pension
plans. The major difference is that the employer carries the "investment
risk" with a defined-benefit plan and the individual carries this risk with
a defined-contribution plan. The good news is that individuals' pension

assets now will be more fully diversified and the likelihood of a severe shock to the standard of living is smaller. The bad news is that the individuals now have to make their own pension decisions and those decisions can be complex. If you have a defined-contribution pension plan such as a 401(k), then the amount of your pension will depend on your cumulative contributions and those of your employers, together with the rates of return on the securities in your plan.

The values in row 4A are relevant for those with defined-benefit pension plans and are the difference between the values in row 1 of the estimates of the amounts needed and the sum of the values in rows 2 and 3 of income from Social Security and the defined-benefit pension. The values in row 4B are relevant for those without a defined-benefit pension; these values are the difference between rows 1 and 2. The estimates of the money needed in rows 4A and 4B must be supplied from the combination of employment-related pensions and accumulated personal savings, lottery prizes, and part-time work in the retirement years.

Note that for those with incomes in one of the columns on the left of both figures, the income from Social Security and employment-related pensions is higher than the estimates of the income needed. The differences in the values in this row reflects that the ratio of Social Security benefits to preretirement income is nearly 60 percent for those with a preretirement income of $25,000 and 15 percent for those with a preretirement income of $150,000.

The values in row 5A are estimates of the prices of an annuity that would provide the cash shown in row 4A for a married couple at age 65; similarly, the values in row 5B show the price of an annuity that would provide the cash shown in row 4B for the same married couple. An annuity is a contract offered by an insurance company that promises to pay you (or you and your designated beneficiary) a specified amount of dollars each year as long as you (or you and your beneficiary) live. Payments stop after the deaths of the owner and the beneficiary. This estimate of the value of the annuity can be considered a target value for your accumulated savings on the date of retirement including your investments in your 401(k) plan and other tax-advantaged accounts.

The assumption is that an annuity that you purchase when you are age 65 will pay eight percent of its face value to both you as the owner and your beneficiary, which is a combination of the rate of return that is embedded in the annuity and the return of part of the funds that you provided the seller of the annuity at the time of purchase. In the first several years more than half of the payment to you will be investment income; as you age, this component declines and an increasingly large share becomes the return of your savings.

Each of the next several chapters deals with one of the major rows in these figures. The next chapter centers on Social Security benefits; your major decision will be whether to begin to collect benefits when you reach 62 or to delay receiving benefits until you reach 65 or 70. The higher your age when you first begin to receive benefits, the larger the monthly payment; in effect, the increase in the monthly payment reflects both the interest income on the funds that you might have received but delayed receiving and a longevity bet that the Social Security Administration made that you may not be around to collect the benefits. The subject of Chapter 13 is the design of a plan for the continuous and gradual accumulation of your savings; one aspect of this plan is to make effective use of tax-advantaged savings programs promoted by the U.S. government. The focus of Chapter 14 is the management of wealth in the retirement years with particular attention to whether you should buy an annuity.

One of the major questions you are going to have to answer is whether you want a "buffer." The replacement ratio approach provides an estimate of how much money you are likely to need if all the pieces fall neatly into place. But there is little margin for error. What happens if there is another surge in the U.S. inflation rate or you must absorb an exceptional health cost? You may decide that you want a 10 or 15 percent margin so you won't have to worry that you will run out of money.

The values in rows 6A and 6B show the price of a perpetuity that would provide the cash associated with rows 4A and 4B, respectively. The distinctive feature of a "perpetuity" is that annual interest payment continues until the end of time; the market value of the perpetuity changes inversely as market interest rates change. If these interest rates decline, the market value of the perpetuity increases. You can bequest the value of the perpetuity to your children or your favorite charity.

You may wish to create your own column if your preretirement income is higher than $150,000; your Social Security benefits will be identical with those in the column on the extreme right. If your preretirement income is between two of the columns, then interpolate; for example, if the preretirement income is $60,000, then you will need $45,000 with a replacement ratio of 75 percent and the annual Social Security benefits will be between $20,376 and $21,576—say, $21,000 as a ballpark estimate.

Once you've identified the appropriate column, work your way down the rows. For instance, you might want to modify the estimate of the retirement benefits from Social Security to reflect that you will not have worked thirty years.

Determine whether you are likely to receive a defined-benefit pension, and, if so, insert your best estimate of the amount in row 3; then revamp the values in row 4A. Once you have a value for row 4A or 4B, multiply that value by 12.5 to get the estimates for row 5A or 5B and by 20 to get the values for row 6A or 6B.

Retirement at Age 55 or 50 or 45

The idea of retiring at age 45 or 50 is immensely attractive to many—sail around the world on your own yacht, start an ostrich farm or an alpaca ranch, study musical composition. All that it will take is money. Note that you won't be able to receive Social Security retirement benefits until you reach age 62 (you can receive disability benefits when you're younger—but only if you are disabled). If you withdraw funds from an employment-related pension before you reach age 59½, the Internal Revenue Service will ask you to pay a 10 percent penalty—and you'll have to pay income tax on the money received.

The annual payout of an annuity with a given face value is lower the younger you are when you first begin to receive the annuity check (because the company that sold you the annuity must make these payments to you for a longer period). The implication is that the younger you are when you expect to receive the first payment under the annuity, the higher the price of the annuity. The difference in the price of the annuity reflects that the capital sum of the annuity will be withdrawn over a longer period, and so the amount of the annual reduction in this capital sum is smaller. The excess of the price of an annuity that will begin to provide payments to you at age 55 over one that will begin to provide payments at age 65 is modest, since most of the payment in the first several years is the investment income. Your life expectancy when you are age 55 is about thirty-five years, and your life expectancy when you are age 65 is twenty-five years.

Develop a Database

You can move beyond the cookbook approach to estimating your annual cash needs in the retirement period by projecting expenditures during this period based on estimates of your current living expenses.

It will be helpful to have some estimates of the amount you now spend each year. That amount will be close to your annual income, but the two might differ because you are repaying various loans and because you are saving 5 or 10 or 15 percent of your income.

You might estimate your living costs in one of several ways. You might be able to use the data from your current budget—if you have one. If you're like most Americans and don't have a budget, take your monthly paycheck and subtract Social Security tax payments, mortgage loan repayments, and other payments that reduce your indebtedness or add to your savings.

Your database should include a personal balance sheet—a list of your assets and how much you owe. Be sure to include the cash value of life insurance policies and the balances in your various retirement accounts. Include the outstanding balance on your mortgage loan.

The data sheet should include pension fund benefits you can expect to receive. Government pensions including Social Security are defined benefits, and the amount you can expect to receive is loosely related to the amount you have contributed.

ACTIONABLES

1. Develop a family financial statement. Estimate the values of your assets and liabilities.
2. Project your accumulated savings for five, ten, and fifteen years into the future.
3. Develop a record of your expenditures.
4. Develop a database of numbers of bank accounts, life insurance policies, auto insurance policies, and other important information.

13   Your Social Security Benefits
Could Be Worth $300,000

In 2007 50 million people—U.S. residents as well as nonresidents—received almost $585 billion from the U.S. Social Security Administration (SSA), which is by far the largest pension program in the world. About 80 percent of the SSA's payments are benefits for retirees and for dependents of those who died before reaching the full retirement age of 65, and nearly 20 percent are made to workers who have become totally disabled before reaching the full retirement age. Social Security benefits provided nearly 60 percent of all of the income received by individuals who were 65 and older, and these benefits were 90 percent of the total income for one-third of those receiving benefits. The average monthly payment is slightly less than $1,000.

Virtually all Americans other than those who work for the federal, state, and local governments are required to participate in the Social Security program. Nearly 100 million individuals pay Social Security taxes. In 2007 these taxes totaled $775 billion, so the U.S. government's "profit" from this program—the difference between the cash received from taxes on workers and employers and the cash paid out in benefits—was $190 billion; the profit in 2006 had been $140 billion. Because taxes have exceeded payments for more than twenty years, the balance in the Social Security trust fund is over $2.4 trillion. Because of this surplus, the U.S. Treasury did not need to raise taxes or borrow more to get the money to pay congressional salaries and for military hardware and farm subsidies.

The U.S. government established the SSA in 1935 to reduce the number of aged poor by providing pensions to retired workers age 65 and older. The cash for these pension payments would come from dedicated taxes—sorry, contributions—on the active members of the labor force and on their employers.

This U.S. initiative followed the development of similar government-sponsored pension programs in other industrial countries. Governments loved to establish pension programs because they appeared to be "doing good" for both the aged and the poor—a "two-fer." Moreover, these programs were immensely "profitable" in their first sixty or eighty years because the cash collected from the taxes on the employed was more than the benefits paid to the elderly retired and other beneficiaries.

When the U.S. Social Security program was established, twenty-five individuals paid Social Security taxes for each individual who received benefits. In 2000, five individuals paid Social Security taxes for each individual receiving benefits. The ratio of those paying in to those receiving benefits will continue to shrink as the American population ages.

Taxes received by the SSA have exceeded the benefits paid in every year since the program was established. Each year the excess of the taxes collected over benefits is allocated to the Social Security trust fund. Moreover, each year this fund is credited with interest income based on the value of the U.S. Treasury securities that it owns and the average interest rate on U.S. Treasury securities.

The Social Security trust fund isn't listed in the Washington, D.C., telephone book. It doesn't have any employees or an address. It's an accounting entry for the difference between the taxes received and imputed interest earned on the accumulated "profits" and the benefits paid.

Because the U.S. government treats the trust fund as a real entity rather than a fictitious one, the federal debt outstanding has been overstated since the 1930s. Similarly, the annual fiscal deficits of the U.S. government have been overstated because of the failure to recognize the excess of Social Security taxes received over benefits paid as a net receipt. (Note that it wouldn't make any difference if there were a real trust fund that bought U.S. Treasury bonds with the excess taxes received over benefits paid; in this case, the U.S. Treasury would issue more bonds.)

Your primary concern should be how to make the most of the benefits you're entitled to as a result of the Social Security taxes that you've

Table 13.1
Delayed Retirement Credits

Year of Birth	Yearly Rate of Increase	Monthly Rate of Increase
1933–1934	5.5%	11/24 of 1%
1935–1936	6.0%	1/2 of 1%
1937–1938	6.5%	13/24 of 1%
1939–1940	7.0%	7/12 of 1%
1941–1942	7.5%	5/8 of 1%
After 1942	8.0%	2/3 of 1%

Source: Data from Increase for Delayed Retirement, Social Security Online, http://www
.socialsecurity.gov/retire2/delayret.htm.

been paying for the last fifteen or thirty years. Initially, the "Normal Retirement Age" (NRA) was 65. Subsequent legislation provided that individuals could begin to receive a reduced benefit at a younger age— when the NRA was 65, they could receive 80 percent of the benefit at 62. The normal retirement age is being raised at the rate of one month for every two calendar years. If you delay receiving Social Security benefits after you reach the NRA, you will receive delayed retirement credits (DRCs); the monthly benefit is higher once you begin to receive benefits. The values of the DRCs for those born in different years is shown in Table 13.1. If you were born in 1940 and begin to receive benefits in 2010, when you turn 70, the monthly benefit would be 35 percent higher than the benefit you would have received if you had first received benefits at the NRA because of the DRCs.

Your principal decision about Social Security is whether you will be better off if you begin to receive Social Security benefits when you reach the NRA or instead when you reach age 62 or 63, or whether instead you should delay receiving Social Security until you reach age 66, 68, or 70.

Social Security: Insurance or Welfare?

A persistent question is whether the U.S. Social Security program is an insurance program or a welfare program masquerading as an insurance program. The answer is not quite either/or. To the extent Social Security is an insurance program, the benefits that each individual receives would be directly related to the taxes that this individual paid. The ratio of benefits to taxes would be similar for those with high incomes and for those with low incomes. To the extent that Social Security is a welfare program, the ratio of benefits to taxes would be significantly higher for those with relatively low incomes.

Each participant in the Social Security program—both those with higher incomes and those with lower incomes—has received more in benefits than he or she has paid in Social Security taxes, and hence the real rate of return on Social Security taxes has been positive for all participants. (Only those who have not worked the minimum number of forty calendar quarters required to qualify for Social Security benefits forfeit their payments.)

The Social Security program has several features that do not have counterparts in an insurance program managed by a private firm. Thus the ratio of benefits received to taxes paid is higher for individuals with relatively low average annual incomes than for those with higher incomes. When the Social Security program was established in the mid-1930s, some individuals then age 64 began to receive benefits that would last a "lifetime," even though they paid Social Security taxes for only one or two months. No private company selling annuities would ever provide benefits so large relative to the amounts paid to buy the annuities. Social Security benefits are "taxed" for those in the 62–65 age range if their annual wage and salary incomes exceed an earnings limit stipulated by the SSA. No private company selling an annuity could ever reduce the benefits paid if individuals continued to work, although the SSA then recalculates and pays a higher benefit for subsequent years. The benefits received by married couples are 50 percent greater than those received by a single individual even though their tax payments may have been the same.

The insurance aspect of the Social Security program reflects that the monthly benefit depends in large part—but not exclusively—on the cumulative Social Security taxes paid. The higher your annual income and the more Social Security taxes you paid, the larger the monthly benefit in the retirement years. Moreover, the more years you paid Social Security taxes, the larger the monthly benefit—although benefit payments peak once you've paid Social Security taxes for thirty-five years.

Payment of additional Social Security taxes will not lead to an increase in the benefits that you will receive.

The ratio of monthly benefits received to taxes paid is four times higher for those with annual incomes of $25,000 than for those with annual incomes of $100,000 and reflects that under the Social Security program, the rate of return on the Social Security taxes paid by those with lower incomes is higher than the rate of return for those with higher incomes. Analysts rely on these data to conclude that those with higher incomes subsidize those with lower incomes. But the individuals in the higher income groups live longer and collect benefits for more years, and hence there is at least a partial offset.

Consider the following experiment to measure the scope of Social Security as a welfare program. Alter the benefits paid to each recipient so that the ratio of benefits to taxes paid is identical for those in the high-income brackets and those in the lower-income brackets—without leading to any change in the aggregate ratio of taxes to benefits for the program as a whole. The benefits to those in the lower-income brackets would decline, while the benefits to those in the high-income brackets would increase. Those with annual incomes in the range of $35,000 to $40,000 would be more or less unaffected by the experiment. The dollar amount of this transfer under the experiment would be several tens of billions a year. The benefits to those in the lower-income groups would decline by this amount, or by about 10 to 15 percent. Because the amount of this transfer under the experiment seems reasonably small relative to the total benefits, Social Security is best described as primarily an insurance program with a nontrivial welfare component.

That's the end of the experiment—but not the end of the story. Assume that benefits paid were proportional to taxes across all income brackets. The number of elderly poor would increase. These individuals and families would receive more of other government benefits, and the taxes to finance these payments would be drawn from those in the upper-income brackets. Social Security taxes are "regressive"—the tax is a larger percentage of the incomes of those in the lower-income groups. In that sense, one motive for the adoption of the Social Security tax may have been to develop a mechanism so that the working poor would be taxed to subsidize their elderly parents.

Why Social Security Won't Go Broke

Newspaper headlines often sound the alarm that Social Security is going to go "broke" in fifteen or twenty years because benefit payments are increasing more rapidly than Social Security taxes. Other headlines note that Social Security has been a bad investment for those who have paid taxes.

If Social Security is going broke, then those who are collecting benefits have found a bonanza relative to the taxes they have paid, and the program will have been a good investment for those already collecting benefits and for some of those who will collect benefits in the future. If instead Social Security has been a bad investment for those who pay Social Security taxes, then the program isn't going broke because benefits have been low relative to taxes paid. The intermediate case that Social Security has been a bad investment and yet isn't going broke might be tenable if the administrative apparatus of the program were extremely costly, but these costs have been very low.

As the American population ages in the next several decades, the number of retired people who receive benefits will increase relative to those in the active labor force. The program's annual "profit" for the U.S. government will decline. Some projections indicate that by 2019 benefits paid each year will be as large as taxes. (Virtually all projections of what will happen ten and fifteen years in the future should be viewed skeptically.) Once benefits exceed taxes, the general view is that the SSA will draw money from its large holdings of government securities in the trust fund, which will sell some of the "securities" to the U.S. Treasury to get the cash to pay the retirees. The U.S. Treasury then would have to borrow more from the public to get the cash to finance the expenditures of the U.S. government.

In 2005 the Bush administration proposed that individual Americans "own" their own Social Security accounts. The thrust of the proposal changed from time to time, but one idea was that individuals might be able to have a portion of their Social Security tax payments directed to the purchase of stocks. The rationale was that since the rate of return on stocks was higher than the rate of return on bonds, the Social Security trust fund would be less likely to face a cash shortage because it would earn a higher rate of return on its investments.

The U.S. Treasury can obtain cash in two ways when Social Security benefits paid exceed Social Security taxes received. It can raise other taxes relative to government expenditures and payments, or it can borrow more in the financial markets.

There is no stack of cash in the trust fund, there never was, and there never will be. If the trust fund sells its "bonds," the U.S. Treasury's choices are to raise taxes and to borrow more from the banks and the public.

Of course the SSA might cut benefits or the projected rate of growth of benefits. This distinction is important; cutting benefits would lead to a rapid turnover in the U.S. Congress and a large number of its members would be in the job market. In contrast, cutting the rate of growth of benefits would solve the program's future financial problem.

As the annual surplus of taxes over benefits declines, Social Security taxes will be increased relative to benefits in one of several possible ways.

Since the Social Security program was established in the 1930s, the NRA has been 65. The first way to increase taxes relative to benefits is to delay the NRA, which already is scheduled to increase to 67 in a step-like fashion for those born after 1937. Thus if you were born in 1938 or thereafter, the age at which you will qualify for full benefits will increase by two months each year so that the NRA for those born in 1943 will be 66; these individuals will pay Social Security taxes for one more year without a corresponding increase in annual benefits—although they may live longer. The retirement age can be increased further.

The second way to increase taxes relative to benefits is to raise the ceiling—$106,800 as of 2010—on the amount of annual wage and salary income that is subject to the Social Security tax. This ceiling is indexed to changes in the consumer price level and increases as the price level increases. At some stage the ceiling will be increased even as the price level remains unchanged, which will increase the Social Security taxes paid by those with higher incomes without any increase in their benefits. One estimate is that raising the cap to $120,000 would lead to an increase in tax revenues that would close two-thirds of the projected gap.

The third way to increase taxes relative to benefits is to increase the share of Social Security benefits that is included in taxable income. Initially Social Security benefits were not included with taxable income (the rationale was that individuals already had paid income tax on the wages that were also subject to the Social Security tax). Now up to 50 percent of these benefits are included in taxable income for those with modest incomes; up to 85 percent of benefits are included in taxable incomes for those with incomes above $34,000 a year. The income taxes collected on these benefits revert directly to the SSA.

The fourth way to increase taxes relative to benefits is to reduce the component of the Medicare payments that is financed by Social Security taxes—which means that other taxes will be increased to finance Medicare payments.

The fifth way to close the gap is to alter the formula for indexing increases in benefits over time. Now benefits are indexed to increases in real wages; until the early 1980s, the increase in benefits had been indexed to the consumer price level. Price-level indexing would lead to a less rapid increase in benefit payments than wage-level indexing. One proposal that has received a lot of favorable attention involves altering the indexing formula so that those with higher incomes have their benefits indexed to the increase in the consumer price level and those with lower incomes would have their benefits indexed to the increase in the wages. The benefits to those in the lower-income groups would increase more rapidly.

Determining Your Social Security Benefits

The SSA is a bare-bones operation. There is a very small chance of an error in the calculation of your monthly benefit, so it can be helpful to know how your benefit is determined. But there's a lot of detail in this section, and you may wish to go directly to the section that deals with when you should begin to receive these benefits.

Your monthly benefit payment from Social Security reflects four principal factors: the Social Security taxes you paid while employed, the number of years you paid these taxes, your marital status, and your age when you first begin to receive benefits. The SSA follows a complex formula in calculating benefits.

The SSA begins with your income up to the cap on taxable earnings for each year you paid taxes, up to and including the year in which you turned 59 years old. The ceiling on taxable wages for different periods is shown in Table 13.2.

Then the SSA adjusts actual earnings to reflect increases in wage rates prior to the year you reach age 60, in a procedure known as indexing. The SSA then computes your actual earnings up to the maximum taxable earnings for each year for the years after you reach age 60 and the year you begin to receive Social Security benefits; these earnings are not indexed to changes in the consumer price level. The result of these three

Table 13.2
Social Security Ceiling on Taxable Wages

Period	Ceiling
1937–1950	$3,000
1950s	3,000–4,800
1960s	4,800–7,800
1970s	7,800–22,900
1980s	25,900–48,000
1990s	51,300–72,600
2000–2010	76,200–106,800

Source: Data from Increase for Delayed Retirement, Social
Security Online, http://www.socialsecurity.gov/retire2/delayret
.htm.

steps is that the SSA has a record of your annual earnings that is partially
indexed to changes in the consumer price level.

The fourth step is that the SSA drops or excludes those years when
your earnings were relatively low to obtain the thirty-five years of your
highest earnings. If you entered the labor force when you were age 21
and retired at age 65, you probably paid Social Security taxes for forty-
four years—but the SSA drops nine of the years of your lowest earnings.
If you have less than thirty-five years of actual earnings, no years are
dropped.

The fifth step is that the SSA adds the total earnings for the best
thirty-five years and divides by the number of months in these years. If
you paid Social Security taxes for thirty-five or forty years or forty-five
years, the divisor is 420. If you paid taxes for thirty years, the divisor is
360. The result of this division operation is your Average Indexed Monthly
Earning (AIME).

Once the SSA has determined your AIME, it computes your Primary
Insurance Amount, or PIA. The PIA is calculated by summing the "replacement rates" for three different ranges or segments of the AIME,
where the term "replacement rate" is the SSA's version of the replacement
ratio noted in Chapter 10.

Social Security has a replacement rate of 90 percent for monthly values of the AIME up to $437, a replacement rate of 32 percent for monthly
values of the AIME between $437 and $2,635, and a replacement rate of
15 percent for monthly values of the AIME between $2,635 and $3,926.

Table 13.3
Determining the Monthly Primary Insurance Amount

(1) AIME Range	(2) Size	(3) Replacement Rate	(4) (4) = (2) × (3)
$437 (or below)	437	90%	$393.30
$437 to $2,635	2,198	32%	703.36
$2,635 to $3,926	1,291	15%	193.65
Total primary insurance amount			$1,290.31

Source: Data from 2010 CCH Social Security Benefits Including Medicare (Chicago: Wolters Kluwer, 2010).

The values of $437 and $2,635 are known as "bend points." The SSA then adds the dollar values for each of these segments to obtain the PIA for those who paid the maximum tax for thirty-five years, as shown in Table 13.3.

Assume Jack Spratt has an AIME of $400. The replacement rate is 90 percent, and the primary insurance amount—the basic monthly benefit check if Jack is unmarried—is $360 a month: $400 × 90 percent. If Jack is married, Mrs. Spratt would receive a benefit payment of $180 a month.

Assume Dawn Sky has an AIME of $2,000 a month. The replacement rate is 90 percent for the first $437 and 32 percent for the next $1,563, so the PIA is $393.30 + $500.16 = $893.46. If Dawn is married, Mr. Sky would receive a monthly benefit of $446.73.

Assume that Snow White has an AIME of $3,500 a month. The replacement rate is 90 percent for the first $437 and 32 percent for the next $2,198 and 15 percent for the next $865, so her PIA is $393.30 + $703.36 + $129.75 = $1,226.41.

Marital Adjustments

If you're married and begin to receive Social Security benefits at age 65, your spouse will receive annual benefits equal to 50 percent of the primary insurance amount shown in Table 13.3—even if your spouse never paid any Social Security taxes.

Now consider the case when both spouses have had somewhat similar employment histories—comparable salaries for a comparable number of years and hence comparable Social Security tax payments. Moreover, the salary histories and Social Security payments are comparable to those in the previous several paragraphs. Both husband and wife have their own PIA. Each spouse will receive Social Security benefits based on the PIA, so the total to this family is one-third larger than the payment to the couple in the previous paragraph.

If there is a large disparity in the employment histories and Social Security taxes paid by a husband and wife, the spouse with the lower PIA will receive benefits equal to 50 percent of the benefits paid the other spouse. (In effect, the rate of return on the Social Security taxes paid by the spouse with the lower income would be zero.)

One last point: one spouse can begin to receive benefits based on his or her own PIA while the other spouse continues to work.

To Retire: 62, the NRA, or 70?

Your primary decision about Social Security is whether to begin to receive benefits at age 65, or at some other age between 62 and 70. (The Social Security program won't pay a retirement benefit to anyone younger than 62, and there is no payoff in the form of an increase in the monthly benefit to delay receiving benefits once you reach 70.) The longer you delay asking for the first payment, the larger the monthly benefit for as long as you live. The benefit payments stop when you die, or, if you have a spouse, the benefit payment is likely to be reduced when one of you dies.

Two narrow financial factors bear on your decision. The first is that if you begin to receive benefits at age 62, your annual benefit is reduced by 20 percent for all future years. (The formula is a reduction of five-ninths of 1 percent for each month for up to thirty-six months before age 65.) The second is that if instead you delay receiving benefits after reaching age 65, you then receive DRCs that range between 6 and 8 percent a year, depending on the year you were born. These credits increase the monthly payment to you. If you were born in 1935 and 1936, these credits are 6 percent for each year after you reach the age of 65; if you were born in 1939 and 1940, these credits are 7 percent for each year. If you were born in 1943, these credits are 8 percent. For example, if you were born in 1943 and begin to receive benefits when you reach age 70, the monthly benefit will be 40 percent more than if you had begun to receive benefits when you turned 65.

Your choices for when you can begin to receive benefits can be considered as follows. Assume you would receive $1,000 a month if you began to receive benefits at age 65; this benefit payment continues as long as you live. You would receive $200 less per month if you begin to receive benefits at age 62 than if you began to receive benefits at age 65.

During the three years between ages 62 and 65, you would receive $28,800 (which is the product of thirty-six monthly payments of $800 a month). If you die when you reach age 66, you clearly were better off to have begun to receive benefits at 62, since you would have collected $28,800 and received a benefit that was $200 a month smaller for twelve months after you turned 65.

If you had started to receive benefits at age 65, you would have received $1,000 a month and hence $60,000. During the five years between ages 65 and 70, you would receive $60,000 (the product of sixty monthly payments of $1,000). If you were born in 1943 or later and decided to delay receiving benefits until you reach age 70, the monthly benefits will be 40 percent greater.

The choice between receiving benefits beginning at age 65 or at an alternative age, perhaps 62, can easily be assessed. Assume that if you begin to receive benefits at age 65 you would receive $1,000 a month—$12,000 a year. But if instead you choose to receive benefits at age 62, your benefit payment is 20 percent smaller, $800 a month or $9,600 a year.

Assume you begin to receive the benefits at age 62 and you send the benefit check to a dedicated savings account at ABC Bank. By age 65, you would have accumulated $28,800. At this stage, assume that you earn no interest on this account. Then after age 65 you begin to draw on these accumulated savings in this dedicated account to make up the difference between the $1,000 you would have received had you waited until age 65 to receive the benefit check and the $800 a month that you are actually receiving; each month you draw $200 from the dedicated savings account at ABC Bank—$2,400 a year.

Note one complication in this comparison. Each year, your monthly Social Security benefit is likely to be increased because the monthly payments are indexed to increases in the money wages of those in the active labor force; in recent years this increase has averaged about 2 percent a year. Thus, although you will receive $800 a month during your sixty-second year, you are likely to receive $816 a month during your sixty-third year and $832 a month during your sixty-fourth year if the adjustment factor is 2 percent a year.

Once you reach age 65, you will begin to withdraw a bit more than $200 a month from the dedicated account to make up for the difference between the monthly benefit that you will be receiving and the monthly benefit you would have received if instead you had waited until you turned 65 to receive benefits. For example, assume that the benefit payments have been increasing at the rate of 2 percent a year. Had you delayed receiving benefits until reaching age 65, your initial monthly benefit would have been $1,061; however, because you chose to receive benefits when you turned 62, your monthly benefit would be $849 when you turn 65. Hence you must withdraw $212 a month from your dedicated account to be in the same financial position you would have been in had you waited until age 65 before receiving benefits.

The amount you need to withdraw from the dedicated account will increase each year. At some stage, you will have withdrawn all the money from this account; call this stage the "crossover age." The crossover age depends on the interest rate on the money you parked in the dedicated account. The higher the interest rate on the funds in this dedicated account, the higher the crossover age. If the interest rate is zero, the crossover age is 77. If you should die before reaching the crossover age, your heirs are better off because of the funds you banked beginning at age 62. When you're 62, the odds are high that you will live to be 77. The implication is that the mortality-adjusted crossover age in a zero interest rate world is probably in the low eighties—that is, you would only be worse off if you began to receive benefits at age 62 if you lived to push 90. But remember, the initial assumption was that the interest rate on the funds in the dedicated account was zero.

Now assume that the funds in this dedicated savings account earn interest; the higher the interest rate, the larger the accumulated balance in this account when you reach age 65. When you reach 65, you begin to draw the same $212 a month from the dedicated account; each year, the amount you withdraw from this account will be higher. Two factors affect the balance in your account: one is the monthly withdrawal to compensate for the difference between your monthly benefit and the amount of the monthly benefit if you had first received benefits at age 65, and the other is the compounding of interest on the money in your dedicated account. The higher the interest rate, the higher the age before the accumulated balances will be exhausted, and hence the higher the crossover age.

The inference is that you should begin to receive benefits at the earliest possible age. You may trigger a 50 percent "tax" on benefits because Social Security has an annual earnings limit for those who receive benefits at ages younger than 65, but eventually you will recover this tax.

A similar experiment can be performed comparing retirement at age 65 and at age 70. If you are scheduled to receive $1,000 a month in retirement benefits at age 65, you would receive $1,400 a month in retirement benefits at age 70 if you were born after 1943. Assume that you receive $1,000 a month at age 65 and place the funds on deposit in the bank; each year your accumulated balances will increase by $12,000 if the interest rate is zero. By the time you reach 70, you will have accumulated $60,000. The higher the interest rates on the funds in the dedicated savings account, the larger the accumulated balance in this account when you reach 70.

When you reach 70 you will begin to withdraw funds from the dedicated account to make up the difference between the benefit that you have been receiving since age 65 and the benefit that you would have received if you had delayed receiving benefit payments until 70. If the annual index factor is 2 percent a year, the first monthly payment would be $1,546. If instead you had begun to receive benefits at age 65, the benefits payment factor would have increased to $1,104. You would then begin to withdraw $442 a month from the dedicated account to compensate for the difference between the two amounts. Each year the amount you would withdraw from this account would increase slightly.

The value of your dedicated savings account would then reflect two factors. One is the amount of the monthly withdrawal to compensate for the difference between the benefit you are receiving and the benefit you would have received if you had delayed receiving benefits until you reached age 70. The second is the interest rate on the funds in the dedicated savings account.

The higher the interest rate, the higher the crossover age. Again, if you die before reaching the crossover age, the funds in your dedicated savings account are part of your estate.

Again, the implication is clear. The delayed retirement benefits may seem generous, but they are a bargain for Social Security. Even with the dramatic increases in longevity, relatively few readers of this book will live to be 124 years old.

Social Security's "Earnings Limit"

One SSA provision that has been carried forward from the 1930s is the "earnings limit," which is sometimes called the "retirement earnings test." This idea probably was adopted to induce individuals to stop working so their jobs would be available for others. If you begin to receive Social Security benefits before you reach age 65 and you earn more than $11,200 a year in wages or salary, then each additional dollar of earned income leads to a 50 percent reduction in a dollar of Social Security benefit. If you earn more than $22,400, then your Social Security benefits are taxed at the rate of 100 percent. (Initially, the earnings limit applied to those age 65 and older; this limit was abandoned a few years ago.)

However, any Social Security benefits that are withheld because of this earnings limit are adjusted once you reach the NRA so that the lost benefits are recovered. One implication of this earnings limit is that some individuals may decide not to work once they have reached the annual earnings limit. Another is that some individuals who might have begun to receive benefits at age 62 or 63 delay doing so until they reach 65.

ACTIONABLES

1. To obtain estimates of your future Social Security benefits, call the SSA at (800) 772-1213 and ask for the earnings and benefits estimate form. Completing this form takes just minutes. After you return the form, the SSA will send you a record of your Social Security tax earnings on a year-by-year basis, the Social Security taxes you have paid, and estimates of your future Social Security benefits. Husband and wife should submit separate benefit forms if each has paid Social Security taxes.

2. Be sure that both husband and wife have paid Social Security taxes for the minimum necessary to qualify for benefits. If not, arrange for part-time employment so that both achieve this target.

3. Remember that one spouse can receive benefits while the other remains employed.

4. Write your Congress members urging that Social Security be modified to increase actuarial fairness in the following ways:

   a. Increase the value of Delayed Retirement Credits.

   b. Abolish the earnings limit for those younger than 65.

   c. Index the earnings for the years after age 59.

   d. Revise the formula for determining the AIME so that benefits will be based on all years of covered employment rather than the thirty-five years with the highest wages.

   e. Abolish Social Security taxes on those older than 70 who remain employed.

5. Finally, if your income needs are large while you are retired and you and your spouse have paid comparable amounts in Social Security taxes in the working years, consider a divorce; the subsidy from the SSA to the elderly who "live in sin" can be as large as a third of their benefits.

14 If You Don't Know How Much to Save for Retirement, You Won't Save Enough

Sometime in your twenties you move into the accumulation stage of your life. Initially, much of the increase in your wealth consists of "real assets"—an automobile, a home, furnishings, and appliances. And you may be paying down educational loans. As you enter your thirties and forties, a larger share of the increase in your wealth will consist of bank deposits, bonds, stocks, shares in mutual funds, and the cash value of life insurance policies. You may have made some real estate investments. The value of your future Social Security benefits increases year by year, and the value of your employment-related pension will increase. Despite the shift toward defined-contribution plans, more than 40 million individuals still have defined-benefit pension plans.

When you retire, you'll be living off your savings rather than off wages and salaries, which may be disconcerting. How well you'll live depends on the amount of your accumulated savings. Most of the money you'll need to pay for your day-to-day living costs in retirement will come from your Social Security benefit, pensions, the income on your accumulated savings, and the value of these savings as you sell some mutual fund shares, bonds, and stocks. The major question when you're in your thirties, forties, and fifties is whether your pension and savings will increase rapidly enough so you will have a glorious retirement. You won't know the answer unless you develop a target for the value of your accumulated savings when you retire.

The great Yogi Berra had it right when he said, "If you don't know where you're going, you'll end up someplace else." The odds are high that if you haven't figured out how much accumulated savings you will need about the time you plan to retire, you'll have much less than you need. To reduce the likelihood that you'll have to become a part-time bagger at the local supermarket, you need a savings program that will track the increases in your personal savings and employment-related pensions so you can compare them with the target values for your accumulated savings as you move along the life cycle.

An effective savings program has three components. First, you need to construct a framework based on the "arithmetic" among four variables: the value of your accumulated savings today, the target values for your accumulated savings when you retire, the rate of return you can expect to earn on your savings as they accumulate, and the number of years until you retire. This framework will help you determine both the target for your accumulated savings at the time of retirement and whether you're on track to achieve this goal at various points along the life cycle.

Second, you need to figure out how you can best use "tax-advantaged" programs that the U.S. government has developed to encourage you to save. The benefit of these accounts is that the interest, dividends, and capital gains are not taxed when earned. If you use one of these programs, you'll park your savings in a "dedicated account" offered by banks, mutual funds, and brokerage firms. Some of these programs provide that the transfer of funds to the tax-advantaged accounts reduces taxable income; in this case the funds withdrawn from these accounts are taxed when the withdrawals occur. Other programs provide that the funds withdrawn from these accounts are not taxed; in this case there is no deduction from taxable income when the funds are transferred to these accounts.

The third component of the savings program involves personal stratagems and gimmicks designed to increase the share of your income that you do not spend. Saving involves delayed gratification. The thrust of Chapter 2 is that there are many ways to reduce the out-of-pocket cash costs of household items and auto transportation. Chapter 3 highlighted the importance of increasing your credit score and minimizing your interest payments. For many people, saving is like dieting; it is often easy to delay the starting date and hope you will be able to catch up. To manage an effective savings program, you must have annual and monthly savings targets, and you need to become accustomed to "paying yourself first"—or at least to moving money into a savings account immediately after you write the monthly checks for the mortgage and property taxes. Some consumption expenditures must be postponed if you don't have enough money for both your savings objective and the mortgage payment.

The Arithmetic of Your Personal Savings Program

Consider first the arithmetic of your savings program—remember the mantra of time-consistency between the target value for your accumulated savings at the time of retirement, the rate of return you can earn on your savings, your current accumulated savings, and the amount you must save each year to meet your savings target. The logic of your personal savings program is straightforward. Start with an estimate of how much you'll need each year to maintain your standard of living in retirement, and then calculate how much will be available from Social Security—revisit tables 12.1 and 12.2. The difference must come from your employment-related pensions and accumulated personal savings.

If you conclude, for example, that you will need $50,000 a year in retirement and that you will receive $20,000 a year in Social Security benefits, you will need an additional $30,000 from employment-related pensions and accumulated personal savings. When you are age 65, an annuity that would provide $8,000 a year would cost $100,000; you would need $375,000 to buy an annuity that would provide $30,000 a year. (See Chapter 15 for a discussion of annuities and their pros and cons.) When you are age 65, a perpetuity that would provide $5,000 a year also would cost $100,000—and you would need $600,000 to buy a perpetuity that would provide $30,000 a year. Once you have decided how much you will need to supplement your Social Security benefit payments and your employment-related pensions, it's a straightforward matter to determine how much you will need to buy an annuity or a perpetuity or some combination of both.

Powerball Lottery, Future Values, and Present Values

Once or twice a year, the newspaper headlines read, "Jack Benny has won $400 million in the Powerball lottery." These headlines are misleading and deliberately so; the story has been written by the flacks who work for the agencies that want to sell more lottery tickets. Jack didn't win $400 million; instead, he won an immediate payment of $20 million and payments of $20 million on each of the next nineteen anniversary dates.

Remember that a dollar today is more valuable than a dollar a year from today; if the interest rate is 5 percent, then the value today of a dollar a year from now is just a fraction more than 95 cents. Similarly, a dollar two years from today is worth just slightly more than 90 cents. The receipt of $20 million this year is more valuable than the receipt of $20 million a year from now, and similarly, the receipt of $20 million a year from now is worth more than the receipt of $20 million two years from now. The difference between the $20 million today and $20 million a year from now depends on the interest rate you use to discount next year's $20 million receipt. Assume that you use an interest rate of 5 percent. Then the $20 million receipt a year from now is worth $19 million today, and the $20 million receipt due in two years is worth $18.1 million today. Once an assumption is made about the interest rate, the "real value" of the lottery price can be readily calculated.

At the 5 percent interest rate, the $400 million lottery prize is worth about $200 million.

Developing a savings program is much easier if you understand two key concepts. One is "future value," which provides an answer to questions like "If I save or invest $10,000 today at an interest rate of 5 percent, how much will I have in ten years?" The two essential data items are the interest rate, the rows in Table 14.1, and the length of the invest-

Table 14.1
Future Value of a One-Time Payment of $1,000

Interest Rate	*Length of the Holding Period in Years*								
	1	2	4	5	6	8	10	20	30
2%	$1,020	$1,040	$1,082	$1,104	$1,126	$1,172	$1,219	$1,486	$1,811
4%	1,040	1,081	1,170	1,217	1,265	1,369	1,482	2,191	3,243
5%	1,050	1,103	1,216	1,276	1,340	1,478	1,629	2,653	4,322
6%	1,060	1,124	1,263	1,338	1,419	1,594	1,791	3,207	5,743
8%	1,080	1,166	1,361	1,469	1,587	1,851	2,159	4,661	10,063
10%	1,100	1,210	1,464	1,611	1,772	2,144	2,594	6,728	17,449

Source: Author.

Table 14.2
Present Value of a One-Time Payment of $1,000

Interest Rate	Number of Years before the Payment Is Made								
	1	2	4	5	6	8	10	20	30
2%	$980	$961	$924	$906	$888	$853	$823	$673	$552
4%	962	925	855	822	790	731	676	456	308
5%	952	907	823	784	747	677	614	377	231
6%	943	890	792	747	705	627	558	312	174
8%	926	857	735	681	630	540	464	215	99
10%	909	826	683	621	564	467	386	149	57

Source: Author.

ment period, the columns. The cell at the intersection of a row and a column is the answer to the question.

The "present value" is the mirror image of the future value and provides the answer to questions like "If I am promised $10,000 in ten years, then how much is that worth today?" You can answer the question only if you have an interest rate. The present values of various combinations of holding periods and interest rates are shown in Table 14.2.

Now it becomes slightly more complicated—be patient. The "future value of a series of payments" provides an answer to the question "If I invest $10,000 today and for each of the next nine anniversary dates, how much money will I have in ten years?" The answer to this question depends on the interest rate or the rate of return on your accumulated savings (see Table 14.3.) This concept helps you understand how rapidly your financial wealth will accumulate if you save on a systematic basis.

The concept "the present value of a series of payments" is the mirror image of the future value of a series of payments and is the answer to the question "If I am promised $10,000 for each of the next ten years, then what is the value of those payments today?" The stream of annual payments of the lottery prize money illustrates the "present value of a series of payments" (see Table 14.4).

One stylized fact is that the amount that individuals save each year generally increases as they move along the life cycle and for three reasons:

Table 14.3

Future Value of a Series of $1,000 Annual Payments

Interest Rate	Number of Annual Payments								
	1	2	4	5	6	8	10	20	30
2%	$1,000	$2,020	$4,122	$5,204	$6,308	$8,583	$10,950	$24,297	$40,568
4%	1,000	2,040	4,247	5,416	6,633	9,214	12,006	29,778	30,832
5%	1,000	2,050	4,310	5,526	6,802	9,549	12,578	33,066	68,439
6%	1,000	2,060	4,375	5,637	6,975	9,898	13,181	36,786	79,058
8%	1,000	2,080	4,506	5,861	7,336	10,637	14,487	45,762	113,283
10%	1,000	2,100	4,641	6,105	7,716	11,436	15,937	57,275	164,494

Source: Author.

Table 14.4

Present Value of a Series of $1,000 Annual Payments

Interest Rate	Number of Annual Payments								
	1	2	4	5	6	8	10	20	30
2%	$980	$1,942	$3,808	$4,714	$5,601	$7,326	$8,926	$16,351	$22,396
4%	962	1,886	3,629	4,452	5,242	6,733	8,111	13,690	17,292
5%	952	1,859	3,546	4,329	5,076	6,463	7,722	12,462	15,372
6%	943	1,833	3,465	4,612	4,917	6,209	7,360	11,469	13,765
8%	926	1,783	3,312	3,993	4,628	5,747	6,710	9,818	11,258
10%	909	1,736	3,169	3,791	4,355	5,335	6,145	8,514	9,427

Source: Author.

they become more serious about saving as they approach the retirement date, their incomes are higher, and their consumption spending is lower because they have purchased many of their durable goods, including their children's educations.

Knowing that the amount saved each year increases as individuals age, you might ask, "If I save $1,000 a year when I am in my thirties, $2,000 a year in my forties, $3,000 a year in my fifties, and $4,000 for the first five years of my sixties, how much will I have accumulated at the time of retirement?" The answer is the sum of four "future value of a series of payments"—and the answer depends on the interest rate (see Table 14.5; the values are taken from Table 14.3).

Note that if the interest rate is 4 percent, the future value of the thirty payments that begin at age 35 is $56,080, and the future value of the twenty payments that begin at age 45 is $29,780—a difference of $26,000 and change. The difference of $16,000 between this value and saving $1,000 a year for ten more years reflects the power of compound interest.

Once you set the target value for your accumulated savings on the eve of retirement, you can readily determine whether you are on track to achieve your goal. The target or lodestone value is shown on the upper right corner in Figure 14.1. The top line in the figure shows the target values for earlier years at an interest rate of 4 percent, while the bottom line shows these values at an interest rate of 6 percent. The target values at an interest rate of 5 percent are shown between these two lines.

There are two ways of getting to the lodestone value. One is to make a one-time payment or investment; in effect you are asking what the present value is of $100,000 five, ten, and twenty years before you reach age 65. The second is to ask what the present value is of a series of annual payments that would lead to the lodestone value of $100,000 at age 65. The earlier you begin to make these payments, the smaller the annual payment.

The assumption in this section is that the lodestone value is $100,000. For most readers, the number is likely to be larger. If the value is $300,000, then multiply the values in Figure 14.1 by three.

Once you have the lodestone value, you can readily determine the intermediate target values for your accumulated savings on earlier dates

Table 14.5
Future Value for Accumulated Savings

| | Interest Rate | | |
	4%	5%	6%
$1,000/year for 30 years (beginning at age 35)	$56,080	$68,439	$79,058
$1,000/year for 20 years (beginning at age 45)	29,780	33,066	36,786
$1,000/year for 10 years (beginning at age 55)	12,011	12,578	13,181
$1,000/year for 5 years (beginning at age 60)	5,416	5,526	5,637
Total accumulated savings at age 65	$103,287	$119,609	$134,662

Source: Author.

Figure 14.1
Amount Needed to Accumulate $100,000 at Terminal Date

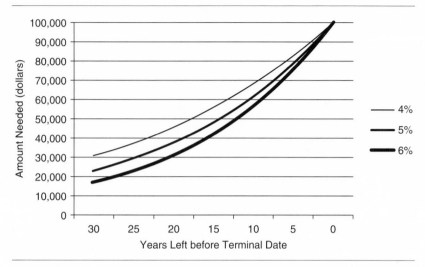

Source: Author.

and can easily determine whether you are on course. The earlier in life that you develop a time-consistent savings program, the smaller the amount that you will need to save each year.

You'll need to make an assumption about the rate of return. The conservative assumption is that the rate of return on your accumulated savings will be about 5 percent a year after adjusting for increases in the consumer price level. (A lot of financial pundits say you can do better than 5 percent, and a few of them may be right. Those who have been proven wrong are no longer financial pundits.) Rates of return were discussed in Chapter 9. Remember: there are no free lunches, and no blood can be squeezed from stones; it's all about the growth of the country.

Management Fees, and Nickels and Dimes

Merrill Lynch got rich by collecting a lot of nickels and dimes that American households thought of as small change. Assume that you plan to save $1,000 a year and that you anticipate an interest rate of 5 percent a year. The management/transaction fee is 1 percent, so the rate of return to you is 4 percent a year.

Table 14.6
Accumulated Values with Different Wedges

	Length of the Holding Period in Years		
	10	20	30
Accumulated value at 5%	12,578	33,066	68,439
Accumulated value at 4%	12,010	29,780	56,080
Difference	578	3,346	12,359

Source: Author.

Now the quiz. With the 4 percent rate, will your accumulated value at the end of ten, twenty, and thirty years be four-fifths the accumulated value with a 5 percent rate? It might seem so, but it isn't (see Table 14.6).

You can't have a major impact on the rate of return unless the current rate of return is exceptionally low, say, below 5 percent a year. You can't have a major impact on the number of years until retirement, although you can delay retirement by two or three years—which may be a major disappointment. The major variable that you can affect is the amount you save each year.

The earlier in life that you develop a savings program, the smaller the annual savings required to achieve your lodestone value. If you start when you're in your thirties, you will need to save a smaller proportion of your income than if you start when you're in your forties. The paradox is that it is hard to save when you are young, because income may be modest relative to consumption needs. When saving becomes easier, there is less time for compound interest to work its magic. You may believe when you're in your thirties that your income is too low to save more than a token amount. But the later you start saving, the larger the amount that you must save each year.

The power of compound interest is evident when you compare how much of the accumulated value of $100,000 represents your annual contribution and how much represents the build-up of interest. Assume an interest rate of 5 percent. If your savings program runs for thirty years, the sum of the annual contributions is $45,000 and the remaining $55,000 represents the accumulation of interest. In contrast, if the savings program lasts ten years, then the sum of the annual contributions amounts to $79,000 and the remaining $21,000 represents the accumulation of interest income.

Remember that the difference in the interest rate has a much more dramatic impact on the amount that must be saved each year in a savings program stretched over an extended period than one that covers a shorter period. For example, assume the interest rate increases from 5 percent to 7 percent; then the amount that must be saved each year declines from $1,505 to $1,059, and if the savings program has a ten-year horizon, the required amount declines from $18,097 to $17,389.

Each year's delay in retirement means that your annual income when you stop working will increase by 5 to 6 percent if you are in your sixties and early seventies. Most of the increase in your annual income results from the compounding of the rates of return for one or more years. But your expected longevity declines as you age.

There are several possible complications to the planning, especially when you are young. As your income increases, your standard of living is likely to increase, and so your cash needs in the retirement years also will be higher. You're going to have to estimate your income when you are in your sixties decades beforehand. Any wealth you may inherit may be an unknown. The rates of return on bonds, stocks, and other investments have been highly variable in the past and are likely to be so in the future.

The only systematic way to cope with these uncertainties is to develop a set of projections on the basis of the best information that is available when you begin your planning. As new information becomes available, you can revise your estimates of the amount you need to save each year.

Recognize the difference in the costs of adjusting to two different types of "errors" that you might make. One is the cost of entering retirement with accumulated savings that are too small to maintain your living standard; your only choices then are to take the hit to your living standard or to delay retirement, perhaps by taking on part-time employment during the early years of what would otherwise be the "golden years." The second type of error is entering retirement with larger accumulated savings than you think you'll need; if you make this sort of error, then you'll be able to sit in the front of the plane. If you don't move to the front of the plane, your children will.

It's likely that, in both cases, the rate of return that you earn on your savings as they accumulate differs from the rate you assumed when you began your savings program. If you compare the actual amount of your accumulated savings with the target values for different dates, you can make frequent small corrections.

TIAA-CREF: The Largest Manager of Pension Plans

The largest manager of defined-contribution pension plans is Teachers Insurance and Annuity Association (TIAA, now TIAA-CREF). TIAA was established in the 1920s to develop pensions for college and university professors and administrative staff. Participating faculty and staff were required to allocate a fixed percentage of their annual salaries—often between 5 and 10 percent—to an individual-specific retirement account; in effect, a contractual savings plan became part of the faculty member's employment arrangement. Most institutions contributed an additional amount to each individual's pension account.

Initially, TIAA used the funds in each individual's retirement account to buy particular bonds for each participant. At the time of retirement, the accumulated balances owned by each individual would be used to buy an annuity from TIAA. TIAA would then forward a check every month to the owner of the annuity for as long as the annuitant lived. In effect, each employed individual was buying a retirement annuity on the installment plan; each annuity would be based on the participant's contributions and the interest rate on bonds, and would be actuarially fair.

In 1952 TIAA established the College Retirement Equities Fund (CREF) so that participants could use part or all of their contributions to buy stocks. One rationale for this innovation was that the rate of return on stocks on average had been several percentage points higher than the rate of return on bonds, and another was that ownership of stocks would provide a better hedge against inflation than the ownership of bonds. Initially, CREF had only one stock fund. Subsequently, CREF established a bond fund, a global stock fund, a growth stock fund, and several different other funds. Now TIAA-CREF has ten different investment accounts. You can move your contributions and your accumulated balances among these different accounts.

Each year more than 1,700,000 individuals contribute to one or several of the TIAA-CREF retirement accounts. Each year TIAA-CREF sends checks to more than 300,000 people. In each recent year, 30,000 individuals have moved from the accumulation stage to the distribution stage. TIAA-CREF had $265 billion under management at the end of 2005.

Until 1998, only individuals employed at a participating academic institution were eligible to enroll in TIAA-CREF investment programs. Now anyone can buy TIAA and CREF mutual funds. Self-employed individuals can buy defined-contribution pensions from TIAA-CREF.

Many of the accounts in TIAA-CREF are tax advantaged; the funds contributed to these accounts reduce taxable income, and the dividends, capital gains, and interest on these accounts are not taxed when earned. The management fees charged by TIAA-CREF generally are 0.5 percent a year or less, much below those charged by most other mutual funds and financial institutions. TIAA-CREF management fees provide a good benchmark for comparison shopping, as do its life and health insurance products.

Until 1988, each participant in the TIAA and CREF programs was obliged to buy one or several annuities on the date of retirement. Since then, the purchase of an annuity has not been mandatory. Now one of the central questions—both for TIAA-CREF participants and for others—is whether the purchase of one or several annuities is a cost-effective decision. (More on that topic in the next chapter.)

Preparing for Bad News

The replacement ratio approach is a useful first step in helping you determine how much you will need to maintain your standard of living in retirement. However, this approach assumes there are no big adverse shocks to your income or expenditures. If there is steep inflation, your income might increase in nominal terms but the purchasing power of your higher income might decline. Congress might raise taxes. Your health insurer might increase your co-insurance payment.

Of course, your finances may sustain good news shocks as well. One way to cope with these shocks is to increase your spending or take a trip around the world or allow your money balances to accumulate, perhaps in anticipation that there will be bad news over the horizon.

Once you've decided how much money you will need to buy an annuity, you might increase the number by 10 or even 20 percent as a buffer so that bad news shocks won't crimp your living standard.

Uncle Sam's Tax Subsidies and Your Savings Program

In the early 1970s the U.S. government began to adopt a number of programs to assist Americans in saving for retirement. More recently, Uncle Sam introduced programs to help save for educational expenses. The generic name for these accounts is individual retirement accounts, or IRAs. The modest complication is that the term "IRA" now is the name of a particular account, sometimes now called the traditional IRA, as well as the family of tax-advantaged accounts. Participation in one of these programs requires a transfer of funds to a "dedicated account" managed by a "plan sponsor," which could be a bank, a mutual fund, or a life insurance company.

One rationale for establishing these accounts was that households would increase the amount they saved each year because the marginal effective income tax rates they paid on funds that were transferred to the dedicated accounts would be lower than the rates on funds invested in traditional accounts. Moreover, these tax-advantaged accounts enable individuals to shift taxable incomes to those years when their marginal income tax rates would be lower than the rates when they were actively employed.

These tax-advantaged accounts have two dominant features. One generic feature common to all of these accounts is that the investment income—the interest, dividends, and capital gains—earned on the money that has been parked in these accounts is not taxed in the year when the income is earned. Then there is an "either-or" feature: if the money transferred to one of these dedicated accounts reduces taxable income in the year when the money is transferred, the money withdrawn from these accounts always is taxed as income. Alternatively, if the money transferred to these accounts does not reduce taxable income, then the money withdrawn from these accounts is not taxed. The judgment call is whether it is more worthwhile to be taxed at the "back end" or at the "front end" (see Table 14.7). Column 1 centers on the tax implications of the transfer of funds to the dedicated account; if this transfer reduces taxable income, the after-tax "cost" to Ben Franklin of the transfer of $1,000 to the dedicated account each year is $650. Ben can then transfer $1,568 to the dedicated account each year at a pretax cost of $1,000 ($1,538 = $1,000 / $650).

Table 14.7
Taxes and Dedicated Savings Accounts

(1) Tax Deduction at Front End	(2) Tax on Distributed Income	(3) Terminal Income
No	No	69,761
Yes	Yes	85,915

Source: Author.

Uncle Sam limits the amount of money that you can transfer annually to the dedicated account. There is either an absolute dollar amount or a ceiling proportional to your income up to an absolute dollar ceiling. The withdrawal of funds from these accounts before a specified age, usually 59.5, generally triggers a 10 percent penalty from the Internal Revenue Service. The IRS requires that you begin to withdraw funds from these tax-advantaged retirement accounts about the time you turn 70—but there are exceptions, especially if you continue to work at the same institution. The amount withdrawn from these accounts to satisfy the minimum distribution rules of the IRS is taxed as ordinary income; more on this in the next chapter.

Consider the increase in the value of the accumulated savings of Ben Franklin under the two scenarios noted in the rows in Table 14.7. These scenarios differ in terms of whether the funds transferred to the dedicated account reduce taxable income in the years when the transfers are made (column 1) or instead whether the distribution of funds from this account increases taxable income (column 2). In each scenario Ben transfers the same annual amounts to his dedicated account for each of the next thirty years; in row 1 he transfers $1,000 a year and in row 2, he transfers $1,588 a year, which has the same after-tax "cost" to him because the transfer reduces his taxable income by $1,000. The interest rate on the funds in each of the dedicated accounts is 5 percent. Interest income is immediately reinvested at the 5 percent rate. Ben's marginal tax rate is 35 percent, both at the time he transfers the money to and when he withdraws the funds from the account.

There are two basic choices. The key feature of row 1 is that money transferred from the account at the end of the thirty-five-year period is not taxable income. In contrast, in row 2 the key feature is that funds transferred from the account at the end of the thirty-five-year period are taxable income.

The unequivocal result is that the preferred choice is to take the tax relief at the "front end," which enables the value of the funds in the dedicated account to accumulate more rapidly. This conclusion seems at variance with the popular understanding that a "Roth IRA" is preferable to the standard IRA.

IRAs are available to everyone who pays U.S. income tax. In 2008 the maximum annual amount an individual could contribute to an IRA was increased to $5,000; this contribution reduces taxable income on a dollar-for-dollar basis, up to the annual $5,000 ceiling. (Moreover, those over age 50 can now contribute an additional $6,000 a year.) Usually the contribution for a particular year must be transferred to the dedicated account by April 15 of the following year; you cannot delay making your contribution even if you request an extension for filing your income tax return.

Some of these dedicated programs are employment related; you may contribute a specified percentage of your earned income to one of these accounts, up to an annual ceiling or cap. (Several accounts—Section 529 and Roth Educational accounts—provide attractive incentives to save for educational expenses—tuition, room and board, books, and supplies—of your children and grandchildren. The details on these programs were discussed in Chapter 8.)

Once your funds have been directed to one or several of the accounts offered by one of these plan sponsors, you'll need to decide whether your funds will be used to buy bonds, stocks, or mutual funds.

The advantages of using these accounts can be illustrated by comparing a traditional IRA account with a Roth IRA. Everyone can have a traditional IRA, but only individuals with an annual income below $110,000 can make a contribution to a Roth IRA ($160,000 for a married couple). You can have both a traditional IRA and a Roth IRA; in years in which your income is above the Roth IRA ceilings, you contribute to the traditional IRA and otherwise you contribute to the Roth IRA.

Assume you're single and have an annual income of $80,000. Are you better off with the traditional IRA, which provides a tax deduction at the front end, or a Roth IRA, which provides for tax-free withdrawal of funds at the back end? First, assume that your marginal tax rate is the same in both the front year and the back year. The answer according to Table 14.7 is that you should prefer the traditional IRA.

Your marginal tax rate might differ because your income is higher in the front-end year than in the back-end year and because of changes in the tax schedules. Thus marginal income tax rates have been declining for more than twenty years, so that had Roth IRAs been available beginning in the 1980s, you would have been better off if you had chosen the Roth IRA.

One more important factor bears on this choice. A very significant part of the rate of return to stockholders in the last twenty years has resulted from increases in the prices of stocks; remember the data in Chapter 9. If you had selected the traditional IRA, then your capital gains would have been taxed at ordinary income tax rates when funds were withdrawn from your IRA account. In contrast, if you had selected the Roth IRA, the capital gains on your stock investments would not have been taxed when the funds were withdrawn. This asymmetry in the taxation of ordinary income and capital gains means that the Roth IRA is preferable to the traditional IRA unless the marginal tax rate in the year of the contribution is 30 to 40 percent higher than the marginal tax rate in the year in which the funds were withdrawn from the dedicated account.

You can participate in several programs simultaneously, provided you satisfy the conditions of each program. For example, you can participate in a 401(k) if you worked for a profit-oriented firm and a 403(b) if you worked for a nonprofit institution and a Keogh plan if you had schedule C income from your own business.

Take an extreme case: assume that you had been working a ninety-hour week, partly for a profit-oriented firm, partly for a tax-exempt institution, and partly for yourself. You can contribute up to $10,500 in the 401(k), $10,500 in the 403(b), and $13,500 in the Keogh programs for the self-employed. You and your spouse can have IRAs (although you won't get any deduction from your current annual income tax payment for the amount transferred to these IRAs because of your high income). You can contribute to the Roth Educational IRAs and to the Section 529 programs of your children and grandchildren.

If your income isn't large enough so that you can take full advantage of all programs for which you qualify, then you'll have to decide which ones are most attractive. The investment income in both types of IRAs is not taxed as the income is earned. Hence the question is whether it is more valuable to have a tax benefit when you contribute to the traditional IRA or a tax benefit when the funds are withdrawn from the Roth IRA.

Moreover, if you prefer to buy growth stocks rather than value stocks (the comparison between the two is discussed in Chapter 9), there is a tax disadvantage to using these programs. If you buy growth stocks, your tax payments would be at the capital gains tax rate of 15 percent. If you invest in one of these tax-advantaged accounts, the effective tax rate would be the rate on ordinary income, perhaps as high as 35 percent.

The first programs you should probably use after the Roth IRA (if your income does not exclude you from using one) are the 401(k) and / or 403(b) defined-contribution pension plans. If your employer contributes to your account, then the value of your savings may increase more rapidly than it would based on your own contribution. The employers' contribution is "free money"—take as much of it as is offered.

The disadvantage of the 401(k) programs is that you may be required to use a significant part of your joint contribution to buy stock in the firm you work for. You may be obliged to hold these shares for a minimum number of years, or until you reach a specified age, say, 55, or as long as you are an employee of the firm. Even the best firms have only fifteen minutes in the sun—or maybe twenty minutes. Since a large part of your human capital is invested in the firm, you should minimize the share of your financial wealth invested in your employer. If you find yourself in this situation, sell these shares at your earliest possible opportunity because you should be diversifying.

Stay tuned; Congress will change the rules.

Saving for Educational Expenses

Section 529 of the Internal Revenue Code initially provided that the investment income on accounts established for the qualified educational expenses of students is no longer taxed. This arrangement now is called the Coverdell Education Savings Plan. A few states do not tax the investment income of these accounts if the funds have been invested with the sponsor chosen by the state. Individual states set limits on the maximum amount that can be invested in these accounts; some states now have limits of nearly $250,000. Each state has designated one or several plan sponsors. Your plan sponsor chooses how your funds are invested, but you choose the sponsor. The annual management fees charged by these plan sponsors differ, and range from 0.65 percent to about 1.50 percent a year.

You may marvel at these programs but conclude that you don't have the cash to take full advantage of them. If so, rethink your savings program. You need to determine whether you are saving enough to achieve your lodestone value. If not, consider increasing your home mortgage and engage in tax arbitrage; the interest payments on the mortgage reduce your taxable income, and the investments in the tax-advantaged accounts accumulate tax free.

Free Money: Your Employer's Matching Contribution

Many employers offer you "free money"—they will match your contribution to your defined-contribution pension plan, dollar for dollar, up to a specified percentage. That's free money—take it when you can get it, and take as much of it as you can get. It's like an interest rate of 100 percent a year, and it's tax free.

Strategies and Gimmicks for Increasing Your Savings

Save for long-term needs; borrow for short-term needs. You should save for the proverbial rainy day, such as an exceptional medical expense, an auto accident, or a period of unemployment. It would not be appropriate to draw on the savings you have dedicated for retirement, in part because you may compromise your retirement and in part because you will forgo the tax advantages. Develop a rainy day fund of three or four months' income. You can also use a home equity loan to finance these rainy day needs.

Saving for retirement is rather like dieting. The key to developing a successful diet is consistency between caloric intake and energy expended. Each diet follows a similar plan—do x or y so that daily caloric intake declines below energy expended, and weight will decline. A more vigorous exercise program will contribute to more rapid weight loss, but a large number of four-minute miles are required to offset the calories in a Big Mac and a medium fries.

A few individuals are natural savers; once their basic needs are met, they don't get much pleasure out of additional consumption and they don't feel the need to keep up with the Joneses. They don't have expensive hobbies, and they are not interested in expensive vacations. They keep their cars for eight or ten years, and they are not tempted to move to more expensive neighborhoods as their incomes increase. Warren Buffett continues to live in the same three-bedroom house in Omaha that he bought in 1950. These individuals tend to have a high saving rate because there is a big gap between their income and their spending.

You can pay someone to help you save. There are 300,000 insurance salesmen who will sell you an annuity that is a contractual savings program. Once a month or once a quarter, you will get a notice from the company that your periodic payment is due. The investment income earned by the insurance company on the bonds and stocks it has bought on your behalf is not taxed—so it's like a tax-advantaged account. When the company distributes funds to you, part of the distribution that represents the accumulated investment income will be subject to income tax. The disadvantage of this annuity is that you might pay the salesperson and the insurance company 2 to 3 percent a year for reminding you to make the periodic payments—that is a large part of the investment income the company is likely to earn.

If you are not a natural saver, you may need some stratagems and gimmicks to increase your savings rate. You might arrange to have your bank transfer $100 or $200 from your checking account to a savings account on the day you deposit your monthly salary. As your salary increases, increase the amount transferred to these accounts.

Assume that you are age 35 and you've decided to stop smoking. You've been a moderate smoker—one pack a day. That's a habit that costs you $4 a day, not a lot of money. But if you instead direct the money you spend every day on smokes into a dedicated tax-exempt account, at age 65, you'll have $65,000—a lot of money. True, you'll have to pay income tax when the funds are distributed from the account. But you'll be wealthier *and* healthier.

Assume that you take a sandwich from home for your lunch twice a week—a savings of, say, $12 a week. Over thirty years, that amounts to nearly $40,000 at a 5 percent interest rate. You can probably think of five or ten such gimmicks. Saving five or ten dollars a day is not likely to make a big dent in your consumption patterns.

Or consider the purchase of a car. Instead of purchasing a new vehicle every third year, buy new wheels every fourth year. In the course of thirty years, you'd buy seven or so cars rather than ten. The trade-off involves the amount of depreciation for the first three years against the additional depreciation of the fourth year. This might amount to $3,000 a year. You can stretch out the cycle of numerous such expenditures to save money.

Now consider the "do-it-yourself" programs. You may have been paying an income tax preparation firm $300 a year. Most of the activity of
such firms involves entering data that you have assembled in a computer
program. You can buy an excellent software program for $15 or $20.

Determining Your Lodestone Value

To get to the target value for your accumulated savings, first estimate the
annual income that you will need in retirement. Refer to Table 13.2,
which is a truncated version of Table 12.2. There are three different estimates of preretirement income: $40,000, $80,000, and $120,000. A re-
placement ratio of 75 percent is used. In the first case, you'll need $30,000
a year; in the second, $60,000; and in the third, $90,000. The values for
the Social Security benefits are the same as those in Table 12.2.

Use a real rate of return, one adjusted for the increase in the inflation
rate.

This example should guide your calculation. Pencil in your estimate of
the amount you'll need each year on line 2 of the column on the right in
Table 13.1. Then pencil in your estimate of your Social Security benefits in
line 3. The amount on line 4 is the difference between the amount on line
2 and the amount on line 3. If you have a defined-benefit pension plan or a
defined-contribution pension plan, pencil in the amount of the annual payments to you on line 5 (you should be able to obtain an approximate value
from your employer). The amount on line 6 is the difference between lines
4 and 5. If you don't have an employment-related pension plan, then the
amount on line on 6 should be identical to the amount on line 4 (see Table
14.8). The amount on line 6 is an estimate of the accumulated personal
savings that you will need to supplement the money from other sources.

Table 14.8
Estimating Wealth Accumulation Targets on the Eve of Retirement

1. Preretirement income	$40,000	$80,000	$120,000
2. Expenditures in retirement	30,000	60,000	90,000
3. Social Security benefits	15,000	20,000	25,000
4. 2 – 3	15,000	40,000	65,000
5. Defined-benefit and defined-contribution pension	5,000	10,000	15,000
6. "Hole"	10,000	30,000	50,000

Source: Author.

Two Life Annuity at Age 65

Once you have the lodestone values in row 6, you can call an insurance agent, a mutual fund salesman, or almost any seller of financial services and ask, "How much must I pay you today so you will pay my spouse and me $x a year for as long as one of us lives?" There are a number of variants of this question that center on the amount of the payment to the surviving spouse and the minimum number of payments. Your savings program for retirement hinges on the consistency among four values. The controlling value is your estimate of your accumulated savings amount at the time you plan to retire. The other values are the rate of return you expect on your accumulated savings, and the value of savings when you begin your savings program. Consistency must be your mantra: you want to be sure that the amount you save each year will enable you to achieve your target for your accumulated savings at the time of your retirement.

ACTIONABLES

1. Estimate how much you will need to maintain your standard of living when you retire.
2. Determine your Social Security benefit.
3. Determine the payout from your defined-benefit pension plan.
4. Determine the value of your defined-contribution pension plan benefit at retirement age.
5. Determine the target value for your accumulated savings—the lodestone value—that you will need at the time of retirement.
6. Develop estimates of intermediate target values for your accumulated savings program.
7. Note the sensitivity of the amount you must save each year to changes in the rates of return on your accumulated savings. The difference between a 6 percent rate of return and a 7 percent rate of return may not seem like much. But over a twenty-year period, the compounding means that the difference in the accumulated totals is much larger than 1 percent.
8. Identify the preferred tax-efficient savings programs.

15   Three Plans So You Won't Outlive Your Assets

The wealth of America has been increasing at an average rate between 3 and 4 percent a year after adjusting for inflation. When stock prices or real estate prices are surging, wealth increases more rapidly than average, and when these prices decline sharply, then wealth may decline for a year or two.

The wealth of most individual Americans peaks about the time they leave the active labor force and embark on a retirement career. Their spending then will exceed their income and their accumulated savings will begin to decline. That's the last chapter in the normal life cycle—and you want to be sure that you do not outlive your assets. Once you've left the labor force, you have fewer opportunities to recover from faulty and expensive financial decisions.

If you have been contributing the maximum amount to Social Security for the last thirty-five years, you will begin to receive the monthly check from Social Security. If you bought an annuity from a private vendor that promised benefits comparable to those that you're likely to receive from Social Security, you would probably have to pay $300,000 at age 65. Even then the monthly annuity checks probably would not be as effectively hedged against an increase in the consumer price level as your Social Security benefit. If both you and your spouse have contributed the maximum amounts to Social Security for thirty-five years, your future benefits are worth between $450,000 and $600,000.

If you have contributed less than the maximum to Social Security, your monthly check will be smaller. The average Social Security benefit is about $1,000 a month or $12,000 a year. An annuity that would pay you $12,000 a year when you are age 65 would cost about $120,000.

You can't outlive your Social Security benefits. Despite all the chatter about Social Security going broke, the monthly payments to you will continue and will be adjusted upward as the living costs for the retired increase. (One of the likely "solutions" to the anticipated financial problems of Social Security is that the scope of wage indexing for upper-income taxpayers will be reduced relative to the scope of wage indexing for lower-income taxpayers, and another is that the cap or ceiling on annual contributions will be raised.)

The single most valuable asset for most families—after Social Security benefits—is the equity in their home, which is larger than the accumulated financial savings in tax-advantaged and other accounts. More than 70 percent of those in the early retirement cohorts own their homes. Some have mortgages. Your home provides you with a valuable "rental service," a nontaxed form of income.

Many empty nesters have more living space than they need—and may want to manage. You can sell your home and move to a less expensive property, and the profit from the sale of the home can be added to your accumulated financial savings. Many individuals are reluctant to move because they're attached to their neighborhoods. Moreover, the real estate commissions and other costs associated with the sale and move could put a dent of 8 or 10 percent in the net proceeds—and an even larger dent if there is a significant mortgage.

A relatively new financial instrument, the reverse mortgage, enables homeowners to borrow against the value of their homes. The key feature of a reverse mortgage is that borrowers do not make any interest payments to the lenders as the indebtedness increases; instead, each month the amount of the interest due is added to the debt (hence the term "reverse"—because the indebtedness continually increases).

The Reverse Mortgage as an Annuity

The traditional thirty-year mortgage provides a loan that is to be repaid with the same fixed monthly payment for 360 months. In the first several months, about 97 percent of the payment is for interest on the indebtedness, and 3 percent reduces the outstanding amount due. Month by month, the loan indebtedness decreases, and the interest payment becomes a smaller component of the monthly payment. The loan indebtedness declines at an increasing rate.

A reverse mortgage is a commitment by a lender to provide a loan based on the market value of your home. The Federal Housing Administration (FHA), which is part of the U.S. Department of Housing and Urban Development (HUD), established reverse mortgages and sets their basic features. The borrowers deal with private lenders. When you take out a reverse mortgage, you can arrange to receive a fixed monthly payment as long as you own and occupy the home, or you can receive a lump sum payment, or you can arrange a line of credit and draw on this line at some future time.

The FHA sets upper limits on the amounts of a reverse mortgage for each city and each county; these limits range from $173,000 to $313,000 in many metropolitan areas (with higher limits in Alaska, Hawaii, and the U.S. Virgin Islands). The lending limits were increased to $625,500 through December 31, 2010.

The key feature of the reverse mortgage loan is that borrowers do not make any interest payment to the lenders; instead, the interest on the indebtedness is added to the indebtedness. You can live in your home as long as you want, and you cannot be forced to move if your indebtedness exceeds the market value of your home perhaps because you live a very long life.

The lenders that provide reverse mortgages are repaid the principal and the interest when the home is sold or refinanced. If the sales proceeds are smaller than the indebtedness, HUD makes up the shortfall to the lender; HUD bears the longevity risk. HUD charges borrowers an insurance premium of about 2.5 percent of the loan amount; the premium receipts are allocated to a reserve that will be drawn on when the lenders incur losses because the amount of the loan exceeds the market value of the property.

If you die soon after arranging for a reverse mortgage, your heirs will sell the house and repay the loan. If you decide to move, you sell the house and repay the loan. If the market value of your home increases sharply, you might refinance the reverse mortgage; you would repay your indebtedness on the first reverse mortgage with the money obtained from the second reverse mortgage.

The amount you can borrow under a reverse mortgage depends on three factors: the market value of your home, the interest rate at the time that you take out the mortgage, and your age. The lower the interest rate at the time you initiate the mortgage, the larger the amount that you may borrow. Similarly, the older you are when you take out the reverse mortgage, the larger the amount you can borrow relative to the market value of your home.

Assume that the market value of your home is $200,000; you and your spouse are 65. The reverse mortgage taken as an annuity would provide an annual payment of $16,000 for as long as one of you lives.

Reverse mortgages have gotten a bum rap because some scamsters induced some elderly couples to take a large lump sum and then invest the proceeds in dubious securities.

Employment-related pensions are the third major source of funds in retirement. More than 40 million individuals have a defined-benefit pension plan, which is like Social Security. Once you reach a specified age, the employer is committed to pay you a specified amount as long as you live. (Often this age is 65, but sometimes the pension benefit begins after twenty or thirty years of employment.) You own the right to the pension payment but not the capital sum. Your employer bears the investment risk and is required by law to invest funds to ensure that the money will be there when the payments to you are scheduled to begin. (Despite the law, many of these pension plans, including those of state and local governments, are underfunded; the assets in the pension accounts are below the present value of the payments that must be made to the employees.) About the only decisions you have to make with a defined-benefit plan center on the choice of the beneficiary and how large a monthly payment the beneficiary should receive if you are the first to die. (You may have to stay with an employer for five or eight years to have the pension "fully vested" so that you own the right to the future payments; if you leave the employer before the plan is vested, you may lose a great deal of the firm's contribution to the pension—but you'll receive the amount you paid.)

The amount of your monthly pension varies with years of paid employment and your income; the longer your period of employment and the higher your income, the larger the monthly payment. For example, the pensions for federal employees are based on the average salary in the five years when they had the highest annual income and the number of years of employment. Members of the U.S. military typically receive pensions equal to 50 percent of their salaries at the time of departure from active duty if they retire after twenty years of active duty, and 75 percent if they retire after thirty years of active duty.

There is some risk that your employer may go bankrupt and not be able to fulfill its obligation to you; you're protected against part or all of the loss because your employer has been paying insurance premiums to a government agency, the U.S. Pension Benefit Guaranty Corporation (PBGC), which will pay the pension if the employer can't. A few of those who had relatively high incomes will take a "haircut" because the pension payment that they will receive from the PBGC is less than the payment they had been receiving from or were scheduled to receive from their employer before the firm went under.

The U.S. Pension Benefit Guaranty Corporation

The U.S. Pension Benefit Guaranty Corporation (PBGC) was established by the Employment Income Security Act of 1974 to ensure that employees of companies with defined-benefit pension plans will not become destitute if these companies go bankrupt. Forty-three million workers in more than 38,000 companies are protected by the PBGC. Currently, more than 200,000 individuals receive checks from the PBGC; these individuals had been employed by nearly 3,000 firms. Another 300,000 individuals will receive checks from the PBGC when they reach age 65. Most individuals receive the same annual benefit from the PBGC that they would have received from their firm; however, the ceiling to the benefit is $41,000 a year.

The funds to pay these benefits come from insurance premiums paid by the firms that offer defined-benefit pension plans. The bankruptcy of the large steel, auto parts, and airline firms has put the PBGC in the red; the payments that it is committed to make exceed its accumulated reserves and anticipated future income.

The PBGC will get out of the red in one of three ways. The premiums charged the firms that still participate in the program might be increased (which will accelerate the pace of firms' switch from defined-benefit plans to defined-contribution plans). A premium might be charged to those workers whose firms have gone bankrupt. The PBGC would receive a "grant" from the U.S. Treasury—in effect, the government would write off the loan to the PBGC as uncollectible.

You may have a defined-contribution plan—a 401(k) or a 403(b)—or some other tax-advantaged account. Currently, 55 percent of employment-related pensions are defined-contribution plans, twice the percentage in 1975. If you've been self-employed even on a part-time basis, you may have a Keogh plan—a tax-advantaged retirement plan.

If you have a defined-contribution plan, you own a specific account. Month by month, year by year, you and your employer have made payments to this tax-advantaged account. You can control—within somewhat narrow limits—the amount of the monthly contribution, how the accumulated balances are invested, and the timing and the form of the distribution of funds. You bear the investment risk because you decided whether the monthly contributions will be used to buy bonds or stocks. If stock prices go up, your income in retirement will be higher—and if stock prices go down . . .

About the time you retire, you'll need to make several decisions about the accumulated balances in your defined-contribution account and any other tax-advantaged accounts. The Internal Revenue Service (IRS) specifies the minimum annual distribution from these accounts once you reach age 70½. The IRS will look over your shoulder to be sure that you comply with its regulations; your plan sponsor is likely to act as an agent of the IRS to ensure compliance. (See the box "IRS Rules on Distribution of Funds from Tax-Advantaged Accounts" for the minimum annual distribution.) The funds withdrawn from these accounts are taxable income (except for the funds withdrawn from a Roth IRA).

Some employers retain rules that limit the ability of the owner of these balances to manage them; a few colleges and universities still require that individuals hold 50 percent of their balances in Teachers Insurance and Annuity Association–College Retirement Equities Fund (TIAA-CREF) accounts. Your plan sponsor may have some rules that constrain your decisions, perhaps by limiting the number of transactions or switches between different types of securities that you can make during a particular period.

IRS Rules on Distribution of Funds from Tax-Advantaged Accounts

1. The minimum annual distribution from each tax-advantaged account must begin in the calendar year that the owner reaches age 70½. However, if you remain at work with your primary employer— even if only on a part-time basis—you can delay the beginning of the distribution of funds until the year after you stop working.

2. The minimum annual distribution from each account is the product of an IRS factor associated with your age and the value of each of your tax-advantaged accounts on December 31 of the previous year. The percent noted in the line below the IRS factor is the reciprocal of the IRS factor or 100/IRS factor (see Table 15.1). For example, if you are age 75 in 2010, the IRS factor is 22.9; divide 100 by 22.9 to obtain 4.37, which is the percentage of your accumulated value in your tax-advantaged account on December 31, 2010, that you must take as your minimum distribution in 2011.

3. Funds distributed from each account (except from Roth IRAs and educational IRAs) are taxed as ordinary income.

4. If the amount distributed from each account is smaller than the required minimum, the IRS applies a 50 percent penalty on the amount that should have been distributed and wasn't.

Table 15.1
Minimum Annual Distribution from Tax-Advantaged Accounts, Various Ages

	70	71	72	73	74	75	76	77	78	79
IRS factor	27.4	26.5	25.6	24.7	23.8	22.9	22.0	21.2	20.3	19.5
Percent	3.65	3.77	3.91	4.05	4.20	4.37	4.55	4.72	4.93	5.13
	80	81	82	83	84	85	86	87	88	89
IRS factor	18.7	17.9	17.1	16.3	15.5	14.8	14.1	13.4	12.7	12.0
Percent	5.35	5.59	5.85	6.13	6.45	6.76	7.09	7.46	7.87	8.33
	90	91	92	93	94	95	96	97	98	99
IRS factor	11.4	10.8	10.2	9.6	9.1	8.6	8.1	7.6	7.1	6.7
Percent	8.77	9.26	9.80	10.42	10.99	11.63	12.35	13.16	14.08	14.93

Source: Data from *J. K. Lasser's Your Income Tax 2010* (New York: John Wiley and Sons, 2010).

5. Funds distributed from these accounts before age 59½ are subject to a penalty of 10 percent—but this penalty can be waived in some hardship circumstances.

6. You have sixty days to move funds from one qualified plan sponsor to another without triggering the need to pay income tax on the funds withdrawn from the first plan sponsor.

7. The Feds declared a holiday for the minimum annual distribution in 2008 and 2009.

If you buy an annuity, you will need to decide on its price or face value, the timing of the purchase, the amount of any payment to a beneficiary, whether the annuity will provide for a minimum number of payments should you and your beneficiary die within five or ten years after the purchase, and whether the annuity should be based on investments in bonds or in stocks. You will also have to choose among the many firms that sell annuities, and you'll have to decide whether to pay for this annuity with funds in a tax-advantaged account or with some other funds.

Most individuals make the transition from the accumulation stage to the distribution stage of life about the time they retire. But you may begin to draw on the accumulated balances in a tax-advantaged account while employed, unless your employer restricts such withdrawals. You can delay drawing on your accumulated balances for some years after you retire and before you reach age 70.

How Likely Are You to Outlive Your Assets?

"How long will my money last?" Monthly checks from the Social Security Administration and defined-benefit pension plans continue as long as you live. If you have a reverse mortgage and take the funds as an annuity, the payments continue as long as you live in the house. This worrisome question applies to the money you have in your defined-contribution pension plan and other tax-advantaged accounts and your other accumulated savings.

The slightly more formal version of the same question is "What is my longevity risk?"

The life expectancies for both females and males at different ages in the "second half" of the life cycle are shown in Table 15.2. These values

Table 15.2
Life Expectancy at Various Ages

	45	55	65	75	85	100
Female	36.6	27.7	19.4	12.3	6.9	2.8
Male	32.5	24.0	16.4	10.2	5.7	2.5

Source: Data from American Council of Life Insurers, *2005 Fact Book* (Washington, DC: American Council of Life Insurers, 2005), p. 153.

are median averages; the good news is that you are likely to be in the 50 percent that will live longer than the average and the bad news is that the longer you live relative to the average for your age cohort, the more likely it is that you will outlive your money. At age 65, a female has a median life expectancy of 19.4 years, three more years than a male. The higher your age, the higher your total life expectancy; at age 65, the median female will live to be 84, and at age 85 the median female will live until 91 or 92.

These data are the aggregate for all Americans. It's a safe bet that life expectancy is higher for readers of this book—a compelling reason for you to buy this book and give it to your friends.

Whether you will outlive your money depends primarily on three factors: the amount of your accumulated savings, the rate of return you earn on your accumulated savings, and the annual "drawdown rate"—the pace at which you withdraw funds from your accumulated savings to pay for your monthly living expenses. Think of the drawdown rate as your personal counterpart of the rate that a college or hospital uses to decide how much money to take from its endowment each year for operating expenses—but with one difference: the college or hospital believes that it is in business until the end of time, so it will never or at least will rarely "eat its capital," but you may be comfortable eating your capital—as long as your capital is not declining at too rapid a rate.

You won't outlive your capital if you adjust the drawdown rate to the value of your accumulated savings and the rate of return on your accumulated savings. You can't really have a big impact on the rate of return on your accumulated savings, since that rate is determined in the market. You chose the drawdown rate. The lower this rate relative to the interest rate on the accumulated savings, the longer your money will last. The columns in Table 15.3 indicate the drawdown rate as a percentage of your accumulated savings; for example, if you have savings of $100,000 and the drawdown rate is 4 percent, you would withdraw $4,000 each year to help with the living expenses. The rows indicate different rates of return on your accumulated savings both in a tax-advantaged and in a non-tax-advantaged account. (Remember that the funds withdrawn from tax-advantaged accounts other than Roth IRAs are taxable income.)

The value in each cell indicates the number of years your money will last for each set of assumptions about the annual dollar value of the drawdown and the product of the drawdown rate and $100,000 and the rate of return on your money. (The $100,000 is chosen for ease of exposition; the results are identical regardless of whether the capital sum is $10,000 or $50,000 or $250,000.)

You can see that if the drawdown rate is equal to the rate of return, your accumulated savings are like a perpetuity and the value of your capital would not decline in the long run, although the market value may change in the short run as interest rates fluctuate. (When the drawdown rate is smaller than the rate of return, your accumulated savings will increase.) The rates of return on your savings—after adjusting for increases in the cost of living—are likely to be in the range of 4 to 6 percent. (These rates of return are after payments to your mutual fund manager or financial advisor; the larger the payments to the fund manager or financial advisor, the smaller the amount available to you.)

Table 15.3
How Long Will My $100,000 Last?

Annual Rate of Return	Drawdown Rates (Annual Amounts in Thousands of Dollars)								
	2	3	4	5	6	7	8	9	10
2%	PER	100	50	33	25	20	17	14	12
3%	INF	PER	100	50	33	25	20	17	14
4%	INF	INF	PER	10	50	33	25	20	16
5%	INF	INF	INF	PER	100	50	33	25	20
6%	INF	INF	INF	INF	PER	100	50	33	25
7%	INF	INF	INF	INF	INF	PER	100	50	33
8%	INF	INF	INF	INF	INF	INF	PER	100	50

Note: PER = perpetuity; INF = infinite.

Source: Author.

Assume that the rate of return is 4 percent and the drawdown rate is 8 percent. Your accumulated savings will decline by $4,000 a year (the excess of the drawdown rate over the rate of return) and your savings will last twenty-five years ($100,000/$4000 = 25). If, in contrast, the rate of return is 5 percent and the drawdown rate is 8 percent, then your money will last thirty-three years; you'll be 98 or 99 before your savings are depleted.

Your accumulated savings are likely to last your lifetime if the drawdown rate is no more than three percentage points higher than the rate of return. For example, again assume $100,000—if the rate of return is 4 percent and the drawdown rate is 7 percent and hence you draw down $7,000 a year, your money will last thirty-three years. To ensure that you do not outlive your assets, set the drawdown rate no more than three percentage points higher than the rate of return. If the rate of return that you can earn on your accumulated savings is 5 percent a year, then you'll be able to draw down your funds at the rate of 8 percent a year. As is evident from Table 15.3, you can make "midterm corrections" if your accumulated savings are being depleted too rapidly. Reduce the drawdown rate slightly.

As you move along the life cycle from your seventies to your eighties, some of your expenditures will decline. You'll do less traveling when you are in the 75-to-85 age cohort than when you're ten years younger. You'll spend less for food and more for pills, less for clothing and more for wheelchairs. You may have fully paid off any mortgage loan on your home or you may have enough equity in the home so that you can refinance so that your monthly payments decline. You can respond to the anticipated declines in your expenditures by drawing down $4,500 a year while you are in your sixties, $4,000 a year when in your seventies, $3,500 a year when in your eighties, and $3,000 a year when you are in your nineties.

The alternative to the steplike reduction in the drawdown is a declining fixed percentage. In this case the amount drawn down each year is a percentage of the remaining balance. Since you would be drawing down the same percentage, you would never exhaust all of your accumulated savings—but in the last ten or fifteen years of the proposed plan, the amount you would be withdrawing each year would be very small. You might decide to draw down the accumulated savings over a thirty-five-year period; all of the funds would be used by the time you reach age 100.

Assume that you begin to draw down your accumulated savings when you are age 65 and that the drawdown rate exceeds the rate of return by four percentage points. By the time you reach age 75, you've drawn down 40 percent of your accumulated savings. If you had $100,000 when you were age 65, you now have $60,000. The midterm correction involves reducing the excess of the drawdown rate over the rate of return to three percentage points, and your funds will last until you are age 95—assuming that you can continue to earn 4 percent a year.

To Annuitize or Not to Annuitize: That's the Question

As you approach retirement, you must decide whether to buy one or several annuities from a plan sponsor, which might be TIAA-CREF or Vanguard or Fidelity or Merrill Lynch. The key advantage of an annuity that the sellers will emphasize is "peace of mind"—the seller panders to your concern that "I might outlive my assets" and promises to make a payment to you (or to you and a designated beneficiary) as long as you live. The assurance that you can't outlive the annuity can be comforting. Be slightly concerned with how long the seller of the annuity will remain in business.

Remember that your Social Security benefit is an annuity. So is a defined-benefit pension plan, and the payments are explicitly guaranteed by the U.S. government, at least as long as the annual payment to you is less than $41,000 a year. You should then ask how much more peace of mind you might obtain from a second annuity, or from a third annuity if you have a defined-benefit pension plan.

If the amount of cash that is likely to be available from Social Security, perhaps a defined-benefit pension plan, and your accumulated savings is large relative to your anticipated payments to maintain your standard of living, another annuity is unnecessary. You'll be paying someone a large fee to provide a service that you don't need. If you're concerned that you may be on the borderline between having and not having enough cash, an annuity can be helpful.

You can buy an annuity when you're in your thirties or forties or even when you're in your nineties, and you may buy as many annuities as you wish. When you buy an annuity, you transfer the longevity risk and the investment risk to the seller of the annuity. The seller promises that as long as you live, you will receive either a fixed amount each month or an amount that varies in response to changes in a market index. The seller bases its promises on your age when you want to receive the first payment from the annuity and its estimates of the rates of return on bonds and on stocks. The seller also has acquired the investment risk, although the seller is likely to have hedged most or all of this by matching the maturity of the bonds that it has acquired with your anticipated longevity. The older you are when the seller begins to make payments to you, the larger the monthly payment for a given face value of the annuity, since your life expectancy then is shorter. The higher the rate of return that the seller anticipates earning on the invested funds, the larger the monthly payment.

What Is the "True Cost" of an Annuity?

Remember the distinction in Chapter 5 between the premium paid to the sellers of various types of insurance policies and the costs of each of these policies, which was to be measured as the difference between the cumulative payments of premiums to the companies and the amounts they paid the insured in the settlement of claims. Remember also that the increase in the cash value projected from the difference between the premium on a term life insurance policy and the premium on a whole life insurance policy was smaller than the amount that would have been forecast based on the difference in the two premiums; it was as if the rate of return on the cash value was negative.

The pattern of cash flows in an annuity is the mirror image of the pattern of cash flows in a cash value life insurance policy. The purchase of an annuity is likely to be costly because the payouts are low relative to the investment returns.

The "longevity risk" is that the sellers of the annuities are "betting the firm" that you and the other owners of annuities will not live significantly longer than their data about life expectancy suggest. The sellers know that Americans are living longer and—surprisingly—that the data available to them cannot capture the lengthening of the life span. Annuity sellers have a conservative bias, for if those who had purchased the annuities were to live much longer than the currently available life-expectancy data suggest, the sellers might go broke. The sellers introduce a fudge factor: they set the payout rates on the annuity modestly below the level they think most accurately reflects your life expectancy to protect themselves if you and other annuity buyers live longer than they expect. If a seller of annuities sets the fudge factor too high, you may conclude that the annuity payment is too low and buy your annuity from a firm that promises larger monthly payments.

To remain competitive, the sellers of annuities must keep their prices low—that is, they must promise a high monthly payment for each $1,000 you might spend to buy the annuity. Similarly, the sellers seek to "price" the different features of the annuities so they are largely indifferent about whether you select a minimum guarantee period and whether you prefer payments based on only the life of the owner of the annuity or on "two lives"—yours and that of your designated beneficiary.

You acquire a credit risk that the seller of the annuity will remain solvent and in a position to fulfill its commitment. The "credit risk" is that the seller may not be able to fulfill its contract, perhaps because of errors in pricing the longevity or investment risk or because of bad management. Someplace in the fine print there is a statement that if the payouts on the annuity contracts are so large that the seller's solvency is threatened, the seller can reduce the payment to you as long as the payments to all the other owners of annuities are similarly reduced. If the seller goes bankrupt, the insurance commissioners in various states are likely to require that the other firms that sell annuities within the state take responsibility for the payment to you. This "private socialism" has been the ad hoc response in the past when insurance companies went bankrupt.

Now that you understand how annuities work, you're at the decision stage. Your first decision is whether to buy an annuity. The principal decisions you need to make if you do decide to buy an annuity are included in Figure 15.1. Since you can buy two $5,000 annuities rather than one $10,000 annuity, you can make more than one choice from each column for each annuity that you purchase. The first decision is the face value of the annuity, which is the one-time payment that you would make to the seller; the price can be $1,000, $10,000, $100,000, or $1 million. (You can buy the annuity on the installment plan; for example, you might decide when you are 55 that you would like to have a $5,000 annuity when you reach 65; the seller of the annuity will send you a reminder of the payment due each quarter or each month.) The second is the date of purchase, which might be this year or the next or five years from now. For example, you might decide to purchase four $25,000 annuities: one this year, one

Figure 15.1

The Annuity Decision Menu

(1)	(2)	(3)	(4)	(5)	(6)	(7)
Face Value	Purchase Date	Source of Funds	First Payment	Investment Choice	One Life/ Two Life	Minimum Payment Period
$1,000	Today	Charitable gifts	Immediately	Bonds Traditional TIPS	One life	
$5,000 $10,000	Next year	Securities	Next year 3 years 5 years 10 years	Stocks	Two life	10 years 15 years 20 years
$25,000	3 years from now	Reverse mortgage				
$50,000		Tax-advantaged funds				
$100,000		Cash				

Source: Author.

two years from now, the third four years from now, and the fourth six years from now. The third decision involves the source of funds to buy the annuity; these might include a reverse mortgage and a gift to a charity as well as funds in a tax-advantaged account. The fourth decision is the date you anticipate that the seller of the annuity will first make a payment to you—you might buy an annuity when you are 65 with the first payment to you scheduled five years later. The fifth decision is whether the payout from the annuity will be based on investments in bonds or in stocks. The sixth decision is whether the annuity will cover two individuals and the amount of the payment to the surviving annuitant as a percentage of the payment to both annuitants. The seventh decision is whether to seek a minimum number of payments in case both annuitants die within a few years after the purchase.

To Buy or Not to Buy an Annuity

There are two arguments for buying an annuity and three principal arguments against the purchase. The principal argument for buying an annuity is peace of mind. You will no longer need to worry that you might outlive your assets. If you pay someone enough, that someone will carry the uncertainty that might keep you up at night. Once a firm has sold you an annuity, you'll receive a monthly check as long as you and your designated beneficiary—if you have one—live.

The fear about outliving your assets might take one of several forms. You might be concerned that you don't trust yourself not to spend your savings at an unsustainable rate. You've worked hard to accumulate the savings, and the money might be exhausted long before you are. You may worry that one or several of your relatives will ask for a loan; their intent to repay may be noble, but they may fall on even harder times. Of course, they might ask for a loan based on your monthly income from the annuity and other sources, but that loan would be smaller and would not make a dent in your capital.

Wealthy individuals are not likely to be obsessed with outliving their assets. Instead, the longevity risk falls on their children or charities or the government; the longer they live, the smaller their residual estate. Those who are concerned that they might outlive their assets should focus on whether they can obtain peace of mind without committing all of their accumulated savings to the purchase of an annuity.

What sort of uncertainty can the seller of the annuity deal with? The seller's promise to send you a check as long as you live can be reassuring, but you should also be interested in how much you can buy with the monthly check—and with the purchasing power of the money received. If the U.S. price level increases, the purchasing power of the check is likely to decline, unless you're one of the few who has bought an annuity that promises to maintain the purchasing power of the monthly check.

It's not an accident that the only annuities that promise to maintain that purchasing power are based on an investment in Treasury Inflation-Protected Securities (TIPS) or on corporate bonds that are indexed to inflation. The U.S. Treasury can get the cash to honor its obligation by asking Congress to raise taxes, or by borrowing.

A second argument some advance for buying an annuity is that the annuity is a "bargain" because you (or you and your beneficiary) have "remarkable genes" and thus are very likely to outlive most of the others in your age cohort—each of your parents reached 100. In this case the monthly payments will include a partial "subsidy" from those whose genes or misfortune cause them to die before most of the others in the same age cohort. (You may want to consider why some of the buyers of annuities would want to subsidize other buyers.)

There may be some self-selection among those who consider buying an annuity; anyone concerned that the purchase of the annuity would be "costly" either would not buy an annuity or would seek to protect themselves—actually their estates—by arranging that the annuity provide for a minimum guarantee payment period, such as fifteen or twenty years. Since most of those who buy securities select a minimum guarantee period, usually twenty years, the "subsidy" from those who would die soon after buying the annuity to those who are likely to live much longer than average is modest, probably no more than 2 or 3 percent in present-value terms. The likelihood that the annuity is a bargain in the sense that the present value of the future checks is high relative to the amount paid to buy the annuity is low.

The Pattern in the U.S. Inflation Rate

If the U.S. price level had been set at 100 in 1900, then the price level would have been nearly 2,000 in 2000—an average annual increase of 4 percent a year. This increase was not continuous and gradual but rather episodic. There were three major inflationary periods: during and after World War I (1917–1921), when the increase in the price level averaged more than 15 percent a year; immediately after World War II (1944–1950), as the price and wage controls that had been adopted to limit inflation during the war were relaxed; and from 1973 to 1985, which was partially the aftermath of a short burst of government spending associated with the Vietnam War. Note that the second episode is modestly longer than the first, and the third episode is longer than the combined duration of the first and the second. On average, there has been one extended inflationary episode every thirty years.

You've heard the cliché "Stocks are a good inflation hedge." Not so—or, more accurately, yes and no. Consider the U.S. inflation that began in the late 1960s and continued through the early 1980s. Stock prices declined during this period. In the very long run, stock prices increase 4 or 5 percent more rapidly than the price level—but these increases in stock prices occur after the inflation rate has declined rather than during the years when the inflation rate is accelerating and interest rates are increasing.

One of your major concerns is how best to protect the purchasing power of your assets or the income on these assets when the cost of living increases. Most annuities aren't helpful—indeed, they can hurt a great deal.

One reason not to buy an annuity is that the purchase of the annuity is an irrevocable event. Once you buy an annuity, you've lost control over the use of your money, and you have fewer assets to draw on to cope with an unanticipated emergency. (Some banks or other lenders lend you money with the stream of monthly annuity checks pledged as collateral against the loan; however, these lenders would be concerned that this stream stops when you die, and so the amount that they would lend would be modest.) You may have a better opportunity to protect the purchasing power of your wealth if you don't buy an annuity.

A second reason not to buy an annuity is that annuities are inefficient— the administrative costs are high, as is evident in the difference in the premiums for term life insurance policies and cash value policies.

A third reason not to buy an annuity is that your cash needs are likely to decline as you move along the life cycle during your retirement. Your cash needs in the first five or ten years after retirement are likely to be greater than in subsequent years. But, again, this concern is important only if you committed all of your funds to buying an annuity; instead, you might commit one-third of your funds to the purchase of annuities, and you might stagger the purchases of several annuities. You might ask, "What is the minimum amount of an annuity payment that together with Social Security would provide me with peace of mind and enable me to maintain a comfortable standard of living?"

A fourth reason not to buy an annuity is that you can't leave assets from it to children, grandchildren, friends, and charities. If you buy an annuity, payments cease on death—unless you have had a minimum guarantee payments feature attached to the annuity. (One exception is that if you purchase an annuity by transfer of assets to charity, the charity receives a capital sum after you die.) Of course it is not ordained that you must spend all the income from Social Security and other annuities; you could save some.

The pros and cons of buying an annuity center on the emotional concern about outliving your assets relative to two other arguments. One is that you already have an annuity in the form of Social Security, and the other is that most annuities do not provide a hedge against a loss of wealth from inflation.

Before you buy an annuity, project your money needs in the first five to ten years of retirement with the monthly benefit from Social Security and from a defined-benefit pension plan (if you have one), and the annual distribution that you might receive if you take the minimum distribution approach to your tax-advantaged funds. To the extent that the cash available from the second approach is likely to approximate the amount needed to maintain the living standard, there is no immediate need to buy the annuity.

Charitable Remainder Trusts and Deferred Gift Annuities

One low-cost approach toward buying an annuity is to transfer an appreciated asset—bonds or stocks or real estate—to a charity, such as a college or university, a hospital, or an environmental group. You avoid paying the capital gains tax on the unrealized capital gain. The charity provides you with an income tax deduction, whose amount depends on the difference between the market value of the gift and the present value of the annuity payments to you as determined by the IRS. The charity then provides you with an annual or quarterly payment for as long as you live.

Assume that you own an asset with a market value of $15,000; your cost or basis is $8,000. If you sell the stock, you would have to pay a tax at the rate of 15 percent on the capital gain of $7,000; the tax payment would be $1,050 and you would have $13,950 in cash that you might use to buy some other asset. (If you are 65, you could use the $9,250 to buy an annuity.) If you give the $15,000 in stock to a charity, you receive an income tax deduction of $15,000; the amount of the gift depends on the present value of the stream of payments to you and varies with your age. If you decide to buy an annuity, first see whether you can pay for it with an appreciated asset.

Choosing the Face Value of an Annuity

If you still want the peace of mind an annuity can bring, consider buying an annuity with a modest face value. Your strategy might be to buy one $10,000 annuity this year, another $10,000 annuity one or two years from now, a third two to four years from now, and so on. One reason for the staggered purchase is to allow you to determine how much money you will spend each year in retirement. Another is to determine whether you will still be as concerned about the peace of mind a year from now and two years from now as you first were, or whether you've become a bit more comfortable carrying the longevity risk.

Timing the Purchase of an Annuity

The usual argument against delaying any purchase is that the price will be higher or that the product will not be available in the future. Neither of these arguments applies to the purchase of an annuity. One feature of an annuity is that the price of an annuity with a given face value declines the older you are at the time of purchase, since your life expectancy then is lower, and the stream of payments that the seller of the annuity expects to pay you is smaller.

The top row in Table 15.4 shows the purchase price of an annuity that would pay $1,000 a month at ages 60, 70, 80, and 90. The price at age 60 is $189,771, and the price at age 70 is $153,085. The bottom row shows the annual payment from a $100,000 annuity at each of these ages; if you had purchased the annuity at age 60, the annual payment to you would be $5,244. If instead you purchase the annuity at 70, the annual payment to you will be $6,264. You can see that the values in the two rows are nearly perfect mirror images of each other—the higher the age, the lower the values in the top row and the higher the values in the bottom row.

Table 15.4
Prices and Payouts on Single Life Annuities, 10 Years Guaranteed, Various Ages

	60	70	80	90
Purchase price	$189,771	$153,085	$120,590	$103,862
$100,000 payment	5,244	6,264	7,452	9,804

Source: TIAA-CREF.

Source of Funds

You can pay for an annuity in four ways. You can buy an annuity with a gift to a charity of either cash or of assets with unrealized capital gains. You can use the funds in your tax-advantaged account, including both IRAs and 401(c) accounts. You can "buy an annuity" by taking a reverse mortgage. And you can buy an annuity with cash. Which approach is preferable, and which has the lowest cost?

First, note that the location of the credit risk differs with the first three annuities. If you buy an annuity from a charity, your credit risk is likely to be with that charity, but if you buy an annuity from an insurance company, the credit risk is with that company. The credit risk with a reverse mortgage is more difficult to isolate; if the bank that offered you the mortgage encounters difficulties, bank regulators will ensure that some other bank acquires it, and the stream of payments to you will continue.

Consider the following instructive comparisons. Should you purchase an annuity from a charity by the transfer of an appreciated asset, or buy an identical annuity? For the purposes of comparison, the effective question is "How much annuity can I purchase for an after-tax cost of $10,000?" If you give stock to a charity, you avoid payment of any capital gains tax and you receive a tax deduction based on the market value of the gift. Assume that your marginal income tax rate is 35 percent. For example, assume that you purchase an annuity by transferring shares in IBM with a market value of $15,000 to a charity; your tax basis or cost for these securities is $8,000. If you sell the stock, you would pay a tax of $1,050 on the capital gain of $7,000 if the capital gains tax rate is 15 percent. If instead you transfer the stock to a charity in exchange for an annuity, you receive an income tax deduction of $15,000, and if you are in the 35 percent tax bracket, the reduction in your income tax payment is $5,250 and the after-tax cost to you is $9,750.

Now assume that you transfer cash to the charity. Since your marginal tax rate is 35 percent, you would pay $15,385 to the charity; the after-tax cost to you would be $10,000. The rate of return on a one-life annuity at age 65 would be 6.5 percent. Note, however, that the rate of return offered by some other charities could be higher or lower. The charity would pay you $1,000 a year. This is a no-brainer; the cost-effective approach is to buy the annuities with appreciated securities.

The second comparison is between the purchase of an annuity from a charity and from a commercial firm like MetLife or Prudential or

TIAA-CREF. The seller would pay you $898 a year. The rate of return on the purchase of the annuity from a charity is higher; remember, however, that the credit risk could be greater. The risk associated with a gift to Harvard or Cal Tech or the Roman Catholic Diocese of New York may seem low; still, these charities are not regulated by insurance commissioners. Note that your tax savings from the favored treatment by the IRS are shared with the charities.

Now consider the comparison between the purchase of an annuity from a commercial seller with cash with the purchase of a similar annuity from the same seller with tax-advantaged funds. The purchase of an annuity with money from a tax-advantaged account is like a rollover; you now have a tax-advantaged annuity. The distribution of the funds from the annuity to you is likely to be subject to income tax. If you had taken a withdrawal or distribution from the tax-advantaged account, that withdrawal would be subject to income tax, and if the distribution is large, the distribution could move you into the highest marginal tax rate. In contrast, if you buy the tax-advantaged annuity, your marginal tax rate when the funds are withdrawn from the tax-advantaged account could be lower. But there is some risk that the marginal tax rates might be increased.

A fifth way to pay for an annuity is to take out a reverse mortgage— assuming that you have some equity in your home. The reverse mortgage differs from traditional annuities in two important ways. One is that there is an upper limit to the amount of the annuity that you can buy with the reverse mortgage, regardless of the market value of your home; that upper limit varies with the city but is about $250,000. The second is that although you can live in your home as long as you want, even if the indebtedness exceeds the market value of the home, you can also undo the reverse mortgage by repaying the accumulated indebtedness. The complication is that you have to be concerned about the interest rate on the reverse mortgage and hence the rate at which your indebtedness would increase. If the market value of your home is much greater than the upper limit to the reverse mortgage, this approach is not likely to be attractive, because you will have paid for the option but can't use it.

Immediate Payment or Deferred Payments

You can arrange it so that the seller of the annuity begins to pay you soon after you buy the annuity or you can ask the seller to delay the first payment. The longer the delay, the lower the price of the annuity. This delay happens more or less automatically when you buy an annuity on the installment plan while employed; the capital sum of the annuity is increasing as a result of the combination of compound interest and the series of annual payments. A general rule of thumb is that each year's delay between the date that the annuity is purchased and the date of the first payment at a time when individuals are age 65 would lead to an increase in the annual payment of about 6 percent.

The Investment Choice

The payment that the seller of the annuity will make to you has two components. One is the investment income on the amount that you paid the seller when you bought the annuity—less the costs that the seller incurred in inducing you to buy the annuity. The second is a return of part of the funds that you paid the seller when you bought the annuity; in effect, this is like the drawdown of your accumulated savings described earlier. In the early years after you buy an annuity, most of the payments to you— perhaps as much as 95 percent—consist of investment income. Year by year, a declining amount of the payment to you will be the investment income on the funds you transferred to the seller, and an increasing share will be the return of your capital.

Stocks

The two principal investment choices are bonds and stocks; there are two subgroups under the bond choice, including a graduated bond account and an inflation-indexed bond account. The key feature of the graduated bond account is that the monthly payment increases at an annual rate of 3 or 4 percent. The initial monthly payment is smaller than with the traditional bond annuity; after about ten or twelve years, the annual payments on the two accounts are about the same, and thereafter the payments on the graduated bond account are higher. The TIPS choice provides an inflation-hedged annuity.

You also can ask the seller of the annuity to make a payment to you based on an investment in bonds. TIAA-CREF sells annuities that are based on investments in bonds and provide for a stipulated scheduled payment which might be fixed at one level forever or may increase at the rate of 3 percent a year. (This configuration is designed to maintain the purchasing power of the money you are paid; the implicit assumption is that the inflation rate is likely to average about 3 percent a year.) In the latter case, the amount of the initial payment will be significantly smaller than if you had chosen a fixed annual payment. It might take ten or twelve years before the amount of the annual payment increases to the value of the fixed annual payment.

You can also ask that the sellers of annuities base their payouts to you on the prices of stocks. These annuities provide a monthly payment to you as long as you live, although the amount of the monthly payment varies with changes in the stock prices. If the price of stocks increases, the monthly payment increases; conversely, if the price of stocks declines, the monthly payment declines. The sellers of these annuities bear the longevity risk, but you bear the investment risk.

If you buy an annuity with a face value of $100,000, you would purchase x annuity units ($x = \$100,000/\$$per annuity unit), depending on the price of each of these annuity units on the date of the purchase. An annuity unit is a percentage participation in a pool of stocks, more or less like a share in a mutual fund.

You can buy a diversified set of annuities, a sort of portfolio of annuities; for example, you might buy a $25,000 annuity based on an investment in bonds, another $25,000 based on a graduated payment in bonds, and a third $25,000 based on an investment in stocks.

Should you prefer a variable-price annuity based on investment in stocks to a fixed-price annuity based on an investment in bonds? Three factors bear on this decision. The first is that historically the rate of return on bonds has been somewhat lower than the rate of return on stocks after adjustment for changes in the price level. The second is that the rate of return on stocks was exceptionally high between 1982 and 2000; the implication is that over the next few years the rate of return on stocks is likely to be modest relative to the rate of return on bonds. The third is that most individuals in the retirement mode should be more conservative in the management of their assets because they are no longer accumulating capital.

One Life or Two—and How Much to the Surviving Annuitant?

You can buy a one-life annuity. The payments stream stops when you die, although you might arrange to receive a minimum number of payments. Or you might buy a two-life annuity; the second annuitant might be a spouse, a significant other, a child, or a friend. The monthly payment on a two-life annuity is smaller than on a one-life annuity, and the difference between the two payments depends on the difference in the ages of the two annuitants and the amount of the payment to the second annuitant as a percentage of the payment.

The Choice of a Minimum Guarantee Period

Many buyers of annuities are worried about "losing their money" if they die soon after buying the annuity. They protect "their interests" by asking for a minimum guaranteed payment of fifteen or twenty years. The sellers of the annuities are indifferent and seek to price the several features so that their own rates of return are similar.

There is an inherent contradiction between the concern with outliving one's assets, which is the primary rationale for buying an annuity, and taking the minimum annual distribution. If your finances are so slender that you think buying an annuity is imperative, do not take the minimum annual distribution.

If you intend to buy an annuity, consider buying a series of annuities over a number of years. For example, assume that you plan to spend $100,000 on an annuity; rather than buy one annuity, buy ten annuities of $10,000 each, one during each of the next ten years. Your average price will be lower by about 10 percent.

The Misplaced Advantages of Buying a Small Annuity

Some individuals commit half—or 40 percent or 60 percent—of the accumulated balances in their defined-contribution pension plan to the purchase of an annuity, perhaps on the rationale that the payments on the annuity together with the Social Security benefit would be sufficient to provide the funds necessary to maintain their desired standard of living in retirement; they would have the peace of mind that they would not outlive their assets. The actual proportion would depend on the estimates of the amount needed together with the funds from Social Security to achieve the minimum living standard.

The logic is baffling; if their accumulated savings are sufficiently large so that the likelihood that they would outlive their assets is trivially small, there is no need to buy an annuity. The case for buying the annuity is that there is some risk there won't be enough money at the distant end of the life cycle, and so the buyers are willing to forgo spending some money in the first few years after they retire to ensure they will have the minimum necessary for comfort and dignity fifteen and twenty years in the future.

Strategy toward Tax-Advantaged Accounts

The bias of most individuals with an IRA or a 401(k) or some other tax-advantaged account is to leave the funds in the account as long as possible so as to take full advantage of the implicit subsidy that the investment income is untaxed. Remember, however, that income tax will be paid when the funds are withdrawn from the account (except for a Roth IRA), and similarly if there are tax-advantaged accounts in your estate, the estate will pay the income tax on these funds. If the tax-advantaged funds are gifted to a charity, no tax will be paid by the charity.

What, then, is the optimal time to withdraw the funds from the account? The mantra from Chapter 6 was that your objective should always be to maximize your after-tax income. Two factors are at issue. One is your marginal tax rates in different years, and the other is the choice between securities that reward investors with capital gains and those that reward investors primarily with either interest income or dividend income.

Consider the second issue first. Assume that the securities in your tax-advantaged accounts reward investors primarily with capital gains, either because you own mutual funds that specialize in holding that group of securities or because you own the securities outright. You pay no tax on the capital gains that you secure on these stocks when the stocks are in your tax-advantaged account. When you withdraw funds from a tax-advantaged account, you will pay tax at the ordinary income tax rate (except when the funds are withdrawn from a Roth IRA). In contrast, if you had held these same securities in a non-tax-advantaged account, you would have paid tax at the capital gains tax rate. If you have both a traditional IRA and a Roth IRA, you should hold the stocks that reward their owners with price appreciation in the Roth IRA and the other stocks in the traditional IRA.

Assume three possible scenarios that relate your marginal income tax rates in the future to the same rates today. The first scenario is that your marginal tax rate will be higher, either because your income will be higher or because the marginal tax rates will be increased. The second scenario is that your marginal tax rate will be lower, either because your income will be less or because future tax rates will be lower. The intermediate scenario is that your marginal tax rates remain unchanged.

Note from Table 15.1 that the minimum annual distribution percentage required by the IRS increases to 8 percent only when individuals reach age 89. If the inflation rate is 3 percent, the value of the tax-advantaged accounts will increase until the owners of these accounts take no more than the minimum annual distribution.

If you anticipate that your marginal tax rate is likely to be higher in the future, the implication is that you should increase the amount that you withdraw from your tax-advantaged account—that is, take the distribution this year when your marginal tax rate is lower than it is likely to be in the future. You could use the funds received to pay for your current living expenses, or you could use them to buy bonds and stocks.

If instead you anticipate that your marginal tax rate is likely to be lower in the future, you should limit the amount that you withdraw from the tax-advantaged account to the minimum necessary to satisfy the IRS rules on the minimum annual distribution. If the funds withdrawn from the accounts exceed the amount you need for your living expenses, you should buy stocks that reward investors with price appreciation in the non-tax-advantaged accounts.

Now consider the intermediate case when you do not expect any change in your marginal income tax rate. To the extent that you want to hold stocks that reward investors through increases in stock prices, it would be advantageous to withdraw funds from the tax-advantaged accounts and buy and hold these stocks in a non-tax-advantaged account.

Assume that you want to hold stocks that reward investors through the payment of dividends. You could withdraw funds from the tax-advantaged accounts, pay the income tax, and reinvest the rest of your funds in the same securities for ten or fifteen years, and pay the tax on the dividend income on a year-by-year basis and sell the stocks at the end of ten or fifteen years. Or you could continue to hold these stocks in the tax-advantaged account and at the end of the period sell the stocks and pay the tax; call this option 2.

On Eating Your Capital in Retirement:
Choices, Choices, Choices

You will have a range of choices about managing your wealth in retirement. You are likely to own your home, and you may have tax-advantaged funds. You also may have accumulated savings.

One of your principal concerns is whether you should first draw on the funds in your tax-advantaged accounts over and above the amount required for the minimum annual distribution or whether instead you should draw on the funds in your non-tax-advantaged accounts or take out a reverse mortgage.

The optimal time for taking out a reverse mortgage is when interest rates are exceptionally low relative to trend. At that time, you will be able to obtain an exceptionally large mortgage loan relative to trend given your age. The market value of your home is also likely to be exceptionally high.

Two factors should primarily affect the choice between these two sources of funds. One is the likelihood of a change in the marginal income tax rate you might pay; the other is your preference for growth and high-dividend stocks. If you prefer growth stocks and think that your marginal tax rate is likely to be higher, draw first on the funds in your tax-advantaged account.

ACTIONABLES

1. Itemize your employment-related pensions, record the contract numbers, and ask the seller to project your accumulated balance(s) at age 60, 65, and 70.

2. Determine the range of investments that can be acquired with the money in your defined-contribution plan and your other tax-advantaged accounts.

3. Determine the fees and charges set by the manager of the funds in the defined-contribution plan.

4. Determine how easily and quickly you can shift back and forth between stocks and bonds.

5. Before funds are transferred from any tax-advantaged account, investigate all of the tax consequences.

6. Do a great deal of comparative shopping before buying an annuity.

16   A Cruel Choice: Paying for Medical
Recoveries or Health Care

The medical establishment has made great strides in extending the life span of Americans in the last several decades. One unintended result is a sharp increase in the health care costs associated with the final years of life because of dramatic changes in the cause of death. Fifty years ago, death often was relatively quick and not very costly because of heart attacks, strokes, and accidents. Now many Americans live into their eighties or nineties, and there is a much higher probability of developing Alzheimer's disease or some other lingering and debilitating ailment. You're likely to have fifteen, twenty, or more good years after you retire, and then you might have three or five years that will require a lot of care—expensive care.

The health care decisions differ from most of the others that you make in two dramatic ways. The first is that you are often dependent on the advice of the seller or supplier of the health care service about what you should do—and the seller or supplier may not provide unbiased advice, since his or her income will be higher if you buy the service. The residents of Miami and Boston buy more health care services than residents of most other U.S. cities, and not surprisingly, there are relatively more sellers of health care services in these two cities—but the residents of Miami and Boston do not live longer than those in other cities. The inference is that some of the expenditures in these cities are not productive in the sense of extending life.

The second difference between the purchase of health care services and most other services is that the buyers pay only a fraction of the cost of many services; a much larger share of the total cost is provided by an insurance company or a health care company or the U.S. government— and this is especially true for seniors. Obviously the total cost has to be covered, usually by insurance premiums or taxes, but there is a large disconnect between the amount paid for a particular service and the total cost of providing that service. Hence there is a tendency to buy more of that service than would otherwise be the case, which leads to higher insurance premiums and higher tax rates.

Still, the newspapers carry sad stories about families that were financially comfortable until an accident or an illness bled their bank accounts and their savings. Will you have enough money to pay the bills should you find yourself in such a situation? Or will you spend down your assets and then be in the position of relying on the government to pay for your maintenance costs in the last few years of life?

Medicare and Medicaid

Medicare and Medicaid are two large U.S. government programs that are often confused. Medicare is a program for all Americans over age 64. Medicaid is for Americans who do not have sufficient income to pay for their own medical and health care costs. Although 65 is the traditional age for eligibility for Medicare, some disabled individuals who are younger than 65 and individuals with Lou Gehrig's disease and end-stage kidney disease also qualify for Medicare. Medicare requires co-payments; some individuals who are over 65 qualify for Medicare if they cannot take care of the co-payments on their own.

Medicare is a national program, with uniform standards. Medicaid is administered by the states.

Seniors incur two different sets of health care costs. There are the expenses associated with recovery from an illness or an accident; the payments are made to doctors, hospitals, pharmacies, and other health care providers. About the only differences from the preretirement costs are that it may take longer to get well and the periods when you're under

the weather may be more frequent. The second set of costs is for maintenance: getting dressed, bathing, eating, and moving between the bed and
a chair. Most of these costs are reimbursements for those who help with
the daily chores of living because seniors don't have the energy or strength
or mental capacity to do these things on their own.

Once you reach age 65, you are eligible for an array of medical services under the U.S. government's Medicare program. You will already
have paid for a large part of the costs of these services through automatic
deductions from your paycheck while you were employed. (When you
were employed, part of your salary was deducted to finance the Medicare
costs incurred by those already 65 and over; now that you're 65, most of
the costs of the services that you receive are paid for by taxes on the actively employed.)

Enrollment in Medicare is more or less automatic once you turn 65.
There are two additional primary decisions about the financial aspects
of your health care needs. One, which occurs either when you enroll in
Medicare or subsequently, is whether to buy one or several insurance
policies popularly known as Medigap policies that will complement the
payments from Medicare and reimburse some or most of the costs that
Medicare will not cover. The other, which can occur either before or after
you reach 65, is whether to buy a health care insurance policy that would
pay you a stipulated daily amount to reimburse the costs of maintenance
if you need extensive help to perform the tasks of daily living, perhaps
in a nursing home or some other assisted-living facility or even in your
own home.

You automatically self-insure if you don't buy insurance—although
the Medicare program will reimburse maintenance costs in an approved
facility if your assets are modest. You need to determine whether the various Medigap policies and the health care policies are expensive or inexpensive relative to your income. Then you need to decide whether you
should buy either or both types of insurance and, if your budget is limited,
which type of insurance is preferable.

Are the year-in, year-out costs associated with recovery from various
illnesses and accidents over the next twenty-five or thirty years likely to
be higher than the costs of maintenance? The recovery costs are certain,
although the amounts involved are uncertain; the maintenance costs are
uncertain because they depend on your general health conditions as you
move toward the end of the life cycle.

The way that Americans pay for medical and health care services has changed drastically in the last fifty years. In the 1950s most doctors were independent practitioners and most hospitals were nonprofits owned by "the community" or by a religious or fraternal group. You were charged for a service soon after you visited your doctor, who mailed you a bill at the end of the month following an office visit or a house call. The hospital presented you a bill as you checked out and politely asked how you planned to pay. You either paid the doctors and the hospitals directly or left the bills unpaid. You might have paid an entry fee on entering a nursing home and then a monthly fee for food and accommodation.

During the last half century, the suppliers of medical services noted in the left column in Table 16.1 have expanded to include many health maintenance organizations (HMOs), which consist of doctors practicing together, often under the umbrella of an insurance company. Now, the U.S. government's Medicare program partially reimburses nearly every American age 65 and over for a wide variety of services provided by doctors and hospitals. Private insurance complements Medicare. A very different type of private health care insurance reimburses the maintenance costs in nursing homes, and even in your own home. You may still write the checks to doctors and hospitals, much as your grandparents did; now you are likely to be reimbursed from government insurance or from private insurance. Or you may pay a fixed fee for medical services when you write the monthly check to your HMO.

Most doctors are salaried and paid by HMOs; many hospitals now are owned by for-profit chains. Similarly, many nursing homes are owned

Table 16.1
Health Care Suppliers and Payment Arrangements

Health Care Suppliers	Sources of Payment
Doctors	Government
Clinics	Government insurance
HMOs	Private insurance
Hospitals	Charities
Retirement/nursing homes	Personal funds
Hospices	
Nurses	
Pharmacies	

Source: Author.

by for-profit firms. More than 1,000 continuing care retirement communities supply comprehensive medical services and health care as part of a package that includes housing, food, and recreational services.

A third party—a government agency, an insurance company, or an HMO—now is more likely to be an intermediary between the suppliers of services and the customer or buyer. There is far less direct connection between the supply of a particular service and the payment for the service. One explanation for the change is that the medical services are now much more expensive because of extensive new diagnostic technologies. Individuals still pay directly for drugs, and they usually pay directly for nursing home care.

Health Savings Accounts or Medical Savings Accounts

Legislation in 2003 made it possible for individuals to establish health savings accounts, which are dedicated accounts like individual retirement accounts (IRAs) in a bank or some other plan sponsor. The funds transferred to these accounts reduce taxable income on a dollar-for-dollar basis (which is an end-run that circumvents the restriction that only those medical expenditures in excess of 7.5 percent of adjustable gross income are deductible from taxable income). Three requirements must be satisfied if you are to qualify for a health savings account: you must be younger than 64, you must have a high-deductible health insurance plan, and you must not have any other health insurance coverage (although you can have dental and long-term health care). The amount of tax-free money you can transfer to this account each year depends on the amount of the deductible; the higher the deductible, the larger the amount of tax-free dollars.

You would draw on the money in this account to pay for medical expenses. And the values in this account would accumulate—apparently without limit—if the amount that you would allocate to the account each year was larger than the amount withdrawn. If you withdrew funds from the account for nonmedical purposes, the IRS would hit you with a 10 percent penalty. When you withdraw funds from the account to pay for medical expenses, the money is not treated as taxable income (unlike a withdrawal from an IRA).

The U.S. government's Medicare program spent $236 billion in 2008, mostly to reimburse Americans for payments to doctors and hospitals. Medicare initially had two parts: Part A, which reimbursed some of the costs of hospitalization, and Part B, which reimbursed some doctors' fees, most outpatient hospital services, and some related services. Then in 2006 Part D began to reimburse some of the costs of drugs. (The funds for Part A are obtained from a tax on wages and salaries like the Social Security tax, and the funds for Part B are obtained by an automatic deduction from your Social Security benefit; Part D is financed both from premiums and from the U.S. Treasury.) Medicare pays the maintenance costs of individuals only when they are in hospitals temporarily. Both Part A and Part B have a deductible for each calendar year and a co-insurance feature for costs over and above the deductibles. Part D has both deductibles and co-insurance features.

Moral Hazard and the Demand for Health Services

The term "moral hazard" means that the economic agent has a self-interest. The companies that sell life insurance encounter the moral hazard that the buyers of one of these policies will take a swan dive from the Golden Gate Bridge; the companies that sell fire insurance encounter the moral hazard that unsuccessful small-business people will torch the store to collect the insurance money. The moral hazard in health insurance is that individuals who are covered by one of the policies will "buy" many more medical and health care services than they would if they had to pay for these services directly with their own money.

The infrequency of direct payment for medical services presents a moral hazard. Because no immediate out-of-pocket cost is attached to the "purchase" of these services, more of these services are demanded than would be the case if the price were related directly to the true economic cost of providing the service; it seems as if the services are "free." But these services may be costly, and the money to pay for them comes from the taxes or the insurance premiums you pay. Both taxes and insurance premiums are higher because individuals demand more medical services than they would if they had to be concerned about the cost of each service.

Part A of Medicare reimburses a large part of the costs of your stay in a hospital. If you're in the hospital for fewer than 61 days, you pay the first $1,100 a year and Medicare pays the rest. If you're in the hospital between 60 and 90 days, you will pay $275 for each day and Medicare pays the rest. Some of the costs of care in a skilled nursing home are covered after you have been in a hospital for three consecutive days. Medicare also covers the costs of care in a hospice.

Part B of Medicare has three principal features. The first is a list of medical services for which you can claim reimbursement and a ceiling on the amount that Medicare will reimburse for each service. (Many suppliers charge this price and some charge more.) Medicare will reimburse the costs that are on its approved list only after you have paid the first $155 of these costs in a calendar year. After the first $155 deductible, Medicare pays 80 percent of these approved costs; you pay the remaining 20 percent (see Table 16.2).

There are three implicit subsidies in the Medicare program. Those with relatively high incomes subsidize those with lower incomes, since they pay more in taxes and receive the same benefits. Those who have had healthy lifestyles are less frequent users of medical services than those who have been heavy smokers or are overweight or otherwise have the misfortune to have a string of maladies, so those in the first group sub-

Table 16.2
Medicare Reimbursement

	Medicare Pays	You Pay
Part A: Hospitalization		
First 60 days	All but $1,100	$1,100
Next 30 days	All but $275/day	$275/day
Part B: Medical expenses		
First $155 of Medicare-approved amounts	0%	$155
Remainder of Medicare-approved excess charges	80%	20%

Note: Thus far Part A of Medicare has been entirely supported by dedicated payroll taxes collected from those at work, and Part B has been supported by those who receive Social Security benefits.

Source: Data from 2010 CCH Social Security Benefits Including Medicare (Chicago: Wolters Kluwer, 2010).

sidize those in the second group, since both pay about the same premium. Finally, the doctors and hospitals are subsidized because Medicare reimburses them for services to the elderly poor who would have been charity patients in an earlier age. (A small sample suggests that hospitals write off about 2 percent of their "revenues" as charity payments.)

Congress required the sellers of Medigap policies to standardize their features so the buyers wouldn't be confused by the razzle-dazzle of the sellers; the sellers compete on price but not on the features of the policy. The result is that there are ten different varieties of "plain vanilla" policies. The basic vanilla is the "A policy." The "B policy" is slightly more comprehensive than the "A policy," and the "C policy" is slightly more comprehensive. The "J" policy is the most comprehensive. Although many firms sell these policies, not every firm sells each of the policies in every state.

The rates for women are likely to differ from the rates for men. Some of the sellers may have a "family discount"—the rate for a husband and wife is modestly lower than the sum of the rates for a man and woman of the same age. Some of the policies including the G policy are shown with and without a deductible of $2,000.

The more comprehensive a policy, the fewer the deductibles and the higher the monthly insurance premium. Your choice is whether to buy a policy with many deductibles and self-insure against the costs that would otherwise be reimbursed if you bought a policy with fewer deductibles.

Some insurance companies set the premiums according to age; senior seniors pay higher premiums than junior seniors. The premiums are higher in some regions of the country than in others. Several of the plans have a high deductible; the benefits are the same, but you pay the first $1,580 each year. The premium for a Plan A Medigap policy for one person is about $600 a year, and the cost of the most upscale policy is about $2,000 a year.

Assume you bought the most upscale policy. Your total out-of-pocket costs for health care policies would then be about $2,000 a year, primarily for insurance premiums; in addition, you would pay some part of the costs for your own drugs.

The companies that sell Medigap policies aren't giving anything away. They probably set the premiums for each of the policies from Plan A to Plan I so that they would fully recover their costs with each type of policy.

But there's a twist—the sellers of automobiles have a much higher profit rate on the sale of options like the built-in navigators and the rearview TV camera when the car is in reverse than they do on the plain vanilla stick-shift model, and the sellers of vodka anticipate much higher profits when the bottle is frosted and stylishly decorated. Similarly, the sellers of the Medigap policies probably have structured their premiums so that the more upscale policies are much more profitable than the basic vanilla policy.

Revisit briefly the principles that should govern your purchase of insurance. You want to buy an insurance policy when the amount of the loss if you self-insure is so large that it would wreak havoc with your finances for a year or two or longer, and when the insurance is fairly priced—that is, the amounts paid in settlement of claims are large relative to the premiums paid.

The minimum cost that would disrupt your finances depends on your income and net worth. Some individuals might find a payment of $1,000 traumatic, although wealthier individuals would not be bothered by a payment of $5,000 or even $10,000. (Remember that medical expenses in excess of 7.5 percent of your taxable income are deductible from your income in computing your tax liability.) Both groups might be greatly pained by out-of-pocket payments of $30,000 or $40,000.

Both groups might be better served by purchasing an insurance policy that reimburses against catastrophic health care and recovery costs. In contrast, Medigap policies reimburse against relatively modest costs.

Comprehensive Health Care Maintenance

The flip side to the good news that you are far less likely to die of a heart attack or a stroke or cancer is that the last lingering illness is likely to be more expensive. As you move into your seventies and eighties, you're more likely to require a lot of expensive attention from caregivers during some extended period of time. The data suggest that about a third of seniors will need expensive care. A significant number of elderly Americans are afflicted with "neurodegenerative diseases"—4 million Americans have Alzheimer's disease, and 1 million have Parkinson's disease.

The costs of a basic nursing home might be $150 a day—$55,000 a year. The daily costs vary by region and by city. Figure seven or eight years, and it's a lot of money. You aren't likely to have any other significant expenditures when you're in one of these facilities, except perhaps for drugs—you won't be traveling, spending money on clothes, or going to many ball games.

There are three basic approaches to these financial costs: you can buy an insurance policy that would reimburse most or all of these costs, you could enter a continuing care retirement community (CCRC), or you could self-insure.

Many insurance companies sell policies that will reimburse the costs of health care. You can choose among policies that provide $100, $200, or $300 a day for three, five, or seven years or even for a lifetime. The policies are Lego-like—you can increase the amount that the policy will pay you each day, and you can extend the length of the payment period. The premiums on the $200-a-day policy are twice as high as those on the $100-a-day policy. Similarly, the premium on the policy that would provide payment for up to five years is generally two-thirds higher than the one on the policy that provides payment for up to three years. These policies generally have a deductible; you can begin to collect in settlement of claims only after you have paid for the first ninety days that you receive the care.

The insurance company probably will ask that you pass a medical exam before it sells you one of these policies. The younger you are when you buy a health care policy, the lower the annual premium; once again, the insurance company is building up a cash reserve. The premiums are somewhat like those for a permanent life insurance policy, in that they are fixed once established.

The companies that sell these policies have set the premiums on the basis of the data on the likelihood that they will have to pay and the length of the payment period. This type of policy is relatively new, and these companies' experience in setting premiums at the levels that correspond with claims is limited. To compensate, they've likely been conservative in setting these premiums—that is, the premiums are somewhat high relative to the prospective claims payments. Perhaps the companies have underestimated longevity, but that's unlikely.

Once an individual has one of these policies and has paid the costs associated with the deductible, the insured has little incentive to economize on the demand for health services. The sellers of the insurance realize that there is a moral hazard and adjust their premiums accordingly. Insurance companies may pay out fifty cents in the settlement of claims for every dollar they receive in premium income. Not an inexpensive policy.

Continuing Care Retirement Communities

The last twenty years have seen the rapid increase in the number of continuing care retirement communities (CCRCs), a very upscale version of the old-line nursing home. Initially, some CCRC sponsors were affiliated with religious groups. Now, some for-profit firms associated with large hotel chains are sponsors of CCRCs. Usually there is a front-end entry fee and a monthly charge, which covers the cost of the rental of an apartment or a small house, a minimum number of meals a week, medical and health costs over and above Medicare Parts A and B, and various housekeeping charges.

The entry fee and the monthly charge vary with the size of the living unit; the charges for a three-bedroom cottage may be three times those for a studio apartment. Additional costs include telephone calls and any meals taken in the dining room beyond the number stipulated in the CCRC contract.

If you join a CCRC, the bill for your health care will be packaged along with the monthly charges for one or two meals a day. Moreover, to the extent that the CCRC has an entry fee, part of the entry fee may be allocated for part of your anticipated future health care costs. The CCRC builds up a financial reserve during the years when you need relatively little health care to cover its costs when you need much more care. Some CCRCs have facilities for the care for individuals with Alzheimer's disease.

The typical CCRC provides three levels of care. Most individuals are fully ambulatory and live in their own apartments when they first enter a CCRC; many of their meals are served in a central dining facility. The next level of care involves the delivery of meals to the individual's apartment. The third level is comparable to a nursing home; the individual moves into a wing of the facility with full-time nursing care. Usually the monthly fees do not increase as the care required increases. There may be an additional charge if one spouse moves into the nursing wing while the other spouse remains in the apartment.

When CCRCs were first established, most had a nonrefundable entry fee that was tied to the size of the living unit. Increasingly, part or all of the entry fee may be refundable, although the larger the proportion of the entry fee that is refundable, the higher the entry fee. You may be able to choose between an entry fee that is 50 percent refundable and one that is 90 percent refundable. (You might prefer a refundable entry fee if you're concerned that you won't find the lifestyle in a CCRC compatible or because you want to leave bequests to children or others.)

The front-end entry fee may seem high, but perhaps you can obtain all or most of the money needed from the proceeds from the sale of your home or condo apartment. Your Social Security check might cover most of the monthly fee.

One appealing feature of the CCRC concept is that the combination of the entry fee and the monthly fee provides a useful benchmark for your living costs in retirement, including implicitly the cost of long-term health care.

Decisions, Decisions: Buying Peace of Mind

The Rolls-Royce approach to the financial costs of health care is either to self-insure or to buy the most comprehensive Medigap policy and, in addition, a health care policy that would reimburse $300 a day for the rest of your life. If you're wealthy, you can self-insure. If self-insurance seems too risky, then the combination of the upscale Medigap policy and a comprehensive health care policy would cost about $8,000 a year when you are 65. Remember that the premium payments on the health care policy will be higher the older you are when you buy the policy. A lot of money, yes. Remember, it's the Rolls-Royce approach and you want to buy peace of mind.

If the premium payments make too big a dent in your budget, then you need to focus on the following question: "If I have only $1,000 or $2,000 a year that can be used to buy insurance for both medical and health care expenses, am I better off buying a Medigap policy or joining an HMO for retirees or buying a long-term health care policy?"

The question is which risks of medicine and health care should be self-insured and which should be prepaid—a complicated choice. One concern is the cost of each type of insurance. (Remember the theme from Chapter 5: the cost of insurance is the difference between the amounts that the companies collect in premiums and the amounts they pay out in settlement of claims.) Both of these insurances are expensive, in that the companies may pay out only fifty cents for every dollar they collect in premiums. The second concern is the hit to your wallet if you incur a medical or a health care expense and are not insured.

Remember that the basic approach when buying insurance is to protect your standard of living and net worth from very large losses from low-probability events. The principle is to self-insure against small losses and buy insurance against large losses. Buy the insurance policies with the highest deductibles.

Distinguish between the costs of each type of insurance and the amount you would pay for each. The costs you might incur because you don't have a health care policy are much, much larger than the costs that you would incur if you don't have a Medigap policy. You should give priority to buying a health care policy.

Consider first the Medigap policies. The premiums range from $600 a year for the plain vanilla version to $2,000 a year for the upscale model. If you buy the upscale policies, you're being reimbursed for the deductibles.

The Medigap policies are "expensive" in that the amounts that the companies pay out in the settlement of claims are much smaller than the amounts that the companies receive in premium payments. Remember that the difference covers the operating costs of the companies, the amounts spent on all those mailings and TV ads, and the efforts of the companies to build up reserves. So stick with a basic Medigap policy.

Now consider the premium for long-term health care. These premiums could amount to $4,000 a year. One way to reduce the premium is to seek a larger deductible—you would pay the costs of the first 180 days of care rather than the costs of the first 90 days.

The federal and state income tax systems have a small bias against buying both Medigap policies and health care policies. If in any year your payments for medical care and health care are exceptionally large, then all of the costs in excess of 7.5 percent of your taxable income can be deducted from your federal and state income taxes. Your premium payments for both Medigap and health care policies also would be tax deductible, but in most years your total medical costs including these costs are likely to be smaller than the 7.5 percent threshold, and so the insurance premiums would not be tax deductible.

For example, assume your taxable income is $60,000 and your medical expenses total $35,000. The 7.5 percent threshold is (7.5% × $60,000), or $4,500. So $31,500 of your medical expenses would be tax deductible.

If you're in the 35 percent income tax bracket, your payment would decline by $11,025. Still, you would be out of pocket $23,975. The larger your medical and health care expenses relative to your income, the greater the tax savings because of the medical expense deduction.

A general rule of thumb is that the taxes will reduce the out-of-pocket costs by about 25 percent. The ideal insurance policy would have a large deductible and a large co-insurance feature; the larger these are, the lower the premium and the lower the economic costs of the policy. You want to minimize the likelihood that you will subsidize those who require a lot of medical services because they feel they've already paid for them.

The implication of the principle of buying only those insurances that will reimburse against catastrophic losses is that the first use of your funds should be to buy a basic health care policy—say, one that would pay $100 a day for three years and with a large deductible. The incremental cost to extend the period of payment is modest and is more attractive than extending the amount of the daily payment.

If your assets are large enough to pay for four or five years in a quality nursing home, then you might ask your children how they feel about the purchase of a health care policy. In effect, they will be "betting" the annual premium payments against the probability that you will need some form of custodial care that will make a dent in their inheritance. The best outcome from their point of view is that you have a short final illness and do not purchase a health care insurance policy. The next best outcome is that you have a short final illness and have purchased a policy. This outcome makes a modest dent in their inheritance because of the amount of the cumulative premium payments and because the costs of the final illness proved smaller than the high deductible in the policy. If the final illness lasts less than ninety days, then the health care policy will not make any payments because of the high deductible. The third best outcome is that you have purchased a health care policy and the final illness is long; this outcome is not quite as attractive as the second because the cost of the final illness is higher before the policy begins to pay the amount above the deductible. The worst outcome from their point is view is that your final illness is long and you have not purchased such a policy; this outcome makes a big dent in their inheritance.

In effect, you're playing the odds with what eventually will be their money.

ACTIONABLES

1. Determine whether you satisfy the conditions for establishing a health savings plan. If you do, establish a health savings plan with the highest feasible deductible.

2. If you decide you need a health care insurance policy, buy one with a large deductible and high co-insurance features.

3. Visit several continuing care retirement communities and discuss the costs of long-term health care.

17 You Can't Take Your Money with You, But You Can Say Where It Goes

When you're hit by the proverbial train, you want your assets to go where you want them to go when you've gone to wherever you hope to go. Since it's difficult to take your money with you on that last trip, you want to be sure that your assets go to the intended beneficiaries. You also may want to minimize the amount of your assets that stick to the hands of the tax collectors and the lawyers.

One of the two sets of issues involved in estate planning centers on the laws that control the disposition or allocation of the property of the recently deceased, and the other deals with the taxes associated with the transfer of the property from individuals and their estates to relatives and friends. If you try to minimize taxes, you may lose control of your assets. If you try to retain control, you will forgo the opportunity to minimize taxes. A difficult choice.

When you die, the law of the state where you live—your legal residence—provides that ownership of all your assets is transferred to your estate. This transfer is automatic; there is nothing you can do about it (except to give some of your assets away prior to death so that the estate will be smaller). Your estate is a fictitious person, more or less like a corporation. The next step, established by law, is that someone—the "executor" of the estate—is required by law to write the checks to pay your debts and taxes and to transfer the legal titles to the assets that are now in your estate to the individuals and charities that you have designated.

The transfer of the assets will follow the terms of your will—if you have one. If you don't have a will, then the transfer will follow the procedures in the state where you had your legal domicile.

"Probate" is the name of this transfer process, which means attesting to the authenticity of your will. The probate process starts when someone—a relative, a trusted friend, a creditor—calls the judge of the probate court in the county where you live with the information that you have died. The probate judge is supposed to protect your creditors and heirs and ensure that the instructions in your will about the disposition of your assets are followed. Probate is a big business. About $500 billion in assets goes through the probate process each year—there are 15,000 probate judges in the United States. (Each county has a probate judge, although in sparsely populated areas the judge may work part time.)

Your will is a legal document that identifies who should receive the assets that you owned before they were transferred to your estate. When someone dies, the original copy of the will is forwarded to the probate court. The will identifies an executor—usually a close relative or trusted friend or a lawyer or a bank—who is legally responsible for paying your outstanding bills and debts and income taxes. The executor may sell some of the assets in the estate to get the cash to make these payments. After these payments have been made, the executor is supposed to follow your instructions about transferring the remaining assets to designated individuals and charities.

If you don't have a will, the distribution of the assets will follow the practices of the state where you live. In most states, all of the assets go to the surviving spouse. In some common-law states, one-half of the assets go the surviving spouse and the other half is divided among the children. The judge of the probate court appoints an administrator to manage the distribution of assets, much as an executor would if you had had a will. The administrator might be a political chum of the judge or a not-so-distant relative (the judge's relative, not yours)—nice work if you can get it.

All estates are subject to the "estate tax" (sometimes referred to as the "death tax"), which is a tax on the transfer of assets more or less like a sales tax. The law provides a threshold credit against the estate tax liability, so that less than 1 percent of estates pay this tax. Very wealthy individuals often have transferred assets to others in anticipation of their deaths to reduce the bite of the estate tax. Estate tax payments are due within nine months of death.

Changes in U.S. tax legislation in 2001 provided for both staged increases in the credit against the estate tax and reductions in the tax rates on estates until 2011; in 2010 the effective estate tax rate is zero. Under the current legislation, in 2011 the tax rates and the credit will revert to their pre-2001 values. A few elderly with large estates might see a tax advantage in calling it quits in 2010, and some of their children will see the difference between the estate tax rates in 2010 and 2011 as an "arbitrage opportunity." However, the likelihood that this reversion will occur is trivially small; the "permanent" law will be changed in 2011, and it's likely that there will be a substantial increase in the unified credit over its 2000 value, perhaps to $4 million or $5 million per individual. And the highest tax rates on estates may be reduced below the levels that prevailed in 2000.

Glossary of Legal Terms

Administrator   The individual appointed by a probate judge to manage assets of the deceased in the absence of a will.

Bypass trust   A trust used to ensure that the estates of both husband and wife benefit fully from the lifetime credit for the estate tax liability.

Executor   The individual designated in the will with the responsibility to distribute the estate's assets.

Generation-skipping tax   A tax of 55 percent applied when assets in excess of $1 million are transferred to the third generation.

Generation-skipping trust   A trust established to take advantage of the $1 million exclusion from the generation-skipping tax.

Intervivos trust ("living trust")   A trust established to facilitate management of an individual's assets in case of incapacitation.

Lifetime credit   Each individual has a lifetime credit that offsets the estate and gift tax liability; this credit was $1.5 million in 2005, $2 million in 2006 through 2008, and $3.5 million in 2009.

Probate   The process of ensuring that the transfer of the ownership of assets of the deceased follows the terms of the will or, in the absence of a will, the common law of the state.

Trusts   Legal entities established to own assets.

Unified estate and gift tax   In 1919 the U.S. government adopted a tax on the transfer of wealth from an estate to family members and other individuals. Most estates are too small to pay any tax because there is a large credit against the tax liability; this credit had been $800,000 in 2000 and was increased to $3.5 million for 2009. Wealthy families have made end-runs around the tax, including initially by transferring wealth to younger family members in anticipation of death. The legislation was modified so that annual gifts to any individual larger than a threshold amount, initially $10,000 a year and $13,000 a year in 2010, would reduce the credit against the estate tax.

Unlimited marital deduction   The provision in the estate tax law that provides no estate tax must be paid on assets distributed to the surviving spouse.

Will   A document that specifies the distribution of assets once they have been transferred to an estate.

If you're like most Americans, you want to minimize the taxes on your estate. You also want to maximize your control over the distribution of your assets. The potential conflict between satisfying these two objectives arises because you are involved with a tax system that is primarily federal and a set of state laws and procedures for transferring ownership of various assets to other individuals at death or in anticipation of death.

The presumption in 2010 is that the credit against the estate tax liability will remain at $3.5 million in subsequent years; if you have a smaller estate, you need not be concerned about the estate tax. This tax will bite if your estate is larger, but this tax is "voluntary" and can be avoided by giving away enough of your assets before you die and instructing the executor to make gifts to charities after you die so that the taxable estate is not larger than the credit. But once you've given the assets away, they're beyond your control even if your personal circumstances or preferences change.

Trusts and the Control over Assets

Wills and trusts are all about control of assets after death. A trust owns assets, receives income on these assets, and pays taxes on the income. Trusts are "ownership vehicles"—fictitious individuals with legal identities. Trusts own assets for the benefit of real individuals.

Trusts differ in their objectives. Some trusts facilitate the management of assets and the transfer of the ownership of assets. These trusts reduce the costs of probate. Other trusts reduce the bite of estate taxes and of capital gains taxes on appreciated assets. Still others extend your control of what had been your assets after you die.

Trusts are either revocable or irrevocable. Remember that after you transfer assets to the trust, the trust owns these assets—you no longer own the assets. Nevertheless, the assets owned by the trust remain in the estate when the estate tax liability is determined. The grantor of a revocable trust can change his or her mind and essentially undo the establishment of the trust by asking that the ownership of the assets be transferred from the trust back to the grantor.

You can change your mind with an irrevocable trust, but it won't do any good. The trust document cannot be undone. The grantor of the trust gives up control of the assets and cannot be the trustee. Once the assets are transferred to the trust, they are no longer in the estate. Irrevocable trusts are used to reduce tax payments. Still, there are tax consequences—the trust may have to pay income taxes, and the transfer of assets to the trust may be subject to the gift tax if the cumulative amount of the annual transfer is larger than the credit against the estate tax liability.

Wills and trusts complement each other. Your will may direct that assets in the estate be transferred to a trust to reduce tax payments and especially estate tax payments. If you want to achieve these tax savings, the instructions in your will must provide that the executor of the estate transfer some of the assets to a trust.

A will is advantageous for several reasons. If you die without a will, the cost of transferring assets is likely to be higher than if you had had a will and named an executor, especially if the executor were a member of your family or a trusted friend. (Their fees and charges and expenses are likely to be lower than those of the lawyers appointed by the probate judge.) If you have a will, there is smaller likelihood of significant bickering among your heirs—and the associated costs of lawyers to straighten out the arguments.

The estate tax law provides for an "unlimited marital deduction," which means that all of the assets left by one spouse to the other are deducted from the taxable estate. The estate tax law also provides that each individual has a lifetime credit against the estate tax liability. The general idea is to calculate the amount of the estate tax as the product of the size of the taxable estate and the schedule of tax rates and then reduce the amount of the estate tax that is payable by applying the lifetime credit.

"Bypass trusts" and "generation-skipping trusts" distinguish between the transfer of the ownership of the assets and the transfer of income that these assets produce, and they make it possible to fully use the lifetime credit while "protecting" the income of the surviving spouse. The bypass trust transfers ownership of some or all of the assets in the estate of each spouse to the trust on death, and the ownership of the income on these assets is transferred to the surviving spouse.

Both husband and wife should establish a "bypass trust" to take full advantage of the lifetime credit. Both husband and wife would stipulate in their wills that on death the assets up to the value of the unified lifetime credit be transferred to the bypass trust—so that if the family's assets are more than the credit, each should own assets equal to the amount of the credit. The trust receives these assets on the death of the first spouse, and the income on these assets flows to the surviving spouse. On the death of the surviving spouse, the will would provide that the ownership of these assets be transferred to children or grandchildren or some other individuals, and the bypass trusts would be dissolved. The law provides that the surviving spouse can dip into the capital of the bypass trust.

A "generation-skipping trust" is, in effect, a second-generation "bypass trust." The gift of the income attached to assets is separated from the gift of the assets themselves. Thus an individual might direct that a specified amount of assets in the estate be transferred to the grandchildren while the income on these assets goes to one or both of their parents for a specified number of years or as long as they live. On the death of their parents, the grandchildren will receive the income on these assets and have control over these assets.

There is an upper limit of $1 million on the amount that can be transferred to a generation-skipping trust without triggering a tax liability; transfers in excess of this amount are taxed at the rate of 55 percent.

The "intervivos" or living trust is usually established to facilitate the management and control of assets of an elderly person. For example, Jack Benny Sr. establishes a living trust and transfers the ownership of some or all of his assets—bonds and stocks, his apartment or home, a checking account—to the Jack Benny Sr. Living Trust. Jack Benny Jr. and Jack Benny Sr. are both trustees; each has the ability to write checks on the trust's accounts. Eventually Jack Jr. will begin to write checks on this account to pay Jack Sr.'s bills.

When Jack Sr. dies, the assets owned by this trust are not subject to probate, but they are included in Jack Sr.'s estate to determine whether a tax must be paid. Jack Sr.'s will indicates how the assets in the trust should be distributed. The trust is dissolved when it no longer owns any assets.

Trusts can be used to reduce the payment of capital gains tax. You may have large unrealized capital gains on stocks and other assets. You may own some rental properties and your "tax cost" or "basis" for these properties may be substantially below current market values, perhaps because of the price appreciation or because of annual depreciation. The market value of your home may be substantially higher than the purchase price.

If you sell one of these assets, you will realize a capital gain, and you will probably have to pay the capital gains tax. If you own these assets when you die, then the cost basis of these assets is "stepped up," and in effect the tax on the capital gain will be avoided.

Rather than sell these assets, you give them to an established charity—your favorite college, university, hospital, or religious institution. The charity sells these assets and uses the proceeds to buy bonds or stocks or some other income-producing assets that will be owned by a trust the charity has established for your benefit. You will receive annual income from this trust. When you (and your designated beneficiary, if you have established one in the trust) die, the ownership of the assets will be transferred from the trust to the charity, and the trust will be dissolved. Before you die, the charity manages the assets owned by the trust for your benefit. The income you receive from the trust is taxable as ordinary income.

One advantage of establishing a trust with assets with large unrealized capital gains is that you avoid paying the capital gains tax. A second advantage is that you receive an immediate income tax deduction for the gift of the assets in the trust to the charity in what may be the distant future year. In effect, the Internal Revenue Service (IRS) looks at the actuarial tables and estimates the year in which you are likely to die and hence the date when the assets in the trust will be transferred to the charity, and then determines the present value of this future gift. A third advantage is that the assets transferred to the trust will not become part of your estate and so your taxable estate is smaller. You also will benefit your favorite charities.

Gifts and Charitable Remainder Trusts

Assume you own stock with a market value of $100,000 and that the cost of the stock to you was $10,000. If you sell the stock, your capital gain of $90,000 will be taxed at the rate of 15 percent so you will pay a tax of $14,500 and have $86,500 to reinvest.

If you give the stock to your favorite charity, you will receive an immediate income tax deduction that might be in the range of $30,000 to $40,000; the actual amount of this deduction depends on your age and the instructions you give the charity about how the funds realized from the sale of the stock will be invested. Assume that the amount of this deduction is $35,000 and that your marginal income tax rate (federal and state) is 40 percent.

In effect, the gift of $100,000 of stock has reduced your net worth by $72,500. Had you sold the stock, you would have had $86,500 in hand after you paid the capital gains tax. Because you gave the stock to the charity, you reduced your income tax payment by $14,000—in effect you have saved $14,000. The $72,500 is the difference between the $86,500 you would have had after paying the capital gains tax and the reduction in your current income tax payment of $14,000.

The trust established with the proceeds from the sale of the $100,000 of stock will provide you with income of $5,000 a year for as long as you and your spouse live. (Remember, this is an example, and the actual values will differ depending on your ages and the instructions you provided the charity about how the proceeds from the sale of the stock should be invested.) If you had sold the stock, then you would have had to earn an interest rate of nearly 7 percent on the $72,500 to be as well off as you are after giving the stock away. You have reduced your taxable estate—but you no longer have any control over the money that you gave away.

If you follow this procedure to make a gift of highly appreciated assets to a charity, the amount of the assets that eventually will be transferred to your children, grandchildren, and other individuals will be smaller. You might find that "the cost" to them of transferring $100 to a charity is $10, since if you had not made the gift, they might have had to pay an estate tax at the rate of 45 percent on the assets that they inherited. Actually, the choice is yours: "If I give these assets to my favorite hospital or college or religious institution, they will receive $100, but if I give these same assets to an individual, that individual will receive $10."

A charitable remainder trust provides that the charity receives the gift after your death. A charitable lead trust provides that the income from the assets in the trust goes to a charity for a specified number of years and then the ownership of the assets is transferred to the individuals designated in the trust agreement.

One of the major questions in estate management involves the timing of the transfer of ownership of assets to your children. One advantage to transferring ownership before death is that the income on the assets builds up your children's wealth rather than yours, and so your taxable estate is smaller and hence the estate tax payment will be smaller. But such transfers involve loss of control.

Trusts can also be used to control the use of assets by an intended beneficiary. You want to transfer ownership of assets to your children or grandchildren but you're worried that they might fritter away funds because of immaturity. You leave the funds to a trust that is established to manage the assets for the benefit of these individuals.

Glossary: Trusts and More Trusts

Charitable lead trust   This trust pays income to charities for a specified period, after which the remainder passes to the children or other individuals. There is an immediate charitable gift deduction and the property's value is frozen.

Charitable remainder trust   This trust pays income to a specified individual and a beneficiary as long as they live; thereafter, the assets in the trust are transferred to a charity.

Grantor retained annuity trust (GRAT)   A trust similar to the QPRT.

Qualified personal residence trust (QPRT)   This trust enables the grantor to transfer titles of real estate to heirs. The trust has a finite life span; at the end of the trust period, the beneficiaries acquire title to the trust.

The U.S. Government's Estate Tax

The U.S. government first established a tax on estates in 1918. (The estate tax is sometimes called the "inheritance tax" and, more recently, the "death tax.") Soon after the estate tax was established, individuals who were anticipating that their estates might be subject to the tax began to transfer assets to their children, grandchildren, and friends to reduce the taxable estate. Subsequently a tax on large gifts was introduced to reduce these end-runs around the estate tax.

In 1976 the law was changed to provide that the tax rates on gifts to individuals and on estates would be the same. Hence, assets transferred to other individuals before death and after death are taxed in a similar—but not quite identical—way.

In 2001 legislation provided that the U.S. estate tax would be phased out primarily by increasing the credit against the estate tax liability on a steplike basis; the legislation also provided that estate tax rates would be decreased slightly.

There are five key features of the U.S. estate tax system. One is the determination of the assets that will be included in the estate for the purpose of determining the tax. This is a distinction between the gross estate and the net estate. Everything you own—bonds, stocks, real estate, computers, books, vehicles, clothing, stamp collections—becomes part of your gross estate. Certain deductions from the gross estate are made before determining the value of your taxable, or net, estate. Gifts to charities reduce the taxable estate. So do all assets left to a surviving spouse. Funeral expenses and the administrative costs of managing your estate can be deducted as well. If you own tax-advantaged funds—Keogh plans, IRAs, and 401(k) accounts—then your estate must pay income tax on these funds when the estate receives them unless these tax-advantaged funds are to be transferred to a charity. The payment of the income tax reduces the taxable estate.

The second feature of the estate tax involves determining the value of the assets that remain in the taxable estate—the tax collectors want to be sure that fair market values are attached to real property, antiques, and family heirlooms. All the assets owned by the estate must be valued at the market prices on the date of death. Experts may be needed to value art, real estate, and family businesses.

The third feature is the set of tax rates that will be applied to the net estate. These rates are shown in Table 17.1. Note that net estates as small as $10,000 are subject to the estate tax. Because each individual has a lifetime credit against the estate tax liability, small estates and medium-sized estates usually do not pay any estate tax. The tax rate on assets in the estates of more than $2 million is 48 percent. So the tax liability on a $3 million estate would be $780,800—but that's before the unified credit.

Table 17.1

Tax Rates on Estates and Gifts

Value of Estate				
Over	But Not Over	The Tax Is	Plus % of the Amount Over	
$0	$10,000	$0	18%	$0
10,000	20,000	1,800	20%	10,000
20,000	40,000	3,800	22%	20,000
40,000	60,000	8,200	24%	40,000
60,000	80,000	13,000	26%	60,000
80,000	100,000	18,200	28%	80,000
100,000	150,000	23,800	30%	100,000
150,000	250,000	38,800	32%	150,000
250,000	500,000	70,800	34%	250,000
500,000	750,000	155,800	37%	500,000
750,000	1,000,000	248,300	39%	750,000
1,000,000	1,250,000	345,800	41%	1,000,000
1,250,000	1,500,000	448,300	43%	1,250,000
1,500,000	2,000,000	555,800	45%	1,500,000
2,000,000		780,800	48%	2,000,000

Source: Data from "Imposition and Rate of Tax," Title 26 *U.S. Code*, Sec. 2001 (2008 edition).

The fourth feature of the estate tax is that each individual has a lifetime credit against the tax due on the estate and on the accumulated value of annual gifts, initially in excess of $10,000 a year and more recently in excess of $13,000 a year.

The amount of the unified credit is shown in the center column of Table 17.2. In 2001 each individual received a one-time credit of $220,550 against the estate and gift tax, which meant that $675,000 of assets was not subject to the estate tax. This credit was increased on a staged basis from $780,800 in 2006 to $1,455,800 in 2009. If the credit remains at the 2009 level in 2011 and in subsequent years, estates of $3.5 million and less will not have to pay the estate tax.

The fifth feature of the estate tax involves the estate tax at the state level and at the federal level. Most of the fifty states also tax estates. But the IRS gives a credit against federal estate tax payments for each dollar of estate tax that was paid at the state level.

Table 17.2
The Unified Credit against the Estate Tax Liability

Year of Death	Unified Credit	Amount of Income Excluded
2006–2008	780,800	2,000,000
2009	1,455,800	3,500,000
2010	1,455,800	3,500,000

Source: Data from U.S. Department of the Treasury, Internal Revenue Service, "Introduction to Estate and Gift Taxes," Publication 950, revised September 2008, http://www.irs.gov/pub/irs-pdf/p950.pdf.

Reducing the Bite of the Estate Tax

In 2007 the U.S. government collected $23.5 billion in estate taxes. The collections have been declining because of the decline in the estate tax rates and the increase in the credit against the estate tax liability, and because many individuals who would be considered rich arranged their financial affairs to "shrink" their taxable estates.

You can give up to $13,000 a year to any other individual without reducing the amount of your lifetime credit; the term for such gifts is "annual exclusion." So a husband and wife can give up to $26,000 each year to each of their children, the spouses of their children, their grandchildren, their siblings, and nonfamily members. There is no limit to the number of individuals to whom you can make such gifts in a year. You can make gifts of $13,000 a year to each of the Jones children and to each of the Smith children. The Joneses and the Smiths can make similar gifts to your children. It's all very legal.

Direct payments to hospitals to settle the medical bills of others and direct payments to colleges for tuition bills of your grandchildren and the Jones and Smith children aren't included in the $13,000 annual exclusion noted in the previous paragraphs. Neither are payments for their summer camp fees.

If you make a gift larger than $13,000 to any individual in a particular tax year, you must file a gift tax form. If you made a gift of $15,000 to one of your children in one year, the gift tax would apply to $2,000. You do not pay the gift tax until the cumulative value of your annual gifts in excess of the annual exclusion of $13,000 exceeds the value of the unified credit.

Since some individuals have an incentive to transfer assets to their grandchildren or great-grandchildren to avoid or reduce the estate tax payments when assets are transferred to the next generation, the "generation-skipping tax rate" of 48 percent is applied to cumulative transfers in excess of $1 million.

Gifts before and after Death

Assume that your estate will be significantly larger than the unified credit. You are considering making a large gift to your children either in the estate or before your death. The tax rates are identical. The intended gifts are large relative to the $13,000 annual exclusion. Should you continue to make gifts to individuals larger than the annual exclusion, or should you wait and let the estate make this gift?

Assume you want your children to receive $100,000 after taxes. How much will that cost you or your estate pretax? As Table 17.3 shows, if you make the gift while you are still alive, the cost to you—the reduction in your assets—will be $155,000; if the estate makes the gift, the pretax cost to the estate is $210,000.

If you make this gift prior to death and pay the highest marginal estate tax, then the cost to you of paying this $100,000 will be $148,000—$100,000 will go to the individual or individuals, and you must pay a gift tax of $48,000 to the IRS on the $100,000.

Assume instead that you have arranged that the $100,000 will be paid to these individuals from your estate. Now the cost to the estate of the $100,000 gift is $196,000 because the estate will have to pay $96,000 in federal estate taxes.

Table 17.3
Direct Gifts versus Gifts through the Estate

	Direct Gift	Legacy Gift
Amount of gift	$100,000	$210,000
Tax at 48%	48,000	110,000
Gift to beneficiary	100,000	100,000
Pretax cost of gift	155,000	210,000

Source: Author.

The explanation for this asymmetry is that the tax payment on the gift prior to death is based on the amount of the gift; the tax is "exclusive." The tax on the gift from the estate is based on the pretax value of the assets; the tax is "inclusive." The takeaway is that with the estate tax you pay a "tax on the tax."

Gifts to charities reduce the taxable estate on a dollar-for-dollar basis. Religious institutions, hospitals, and colleges and universities receive substantial funds that might otherwise have gone to the IRS.

A "generation-skipping trust" is, in effect, a second-generation "bypass trust." The gift of the income attached to assets is separated from the gift of the assets themselves. Thus an individual might direct that a specified amount of assets in the estate be transferred to the grandchildren while the income on these assets goes to one or both of their parents for a specified number of years or as long as they live. On the death of their parents, the grandchildren will receive the income on these assets and have control over them. There is an upper limit of $1 million on a generation-skipping trust.

"Second-to-Die" Insurance Policies

The estate tax payment is due only after the death of the surviving spouse. Life insurance sales forces have made fortunes selling "second-to-die" or survivorship life insurance policies. The main feature is that the insurance companies pay the beneficiaries only after the death of the second spouse—which means that the premiums must be paid for a longer time and the cash values accumulate for a longer time. Their sales pitch is that the proceeds from the life insurance policies can be used to pay the estate tax. The premium on the second-to-die life insurance policy is somewhat lower than on a policy sold to an individual of the same age because the mortality data indicate that one of the spouses is likely to outlive the other by three or four years.

The second come-on in the sales pitch is that the payment of the life insurance premium reduces the value of the taxable estate while the proceeds of the life insurance policy are not taxable to the beneficiary, provided the policy is owned by an irrevocable trust. So there is a form of "tax arbitrage."

The sales pitch suggests that the policy might pay off after only one or two premium payments, so the insurance company will pay your heirs much more than you paid the insurance company. The sales pitch fails to mention this: life insurance companies never give anything away. If in some cases the payoff from the life insurance policy is extremely large relative to the sum of premiums paid, then in other cases the payoff from the life insurance policy will be low relative to the sum of premium payments and compound interest if both spouses live to be 100. And the insurance salespeople also fail to disclose that the payment of the premium reduces the amount that can be given to the beneficiary each year under the $13,000 exclusion or exemption from the gift tax, unless the policy is owned by an irrevocable trust.

Should you buy one of these policies? Will the amount that you will leave your children be larger if you buy the policy or if you don't? You might want to discuss the purchase of a policy with your children, assuming they are the major beneficiaries of your estate. If you buy the policy and both your spouse and you die soon thereafter, then the payoff from the policy will be large relative to the total of the premiums paid; your children will be better off because you bought the policy. If instead you and your spouse have Methuselah's genes, then the sum of the premium payments will be large relative to the value of the policy, and your children may conclude that they would have been better off if you hadn't bought the policy.

ACTIONABLES

1. If you do not have a will and have significant assets, make an appointment with a lawyer to write a will. Review your will if you already have one.

2. Establish a "bypass trust" if your assets are greater than $3.5 million in 2010. Similarly, establish a bypass trust for your spouse. Be sure that both you and your spouse have $700,000 in your own names.

3. Establish a "generation-skipping trust" if your children's estates are large enough that they might be subject to the estate tax.

4. Establish an intervivos trust to facilitate transfer of property, especially if you are somewhat elderly.

5. Make a "dry run" to ascertain whether your estates would be subject to tax if you and your spouse were hit by a train today. If your estate is likely to be taxed, develop a plan to reduce the taxable estate by making gifts to children, grandchildren, friends, and charities prior to death.

6. Project the value of your estate at the likely age of retirement. Consider annual gifts to children and grandchildren to reduce the taxable estate.

7. If you contemplate significant gifts to charitable institutions, consider establishing a charitable remainder trust or a charitable lead trust, especially if you have large unrealized capital gains.

18   Ciao and Shalom

The forty years since the late 1960s have been extremely turbulent for Americans. There were three massive oil price shocks and one modest one. The U.S. price level more than doubled in the 1970s, and the inflation rate reached 13 percent in 1980. A tight money policy adopted at the end of 1979 to bring inflation under control led to a surge in interest rates and bankruptcies, and the unemployment rate climbed above 10 percent. Interest rates declined after 1982 and the economy began to grow again; stock prices at the end of the decade were three times higher than at the beginning. A dot-com bubble in the second half of the 1990s led to a sharp increase in stock prices, which contributed to economic well-being. Then there was a mild recession in 2001, and stock prices declined by 40 percent between 2001 and 2004. The year 2002 was the beginning of a bubble in residential and commercial real estate; home prices doubled in many regional markets and construction activity surged. The implosion of the bubble in 2008 toppled some of the largest banks and investment banks, and some of the icons of American industry and finance—General Motors, Citicorp, Bank of America, AIG—were in great financial difficulty and used government money to stay in business.

Despite the turbulence associated with these financial swings, the U.S. economy grew at a rate of 3 percent over much of the period. Financial turbulence means larger swings in the values of stocks, real estate, and currency and in the rate of unemployment. Periods of unemployment and declining income are more extensive.

The quality of your life both when you are in the active labor force and then in retirement will depend in part on the success of the United States in achieving a rate of economic growth comparable to that in the second half of the twentieth century. "A rising tide lifts all ships," and the difference between an average rate of growth of 3 percent and one of 2 percent amounts to a difference of 40 percent in per capita gross domestic product over a generation. That's a lot of money—and the higher the rate of growth, the higher the rate of return on some of the assets that you will have acquired with your savings.

Are the last forty years a prelude to the next forty, or will there be a return toward greater financial stability? The implication of greater stability is that the rate of economic growth will increase.

There is little you can do to dampen the turbulence in the macroeconomy. Recognize that there is a nontrivial likelihood that there will be more turbulence, and be prepared—if there is a return to stability, then you will be in bonus territory because of the precautions that you will have taken to cope with a less stable world. The problem with living too close to the edge is that the edge can suddenly shift inward and you will find yourself on the deep side.

Your primary objective as you move along the life cycle is to smooth your consumption spending from one month to the next and one year to the next. You will want to buffer or insulate the amount that you will have available to spend from shocks to your income and sudden emergencies that involve a surge—often and hopefully one time—in your expenditures. The greater the turbulence in the future, the more important it is for you to have buffers to insulate your consumption spending from expensive shocks to your income and wealth. You will need both personal savings and credit to enable you to minimize the likelihood that you'll need lots of Hamburger Helper in the down times when the income takes a hit. If you're one of the fortunate ones, you will be involuntarily furloughed—in effect a disguised reduction in your income—and if you are less lucky, you may be searching for new employment opportunities. Smoothing consumption also means preparing for the inevitable departure from the active labor force; the monthly or weekly paycheck stops, and you're then on your own.

The key aspect for financial planning is to "pay yourself first" and to commit to saving 10, 12, or 15 percent of your monthly income, including the amount that is being used to reduce your mortgage indebtedness month by month by month. Yes, saving is difficult, but recognize the likelihood that you had a comfortable lifestyle when your income was lower. As your income increases, increase the amount that you save by a nontrivial percent—say, 20 percent. Similarly, save at least 20 percent of any windfall.

One of the key attributes that will help you achieve your savings targets is to become more conscious about the relative cost of achieving your objectives. Enter the marketplace with healthy skepticism toward the sellers of soap, automobiles, and stocks. Most of them are specialists in a narrow sector, and you are a generalist in many different markets. They have advantages in terms of providing information, providing misinformation, and withholding information.

When you're in the supermarket, minimize loyalty to particular brands and scout out the generics—remember, every branded good was a generic before it was rechristened and branded. Remember that day-old bread is a bargain and that the strategy of buying last year's model can reduce the amount you spend. Increasing the length of time you own a car—before you acquire a replacement that is one or two years old—can have a major impact in enabling you to increase the amount you save. Similarly, when you're dealing in the financial markets, be cost conscious—seek to minimize the management fees and the transaction costs. Remember that you're at the receiving end of an industry that wants you to spend.

The motive for this book was to provide a framework that will help you gain control of your financial life. Your objective is to ensure that your standard of living in retirement will not be significantly different from your standard of living while you were employed; if your standard of living declines, the inference is that there were some costly accidents or that you failed to plan. You need a plan for saving in the years you're in the active labor force so that the combination of your accumulated saving in both tax-advantaged and regular accounts, together with Social Security and a defined-benefit pension, will be sufficient to provide 70 or 80 percent of your preretirement income.

Glossary

AARP (formerly known as the American Association for Retired Persons) AARP is a trade union for seniors that works for the protection of Social Security benefits and Medicare benefits. Membership is open to those age 50 and older. AARP members receive discounts on car rentals and hotels. *AARP The Magazine* has a circulation larger than that of any other magazine. The magazine has exclusive arrangements with companies that sell life insurance, Medigap insurance, and auto insurance; these firms pay fees to AARP, which accounts for a substantial part of its income and enables AARP to maintain a low annual membership fee. One result is that its members do not benefit from price competition among the companies when they buy various types of insurance.

Active management versus passive management Strategic alternative choices to the selection of securities by the managers of mutual funds. Actively managed funds seek above-average performance from "professional" stock selection and timing, while passively managed funds seek average performance by replicating the performance of an index at the lowest possible cost.

American Association of Individual Investors (AAII) A Chicago-based nonprofit group that publishes much relevant and useful information for investors. AAII has clubs in various U.S. cities.

Amortization   The process of reducing indebtedness with serial payments over a fixed number of years.

Annuity   A contract usually sold by an insurance company that provides a fixed annual payment to its owner as long as the owner (and if included, a designated beneficiary) lives. The appeal is that "one cannot outlive an annuity," although the purchasing power of the monthly check may decline as the consumer price level increases. Social Security retirement benefits are an annuity, and the payments are increased to reflect increases in living costs. The private firms that sell annuities are concerned with the longevity risk that individuals are living much longer, and the price of annuities probably has been increased relative to the benefits to reflect this risk.

APR   A shorthand term applied to the presentation of an annual percentage interest rate. Interest rates generally are quoted in terms of a flat rate, and then the annual percentage rate allows for continuous compounding of interest.

Arbitrage   A process of taking advantage of differences in prices of the identical or nearly identical good or service available in different markets or at different times. These price differences may reflect that sales taxes are higher in some jurisdictions than in others; for example, sales taxes, cigarette taxes, and alcohol taxes differ among states. The price differences may reflect that sellers are engaged in price discrimination and have set lower prices in communities with lower incomes. Some stores charge lower prices on Tuesdays, and movie theaters charge lower prices at matinees. Individuals arbitrage the differences in state taxes on income by moving to those states that have zero tax rates on income; similarly, individuals arbitrage the difference in state tax rates on estates by moving to those states that do not tax estates.

Blodgett, Henry   A Yale-educated history major who pimped new-era stocks for Merrill Lynch during the dot-com boom of the late 1990s. Blodgett would set price targets for firms, and everyone—well, nearly everyone—would buy the shares until they nearly reached the target. At the same time that Blodgett was singing the praises of the particular firms to the public, he was describing several of them in e-mails to friends as pieces of shit. Blodgett was scolded by the SEC but kept his fortune, even though many of those who believed him and followed his advice lost a substantial part of their fortunes. You have to believe that the top management of Merrill knew that Blodgett's act was a con. Jack Grubman was a tout for MCI WorldCom and made a fortune hustling for a firm that eventually went bankrupt.

Board of Governors of the Federal Reserve System   The institution established by the U.S. Congress in 1913 to reduce the susceptibility of the U.S. economy to financial crises.

"Boiler shop"   A firm that sells stocks over the phone, usually penny stocks (those with a market price of less than $1.00). The scripted story is that the price of the stock has rapidly increased in the last two weeks and will continue to increase because the firm has discovered a new battery that will last twelve years or a new formula for automobile tires that will outlast the car. The initial pitches for these firms now are made over the Internet. If the stock price is less than $2.00 a share, pass.

Bonds   A financial instrument of indebtedness issued by private borrowers and government borrowers. The instrument specifies the interest rate on the bond, the frequency of interest payments, and the date that the borrower is scheduled to repay the amount borrowed. The riskiness of bonds is evaluated by the credit rating agencies.

"Bubbles"   Nonsustainable financial processes that involve a short-term feedback from increases in prices to increases in demand. The increase in Japanese real estate prices and stock prices in the second half of the 1980s was a bubble; individuals and firms were buying these assets because their prices were increasing, and their prices were increasing because individuals and firms were buying these assets. These price increases were much larger than could be explained by the fundamentals; for example, real estate prices were extraordinarily high relative to the rental income on the properties. Similarly, the increase in U.S. stock prices in the second half of the 1990s was a bubble; when the prices stopped increasing, they immediately began to decline. And the increase in real estate prices in the United States, Britain, and five or six other countries between 2002 and 2007 was a bubble. Changes in asset prices that cannot be explained by the changes in "fundamentals" can be attributed to bubbles; stock prices are then high relative to the corporate earnings and home prices are high relative to rents.

Capital gain   A profit from the excess of the current market value of an asset or security over the purchase price of that asset or security. The capital gain is "realized" if the asset or security has been sold and the seller has the cash in hand; otherwise, the capital gain is unrealized—a paper profit.

"Caveat emptor"   "Let the buyer beware." A polite Latin phrase for the practice of the sellers in seeking to take advantage of the ignorance, goodwill, or laziness of the buyers. A seller who says he is looking out for the buyers' interest is a naïf or thinks the buyers are naïfs.

Closed-end mutual funds   Closed-end mutual funds have a fixed number of shares, and the prices of these shares change continuously in response to changes in demand and supply; the prices can differ significantly from net asset value. Open-end funds have a variable number of shares, and the prices are closely linked to net asset value. Exchange-traded funds combine some of the elements of open-end funds in that the number of shares outstanding increases or decreases in response to changes in demand, and some of the elements of closed-end funds in that the prices change continuously during the day.

Co-insurance, often "copay"   The share of any loss above the deductible that must be paid by the insured. For example, the insurance policy may state that the company will reimburse 80 percent of reimbursable costs above a fixed amount known as the deductible. The owner of the policy pays the deductible. Alternatively, the copay might be a fixed dollar amount.

Continuing care retirement community (CCRC)   A village for seniors that provides a package of housing in the form of either apartments or cottages, one or two meals a day, and health care. The seniors often pay a front-end entry fee (which may be partly refundable when they leave) and an all-in monthly fee. CCRCs often have three levels of care: one for individuals who are fully ambulatory, a second for those who continue to live in their apartments but are no longer ambulatory, and a third for those who need nursing care, perhaps on a continuing basis.

Credit cards and debit cards   A credit card is a "package" that combines a means of payment and a short-term loan. If payment to the issuer of the credit card is made within a grace period, the loan is interest free. A debit card is like an instant electronic signal to the bank to transfer funds from the owner of the card or payor to the payee.

Credit rating agencies   These firms, including Standard & Poor's, Moody's, and Fitch Ratings, place bonds issued by private sector borrowers and public sector borrowers in one of eight or ten ranks, depending on their assessment of the likelihood that the borrowers will make the scheduled payments on a timely basis. The rating agencies are paid by the firms that want to sell the bonds. An inherent conflict of interest may occur because the borrowers "shop around" for the firms that would give them the highest credit rating, since the higher the rating, the lower the interest rate that they would pay.

Credit scores   Ratings that provide lenders with the projections about the likelihood that individuals will make the payments on their home mortgages, their credit cards, their installment sales contracts, and other debts on a timely basis, based on their history of previous payments, the total of their indebtedness relative to their incomes, and other factors.

Credit union   A cooperative or mutually owned institution that accepts deposits and makes loans; an alternative and competitor to traditional banks. Deposits in credit unions are federally insured.

"Day-old bread"   A euphemism for goods that may be slightly dated, like last year's Ford, Chevy, or Toyota, or last season's skirts.

Deadbeat   A polite term for someone who fails to repay.

Deductible   A threshold value on an insurance policy. The loss must be larger than the deductible before the insurer will pay the insured in the settlement of the loss.

Defined-benefit pension plan   A plan that provides a fixed monthly payment based on annual income, length of service, and perhaps the average salary for the five highest years. The company bears the investment risk. The federal, state, and local governments have defined-benefit pension plans. More recently, defined-contribution pension plans provide that the individual bears the investment risk; these defined-contribution plans are identified as 401 and 403 plans.

Derivative   A security whose price is based on the price of some other security. For example, a futures contract or an option is a derivative, as is an asset-backed security or a mortgage-backed security. Shares in mutual funds are derivatives.

Disability insurance   An insurance policy that provides for payments to the insured if some physical or other ailment prevents or limits the insured's ability to be gainfully employed. One of the major programs of the U.S. Social Security Administration provides monthly payments to disabled workers.

Diversification   One of the central themes of investing and the selection of securities for a portfolio; a ten-dollar term for the aphorism "Don't put all your eggs in one basket."

"Efficient market view"   The proposition that prices of stocks and other securities adjust immediately and fully to new information, so that exceptional profits are not "left on the table." The random-walk view of stock prices is associated with efficient markets and is the rationale for passively managed index funds.

Enron   Initially a gas pipeline company that expanded into many different businesses, including water distribution and power generation as well as trading electricity and other services. *Fortune* magazine considered Enron one of the best-managed firms in the country. For eight or ten years, Enron falsified its profits and conned its auditors. Enron is in the *Guinness Book of World Records*: more of its employees have gone to jail than of any firm other than the Brooklyn mob.

Equity risk premium   A value for the difference between the rate of return on bonds and the rate of return on stocks, otherwise known as equities. The higher rate of return on stocks is a measure of the payment that investors want for carrying the greater risks associated with the ownership of stocks.

Estate tax insurance   A life insurance policy that is sold to those with large estates that will provide their heirs with the money to pay the estate tax. The gimmick is that the premiums that are paid for the insurance reduce the taxable estate, while the proceeds from the insured's policy are not taxable.

Exchange-traded fund (ETF)   A type of mutual fund that combines some of the elements of an open-ended fund and some of the elements of a closed-end fund. The number of shares outstanding of an exchange-traded fund increases in response to the increases in the demand. The prices of these funds change continuously during the day.

Extended warranty   A rip-off form of insurance that promises to reimburse the loss due to failure of the automatic garage door to open, the toaster to accommodate Pop-Tarts, and such. The premiums paid for these warranties are a thousand times larger than the payments in the settlement of claims. Anyone who tries to sell you one of these policies is not your best friend.

Federal Deposit Insurance Corporation (FDIC)   A U.S. government corporation established in the 1930s to insure bank deposits up to $10,000; subsequently the ceiling was increased to $40,000, then $100,000, and then $250,000 in the financial crisis of 2008. Each bank pays an insurance premium, and the FDIC builds up a reserve when the economy is doing well. When a bank fails, the FDIC takes money from this reserve to ensure that depositors do not incur losses. When the reserve has been exhausted, the FDIC has the authority to borrow up to $500 billion from the U.S. Treasury.

FICO score   A score that purports to measure the likelihood that the borrower will adhere to the terms of the loan. FICO is the acronym of the Fair Issacs Corporation, the firm that developed the formulaic approach that each of the three credit-scoring firms uses. Experian, TransUnion, and Equifax are the major suppliers of credit scores.

Fine print   The terms and practices that you agreed to when you accepted a credit card that will allow the supplier of the card to screw you with fees and cascading interest rates—legally, of course.

"Free lunch"   The "no such thing" that millions of individuals continue to seek and that thousands of sellers suggest they are ready to provide.

Futures contracts   Derivative contracts to buy and sell commodities such as crude petroleum, wheat, pork bellies, and currencies including the British pound and the Canadian dollar at specified future dates. These contracts are traded on organized exchanges, including the New York Mercantile Exchange.

Future value   The value of a sum of money at a specified date in the future if invested today at a particular interest rate. The mirror is "present value," which is the value today of a sum of money at a specified date in the future at a particular interest rate.

"Generic"   A nonbranded product. Rice and wheat and coffee and chickens leave the farms as generics, and then some of these products are moved into "factories" and emerge as "branded" goods. Some inexpensive generic products have "brand names," but sellers make no effort to market the product.

Government-sponsored enterprises (GSEs)   Firms chartered by the U.S. Congress to provide credit to particular groups of borrowers. Because of the federal charter, the interest rates on their loans are lower than they would be otherwise. The Federal National Mortgage Corporation

(Fannie Mae) and Federal Home Loan Mortgage Corporation (Freddie Mac) were established to increase the credit available for home mortgages. The Federal Student Loan Association (Sallie Mae) provides student loans and guarantees the loans of other lenders.

"Growth versus value"   A distinction sometimes applied to different stocks. Growth stocks are those whose earnings are projected to increase several times more rapidly than GDP, while value stocks are those whose earnings are likely to increase about as rapidly as GDP.

Health insurance   A policy that provides a specified daily amount—$100, $200, or $300—for up to three, five, or seven years to reimburse the expenses incurred in an assisted-living facility. The deductible may take the form that payments begin only after the insured has been in the facility for ninety days.

Hedge fund   A limited partnership that resembles a mutual fund and seeks above-average returns from speculative transactions in stocks, bonds, and currencies. Initially some of the hedge funds hedged their exposures; they might be "long" twenty stocks and "short" twenty other stocks, with the market values of the long position and the short position of the same approximate value. Few of their investments are hedged, so the term is now a misnomer. Long Term Capital Management was the most successful hedge fund in the 1990s until it crashed in 1998.

Index   A scorecard for measuring changes in the value of groups of stocks and other assets by providing one number that summarizes the changes in the value of a large group of securities or assets. The Dow Jones index summarizes the changes in the price of 30 stocks, while the S&P 500 index summarizes the changes in the value of 500 stocks. The S&P 500 comes in two versions; one is adjusted to show that dividends have been reinvested.

Index fund   A mutual fund that seeks to replicate the rate of return on a particular stock index. Index funds are passively managed; the managers of the funds spend no time in stock selection. Actively managed funds seek above-average returns from stock selection.

Individual retirement account (IRA)   A designated savings program developed to encourage Americans to save for their retirement by "parking money" in designated accounts with plan sponsors, such as a bank or a mutual fund or an insurance company. The generic feature is that the investment income in these accounts is not taxed when earned.

If the plan had been funded with post-tax dollars, as with a Roth IRA, the distribution of the money from the account is not taxed. In contrast, if the plan had been funded with pretax dollars (the allocation of money to the account reduces taxable income), then the distribution of money from the account is taxable at ordinary income tax rates. Initially the annual limit to the amount that could be transferred to these designated accounts was $2,000. That limit has been increased to $5,000, and the limits are higher for individuals over age 50.

Interest rate An arithmetic term that links a value at a specified future date with a value today. Assume John Doe promises to pay $100 today or $300 in five years; an interest rate can be inferred. The $300 is a future value.

Investment bank A financial institution established after the passage of the Glass-Steagall Act of 1934, which was designed to separate the commercial banks from the riskier investment banks. Investment banks do not issue demand deposits. Morgan Stanley was a "white shoe" investment bank, created from the JPMorgan Bank. Goldman Sachs was not white shoe. Both firms were clobbered in the 2008 crisis, and Morgan Stanley acquired a substantial capital injection from Mitsubishi Bank in Tokyo.

"Jumbo loans" Mortgage loans with a principal larger than $417,000, which was the largest that Fannie Mae and Freddie Mac would buy before the 2008 financial crisis; smaller mortgages are known as "conventional conforming." The ceiling was then increased to $761,000. Interest rates on jumbo loans are higher than those on smaller loans.

"Junk bonds" A colloquial term for high-risk bonds, those that are judged too risky to be ranked as investment grade by the credit rating agencies. Junk bonds should be viewed as stocks with high dividends. "Fallen angels" are bonds that once had a credit rating but are no longer rated because the risk of default has increased. The term "high-yield bonds" is a euphemism for junk bonds.

Keogh plan A plan similar to an IRA that allows self-employed individuals to have dedicated retirement accounts. The transfer of money to one of these dedicated accounts reduces taxable income. Funds withdrawn from these accounts are taxable income.

Leverage   The use of borrowed money to facilitate the purchase of a property or a security. For example, if John Doe buys a $200,000 home and makes a down payment of $40,000, the leverage ratio is 5:1.

Life insurance policy   A policy that pays a stipulated amount should the insured die. There are two basic types of life insurance, which can be identified by whether the annual premiums increase year by year or every five or ten years, or whether instead the premiums remain unchanged from one year to the next. Term insurance is one of the two basic forms of life insurance; the annual premium increases continuously or at five- or ten-year intervals to reflect the increases in the mortality rate as individuals age—the older they are, the greater the likelihood that they will die in the next year. In contrast, the annual premiums on permanent life or whole life or universal life are "fixed forever" at the time of purchase and do not increase as mortality increases. These permanent life policies adjust to the higher mortality by building up a "cash reserve"as longevity declines.

"Loads"   Open-end mutual funds that have front-end sales charges or back-end redemption charges that compensate the sales personnel.

Longevity   The estimate of the number of years that an individual will live. Medical science has led to a phenomenal increase in longevity in the last fifty years. Longevity risk is the risk that an individual will live much longer than the estimate. Mortality risk is the risk that an individual will die within a particular period, usually a year.

Lottery   A game of chance with extremely low odds of winning. A device by which states like Vermont, that are reluctant to raise taxes to pay for better schools, tax those who participate in these lotteries, primarily the poor, to raise money to pay for better schools. Consumer's Union has organized a lottery to raise money for its good deeds.

Madoff, Bernie   A sleaze who stole other people's money to support a $10 million lifestyle for nearly twenty years. He managed the largest Ponzi scheme in history, with more than 4,000 clients, including widows and orphans and various charities. Sleaze may be too polite.

Marginal tax rate   The increase in the total tax payment as a percent of the increase in income.

"Mean reversion"   The view that prices of securities and real estate return to their long-run average values when some form of shock causes the prices to increase significantly above these values. The mean or average price-earnings ratio for stocks is seventeen.

Medicare and Medicaid   Medicare is a U.S. government policy to help individuals over age 65 with the costs of various medical services. Medicaid is designed to help individuals not yet age 65 pay for some of the medical services. Medicare is available to individuals younger than 65 with exceptional diseases, such as Lou Gehrig's disease. Individuals older than 65 who have limited incomes can use Medicaid to help pay for those medical expenses that are not covered by Medicare.

Medigap insurance   Standardized policies sold by private companies designed to reimburse the insured for the some of the costs that Medicare will not reimburse, in part because of its deductibles or its co-payments.

Momentum investing   The proposition that changes in prices of stocks and of currencies in the near future can be profitably forecast from the changes in these prices in the recent past, as reflected in the cliché "The trend is your friend."

Money market fund   A mutual fund that sells short-term IOUs that are more or less the equivalent of bank deposits, with the difference that funds were not guaranteed against credit loss by the U.S. government—until they were guaranteed during the 2008 crisis.

"Moral hazard"   The risk that the party to a transaction or a contract will alter his or her behavior to capitalize on the transaction or contract. For example, John Doe buys a life insurance policy two days before he undertakes to fly from the Golden Gate Bridge, or he sets fire to his bankrupt store to collect the insurance money. Insurance companies are especially concerned with this behavior.

Mortality risk   The likelihood that an individual will die in the next year.

Mortgage   A loan that uses homes and apartments and other real property as collateral; if the borrower fails to adhere to repayment terms of the loan, the lender has the right to acquire title to the property. Most home mortgages have fixed interest rates, based on the maturity of the loan. The most frequent is the thirty-year mortgage, but there are also fifteen-year mortgages. Most home mortgages are amortizing; that is, part of the monthly interest payment reduces the amount owed. Mortgages with a fifteen-year maturity and a ten-year maturity are less common. Adjustable-rate mortgages (ARMs) stipulate that the interest rate paid by a borrower will increase or decrease in response to changes in some base interest rate; most ARMs have limits on the maximum amount of the change in any one year and the maximum amount of the change in the lifetime of the contract. Option mortgages provide that the monthly payment for the first three or five years is less than the monthly payment consistent with the interest rate, so the borrower's indebtedness increases. The term "negative amortization" can be applied to the period when the indebtedness is increasing.

Mutual fund A financial instrument or evidence of ownership like a bond or a share or a mortgage; also, a financial institution that issues or sells these instruments. Mutual funds as institutions sell shares and use the money collected from the sale of these shares to buy bonds, shares, other types of securities, and commodities. Mutual funds provide investors—especially small investors, those with security wealth of $50,000 or less—with the opportunity to diversify their holdings of securities at lower cost than if they attempted to do so on their own. One principal distinction is between closed-end funds, which have a fixed number of shares, and open-end funds, which have a variable number of shares. A second distinction is between the open-end funds that have sales or redemption fees and those that do not. A third distinction is between actively managed funds that seek above-average rates of return from professional selection of securities and passively managed funds that seek to mimic the performance of an index.

Option A contract that provides its owner with the right to buy or sell a security or an asset before a stipulated date at a specified price.

"Payday loan" A short-term loan, usually secured by title to an automobile, that has an interest rate of several hundred percent a year.

Perpetuity A perpetuity contract provides a fixed annual payment until the end of time; the difference is that the owner of an annuity is "eating the capital or principal," while the capital or principal of a perpetuity remains unchanged, although the market price of the perpetuity changes and the purchasing power of the interest payment may decline as the consumer price level increases. The annual payments on an annuity and on a perpetuity differ, depending on age at time of purchase; at age 65, the difference is probably in the range of 3 to 4 percent.

"Pigeon Drop"   A scam that involves the "discovery" of a cache of cash that has no apparent owner, as if the money had been dropped by a pigeon.

Points   Money added to the face value of a mortgage to compensate lenders for the administrative costs that they have incurred in arranging the mortgage.

Ponzi scheme   An arrangement whereby a manager agrees to pay an interest rate that usually is much higher than that paid by banks and credit unions. The manager uses the money received from those who buy these IOUs on Tuesday to pay some of the interest to those who bought these IOUs on Monday. Bernie Madoff ran one of the largest Ponzi schemes ever; his gimmick was that those who invested with Madoff thought they were buying shares in traditional firms—he provided phony statements indicating the securities they owned. Some of those who invested with Madoff in the early years withdrew more money from their accounts than they had initially placed with Madoff.

Price discrimination   A practice of the sellers to charge different buyers different prices for the same good or service. Airlines engage extensively in price discrimination and charge very different prices for travel between the city pairs; the price may depend on when the ticket was purchased. Colleges engage extensively in price discrimination when they award scholarships of varying amounts to different individuals.

Private mortgage insurance (PMI)   A form of credit insurance that is a substitute for the traditional 20 percent down payment that individuals make when they have purchased a home.

Real rate of return   The rate of return on a stock or other security adjusted for the changes in the price level, usually the consumer price level.

Replacement ratio   The estimate of the money needs in retirement that will be required to pay for the same standard of living as the preretirement income.

Reverse mortgage   A mortgage loan whose defining feature is that the amount of the indebtedness increases over time because the interest payments are added to the principal of the loan. Individuals can continue to live in their homes even though the mortgage indebtedness may be larger than the market value of the property. The terms of the reverse mortgage are set by a U.S. government agency, the Department of Housing and Urban Development (HUD). Individuals who take out a reverse mortgage pay an insurance premium to HUD. The lenders are guaranteed against loss by HUD.

"Rip-off" A colloquial expression for a payment that is excessively high for the value of the good or service that is being provided.

Risk The likelihood or probability of an event, such as death or home fires, based on the analysis of the frequency of the events in the past. Risk is distinguished from uncertainty, where the events are so infrequent that there is no good basis for estimating their likelihood in the future.

Shadow price The implicit price for x or y, which can be inferred from two other data points. For example, ABC Motors offers to sell a new car for $30,000 without a down payment and with monthly payments over five years at zero interest rate. The shadow price of the car involves subtracting the dollar value of the "cheap credit" from the $30,000.

Stepped-up basis A term from the tax code that allows those who have acquired property from inheritance to use the value of the property on the date of the death of the donor as the cost basis for calculating capital gains taxes.

Tax-advantaged accounts Accounts at a plan sponsor including banks, insurance companies, and mutual funds that allow investment income on the value of the assets in the accounts to accumulate tax free. IRAs, Keogh plan accounts, and health savings accounts are tax advantaged. The withdrawal of the money from these accounts may or may not be taxable income.

Tax base The value for computing a tax. The tax base may be income earned in a particular period, or wealth, or the assessed value of a home.

Tax credit A reduced tax payment on a dollar-for-dollar basis. Congress legislates tax credits to deal with noble social issues like energy conservation or to deal with losses due to natural disasters like Hurricane Katrina. Tax credits are more valuable than tax deductions on a dollar-for-dollar basis.

Tax deduction   A payment for interest, state or local income or sales tax, or medical expenses that reduces taxable income on a dollar-for-dollar basis.

Teaser   A price or charge for the first month or two that is much below the price or charge for subsequent months.

TIPS   The acronym for Treasury Inflation-Protected Securities, which have been issued by the U.S. Treasury for more than ten years. The interest payments and the principal repayment are indexed to the changes in the U.S. consumer price level.

Title insurance   An insurance policy that protects against the risk that there are liens or prior claims on a home or other property.

Transaction costs   The costs associated with buying or selling, or both buying and selling, stocks, bonds, mutual funds, real estate, coins, impressionist paintings, and other assets.

12b1   A section of the Investment Company Act of 1940 that allows the owners of firms that sell mutual funds to charge the owners of shares in these funds fees of up to 0.50 percent a year, to compensate for the costs that they would incur in marketing the funds in the belief that the economies of scale from much larger funds would enable them to charge much lower fees. It hasn't worked out that way. These fees are a data point that suggest that the Securities and Exchange Commission has been captured by the firms that own the mutual funds.

Unified estate and gift tax   In 1919 the U.S. government adopted a tax on the transfer of wealth from an estate to family members and other individuals. The estate tax is called the "death tax" by its critics. Every estate is subject to the estate tax, but less than 1 percent of the estates actually pay the tax. Most estates are too small to pay any tax because there is a large credit against the tax liability; this credit had been $800,000 in 2000 and was increased to $3.5 million for 2009. Wealthy families have made end-runs around the tax, including initially by transferring wealth to younger family members in anticipation of death. The legislation was modified so that annual gifts to any individual larger than a threshold amount, initially $10,000 a year and $13,000 a year in 2010, would reduce the credit against the estate tax.

U.S. Pension Benefit Guaranty Corporation (PBGC)   A U.S. government corporation established by the Employment Retirement Income

Security Act of 1975 to insure defined-benefit pension plans. The level of payments made by the PBGC is the same as that made by the private firm, except that the annual payment to any one individual cannot be larger than $41,000. Every firm with one of these pension plans pays a premium to the agency, which led to an increase in its reserves; however, the bankruptcy of steel, auto, and auto parts firms means that the payments of the PBGC are likely to exhaust its reserves.

U.S. Securities and Exchange Commission   The U.S. government agency established as the consumer watchdog in financial issues. The agency has been a massive screw-up, and its competence was sharply questioned because it didn't follow through on suggestions that Bernie Madoff was running a Ponzi scheme.

U.S. Social Security Administration   The U.S. government agency established in 1936 to provide retirement benefits for Americans over the age of 65. Initially individuals were eligible to receive a lifetime of benefits, event though they may have paid the tax for one or two months. These benefits are an annuity. Benefits have been increased to compensate for the increases in the living costs of the senior citizens. Workers are taxed; sorry, workers and their employers make contributions, now of 6 percent of their annual income. Initially, 65 was the normal retirement age; subsequently, individuals were eligible to receive reduced benefits at the age of 62. The program has been amended to provide benefits for disabled workers and for the survivors of those who have paid Social Security benefits. A very consumer-friendly culture. The 800 number is 1-800-772-1213, and the Web site is www.socialsecurity.gov.

Index